PREHISTORIC WARFARE IN THE AMERICAN SOUTHWEST

PREHISTORIC WARFARE IN THE AMERICAN SOUTHWEST

Steven A. LeBlanc

THE UNIVERSITY OF UTAH PRESS

Salt Lake City

Figures 2.1, 2.5, 4.6, 5.2, 5.6, 6.11, 6.20, 7.1 ©Baker Aerial Archaeology

01 02 03 04
2 3 4 5 6
This book is printed on acid-free, archival-quality paper.
Manufactured in the United States of America

Library of Congress Cataloging-in-Publication Data

LeBlanc, Steven A.
    Prehistoric warfare in the American Southwest / Steven A. Leblanc.
        p.   cm.
    Includes bibliographical references and index.
    ISBN 0-87480-581-3 (alk. paper)
        1. Pueblo Indians—Warfare.   2. Pueblo Indians—Wars.   3. Pueblo
Indians—Antiquities.   4. Southwest, New—Antiquities.   5. Mexico, North—
Antiquities.   I. Title.
E99.P9L42   1999
979'.01—dc21   98-42327

CONTENTS

FIGURES

TABLES

PREFACE

Warfare is a subject we would all like to ignore. Unfortunately, it is becoming more and more clear that we cannot ignore it if we want to understand human behavior. Warfare is more common and more involved in shaping human societies than anthropologists have recognized. As unpleasant as it may be to deal with this topic, we cannot objectively begin to understand the past without coming to grips with warfare.

This book deals with the warfare issue in one small area of the world over the relatively short span of less than two millennia. As such, it does not tell us much about the overall relationship between human societies and warfare, but it does begin to provide a piece of the broader relationship.

I did not set out to study warfare; it found me. It had become clear to me since beginning research in the area in 1972 that I could never explain the events in the El Morro Valley near Zuni, New Mexico, except by warfare. *How* it explained them, I had no idea, which is where things remained for more than twenty years. Then in rapid succession, several events transformed my perception of warfare. First, Patty Jo Watson and I spent a brief time visiting sites and excavations in the Southwest in the summer of 1995. We visited Keith Kintigh's project in the Upper Little Colorado River area. I saw patterns that fit with the El Morro patterns and began to take a pan-Anasazi view instead of an El Morro view of warfare. As we traveled, I was reading Haas and Creamer's *Stress and Warfare among the Kayenta Anasazi of the 13th Century* A.D. Once again, the similarity with El Morro was remarkable. But Haas and Creamer had made sense of the intervisibility of sites in the Kayenta as being visual links between allied villages. We had noted the same site intervisibility in El Morro, but had not interpreted it. We went back to El Morro and upon reexamination, I decided that the Haas and Creamer interpretation—intervisibility was for defense among allies—was obviously correct. For the first time, I had an explanatory model and a way of looking at warfare. I was then committed to working out the larger picture.

But, it was a job I found far harder to do at this stage in my life than earlier. Reading about thirty children burned to death in a tower kiva when one has small children is not particularly pleasant. I was also hoping that an academic interest in warfare would not spill over to my children in the form of their becoming interested in actual war.

Now interested in the topic, I produced a couple of small papers on particular aspects of the problem. These were quickly rejected by journals. When I tried to ferret out from the reviews what the objections were, I concluded that they simply *a priori* had rejected warfare as neither common nor important. However, at about this time Lawrence Keeley's seminal work, *War before Civilization*, appeared. I decided Keeley was right and the reviewers were wrong. Steadman Upham then encouraged me to put my ideas in book form so the arguments could be presented in their entirety. While some of the ideas presented here support some of Upham's theories, many others do not. Knowing this full well, he was still supportive. Finally, it was David Wilcox, who has some of the clearest ideas on Southwestern warfare and who has produced the broadest syntheses to date, who provided the strongest encouragement and the greatest number of suggestions to turn my ideas into book form. Again, even though his interpretation of Southwestern warfare signficantly differs from mine in places, he unfailingly continued to support this effort and provide invaluable critiques of it.

Probably the only individuals who "like" war are those who are confident that they will not have to take part in one. This does not mean that individuals and society do not consider success in war important. Societies regularly reward those who prove themselves good at making war. The fact that the United States rather regularly elects its top generals to the office of president after successful wars is but one such example. At the same time, descriptions about the consequences of war can be very unpleasant. Even the great distance of time cannot make reading about the slaughter of the children in the Salmon Ruin tower easy. The only difference in our perception of the degree of suffering in the prehistoric past and World War II is the absence of firsthand accounts and photographs of the former. Were we to have those, we would undoubtedly react with horror at prehistoric warfare, just as we do with more familiar conflicts.

If war is so unpleasant, then why study it? Can we not simply ignore it? Unfortunately, if warfare is an important cultural process, we cannot ignore it. We cannot study the ecology of the Serengeti without understanding the predator/prey relations. We may all find watching footage of a lion killing an immature zebra while its mother frantically tries to protect it both sad and even distressing, but that does not mean biologists can ignore lions.

Writing this book would not have been possible without the generous help of a great number of people who have provided me with information, ideas, and suggestions. Much of this information was from archival sources or work that was still in progress, so the efforts made to get me information were sometimes quite substantial. I am very grateful for this effort on everyone's part. This is especially satisfying since some of these people by no means agree with my interpretations of the material, but in the spirit of open inquiry and a common goal of understanding the past, they were willing to be of assistance. Before acknowledging these people, a list that I fear is not complete, special mention must be made of Christy Turner and David Wilcox, whose sharing of information and continued encouragement were key factors in my even beginning to make useful headway on this topic. Also, Patty Jo Watson made extensive helpful suggestions on an earlier draft. Special thanks go to my wife Katherine E. Register, who provided substantial editorial assistance and suggestions and who put up with the project. The list of people who also contributed to my efforts includes Mark Alder, Bruce Anderson, Roger Anyon, Bruce Bradley, Cory Breternitz, Tom Cartledge, Linda Cordell, Winifred Creamer, Helen Crotty, David Cushman, Carolyn Davis, Jeffrey Dean, William Doelle, Andrew Duff, Paul and Suzanne Fish, Dennis Gilpin, Larry and Nancy Hammack, Genevieve Head, Michelle Hegmon, John Hohmann, Winston Hurst, Kristin Kuckelman, Susan Kenzle, Keith Kintigh, Richard Lange, Signa Larralde, Karl Laumbach, Ricky Lightfoot, William Lipe, Joan Mathien, Barbara Mills, Kenneth Peterson, Peter Pilles, Judy Propper, Glen Rice, Charles Riggs, John Roney, John Speth, Katherine Spielmann, John Stein, Steadman Upham, Kim Walters and the staff of the Braun Library of the Southwest Museum, Los Angeles, Christopher White, and Richard Wilshusen.

A note on the illustrations: Having published maps and photographs in the past that I now believe led to the pot-hunting of sites, here I am deliberately vague about the names, locations, and other aspects of some of the figures and maps. I believe I have provided enough information for the general reader. The specialist who needs more specific information can simply ask me for it.

PREHISTORIC WARFARE IN THE AMERICAN SOUTHWEST

FIGURE I.I
Map of the Southwest
showing the locations
of the major cultural
divisions.

CHAPTER ONE

INTRODUCTION

The facts recovered by ethnographers and archaeologists indicate unequivocally that primitive and prehistoric warfare was just as terrible and effective as the historic and civilized version. War is hell whether it is fought with wooden spears or napalm.

—Lawrence Keeley, *War before Civilization* (1996)

Massacres, raiding parties, ambush, pillage, scalping, and captive taking—all the things we know and sometimes dread to admit occur in times of war—happened in the prehistoric Southwest. There is ample archaeological evidence for such aggressive, militaristic behavior, and the purpose of this book is to show that there was, indeed, early warfare in the Southwest. It not only occurred but it also was far from a minor aspect of early Southwestern society.

The vast depth of the region's archaeological record shows that conflict between the people of the Southwest was not simply based on revenge or anger, but was decidedly purposeful. Warfare in this area could be swift or smoldering as well as certainly severe. It was directly related to ecological and social factors that were critical to the survival of the groups involved. During certain times and places, entire societies probably ceased to exist because their defensive and offensive abilities were inadequate.

Early warfare in the Southwest was not a tangential activity. In many circumstances, success at warfare and the social milieu directly related to it—including alliance formation and trade—were essential group survival skills. The people who mastered these accomplishments grew and prospered. Those who failed were eliminated or absorbed into new configurations.

In fact, the very concept of pueblo-dwelling people is the result of warfare. The term "pueblo" refers to the compact, often multistoried communities—in contrast to the more spatially dispersed settlements occupied intially in the Southwest. In spite of their modern-day peaceful reputation, the reason the people of the Southwest ended up residing in pueblos was because of military conflict. Through evidence such as site locations and settlement patterns, it is clear that over time these early residents moved into larger and larger sites specifically designed to be defensive. The pueblos known today, such as Acoma, Zuni, and Hopi, were fundamentally designed for defense by way of their geographic setting or their architectural layout, and sometimes both setting and layout made them supremely defensive. This very clear pattern evolved as a result of and a response to prehistoric war.

When seen in this light, the nature and role of warfare in Southwestern prehistory takes on a new importance. Almost every major area of interest in the region's prehistory has, or potentially has, an important link to warfare. And yet, this exploration, like warfare itself, can be fraught with pitfalls. In striving to understand prehistoric conflict, anthropologists must be careful not to place value judgments on the behaviors related to warfare. Because mainstream anthropology has, until recently, been loathe to recognize warfare as a major force in social evolution, researchers often look for evidence that people fought only because they had to. There are numerous accounts throughout the world of particular groups *defending* themselves against the aggression of others.

As Florence Hawley Ellis noted about the ethnographically known groups in the Southwest, everyone seemed to be involved only in defensive warfare. This, of course, is an impossibility. Warfare was real in the past, just as it is today. There were, and always will be, winners and losers. If the winners are automatically labeled "aggressors" and therefore bad, then you are not studying the past, you are simply using ethnocentric values to interpret it.

Also, to accept the simple statement that a particular group was only "defending itself" and was never the aggressor, ignores all that is known about warfare—whether prehistoric, historic, or modern. No group will be solely on the defensive if avoidable. Some form of offense is necessary to make the other side spend resources on defense. Otherwise, the opposing force gains an enormous military advantage. If members of a group know you will never attack them, then they do not suffer the costs of defense—from building fortresses to leaving warriors behind to defend their settlements when they come to attack you.

The calculus of war requires some offense, even from the group that expects no material gain from its own aggression. Thus, the whole notion of "good guys" and "bad guys," "aggressors" and "defenders" becomes essentially meaningless.

If each group perceives that its survival depends on successful war, then each perceives itself to be the "good guys." If we accept the proposition that there is little utility in trying to determine who was in the right in prehistoric warfare, then what does that say about the perpetrators of modern war? Don't we regularly condemn aggressors today? Without moving far beyond the scope of this book, it would seem that major modern wars have not been about survival. In fact, many of the defeated parties are far better off now than when they went to war initially.

Perhaps that is what most upsets us about modern war. It is not usually necessary for survival, and therefore seems senseless. But this does not mean we can have the same attitude about prehistoric warfare. Groups were exterminated in the past. Given the lack of overreaching political organization, most prehistoric people had no choice about warfare much of the time. They could not declare themselves pacifists—to do so would have meant certain extermination. In the past, war often does seem to have been about survival. Just because we live in an era of senseless wars does not mean war was always senseless.

PERCEPTIONS OF WARFARE

Although it is not the purpose of this book to address the extent, nature, and importance of warfare on a worldwide basis, the issues considered here for the Southwest have worldwide implications in their more general form. In terms of building general models of why social organizations evolve and why warfare takes place, the Southwest provides an important case study, it being one of the archaeologically best known places in the world. It should provide one of the best examples we can find for why people fight, when they fight, and the consequences of their fighting. The Southwest should be looked at in terms of the broader models, and it should be used in helping to construct those models.

So, it seems appropriate to briefly consider previous attitudes toward the prevalence of warfare in general, its significance, and causes—not so much to critique these issues, but to provide a general framework for the discussion that follows.

Until recently, there has been a prevailing opinion among archaeologists and anthropologists that human societies were, in the past, mainly peaceful. It was believed that war was uncommon—and often was just "ritual warfare" with few fatalities and even fewer social consequences. Thus, in formulating models for how societies worked, warfare could be, and has been, generally ignored. This attitude has recently begun to change, a good example being the recent recognition that the Classic Maya—long considered a peaceful society—regularly engaged in warfare.

The recent publication of Lawrence Keeley's *War before Civilization* (1996) is sure to be a major factor in changing the anthropological perception of warfare. Keeley provides an excellent critique of archeologists' prior attitudes toward warfare and a summation of the worldwide evidence for ancient warfare. Much of what follows in this chapter is inspired and supported by that significant work.

The actual ethnographic evidence for warfare—which is quite extensive—has sometimes been explained as the result of indigenous peoples being affected by colonial, meaning usually Western, states. It is argued that this "abnormal" influence is the true causal factor of the observed warfare and that it is incorrect to use these ethnographic cases as models for prehistoric behavior (R. Ferguson and Whitehead 1992).

At the same time, archaeologists have often observed clear evidence for warfare—as seen in the construction of defensive sites, burned sites, bodies that show evidence of violent death, and the prevalence of weapons of war used as funerary goods—and simply ignored it. And, while other archaeologists may recognize evidence for the existence of warfare, they often ignore that warfare *did* occur when it comes time to attempt an understanding of past behavior. The above generalizations do not mean to imply that all archaeologists and anthropologists have ignored the evidence and implications of warfare. My point is that those who have recognized warfare for the force it is have been such a small voice that they have gone unheard by the larger academic community.

The orientation of this book toward the importance of warfare as a factor in cultural behavior in the Southwest is far from the norm. The emphasis and interpretations presented here will surely be met with both considerable skepticism and opposition. There is nothing wrong with scholars turning a critical eye toward the issue of warfare, so long as any opposition is based on sound data and substantive arguments and not simply on distaste for the subject.

In fairness, however, to reverse the logic is equally valid. Because there is no *a priori* reason to believe that any particular group, time, or place was peaceful, there is also no reason, more or less, to have to demonstrate the existence of warfare than there is to have to demonstrate the existence of peace. It simply cannot be assumed that most people were peaceful most of the time. Therefore, it is just as much of an obligation to show that *peace* prevailed in a particular situation as it is to show that *warfare* took place.

Such an attitude flies in the face of traditional anthropological attitudes that assume everyone in the past was peaceful, that warfare was uncommon, and—even when it did exist—that it was unimportant. Such a demand that peace be demonstrated and not assumed is a significant challenge. And, if it is difficult to demonstrate the existence of warfare in the archaeological record, it is even more difficult to demonstrate its absence. So, if the argument intends to show that a particular period or region was peaceful, then it must show something that is not easily shown.

Nevertheless, without making an attempt at firmly demonstrating a lack of warfare—but simply assuming it—we are likely both to miss instances of significant warfare as well as to fail to examine the existence of peace when it did exist. Our understanding of the past will be enhanced by carefully addressing this issue.

THE NATURE OF PREHISTORIC WARFARE

Despite evidence of significant new thinking on the relevance of martial conflict during prehistoric times, Keeley clearly illustrates anthropologists', including archaeologists', continuing tendency to brush aside warfare. In *War before Civilization* he contrasts a Hobbesian view of the world—where everyone is always ready and eager to fight everyone else—and the Rousseauean view—in which "noble savages" live peacefully together. Kelley persuasively argues that, to some degree, both the existence and importance of warfare have been ignored because of preconceived notions about human behavior. In essence, the aggressive Hobbesian view was rejected and the peaceful Rousseauean view was embraced. Searching for warfare has been widely considered "politically incorrect," plain and simple. However, once it is acknowledged how common and likely warfare was, then the evidence for warfare in the archaeological record is obvious in any area of the world for which there is a reasonable amount of information.

Keeley continues by destroying several theories that have almost become anthropological dogma. These popular tenets include the ideas that "primitive" warfare is a result of colonial contact and a matter of ritual involving few deaths and fewer sociopolitical consequences, as well as the notion that when there are proven, significant instances of warfare they are rare and, consequentially, irrelevant.

These myths are quashed with overwhelming evidence. Keeley persuasively argues there is nothing primitive about primitive warfare. It is purposeful, organized, and effective—and he backs up this claim with shocking data about fatalities. Primitive warfare was indeed deadly. Moreover, he points out that the social consequences of early warfare—including extinction of whole groups—and its effects on external group relations were both significant and pervasive. In spite of the previous reluctance to see and deal with warfare, he proves that there is considerable evidence for it in the archaeological record throughout the world and that it is far more prevalent than has been generally considered.

In an eye-opening contrast to modern warfare, Keeley demonstrates that casualties—on a per capita basis—were much greater in nonstate warfare. And he shows that there were, indeed, tangible profits and losses to primitive war.

Assuming Keeley is correct, then there should be evidence for the general consequences of warfare affecting the overall population size and its composition. Also, the role and importance of warfare should, over the long haul, be reflected in social organization and the stature of warriors. Sure enough, there appears to be convincing evidence from the Americas and elsewhere that celebrated warriors, or perhaps war leaders, attained a higher status and had greater access to resources—including wives—than those combatants who were not as successful.

Anthropologists on War

Keeley is not alone among anthropologists in addressing prehistoric warfare. However, in spite of interest in the role of warfare as a force in culture change (e.g., Service 1962, 1975; Carneiro 1970), there are only a few broadly synthetic anthropological works on the subject. Virtually all are collections of papers by various authors. These compilations include Fried et al.'s *War: The Anthropology of Conflict and Aggression* (1968); and R. Ferguson's *Warfare, Culture, and Environment* (1984); Haas's *Anthropology of War* (ed., 1990), Tkaczuk and Vivian's *Cultures in Conflict* (1989), and R. Ferguson and Whitehead's *War in the Tribal Zone* (1992). To a large extent, the authors of most of these papers are guilty of Keeley's criticism in arguing that ethnographic warfare is a product of colonialism and, by implication, that in the prehistoric past warfare was minimal. Or, the volumes are too generalized to advance the topic very far. Turney-High's classic *Primitive War: Its Practice and Concepts* ([1949] 1971) has been resoundingly refuted for what (now) appear to be obvious major misinterpretations.

There are other enlightening studies: Ember and Ember (1992) give a cross-cultural summary of warfare. And several researchers have found numerous ethnographic examples of warfare in New Guinea: Meggitt's classic *Blood Is Their Argument* (1977) is the most lucid, but see also Heider (1979), Morren (1984), Sillitoe (1977), and Berndt (1964). Careful reading of this literature provides not only considerable evidence for the pervasive presence of warfare but also an insight into how it was executed in the past and its impact on society as a whole.

The archaeological community simply has not come to grips with warfare, either in building models or in digesting hard, direct evidence of war and the making of war. This failure is every bit as acute for the rest of the world as it is for the Southwest. A recent example in which warfare is simply ignored as a meaningful social or political factor, despite otherwise convincing evidence, is Cunliffe's 1994 work on European prehistory. While a significant number of the book's illustrations are of hill forts, chariots, and weapons, the region's social organization—and especially trade—are discussed as if warfare was either nonexistent or only of the "ritual" type.

Keeley also demonstrates that most introductory textbooks in archaeology ignore warfare except at the state level of sociopolitical organization. And, similar omissions characterize texts on the Southwest (which are analyzed further, below). It is simply not possible to reconcile Keeley's data and arguments with this major lapse.

Certainly, it is possible—though rare—to find good examples of anthropological examinations of warfare, its change in intensity over time, and its overall importance to understanding past behavior, such as Moss and Erlandson (1992), Tuck (1978), and Milner et al. (1991). The most dramatic transformation of interpretation in the last few years is the radical rethinking of the role of warfare in Classic Maya society. Although Webster (1975) provided the first formal argument for significant Mayan warfare, it was not until advances were made in deciphering Mayan writing that this reality was accepted. Yet, once looked for, it was obvious there was previously ample evidence of warfare, and reading the actual texts was not necessary to demonstrate its existence or its importance (e.g., Culbert 1988; Demarest 1992).

Models and Definitions of War

There are several issues surrounding the traditional anthropological models of warfare. One is the extent to which warfare is directed toward material gain. (Land is usually considered the most coveted prize, but other scarce resources are also deemed important.) Those on one side of the argument tend to claim materialist or environmental necessities are the driving forces behind warfare. Those on the other side believe social and emotional factors (such as revenge, status seeking, etc.) are the driving forces behind most conflicts and see any material gains as incidental. Another major issue in creating warfare models, mentioned above, is the extent to which observed warfare is the result of colonial impact. While this book is about the Southwest, these more general issues are always in the background.

The definitions for war can be as varied as the various anthropological models. Meggitt's 1977 straightforward definition of war seems to be the most useful. He considers war "a state or period of armed hostility existing between politically autonomous communities, which at such times regard the actions (violent or otherwise) of their members against the opponents as legitimate expressions of the sovereign policy of the community."[1]

Meggitt's definition does not make a distinction between "raiding" and "warfare," although such a distinction is commonly used. This is important because Keeley and others show that warfare can take many forms—even among the same people at roughly the same time. Raiding is an integral tactic of warfare. It is used in conjunction with other types of tactics, and it is deadly. Over time, raiding can result in very substantial numbers of deaths and elicit significant cultural responses to it. The tendency to falsely differentiate between raiding and warfare is probably related to the desire to play down the role of conflict in human history. By labeling what is as deadly and common as "raiding," instead of recognizing it as simply

---

1. Although warfare has been variously defined, such definitions usually revolve around violence between independent political entities in order to distinguish it from homicide and intragroup feuding. A case can be made that such a distinction is partially invalid. When the group size becomes small and the nature of political groups becomes very fluid, the distinction between homicide and warfare becomes fuzzy. Since my stance is that most, but not all, of the archaeological indicators of warfare relate to between-group activity, the problem with those distinctions is not critical for the present discussion.

another component of warfare, is to minimize its importance. Regardless of the tactics, war is war.

However, even this broad definition of warfare is problematic and may be too restrictive, in that it assumes open conflict. Perhaps a more useful archaeological conception of warfare is one in which the potential opponents are making risk calculations that result in considerable defensive efforts or *potential* defensive efforts. Actual open conflict between forces could be almost continuous, or intermittent (but endemic), or relatively rare.

From an archeological perspective, it is not required to find "bodies draped over the parapets" to demonstrate the presence of warfare. If the *threat* of attack is great enough, people will respond with various defensive measures—from fortifying their defenses, to moving away, or to forming strategic alliances. And, if the threat of attack is the underlying cause of this behavior, then the behavior cannot be understood without reference to the perceived menace. Therefore, both the role of warfare and/or its threat must be taken into account as relevant to understanding past behavior (see Boulding 1963).

In short, the threat of warfare will result in many of the same behaviors as will outright conflict. If you expect warfare in your lifetime, you will build and locate your community accordingly. You will maintain weapons, you will train your youth for fighting, you will develop military leadership, and you will seek and maintain alliances. Some of the archaeological evidence for warfare will therefore be the same, whether conflict was taking place or only if the threat of it was high.

Thus, a problem with the term *warfare* is that it becomes equated with actual fighting. Intensification of warfare can be more broadly looked at in terms of defensive needs, with actual serious hostilities possibly being less common. Because attacking usually requires more resources and is riskier than defending, fairly equally matched foes can expend enough energy on defense so that offense becomes impractical and a stalemate may result. For example, more than 900 castles were built in Great Britain within 100 years after the Norman Conquest (Keegan 1993), but only a small fraction were ever successfully sacked. In other words, for almost 400 years, castles were built and used because they worked as good defenses.

However, people sometimes miscalculate the odds and either do not fortify adequately or attack recklessly. Once open conflict starts, cultural forces—including the institutionalization of the military and group anger with enemies—can make cessation of hostilities very difficult, even if rational evaluation would dictate otherwise. Truces in some societies are hard to maintain. Even though a truce may be the wish of the majority, a few "hotheads" can break the peace to satisfy personal grudges or family revenge.

So, looking at warfare during a particular time period can be a fluid process. At some times, there may be archaeological evidence in the form of defensive sites, alliances, etc., with little evidence of outright conflict. Or, there may be evidence of actual fighting which was apparently ecologically driven at the outset, but which continued long after the underlying causes had changed and was perpetuated on the basis of revenge and long-standing feuds. Examples of both are there in the archaeological record of the Southwest.

Prehistoric War—Common and Deadly

Perhaps the most important point Keeley makes is that primitive war is deadly. He shows that both tribal- and chiefdom-level warfare generally resulted in fatalities far greater than those experienced by Europe during World Wars I and II. Modern wars typically result in considerable casualties for the soldiers involved (and sometimes civilians) and last for several years, with intervals of relative or complete peace in between. The proportion of dead on an annualized basis over long periods of time is relatively small, representing a low percentage of the population.

In *War before Civilization*, Keeley summarizes data on the number of dead from numerous single historical battles. The Maori, Chumash, Dani, Maring, and Mohave-Yuma have recorded battles where more than 15 percent of the combatants were killed. However, such major battles were rare. In reality, primitive war seems to have consisted of smaller numbers of dead in most engagements—battles or ambushes—but, the number of engagements was quite high. So, the cumulative death rate for males was very high—and was significant for women and children as well.

Keeley demonstrates that nonstate societies regularly had casualty rates, as measured over a human life-span, greatly in excess of those for Europe in the twentieth century. Keeley (1996) and Meggitt (1977) both present a range of death rates, due to warfare, for groups throughout the world of 20 to 30 percent of all males and 2 to 7 percent of all females. The result of these discussions is the realization that, apparently, for much of human history, about 25 percent of men and 3 to 5 percent of women died as a result of war.

These deaths came from several different aspects of fighting: formal battles, ambushes, surprise attacks, and massacres. Perhaps the greatest misunderstanding about primitive warfare involves formal battles. Such battles were usually agreed upon in advance as to time and place by both sides, and they were usually stopped before one side was clearly victorious. Because few deaths occurred in any given battle, the idea that such battles were only ritual in nature has become popularized. However, lives were lost in these major conflicts, and over the cumulative time of a person's life the chance of being killed in a formal battle was significant. One death in a battle that involves 100 to 200 men may not seem like much, but if even six such conflicts took place in a year, and a man was involved in the fighting for twenty years, then 120 deaths would occur in battles he fought in. That is, he would have a greater than a 50 percent chance of dying in one of those formal battles.

Information summarized by Keeley shows that ambushes and surprise attacks, with consequent massacring of an entire community, resulted in more fatalities than did formal battles. On an annualized basis, deaths from both the more common ambushes and the relatively rare massacres were quite significant. It is however, the total number of fatalities from all forms of warfare that is important. To look only at one form of warfare, and only for a short interval, is to miss the point. In combination, the cumulative effect on a population resulted in extraordinarily high death rates.

Not only was prehistoric warfare deadly but it was also common. Both Keeley (1996) and Ember and Ember (1992) provide evidence that in many societies warfare was endemic—with some sort of military conflict usually taking place annually or at least every few years. Thus, the actual likelihood of there being a prehistoric interval of several hundred years' duration without any warfare seems small, and we should be suspicious of such interpretations. When these times of peace are found, they should be of considerable interest, for they are the unlikely event, the exception within the general trend.

THE CAUSES OF WARFARE

Exactly what causes warfare is, of course, a subject of extreme interest. European literature begins with the *Iliad*, and the motives of the protagonists are ever present in Homer's account. Much of the literature on the causes of warfare is more philosophical than factual, and it raises most of the problems inherent in anthropological understanding: Do we try to understand *what* people do, or what they *say* they do? Just what constitutes the nature of an explanation of warfare?

The various explanations for war can be put into two broad categories. The first involves whether fighting erupts over competition for scarce resources (i.e., a materialist or ecological causality) or is sparked by nonmaterialist explanations. Part of this debate is only a different formulation of the arguments previously discussed: that what is labeled warfare in some societies is not anything like modern warfare and is more ritual than real. Even without that issue, the debate over materialist and nonmaterialist causality is still an important one.

The second frequently debated issue is whether ethnographically observed warfare reflects anything but the effects of colonial activity. Many papers in the R. Ferguson volumes mentioned above are good examples of the affirmative argument. Both sides of this debate and the associated literature are nicely laid out in a recent exchange of comments by Shankman (1991) and Blick (1988). Shankman criticizes Blick for arguing that New

Guinea warfare was colonial-impact induced, and then goes on to make a very strong case for material gain and ecological pressure as the underlying cause. (A counter argument is provided by Knauft [1992].)

The Shankman argument that New Guinea warfare cannot be explained by colonial impact and that population growth and ecological factors were the root causes seems very credible, in large part because he is able to provide some time depth to the data and extend them beyond the small area of any one group. Keeley provides additional arguments against the colonial-impact model, and the overall weight of evidence is very telling. That is, while the causes of war in general will remain a topic of debate, the colonial-impact explanation seems close to being laid to rest with Keeley's general work and the careful evaluation of some of the particular examples.

Regardless of how the ethnographic evidence is interpreted, the point is quickly reached where archaeological evidence is critical to the argument. To further our understanding of warfare we must come to grips with the precolonial situation and gain a long-term perspective on warfare. Studies of long time intervals are very useful, and it is the ethnographic cases with the greatest time depth that are the most revealing. Extending our knowledge into the archaeological past is an enhancement of this strength. Moreover, even if many of the particulars of the ethnographically known warfare situations were being heavily influenced by colonial factors, they represent only a fraction of human history. What went on the rest of the time? If we interpret the archaeology with the assumption that there was no warfare, archaeologists cannot contribute to the debate.

The Scarce-Resources–Carrying-Capacity Model

The "scarce-resources" model for warfare basically argues that resources were limited and people ultimately fought for them (Vayda 1968; Durham 1976). Scarce resources are closely related to the concept of carrying capacity. The carrying capacity would be the number of people who can be supported by a given amount of land. The concept of carrying capacity is both useful and open to difficulties. There is both the practical matter of trying to measure it as well as several theoretical issues, such as: If you do not eat a class of food (via taboo or other cultural-behavioral reasons), is it part of your groups' carrying capacity or not? Obviously, the carrying capacity can vary between good and bad years, with long-term changes in climate and with the introduction of new technologies and cultigens. Nevertheless, in the short run, the resources available to a given group in a particular locality will be finite. There will be a carrying capacity maximum. The closer a group's size is to the maximum possible group size, the more food stress there will be. Even minor variances in annual food availability will potentially cause shortfalls that may lead to hunger or even starvation.

Without my getting deep into this issue, one argument has been made that people go to war because they were pressing against their carrying capacity and needed the resources of adjacent groups. While competition over land seems to have been the primary concern in the scarce-resource model, the argument can be broadened to include other limited resources, such as access to exotic goods or even access to wives. Part of this debate centers around the "raiding is an extension of trading" model.

The difficulty with evaluating the scarce-resource model for warfare is that the time frame in which it was played out was often much longer than is usually afforded by most ethnographic studies. As Heider (1979) noted in his study of the Grand Valley Dani in the central highlands of New Guinea (the people of the film, "Dead Birds"), had he not returned to this group after some years he would not have seen nearly as much evidence for the relationship between warfare and resource competition. Similarly, Shankman's analysis (1991) of the same general area relied upon even greater time depth, with information from adjacent valleys as well. When a more regional, long time-depth analysis was undertaken, the case for warfare over resources became much stronger. Groups can be exterminated or they can migrate and territories can be reallocated, and all these occurrences can happen over considerable intervals of time.

Linguistic maps provide further large-scale evidence for long-term competition over land. As discussed below, these maps are filled with evidence of one language group forming a wedge between other, more closely related groups. The idea that the abrupt population shifts represented by these language distributions were from peaceful migrations is so unlikely it's close to being preposterous. Granted, a few such movements may have been the result of a population decline by the original group and the empty niche being filled by another group. But these examples must be relatively rare.

As Kirch (1984) points out, the New Zealand Maori could choose between agricultural intensification and warfare. They could clear more forest for new farmland or they could try to take already cleared land from their neighbors. Apparently, most of the time the Maori chose taking rather than clearing—with intense warfare erupting. This example points up the central role warfare must play in agricultural intensification. Except on small islands or where the state imposed peace, a group could choose between intensification or seizure. We cannot understand the decision to intensify without understanding the nature of the choice available to that group. To ignore the warfare option is to place the decision to intensify in a culturally void context. In different terms, if we study intensification only in places with colonial—or with state-imposed—peace, we cannot extrapolate these models to the general prehistoric record, where such conditions were the exception rather than the rule.

The Yanomamö of South America present an interesting case. Chagnon (1968:110) states at one point that "the conflicts are not initiated or perpetuated with territorial gain as an objective or consequence" (1968:110), and R. Ferguson (1992) has argued that Yanomami warfare is a result of colonial impact. However, several other observations by the same authors seem to belie these opinions. Consider this: "Where the Yanomamö have bordered the territory of other people they have fought with them and consistently pushed them out. They are presently forcing the Carib-speaking Makiritare Indians farther north and have virtually exterminated the Maku Indians" (Chagnon 1968:129). Chagnon continues (117): "Mutually hostile villages are separated by at least two or three days' march: If they are separated by a distance of less than two days and intensify their hostilities, one of the two will move to a new, more distant location, abandoning its old garden."

The Vengeance Motive

In contrast to the scarce-resource model of warfare, the "vengeance" model ascribes much "primitive warfare" to simply "getting even." Revenge—whether for the killing of one's family members or members of one's group or simply a historical "they are the enemy" attitude—is considered the motive behind such warfare. Unquestionably, over the ages, when groups engaged in discussions about whether to go to war, factors such as revenge were frequently brought up and they carried weight. Also, when ethnologists have asked why people fought, such explanations were often given. For example, demands by Apache women of vengeance for previous deaths were a factor in deciding to undertake raids (Basso 1971).

However, as Keeley notes, most prehistoric peoples did not like warfare. Even the victors suffered wounds and fatalities. How often would the revenge motive actually outweigh this distaste for the ugly consequences of a conflict? War is also very disruptive in terms of food procurement. For example, in New Guinea when warfare resulted in a stalemate, a truce was often arranged because farming was interrupted to the point that the cost of continuing the conflict became too great.

Also, if, as some anthropologists believe, warfare was uncommon and unnecessary, why would such "get even" animosities develop in the first place? And why would they not be suppressed? More insightful are examples put forth by Boehm (1996) showing very careful calculation on the part of warfare decision makers, including the Mae Enga and the East African Mursi. He demonstrates such studied military reasoning as "if we don't retaliate, we will appear weak and will leave ourselves open to further attack" and the careful selection of ways to stage retaliation so as not to cause the other side to overreact in turn. That is, while there were frequently "hotheads" who wanted revenge, groups tended to make more calculated decisions as to when, with whom, and where to fight.

Controlling the revenge motive can also be seen in the social mechanisms in place to moderate warfare behavior. Communal discussions were common in the decision-making process, and often they had to be ratified by omens or religious leaders before any action was taken. Could not this ratification process have been used to temper hotheaded decisions or situations where the chances of success were deemed low by more knowledgeable individuals?

Such social mechanisms seem to have been effective, and if there was no gain and only loss from such "get even at any cost" conflicts, those engagements would be expected to be rare and minor. However, it cannot be said that revenge was not used as justification for warfare or that such attitudes did not become entrenched over a long period of conflict between two groups. Quite the contrary. As is the case in the Southwest, warfare that may have been "rational" earlier, continued long after such logical reasons ceased to exist. It is quite possible that scarce-resource-induced warfare was an underlying cause of long-term conflict and short-term militaristic behavior was couched in a vengeance mode.

The Ritual Model

Another explanation for prehistoric warfare is that it is indeed "ritual" warfare. This theory proposes that conflicts were staged to adjudicate disputes or to allow men to "show their stuff." This behavior was carefully controlled by the society at large, however, and resulted in few deaths and few major consequences. It is the myth of the prevalence of this type of warfare that Keeley demolishes. Like the "vengeance motive" theory, it is better explained in terms of short-term behavior or as part of a larger corpus of behavior that included other forms of warfare as well.

In summary, we cannot assume that prehistoric warfare does not have genuine underlying causes and does not result in genuine consequences in terms of territorial and resource allocations. While it is incorrect to simply assume such causes—and we must certainly look and test for them—researchers should not assume that warfare does not have competition as the major cause; instead, competition should be suspected and looked for.

METHODS OF WAR

Any discussion of prehistoric warfare must include the methodology of war. There are indeed standard, predictable ways of making war that have worldwide applicability. As mentioned earlier, formal battles—those agreed to by both sides as to time and place—are the most obvious type of warfare, although they may not have been the most deadly. However, such formal battles certainly had a place in the "repertory of war" and probably served other functions beyond direct aggression. For example, they would have given each side the opportunity to evaluate the military power of their adversaries. How many men could each field? How well were the troops trained? How well were they being led? Presumably, each side would try to appear stronger than it actually was in order to reduce the threat of a serious attack. Such formal battles may have been more like today's military maneuvers—or a pure show of force, like the former Soviet Union's May Day parades.

Ambushes, by way of contrast, were strategically a much more important form of warfare. In the famous "Dead Birds" film by Robert Gardner, which recorded war in New Guinea, formal battles were shown in which very few casualties occurred, while several times that number were killed by ambush. With the Yanomamö, most raid victims were shot while bathing, fetching drinking water, or relieving themselves (Chagnon 1968:137). Small parties of hunters, women out collecting firewood, and those answering a nighttime call of nature were all targets for ambush. The death toll from such ambushes, cumulative over time, could represent a large fraction of the population. Moreover, the threat of ambush would have resulted in fewer hunting forays, less wild-food procurement by women, and otherwise less efficient subsistence procurement. So, a population that was seriously harassed by ambush would have suffered nutritionally as well as from actual fatalities.

An extension of the ambush is the surprise attack. A quick strike against part of a settlement or an isolated piece of a community, especially at night, seems to be a common pattern. The goal is not the complete annihilation of the enemy, but the hope that a significant number of people, particularly men, could be killed. Each successful surprise attack would weaken the enemy, making future attacks easier.

A massacre could occur under several circumstances. There are instances where formal battles resulted in a rout of one side, leading to wholesale massacre. Similarly, a surprise attack, when perfectly executed, could also result in the complete annihilation of the enemy. Planned attacks with the expectation of a massacre did take place, although they did not always succeed. However, information gleaned from New Guinea and from archaeology shows that these premeditated onslaughts were occasionally successful. Such events occurred about once a generation in New Guinea, often killing as many as 8 to 10 percent of the overall groups under consideration. Based on Keeley's information, planned massacres are also known to have affected a number of other groups in various parts of the world. As in New Guinea, such catastrophic events seem to have been rare, killing 10 percent of the total area's population, with occasional incidents resulting in as much as 20 percent. It is likely that most of these planned massacres were preceded by other forms of warfare in which the enemy was subsequently weakened. Then, only after the targeted group's weak points were uncovered would such a drastic plan of annihilation be undertaken.

And certainly, a reversal of fortune could also occur: An attack could miscarry and the aggressors could be annihilated. Or, in a worst-case scenario, while the attack force was away, the underdefended home community could find itself under attack from another quarter. It is this fear that provides strong motivation for the formation of alliances, which reduce the risk of such unforeseen attacks.

A classic case of such an attack gone awry, reconstructed by Kroeber and Fontana (1986), was a battle between the Quechans (Yumans) and the Maricopa, who were allied with the Pima. Briefly, in 1857 more than 100 Quechans traveled on foot from the Colorado River to an area near modern-day Phoenix, planning to attack a Maricopa village. The invaders successfully surprised the Maricopa and a slaughter was about to ensue. However, unknown to the Quechans, the Piman allies of the Maricopa were residing nearby. The Pima had horses and greatly outnumbered the Yumans. They counterattacked and the Quechans were killed, almost to the man.

This example contains several key points worth reiterating that are relevant to future discussions of prehistoric warfare in the Southwest. First, the Quechans walked more than 150 miles (242 km) to make this attack. It is certainly reasonable to expect prehistoric people, including those in the Southwest, to move equally long distances for the same purpose. And secondly, military intelligence can be faulty, often resulting in major miscalculations such as the Quechan attack against much more powerful allied forces. Researchers should be willing to accept the possibility that a prehistoric group might attack another in circumstances that would be considered irrational by modern-day assessments. Such an attack may not have been wise at the time, but the perpetrators may have had inadequate knowledge to recognize it as such.

Finally, massacres did occur. In this case, it is known, ethnographically, that a significant number of Quechans were killed. (Incidentally, this massacre would be archaeologically unobservable today because the warriors were killed some distance from any site and would not have been buried in their home community.) Also of interest is that, during the preceding twenty-five years, there are records of thirteen previous attacks by the Quechans on the Maricopa and eight attacks by the Maricopa on the Quechans. Thus, one side made an attack on the other almost annually for at least a generation.

The various forms of warfare seem to take place at all levels of social complexity. It is important to recognize that "real" warfare did take place where social systems were simple and population densities were low. Hunters and gatherers, especially those in areas where survival itself was precarious and where kinship links between groups would serve to mitigate disputes, would be expected to have little, if any, warfare. The Eskimos and Aleuts would seem to fit such a pattern. However, they had considerable warfare, most often in the form of ambush or surprise attack. For example, the Aleut fielded large war parties, and attacks involving deceit and surprising sleeping people were preferred. Defiling bodies was common. The son of a chief might be held captive, but customarily the enemy warriors would be killed and the women taken prisoner (Lantis 1984a). The Nunivak were raided by mainland Eskimos, who were raided in return. Again, the strategy was to surprise people in their houses and try to kill everyone, taking only a few women and children captive (Lantis 1984b).

Warfare also was common among the Asiatic Eskimos, and the typical military tool kit included armor and shields made of wood, ivory, sealskin, and baleen (Hughes 1984). Edwin Hall (1984) also notes that for the Eskimos of the interior of northern Alaska, interregional warfare involved up to several dozen men who often used bows and arrows in ambush. The same groups that warred also had marriage and partnership bonds; they might meet peacefully and engage in war in the same year. Finally, the boundaries between Eskimo and other groups were areas of conflict. The Cree, living to the south of the Quebec Inuit, massacred any Inuit they encountered; they took scalps and spared only some infants (d'Anglure 1984). Similarly, Chippewa boundaries and empty zones (no-man's-lands) were also the focus of conflicts (Hickerson 1967). Thus, warfare for these hunters and gatherers seems little different from that of horticulturists. For future reference, there is every reason to believe that the early-period people of the Southwest had greater numbers, greater population density, and a greater degree of sedentariness than did Eskimos, so there is no reason to assume that warfare should have been rare or unimportant in the Southwest.

One other important aspect of warfare at this level was the capture of women and children—and their incorporation into the victorious group. Such behavior can be seen in chimpanzees, and it has occurred in various human societies throughout the world. It has important implications not only for the growth of the victorious group but also for the distribution of design attributes and other cultural traits known and carried by women. If warfare was common in the past and if the capture and incorporation of women into victorious groups was also common, then the implications for cultural change and variability must be considered.

ALLIANCES AND WARFARE

The formation and maintenance of alliances—a close association for a common objective—between independent political entities is certainly a fundamental aspect of social behavior. And the formation of alliances due to the threat of war, which is considered in chapter 7, was a very important aspect of intergroup political behavior—much more important than has generally been credited previously. Similarly, the nature and frequency of trade must have been intimately related to such alliances. Thus, many aspects of social behavior can be usefully viewed in the context of war or its threat. If warfare was almost ubiquitous in the past, then alliances must have been key to group survival. Where were these alliances and what was maintaining them? Perhaps trade in exotics should be seen as the coinage of diplomacy, not simply as supplying status signals for the elite.

In virtually all types of societies, there exists great motivation for the formation of alliances with other groups. This may well be one of the attributes that separates human warfare from that of chimpanzees. With the benefits of negotiated peace and alliances with some groups so valuable, considerable effort was probably routinely devoted to forming and maintaining close associations. The exchange of goods and of individuals could have been used to cement close ties with potential or extant allies. Exchanging marriage partners was a common method for linking communities, and requiring members of the families of subordinate leaders to reside with the paramount leader was a method for reducing rebellion. Even in rather recent times, relatives of nobility were often forced to live at the king's court so the nobles would be constrained from revolting.

However, all evidence seems to show that such alliances were fragile and subject to disintegration because the calculus of advantage for each group would have been slightly different and, over time, the possibility of more advantageous new alliances would have been likely. In addition, the unsanctioned breaking of a truce by individuals with old grudges, or by parties that were not in favor of the new alliance to begin with, must have occurred.

If the formation and dissolution of alliances or truces took place during one generation, or even a century, it may be very difficult to see these processes in the archaeological record. That is, several groups may alternately be at war and in alliance with each other (a Southwestern example is given by J. Charles Kelley [1952]). During alliance periods, exchange of goods between allied groups might have been very common; during periods of animosity, no exchange might have taken place between the same groups. However, over the span of several cycles of truce/alliance and warfare, there might be apparent evidence of trade among all groups, whereas finer temporal resolution might show alternating intervals of trade and no trade between various pairs of the groups. As with the Eskimo example above, such shifts could even have taken place on an annual basis.

Conversely, some alliances and nonalliances might have been very basic, resulting in long-standing boundaries where interaction was greatly reduced, at least directly. The English-Spanish relationship in Europe did not oscillate between war and alliance over hundreds of years. It may have resulted in periods of truce and war, but the two countries rarely joined against a common enemy. Similarly, the western and central Mexican boundary seems to have been very strong for more than 1,000 years in Mesoamerica. It is not difficult to suggest that this boundary was formed, in part, due to the nature of warfare and alliances over much of this period, as it was at the time of Spanish contact.

Another lesson learned from ethnographic and historical accounts of warfare is that conflict was more likely to take place between related groups than might be expected. For example, while the Mae Enga fought most often with groups with which they did not believe themselves related, they also fought within their own clan and phratry groups. They also fought with groups from which their wives originated and with whom their daughters lived. In fact, special precautions were often taken to reduce the likelihood that blood relatives of the intended victims, who were living with the aggressors, didn't warn their family members of an impending attack. Individuals also positioned themselves on the battlefield so as to minimize the likelihood that they would fight directly with a relative. In spite of these linkages and the unwillingness to fight directly with relatives in another group, warfare still took place between those groups.

Similarly, as discussed in chapter 6, oral traditions of the Hopi and historical records reveal that they attacked other villages in their own area—previously erstwhile allies—on several occasions (Malotki 1993). Thus, it is important to keep in mind that relatedness and alliances are matters of degree. There is little reason to expect that villages in the same area were always allied and friendly. While it is likely that nearby villages were allies most of the time and that competition mainly occurred between alliances of settlements, under some circumstances warfare between villages of the same nominal alliance must have taken place.

RESULTS OF WARFARE

The extraordinarily high number of deaths due to prehistoric warfare has previously been discussed; but in addition to population loss, warfare results in territorial loss. Cultural groups did replace each other, usually via success in warfare. Direct evidence from New Guinea and other peoples as well as historical evidence from the Tupi of Brazil (Balée 1984), the Yanomamö, and numerous linguistic distribution maps all show the same thing: Over time, group replacements can occur in large areas.

Keeley (1996) presents a summary of some territorial gains (and losses) over time due to warfare for a variety of societies. On a per-generation basis, hunters and gatherers, such as the Walbiri, Ingalik, Kutchin, and Comox, gained or lost from 3 to 50 percent of their territory in one generation. Similarly, farmers and herders, such as the Mohave, the Cuka, Meur, Telefoimin, Nuer, and Maring, had gains or losses of 5 to 60 percent. Thus, significant territorial loss was prevalent both for hunters and gathers and for farmers.

Meggitt (1977) has carefully analyzed the nature of territorial gain from Mae Enga warfare. In three-quarters of the approximately thirty-four wars he was able to track, the aggressors took over all or part of the other group's territory. In 17 percent of the cases, defeat led to the complete eviction of the losers, who numbered, in aggregate, some 1,500 people.

Since this information represented, at best, two generations of history, a figure of 30 percent group replacement per century is probably accurate. Shankman (1991) summarized other New Guinea data and found instances where 25 percent of a valley's population was completely displaced by war and upward of 25 percent of adult populations had come to reside where they did due to loss of their own territory. Based on this evidence, it is safe to conclude that extinctions of autonomous groups were commonplace, although all of the people in the group might not be killed. The sum of these cases suggests that perhaps as much as 20 percent of a region's independent groups could disappear per century under instances of intense warfare.

Linguistic distributions provide a very interesting line of evidence for group replacements, sometimes on very large scales. In the Southwest, as discussed later, the Keres speakers moved into the middle of the Tanoan-speaking groups of the Rio Grande Valley. Such a "linguistic wedge" seems most likely to have been the result of one group expanding at the expense of others. Nearby California presents a classic case of such patterns. For example, Moratto (1984) presents a series of maps showing the location of linguistic groups in California over time. He suggests that initially most of the state was occupied by Hokan speakers. Then, speakers of Penutian and Uto-Aztecan languages displaced the Hokans over much of their range, driving great wedges in the original linguistic distributions. While the details are quite complex and other language groups were also involved, the intrusion of these two major linguistic groups is very clearly patterned. Why should it not be seen as a forced displacement?

There is some archaeological evidence to support this argument. The Windmiller sites in California have yielded skeletal populations that have skulls fractured from blows and bones with embedded projectile points. There were also human bone artifacts recovered, as well as skull caches and isolated skulls (Ragir 1972; Heizer 1974). The Windmiller sites seem to indicate an intrusive group of people into California's central valley; perhaps they also introduced a new linguistic stock. Interestingly, the Windmiller sites date somewhere in the 2500 to 1800 B.C. range, before acorns became a staple in California, and the sites' inhabitants were classic hunter-gatherers. Thus, these sites provide evidence for significant hunter-gatherer warfare at a time when population densities were lower than later and perhaps for the expansion of one linguistic group at the expense of others via warfare.

On the Northwest Coast, the reverse seems to have happened. Penutian speakers were apparently displaced by Salishan speakers, who were, over time, displaced by people speaking other language groups (Thompson and Kinkade 1990). Such patterns are also seen in eastern North America where the Algonquian speakers seem to have been split by the Iroquoian speakers, who expanded to the north, south, and west from their initial area in the greater New York area (Lounsbury 1978). In all these cases, the idea that great expanses of territory were given up by the initial language-family speakers without conflict is so implausible that a model of how it might occur is difficult to envision—except for a drastic depopulation among the original inhabitants.

In none of these cases can such linguistic distributions be explained by appealing to colonial-impact warfare (although other examples of linguistic distributions can). The best explanation is that some groups had a technological or other cultural advantage that led to faster growth rates than their neighbors had. As they increased in population, there would likely have been warfare with neighboring groups. There most likely would have been warfare between subunits of the growing group, but there would have also been warfare between various components of the growing group and its neighbors. And, the more advantaged group would have expanded at the less advantaged groups' expense. So, most likely there would not have been a monolithic, internally peaceful group deliberately expanding at the expense of its neighbors. Instead, there would have been competition among many smaller groups, with one set of groups more similar in some advantageous way expanding at the expense of other groups who did not share this advantage.

While it is possible that some of the historical examples of linguistic replacements occurred because the range of the prior people was diminished—such as in the Great Basin or parts of the Southwest—and a new group moved in before the original group could build its numbers back up, the possibility that this was a peaceful process seems relatively unlikely. In the Southwest, the Athapaskans did move into some empty zones, but as soon as they began to expand they came into conflict with the Pueblo people. Similarly, while the so-called Numic expansion (if there was one, and not an evolution in place [see Madsen 1994]) may have been initially into an empty zone, there was ultimately conflict on the southern edge of the Numa range (Ute), the far southeast (Comanche), and the northeast (Shoshone). That is, the further expansion of the Numic speakers was not into empty territory and was accompanied, or most likely was accomplished, by warfare.

Why did these linguistic groups succeed in expanding? They may have had a superior military ability, which could have been due to better weapons, to a social structure more suited to military behavior, to better childhood training of future warriors, etc. More likely, it was partially due to an ability to reproduce faster than the other groups, through either technological differences or cultural differences that led to more rapid growth. Even if groups were equally matched militarily on a one-to-one basis, the steady attrition brought about by warfare would have resulted in the faster-growing group slowly replacing the slower-growing one. And, if the capture and incorporation of women from defeated groups into victorious ones was extensively and effectively practiced, then the process could have been even faster. Thus, group expansion as a result of technological or adaptation differences and expansion due to warfare were probably so intertwined that the former should not be considered without the latter.

SOUTHWESTERN WARFARE

The Southwest of the United States is a good place to tackle the concept of warfare from a prehistoric perspective. The archaeological information is probably as good as for anywhere else in the world for this purpose. If the causes of warfare are ultimately related to ecological factors, then the Southwest is also a very relevant place to test that proposition. The area is marginal for agriculture and has periods of drought, flood, and arroyo cutting as well as periods of increased or decreased climatic variability. These factors have long been postulated as important in shaping human behavior in the Southwest. If such ecological factors can determine group survival, then warfare should be considered, at least for some of the time, a response to any major ecological changes.

In sharp contrast to this rationale, the Pueblo people of the Southwest have come to be known as "the peaceful Pueblo people." It is not at all clear that they initially ascribed this penchant for nonviolence to themselves, but today it is certainly ingrained in the general public's perception as well as in the anthropological literature for the region. Ruth Benedict's "Apollonian Zuni" (1934:73) is the classic "peaceful people" model.

Thus, if there is any place in the world where there is conflict between an ecological model of warfare and the broad perception of the region's long-term inhabitants having been peaceful for millennia, it is the Southwest. If the Pueblo people were able to deal with the periods of extreme resource stress so well documented in the prehistory of the Southwest without warfare, then any ecologically based model would seem far from correct. Conversely, if warfare can be shown to have been a significant cultural factor in the Southwest and if its form and intensity can be correlated with ecological changes, then the modern-day concept of the "peaceful Pueblo people" becomes a myth. To the extent that this work successfully makes such a demonstration, then ethnologists and archaeologists have been perpetuating the myth and using it for the basis of interpreting behavior for over a century. This would imply that more care is required in the assumptions we make and the preconceived ideas we bring to the interpretive framework.

This book is about warfare, and as such does not fully consider other aspects of Southwestern cultural systems. The book's focus in isolation from other cultural factors is undertaken, in large part, because of the need to establish the parameters of the recognition and importance of prehistoric warfare. This approach is certainly not ideal. War should no more

be singled out from other institutions than should trade or status differentiation. Indeed, the opposite is true: Warfare was probably so integral a
part of most cultural systems that it could hardly be separated out. If, as is
considered below, warfare was closely related to carrying capacity and
other aspects of subsistence—and its practice affected, and was affected
by, social alliances, individual status positions, settlement sizes and locations, and so on—then even a pretense to see warfare in isolation misses
its major relevance.

Previous Considerations of Southwestern Warfare

In order to put the present interpretation in perspective, it is necessary to
review, briefly, previous ideas about Southwestern warfare. Given the cov-
erage of some of the recent discussions (Haas and Creamer 1993, 1996;
Haas 1990; Wilcox and Haas 1994), there is no need to address this history in detail. As mentioned earlier, archeologists have traditionally under-
estimated the presence and significance of warfare in the prehistoric record,
both in the Southwest and elsewhere. Nevertheless, the suggestion that
warfare played a role in Southwestern prehistory has been made repeatedly for over a century. Bandelier and others recognized some sites as
"forts" (Bandelier 1892; Colton 1932; Hargrave 1933; Gladwin 1943;
Hibben 1937). Warfare as a possible cause of abandonments—with nomads frequently considered the enemy—was suggested by Schwartz (1956),
Danson (1957), P. Martin (1959), Kidder ([1924] 1962), P. Martin et al.
(1964), and Jett (1964). Linton (1944) may have been the first to make a
coherent argument that warfare was more likely to have been interpueblo,
and Woodbury (1959) is generally credited with providing substantive evidence of significant interpueblo warfare. Similar observations had been
regularly made before (Schulman 1950; F. Ellis 1951; Wormington 1947;
Smith 1952a; W. Taylor 1958). In particular, see Haas and Creamer (1993)
on the history of research and interest in Southwestern warfare.

It is probably no accident that Woodbury (1956) was the first to make a
good argument for interpueblo warfare. He had just worked at Atsinna
Pueblo at El Morro, when he proposed that interpueblo warfare was important prehistorically. Subsequently, a very similar argument for the same
region was made by Watson et al. (1980) and S. LeBlanc (1989a) in sum-
marizing work in the El Morro Valley. This area has particularly clear
evidence for Late Period warfare (discussed later). Not surprisingly, warfare is recognized most easily in places where it was most intense. Lipe and
Matson (1971) make a similar argument for the importance of Anasazi
warfare in the northern Southwest—again, an area that has particularly
good evidence for warfare—and Wilcox (1979) provides an equally co-
gent argument for warfare in the Hohokam area.
There have been some strong statements about the overall role of warfare
in the Southwest. Perhaps the most succinct is by Peckham: "Warfare,

whether with neighboring Anasazi or raiding Plains Indians, seems to have been an Anasazi preoccupation, as evidenced in rock art, oral history, and the Historic Period survival of formal warrior societies that probably had their beginnings in the Coalition or Classic period" (1981:137). Haas and Creamer also make a strong statement: "[W]arfare was endemic throughout the northern Southwest in the 13th century, and any explanations of settlement, political relations and abandonment must incorporate warfare as a central causal variable" (1993:483). There has been a notable recent recognition of warfare in the Southwest, with both data and interpretations providing increasing evidence for its importance, including Haas and Creamer (1993, 1995, 1996); Wilcox and Haas (1994); R. Lightfoot and Kuckelman (1995); and S. LeBlanc (1996, 1997). Whether this is due simply to more available information or a new perspective is open to interpretation.

Yet, in spite of a few broad statements, the orientation of these interpretations for warfare has been quite localized. Most archaeologists who have recognized warfare have done so for a particular site or a small area, and have not tried to extrapolate their findings to the larger region. Wilcox and Haas (1994) come the closest to a pan-Southwestern view, but they lack an explanatory model and mainly argue (quite correctly) that warfare must be taken far more seriously in future model building.

Thus, there has been an evolution from initially just admitting to the existence of Southwestern warfare to the recognition that it was important in some areas, to the realization that it had broad relevance, and, finally, to the actual demonstration that it was possible to examine it in terms of why it happened, who it happened to, and how it worked. Haas and Creamer (1993) should be credited with providing the first good evidence—in the form of site distribution data—that points to interpueblo conflict and to its importance in cultural change in the Kayenta area. Prior to their work, such arguments were based more on gut feelings than on hard evidence—and many archaeologists believed warfare simply existed rather than its being critical to their interpretations. For example, I have argued that warfare was responsible for the settlement patterns seen in the early Mogollon periods (1989b) and in both settlement pattern changes and site layouts in the El Morro Valley and west-central New Mexico (1978, 1986, 1989a), but did so with little supporting evidence.

There have been, and continue to be, many researchers who have rejected warfare as an important element in Southwestern history. In spite of the previous suggestions that warfare must have been important for the understanding of Southwestern prehistory, most syntheses of the area's prehistory virtually ignore warfare or claim it to be a minor, if not irrelevant, factor (P. Martin and Plog 1973; Cordell 1984, 1994). Most of the articles in Gumerman (1994) overlook warfare, with the notable exception of Wilcox and Haas (1994). Some synthesizers, such as Stephen Plog

(1997), make a much stronger case for its relevance. But Plog relegates the discussion to four pages and does not integrate warfare as an important cultural factor in the overall discussion of culture change or adaptation.

Even the authors in a volume specifically devoted to conflict and warfare (P. Fish and Fish 1989; Rohn 1989; Cordell 1989) paint Southwestern warfare as a minor factor and make only a passing attempt at producing actual evidence on the subject. Cameron and Tomka's collection of papers (1993) on site abandonments does not mention warfare as a possible cause. Incidentally, a similar omission exists for adjacent California. Moratto (1984) mentions warfare only twice in his exhaustive summary of California archaeology, and the other major synthesis, by Chartkoff and Chartkoff (1984), has even less to say on the subject. These lacunae occur in spite of ample evidence in California for prehistoric warfare, historical warfare, and the linguistic-family distribution evidence for warfare discussed above.

There is little to be gained in reviewing researchers' statements about the lack of importance of warfare because, for the most part, that is just what they are: opinions that warfare was not important. Nothing to that effect is based on any actual evidence. To further obscure the situation, most of the researchers who have espoused the importance of Puebloan warfare (particularly in the late prehistoric period) have usually evoked nonpueblo peoples—in most cases Athapaskans—as the aggressive enemy. Such assumptions have not been accompanied by any hard analysis. I believe this is because of the implicit assumption that the Pueblo people were peaceful and had been so in the prehistoric period. Although, again, as is discussed in upcoming chapters, there is a small minority of archaeologists who have argued for interpueblo warfare.

Thus, at this time it is easy to compile a short list of researchers who see warfare as significant in the Southwest, a longer list of those who see some evidence for warfare but are unsure about its significance, and perhaps an even longer list of those who completely discount warfare in the Southwest as a significant social factor. Obviously, this is not an issue to be determined by popular vote. Simply saying you are for or against warfare as an explanatory factor is irrelevant. A coherent argument is needed, not just for the *presence* of warfare, but for its *form* and *consequences*. In not accepting the argument, you must show its fallacies and provide alternative explanations for the observed data. The converse is also true. In light of Keeley's evidence for how commonplace prehistoric warfare was in general, you should have to present actual evidence that there was a lack of warfare.

In summary, except for a very few studies, the literature on prehistoric Southwestern people consists mainly of intuitive statements about the presence or absence of warfare, with little evidence presented in either vein. Moreover, even while allowing that such warfare existed, researchers have virtually ignored the questions as to its causes, its nature, and its consequences. The reason for this may be that there is no model available to explain the role warfare played. I believe that enough evidence exists about Southwestern warfare that such models can be made and tested.

A SUMMARY OF SOUTHWESTERN CULTURE HISTORY

For those readers who may not be familiar with the prehistory of the Southwest, a very brief summary follows as a reference. It focuses on only those aspects directly related to the discussion herein and is not meant to cover all topics, even briefly. See Cordell (1984, 1994, 1997) and Plog (1997) for more extensive summaries.

One catchy, but nonetheless serviceable, description of the geographic area known as the Southwest is that it extends from Las Vegas, Nevada, to Las Vegas, New Mexico, and from Durango, Colorado, to Durango, Zacatecas, in Mexico. The core of this region can be divided into three major physiographic and cultural zones: the Anasazi, the Mogollon, and the Hohokam. (See Figure 1.1.) In spite of the problems with such a simple description, the terms are a useful shorthand. The Anasazi area consists of the Colorado Plateau, the northern portion of the Southwest. It also includes the upper Rio Grande Valley, but for most of this discussion the Rio Grande area will be kept nomenclaturally separate.

The Mogollon area includes the mountains in the middle of the Southwest and the lower desert area to the south, primarily in southern New Mexico and northern Chihuahua. The Jornada Mogollon—that area east of the Rio Grande in southern New Mexico—will be so referenced. The Hohokam area generally coincides with the low Sonoran Desert of the Phoenix and Tucson basins and surrounding areas. These broad cultural divisions generally refer to the peoples in those areas after they began making pottery and up to about A.D. 1400, when the terminology ceases to be very useful.

I divide the temporal sequence of the Southwest into three broad periods, due in part to real changes in the intensity of warfare during these intervals but also due to the degree of archaeological information available. For example, the first time period I consider lasted more than 1,000 years. There is little, if any, reason to believe that warfare was equally intense during this entire span of time. However, I cannot find enough evidence of meaningful changes within the period—so, it is considered as a block. Perhaps such refinements can be made in the future.

The Early Period: Up to A.D. *900*

The Southwest experienced a long period of time during which the population was composed of hunters and gatherers—although some cultigens were present (see Matson 1991; Wills 1988; Huckell 1995). Then, during the last millennium B.C. and the first few centuries A.D., the use of corn seems to have increased significantly, despite its presence prior to this time. In the north, or Anasazi region, during the later period—known as Basketmaker II—the people built small, shallow pit houses and large storage cists. (See Figure 1.2.) There was also frequent use of rock overhangs—cliff alcoves—or caves as habitation sites. Recent finds in the low desert area of the Hohokam also show evidence for significant reliance on corn farming and pit houses clustered into villages. There were a few similar sites in the first centuries A.D. in the Mogollon area. And, in particular, there were large, apparently preceramic hilltop sites in northern Chihuahua that may also indicate an intensification of farming. In summary, the late preceramic period—Huckell's early agricultural period—all over the Southwest appears to reflect more use of corn, more permanency to sites, and larger populations living in one place. This is in contrast to the previous millennia, when a sparse number of highly mobile hunters and gatherers was apparently the norm.

Later, ceramics, larger and more substantial pit houses, new metate types, ground stone axes, and other traits appeared around A.D. 200 in the southern portion of the Southwest—the Mogollon and Hohokam areas—and by around A.D. 500 in the most northern reaches of the Anasazi area. This period is referred to as Basketmaker III in the Anasazi area, the Red Mountain phase in the Hohokam, and the Early Pithouse period in the Mogollon (which can be further divided into temporal and regional phases). During this time, relatively large villages became common—some with more than fifty pit structures, which were not necessarily all contemporary—and large, presumably more public, buildings appeared. (Site locations and site configurations and sizes are discussed in chapter 4.)

Anasazi public structures began simply as larger pit houses, over time evolving into more distinctive buildings known archaeologically as "kivas." At around A.D. 900, the structures were in transition—often referred to as "proto-kivas." Until very late in the prehistoric sequence, they remained underground structures, or at least conceptually so. (Sometimes they were actually situated aboveground, but were entered via the roof from a plazalike area as if located underground.) While they were labeled kivas in reference to the modern pueblo ceremonial structures to which they are clearly related, there is no reason to believe their function remained constant over almost 2,000 years. Likewise, it is not safe to assume that even in the historic period kivas were used solely for religious activities. They seem to have served, over time and space, variously as men's houses, winter domestic space and communal gathering places, as well as places for both community and subgroup ceremonies, depending on the size of the structure. In the Anasazi area, tall, towerlike structures that were round like kivas are sometimes called "tower kivas," but their actual use is far from clear.

To continue the timeline: there was a long and gradual trend toward larger villages; use of pit structures as the primary living space persisted up to around A.D. 800–900, when the first aboveground habitation units (as opposed to aboveground storage rooms) came into use in the Anasazi area (pit structures continued to be used at least part of the time for habitation until the 1200s). This interval coincides with the Pueblo I period in the Anasazi region, the Late Pithouse period in the Mogollon area, and the Snaketown, Gila Butte, and (partially) Santa Cruz phases of the Hohokam. Significant aggregation occurred in the Pueblo I period and substantial village sites developed among the Hohokam and Mogollon. Nonetheless, there is little evidence that the largest group that resided in one place ever numbered more than 100 to 200 people, and numbers this large are presumed to have existed only at the very end of the interval.

There is also little evidence of large-scale irrigation systems at this time, although in the Hohokam area there were the beginnings of such works. Burials were formal (although with fewer grave goods than appear later, the exception being the burials in caves in the northern area, which resulted in excellent preservation of what would have perished in other contexts.)

Although a large amount of research has been done on these early sites, they are harder to find and harder to study than later sites, and relatively less is known about them. This is particularly true for the preceramic sites. I consider this entire time range—the early agricultural period (the late preceramic) and the early, primarily pit-house–oriented periods, up to around A.D. 900—as the Early Period. By lumping this more than 1,000-year interval into one broad category, I am doing a huge injustice to the great range of variability and change that took place in the Southwest. But, for my purpose of evaluating warfare, it seems acceptable.

The Middle Period: A.D. *900–1250*

Beginning around A.D. 900, a series of significant changes began to take place over the Southwest, with the most dramatic changes appearing in the Anasazi area. First, the sites later to become the major centers of the "Chaco interaction sphere" had their initial constructions. Over the next 200–250 years, the Chaco system—which extended from southwestern Colorado and extreme southeastern Utah to the southern end of the Colorado Plateau around Quemado in west-central New Mexico—came to dominate the Anasazi area. Interestingly, it did not include most of the western Anasazi area—the Kayenta area in Arizona and farther west—nor the Rio Grande area to the east, and it is far from clear exactly what the vast Chaco sphere represented.

The Chaco system appears to have consisted of major buildings, the largest being about 900 rooms. A number of these large buildings were clustered in Chaco Canyon in northern New Mexico. They all had a distinctive masonry style and extra-large rooms, were often multistoried, and had unique features, such as round kivas within the blocks of rooms. Other very large buildings existed to the north, along the San Juan River. However, there were more than 100 smaller buildings—termed "Chaco outliers or Great Houses"—extending from southeastern Utah, through southwestern Colorado, and down to the edge of the Mogollon area.

It is unclear whether the Chaco interaction sphere was a monolithic political entity, a group of competing polities, or simply an architectural fad-like gloss overlying very different societies. Of particular importance to this discussion is that the Chaco-styled Great Houses were only part of the surrounding local communities. There were almost invariably clusters of small room blocks spreading out from the Great House, which often had a very large, round and presumably public building—a "Great Kiva"—in close association. The small room blocks were one story, typically consisting of ten to twenty rooms, with kivas in front of them, and they might be located as much as a mile or more from the Great House. The Great Houses were, in some localities, spaced about 8 miles apart; and, with the small room blocks spreading out 1 or 2 more miles, the result of this pattern would have been an almost continuous distribution of habitation sites.

As discussed below, this is the only time in the Anasazi sequence when there seems to have been a dichotomy in habitations. The landscape consisted of large, imposing structures with very big rooms and other labor-intensive aspects to the constructions, surrounded by groups of small rooms that would have required much less of an investment in labor. In other words, a minority of the people lived in structures much more impressive than the majority. Such differentiation was unknown prior to the existence of the Great Houses, and did not reoccur after their disuse. It is easy to conclude that this form of social differentiation was unlike that seen at any other time in the Southwest.

During the same time period, south of the Chaco-sphere Anasazi, the Mogollon had started to build aboveground houses. However, communities in this area were still in the range of 200 or fewer people. A number of regional differences can be detected in the Mogollon, and no one has suggested any panregional political integration for this area. Here, there was a well-developed tradition of Great Kivas that began earlier than in the Anasazi area and continued up to the A.D. 1100s. Smaller kiva-like structures were known, but they were less common and less distinctive than the kivas in the Anasazi area. In both the Anasazi and Mogollon areas, the dead were almost always buried in flexed positions, in burial pits, and often with some grave goods. Burials were usually in distinctive areas, such as in trash middens, under the floors of rooms, or in abandoned structures. Even when no grave goods were present, there was evidence of great care in conforming to general conventions of how the bodies should be treated. While there were a few rooms, or even room blocks, that seem to have been built better than others in the Mogollon area at this time, there was nothing that even remotely resembled the difference between a Great House and a typical small dwelling in the Anasazi area.

By this time, the Hohokam of the low desert were utilizing long and sophisticated irrigation canals (also known from the Anasazi and Mogollon areas, but they were much less extensive). Dwellings in the Hohokam remained pit houses, but small platform mounds became associated with ceremonial activities. Villages may have been linked politically along canals, and the large number of ball courts may have been utilized in some fashion to integrate separate communities. Hohokam interments were usually cremations and were located in cemeteries that were distinct locales. Public architecture was in the form of large oval rings of earth, thought to be ball courts analogous to those made of stone in Mexico.

In each of the three Southwestern cultural areas, there does seem to have been some sort of core-periphery relationship. The Hohokam had a dense habitation pattern, with large sites in the major valleys and much smaller sites (with many fewer exotic goods) in the uplands. Similarly, the Mimbres River area and similar drainages in the Mogollon area had large concentrations of sites with lots of painted ceramics, plus exotic shell and turquoise; but in surrounding areas, sites were small with few painted ceramics and fewer exotic materials. The Chaco-linked sites in the eastern Anasazi area encompassed a much larger area than the above core areas did, but the Chaco region, too, was surrounded by areas, such as the Gallina, the Rio Grande, the Kayenta, and the Fremont, all with smaller sites and fewer exotics (although they had more painted ceramics than their periphery counterparts to the south). Thus, not all communities were equal during the Middle Period.

During this interval, population growth was substantial, with most reconstructions showing an increased rate of growth—although the increase probably began somewhat before A.D. 900. Prior to this period, it is difficult to measure growth rates because the earlier sites had much less time-diagnostic pottery and were smaller, which makes them harder to find and date. Consequently, comparing rates of growth between the two periods cannot be done with much confidence. Nevertheless, the intuitive feeling is that population growth during the preceding Early Period was at a slower rate than that for the Middle Period.

Then, around A.D. 1150, there was a marked change over most of the Southwest. The Chaco interaction sphere underwent a major restructuring—or a complete collapse, depending on one's perspective. The Mogollon area was also altered significantly in terms of a major population and social change in the Mimbres area, its most densely populated sector. Similarly, the Hohokam region underwent some form of cultural change, with major sites abandoned and the population redistributed over the landscape. The nature of the cultural systems for the period from A.D. 1150 to 1250 is surprisingly unclear in all these areas, despite the impressive amount of work that has been done. There does not appear to have been a major population decline, but there is also no evidence of substantial growth from about A.D. 1150 on. A few sites, such as Aztec and Yellow Jacket, in the northern Anasazi area were quite large at this time, but most were smaller than the largest settlements of the previous century. Also, there were few examples of community differentiation in terms of big multistoried buildings combined with small single-story structures in the same community.

My Middle Period directly corresponds to the A.D. 900–1150 interval, with the period from A.D. 1150 to 1250 considered either the end of the Middle Period or the beginning of the Late Period. That interval of time is variously discussed in both contexts and is clearly transitional, regardless of its classification.

The Late Period: A.D. 1250–1500s

Beginning around A.D. 1200—but becoming increasingly obvious by around A.D. 1250—very distinctive changes started taking place in all three Southwest cultural areas. In the Anasazi region, sites began to become larger, with smaller sites soon disappearing completely. In the Mogollon, the same process began to take place, but slightly later in time. Similarly, in the Hohokam area a new class of site, the adobe compound, began to appear; although in this case, small habitation units surrounded the larger adobe sites, at least for a time. (This is the other instance in the Southwest where it appears that people of the same community resided in markedly different forms of architecture.)

These changes did not occur synchronously throughout the Southwest, so a beginning date for the Late Period is somewhat arbitrary. Sometime between A.D. 1200 and 1300 seems appropriate. Beginning around A.D. 1300, large areas of the Southwest became uninhabited, a process that continued over the next two centuries. The one exception to this pattern was the Rio Grande Valley, which experienced a population influx and was ultimately the largest population center at Spanish contact. However, the pattern of small sites replaced by fewer, larger sites also occurred in the Rio Grande region. Northwestern Chihuahua may also have had a population increase after A.D. 1300, followed by a population decline before the end of the 1400s.

At Contact in 1540, there was some population in southeastern Arizona, apparently arranged in fairly small communities; the Mogollon area was essentially empty; and the heartland of the Hohokam was empty or greatly reduced in population. The old Anasazi area to the north had three groups of sites—Acoma, Zuni, and Hopi—and perhaps eighty pueblos scattered along the Rio Grande, its tributaries, and the upper Pecos. The Acoma (speaking Keres), Zuni, and Hopi spoke unrelated languages, and the Rio Grande communities were divided into several language groups, with most people speaking related languages of the Tanoan family, but with a group of Keres speakers residing in the center of the valley.

While the vast majority of researchers accept the idea that much of the Southwest was abandoned at the time of Spanish contact and seek to explain this phenomenon, a few feel that there was a shift from farming to hunting and gathering over much of this area and that the suddenly nomadic people simply became archaeologically invisible (e.g., Upham 1982). Of course, acceptance of such a shift requires solid supporting data, which is currently lacking. Also to be considered is that sometime in the late prehistoric period or the late 1500s (an important distinction that is hotly debated), the Athapaskans—ancestors of the Navajos and Apaches—as well as the Numic speakers—ancestors of the Utes—entered this area. In addition, people from the Colorado River area and from the Great Plains may have moved farther into the Southwest than they had previously.

In the historic period, all the farming people in the Southwest underwent a considerable population decline due to exposure to European diseases, exploitation by the Spaniards, and conflicts with the Athapaskans and Utes. Cultural traditions were suppressed, and evolved to cope with these changed conditions. The issue of Southwestern warfare relates directly to the questions surrounding population growth, abandonments over much of the Southwest, and the changing cultural traditions.

AN ENVIRONMENTAL EXPLANATION
FOR SOUTHWESTERN WARFARE

Here, I present a synopsis of a heuristic model for Southwestern warfare. This is more a framework than a formal model, and it must be stressed that the model is not demonstrated in this book. It is presented here to facilitate the reader's ability to place the ensuing discussion into an overall context. While I believe, over time, the broad aspects of this model will turn out to be correct, that is not the point. Rather, the point is that prehistoric Southwestern warfare seems to be patterned and that this patterning will turn out to be explainable. Whether or not the following discussion is found to be correct, it is a point of departure for future testing and model building.

The environmental explanation for prehistoric Southwestern warfare, simply put, is that the region's population size was, in general, closely related to the carrying capacity. Over long spans of time, changes in carrying capacity must have affected the number of people that could be supported. Over short intervals, successive bad years must have resulted in food stress approaching starvation, and outbreaks of warfare were likely to have ensued. In more abstract terms, during good times the Southwestern people must have been capable of moderate rates of growth, and this, combined with high short-term variability in rainfall and other critical aspects of the environment plus long-term major changes in carrying capacity, must have sown the seeds for periods of both relative peace and intense warfare. When the carrying capacity rose, the population rose. When the carrying capacity later fell, the population would then have been too large to be supported and would have contracted, and intense warfare seems to have been involved in the contractions. This relationship appears to hold for the last 2,000 years or so—the time for which there is enough evidence to evaluate the model.

Certainly, the concept of carrying capacity in the Southwest and elsewhere is complex. In particular, it could be asked how much was the carrying capacity a consequence of cultural behavior and norms, and how much was it affected by various factors, especially technological innovation. The purpose here is not to debate the nature and complexity of the concept of carrying capacity, but simply to point out that in all probability the effective carrying capacity did change over time and that the human population had to respond to these changes.

In particular, it is the probability of the Southwest's having experienced long-term changes in climate that is presently of most interest. Much of the focus of previous climatic reconstructions for the area has involved short-term changes in rainfall patterns and associated streamflow from runoff. While these data are of considerable interest, so is the possibility of demonstrating more long-term trends. Short-term variability can exist within the context of long-term trends (see Dean et al. [1994] and Dean [1996a] for extended discussions). In spite of the good quality of much of the climatic information on the Southwest, such long-term data are hard to come by, as they are for the rest of the world. An emphasis on short-term variability does not mean that long-term trends were not real and important. Rather, because long-range trends are harder to see may be why they are dealt with less often.

Just how changes in climate would have affected the prehistoric people of the Southwest is not obvious. But certainly, any overall global weather changes, which in turn prompted regional changes in temperature and precipitation, would have affected the area. Precipitation is critical in such an agriculturally marginal area, but temperature also plays an important role. Both the length of the growing season and the summer nighttime temperatures are critical for crop maturity in the Southwest's higher elevations. In lower elevations, local temperature may have been of limited concern. However, most of the water for farming in the lower areas is exotic, flowing down from higher elevations. Any change in temperatures higher up—affecting the depth of snowpacks, the timing of spring thaws, and so forth—would have affected farmers who were using exotic water resources, even if the amount of precipitation did not change. Thus, any change in temperature could have had major effects on Southwestern crop yields, not only in higher elevations but also in lower ones.

Examining global weather changes for trends that might have affected the Southwest is challenging, especially since the climate history of the world for the last 2,000 years is only partially understood. Yet, the best evidence comes from Europe, where historical records augment, if not provide, the primary climatic evidence. The extent to which European climate can be extrapolated to the rest of the world is debatable. In fact, a climate shift for the better in Europe may well have resulted in worsening conditions elsewhere. Nevertheless, the broad patterns seem to be synchronous over the Northern Hemisphere: when it was cold in Europe, for example, it was cold elsewhere.

Tree-ring data from the Southwest and, primarily, the historical record in Europe (Northern Hemispheric basis) indicate that, in general, the period from around A.D. 0 to about A.D. 900 was one of "average" climate. There were some fluctuations, but they were relatively minor and not as great as what was to follow. From the period A.D. 900 to around A.D. 1200 or so, the climate was warmer than the long-term average. This interval has been termed "the Medieval Warm Period" (see Lamb 1995). The subsequent time period, from around A.D. 1300 to the early 1800s, was colder than average. This later span can be divided into a period of initial cooling, followed by an interval that was a bit warmer, then an even colder time beginning around 1500. This last period is sometimes called "the Little Ice Age" (although some scholars such as Lamb [1995] see the entire A.D. 1300–1800 interval as the Little Ice Age). In Europe, the Medieval Warm Period correlates with population growth and relative economic prosperity. The building of the great Gothic cathedrals began at that time. Then, the following cooling trend brought demographic and economic catastrophe, which became intertwined with the Black Death.

Of particular relevance to subsequent arguments is the transition between the Medieval Warm Period and the Little Ice Age. The timing of this transition is variously interpreted. It is considered by some scholars to be as early as the mid-1200s in some regions and as late as the 1400s by others (Broecher 1992; Grove 1990; Lamb 1995; LeRoy Ladurie 1988). However, the Little Ice Age is usually defined as starting when the glaciers began to advance, which was clearly later than the initial shift to colder weather. As Grove and Lamb note, possible evidence for the cooling trend may be seen in the terrible harvests recorded in England starting in the late A.D. 1270s, with famine present by the early 1300s. These dates are extremely close to those proposed here for evidence of a major cultural change in the Southwest. *A priori*, the climatic changes would seem to fit the Southwestern data close enough to merit consideration as a possible causal factor.

Based on the above interpretation, I think the first centuries A.D. would have been adequate for farming over much of the Southwest, but not optimal. The subsequent Medieval Warm Period appears to have been a time when the climate was very good for agriculture throughout most of the Southwest, and the population would be expected to increase; and there is

TIME PERIOD	ANASAZI	MOGOLLON	HOHOKAM
Late Period	Pueblo IV Pueblo III	Salado Western Pueblo Animas Tularosa	Classic
1250 A.D.			
Middle Period	Pueblo II	Mimbres Reserve Three Circle	Sedentary
900 A.D.			
Early Period	Pueblo I Basketmaker III Basketmaker II	Late Pithouse Early Pithouse Archaic	Colonial Pioneer Archaic

FIGURE I.2
Chart of the cultural sequences for the Southwest.

substantial evidence that it did so. Population does seem to have increased prior to the 1200s, and sites seem to have been everywhere. The subsequent Little Ice Age period would, presumably, have been a time of much worsened agricultural potential, with some areas rendered unusable and others much more marginal. And, there is evidence for warfare and the abandonment of vast regions, particularly those at higher elevations. Only a few areas of the Southwest are likely to have actually benefited from the colder conditions.

While there is good evidence for global warming, then cooling, in Europe and elsewhere, it is far less clear how much these changes were felt in the Southwest. Dean (1988, 1994, 1996a) and Peterson (1988, 1994) lay out the arguments and evidence in detail for the Medieval Warm and the Little Ice Age periods in the Southwest. Peterson's data, which support the presence of both the warmer and cooler time periods, are derived from the very northern edge of the geographical area in this discussion. And, although it is agreed that tree-ring data are better suited for revealing short-term changes rather than long-term trends, Dean argues that the tree-ring data do not show clear evidence of either the Medieval Warm Period or the Little Ice Age. In sum, Peterson is more strongly inclined to accept a Medieval Warm Period followed by a Little Ice Age for the Southwest, and Dean is much more cautious. Archaeologists are far from being able to accept outright a simple scenario of a population buildup during the warm period, followed by a population crisis during a cold period; certainly, caution remains appropriate. Yet, such a comprehensive model should be considered in any overall explanation of this time period.

Although population growth and then its decline seen for the Southwest follows the pattern found in Europe and elsewhere very closely, it does not automatically follow that similar climatic changes occurred in the Southwest—the evidence for this is unclear. But, neither is there strong evidence that such changes did *not* occur in the Southwest. The following model assumes that these changes were worldwide in impact. And, even if the effects in the Southwest were subtle, they were enough to have had significant impact on the carrying capacity.

Initial Warfare

As discussed in chapter 4, the Early Period in the Southwest, especially from about A.D. 0 to around A.D. 900, shows a significant amount of warfare. During this initial period, which saw a shift to agriculture and to larger, more permanent villages—including Basketmaker II, Basketmaker III, and Pueblo I of the Anasazi sequence; the Early Pithouse period of the Mogollon; and the Pioneer and early Colonial periods of the Hohokam—there was significant warfare in most areas. In fact, there was much more warfare than might be expected, which is probably explained by resources becoming differentially valuable and by disputes over their ownership as well as by general population pressure.

Early Period warfare seems to have been chronic, but with only limited impact on settlement patterns or social organization. Fortifications were common, but they were relatively minor affairs, and major no-man's-lands (empty zones) did not seem to open up—or if they did, they were local, not regional, phenomena. It may be that there was a slow increase in carrying capacity over the entire Southwest, primarily due to the continual selection for greater yield in the domesticated plants and the development of other technological improvements (see Matson 1991).

Population growth was relatively slow at this time, and there was surely some carrying-capacity pressure. But, the carrying capacity was being raised enough so that severe resource stress was avoided and, consequently, warfare was sporadic. In other words, growth in the population was constrained by the carrying capacity, and warfare was a consequence of the resulting stress. Then, with the carrying capacity slowly rising, the carrying-capacity pressure would have lessened.

More subtle factors may also have been at play: the warfare—or the threat of it—that took place in the Early Period may also have been caused by shifting subsistence strategies. As farming became widespread, between 800 B.C. and A.D. 200, the desirability of some geographic areas over others may have changed. Land that may have been good hunting and gathering territory could have included poor farmable areas. And, conversely, locations that may have held relatively poor prospects for foragers, suddenly might have had some excellent farming areas. As the people shifted from one subsistence mode to the other, what had been desirable or undesirable probably changed, and people would have wanted to reposition themselves over the landscape. In other words, resources may have become differentially valuable and disputes over their ownership may have risen.

In sum, the Early Period may be viewed as a sort of baseline of carrying capacity, population growth, and cultural responses to those factors. In this sense, the Early Period in the Southwest was probably typical of what transpired throughout much of the world for much of this time. It is in precisely this kind of situation that Keeley argues warfare is chronic. The lack of any central political authority, combined with continuous or intermittent resource stress should be expected to result in continuous or intermittent warfare—which is exactly what is found for the Southwest at this time.

A Decline in Warfare

During the Middle Period, lasting from A.D. 900 to about A.D. 1200, when the climate seems to have been particularly good, warfare appears to have been at a minimum. It was not completely absent, as is discussed in chapter 6, but visible evidence for warfare noticeably diminishes in the ensuing centuries. In fact, it was remarkably uncommon—in stark contrast to what preceded and what followed. In particular, during the period of the Chaco interaction sphere and its expansion (A.D. 900–1130), there was apparently some form of *Pax* Chaco (see Lekson 1992). Equally important, from around A.D. 900 to the mid-1100s, for reasons that are still unclear, apparently most of the rest of the Anasazi area experienced insignificant warfare, as did the Mogollon and Hohokam regions.

The population also grew substantially during the climatically optimum Middle Period (Dean et al. 1994). The best current estimates show the overall population tripling—the highest level ever for the prehistoric Southwest. And, in almost every part of the region, farming settlements were established. Localities that in prior times had been too marginal for successful farming were now utilized. It appears that the carrying capacity rose sufficiently to accommodate the population growth. Or, perhaps more accurately, the increase in population took place because of the increased carrying capacity.

It may be that the integrative forces of the Chaco interaction sphere, as well as the contemporary Hohokam integrative social mechanisms, provided additional means to minimize conflict. Regardless of the interplay, a rising carrying capacity and increasing population were correlated with minimal to nonexistent warfare. Nonetheless, another form of conflict was taking place in the Anasazi area. Simply put, some people were being treated very badly in life and at death. The violence does not appear to have been warfare related. Instead, it seems to have taken place within the political units, not between them. This topic is considered in chapter 5.

Then, sometime in the mid-1100s, the Chaco interaction sphere went into decline. The Hohokam system also experienced considerable change, and the pattern of peace began to break down. At first, as the climate

began to deteriorate, there must have been local and short-duration subsistence problems. Based on evidence, warfare during this transitional period began to increase slightly. Then, beginning in the 1200s, population
growth seemed to slow abruptly and there was more warfare. That is,
between the middle of the 1100s and the late 1200s the situation reversed.
The climate went from optimal to very poor (Peterson 1994), and by then
the integrative forces of the Chaco sphere were no longer in place. Competition began to increase as a very large population was suddenly faced
with increasingly limited resources. This caused significant destabilization,
resulting in very serious warfare with concomitant population loss.

Intense Warfare

Sometime around A.D. 1250, the rapid shift to a significant level of warfare
became increasingly apparent. During this Late Period, population ceased
to grow and began to decline. For the first time, there were major changes
in settlement patterns that reflected the existence of warfare. As the 1200s
drew to a close, conflict became intense, population migrations began to
take place on a massive scale, and the societies of the Southwest began to
undergo considerable changes. Warfare as a means of gaining access to
limited resources became common—and progressively more intense. A case
can be made that warfare was particularly intense for a period of fifty to
seventy-five years, and then began to diminish as, presumably, the original
motivation faded and social mechanisms to control conflict evolved. Because resource stress would have eased up somewhat during the slightly
warmer interval between the 1300s and the major cold snap of the late
1400s and 1500s, warfare could also have declined in intensity during
that time period.

Overall, the following scenario would appear to be a classic ecological
model of warfare: An initial period of chronic warfare caused by carrying-
capacity stress followed by a greatly improved carrying capacity as a result of the Medieval Warm Period. There was not only an increase in the
population but also a decline in warfare—and the most extravagantly large
architectural constructions ever created in the Southwest were built. (Later
sites were larger absolutely, but they were occupied by many more people.)
These Middle Period sites were much larger than was necessary and were
monumental in scope. The realization of a comfortable carrying capacity
continued over 200 years. It ended somewhat gradually, perhaps when the
capacity was finally reached. More likely, the optimal time period ceased
when the climatic changes leading up to the Little Ice Age began with an
interval of increased variability, causing resource stress at an ever more
frequent rate. Social behavior began to change and warfare began to show
up. As the climate cooled, the carrying capacity rapidly deteriorated, leaving a large population to compete over a now-smaller resource base.

The benign climate, which allowed the population to grow beyond the long-term carrying capacity, did not, however, revert to the long-term mean. Instead, it deteriorated to a new low. The population was then many times greater than the area could support, and it crashed—with intense warfare playing an integral part in the decline and response.

To make the situation even more complex, throughout this overall time period, technological advances also occurred that may well have exacerbated the ecological changes that were taking place. For example, during the Late Period the sinew-backed recurved bow was introduced into the Southwest (see chapter 3). It's unclear whether the recurved bow played a major role in the intensification of warfare in the region, but certainly this much more powerful weapon was probably available to some groups in the Southwest before it was to others. Such inequities could have upset the fragile relationships between communities, rapidly altering the previous balance of power and making warfare more deadly. Thus, the introduction of the recurved bow could have intensified a cycle of warfare that then went on for centuries—and greatly altered many fundamental aspects of Southwestern behavior. Yet, its introduction would have had a major impact only under proper conditions. This powerful new bow, deadly when used against other human beings, may have contributed to the overall chaos of the times, but surely was not the underlying cause.

The intense warfare of the late 1200s seemed to spark an initial set of changes that subsequently caused a chain reaction of significant events that eventually engulfed most of the Southwest. The resulting depopulation, migration, settlement clustering, and community structural changes were still being played out when the Spanish entered the area in the mid-1500s. Thus, from the late 1200s to the 1550s the Southwest cannot be fully understood without considering the significant consequences of intensified warfare. All settlement patterns, population dynamics, and formations of larger social groupings should be assessed on the basis of defense and defensive alliances as well as the apparent need to eliminate competition for resources—or, more specifically, to keep competitors at bay.

As it turns out, the Late Period is the time for which a huge amount of archaeological information is available, so the entire process can be examined in greater detail and with far more resolution than is possible in the earlier periods. Admittedly, there is a bias in this book toward the Late Period. That's unfortunate, because the nature of warfare during the time when agriculture was first established is of considerable theoretical importance. Also, the process by which the Chaco interaction sphere seems to have diminished conflict—possibly even beyond its boundaries—is of great interest. But, these, the most compelling times, are the hardest to address. Nevertheless, the intense warfare of the Late Period is equally important—especially in terms of studying alliance formation and interaction.

This overall model for the Southwest does not intend to imply that warfare is an explanation for all of the events that occurred or that even where war was an important cause its existence is a full explanation of events. The point is, if warfare was having an important impact on parts of the system, it must have been having some impact on the whole system as well.

One important, final note: The increase in warfare in the Southwest beginning in the 1200s, was not unique to this region. It was a continent-wide phenomenon. There was an increase in warfare in the Northwest Coast area, as seen in an increase in fortifications dating to around this time (Moss and Erlandson 1992; Maschner 1991). There is also considerable evidence from the plains and the central United States for increased warfare in general (Bamforth 1994; Owsley and Jantz 1994) and in particular at warfare-related sites such as Crow Creek (Zimmerman and Whitten 1980; Willey 1990), the Lawson Site (Owsely et al. 1977), and Norris Farm No. 36 (Milner et al. 1991). Also, shifts in settlement patterns and site layouts similar to those seen in the Southwest are known for the Northeast (Tuck 1978). And, palisaded villages and the development of no-man's-lands also occurred at around this time in the Southeast (D. Anderson 1990; Larson 1972). The number of individuals who died from fighting also greatly increased at this time in Southern California (Lambert 1997b). That all these geographic areas would have had an observable increase in warfare at the same time strengthens the likelihood that there was a significant phenomenon in the Southwest and that it had continent-wide, if not worldwide, causes.

The close parallels with Europe involve not only changes in population— a period of low growth, followed by growth and then decline—but also an architectural happening. The great Chaco sites were being built at the same time the great Gothic cathedrals were under construction. Furthermore, on both continents, the subsequent fourteenth century was calamitous. The Southwest also evidences parallels with the rest of North America. Warfare increased at the same time elsewhere on the continent; the great site of Cahokia, near St. Louis, Missouri—location of the biggest prehistoric site and the largest pyramid north of Mexico—flourished at the same time as the Chaco and Gothic architectural events. In other words, these inter- and intracontinental patterns of cultural florescence and decline are so closely correlated that they must be explainable by broad trends and similar causes and not by local idiosyncratic events.

Finally, there are several aspects to the overall model for warfare in the Southwest that must be kept in mind. First, the chronic warfare of the Early Period is to be expected. It was probably a typical worldwide human behavioral response to conditions of the time. That Southwestern archaeologists have not focused on the warfare during this period does not mean it is unusual or is in particular need of explanation. It is the lack of warfare during the Middle Period that is really the unexpected phenomenon. Once evidence of prehistoric warfare as a common phenomenon is accepted, then the existence of a 250- to 300-year period during which there was almost no warfare becomes very intriguing. Was this simply a case of population growth not being able to exceed the carrying capacity? Or, did the good climate lead to new social organizations that, in turn, were able to minimize warfare at least for awhile? And, finally, the shift to intense warfare in the Late Period should be expected after the supranormal growth of the preceding period. Its absence would have been the surprise. After a tripling of the region's population, followed by a deteriorating climate, what else could the results have been? The only alternative would have been emigration out of the stressed region. But this would have been possible only if other geographic areas had not also experienced equally large population growth and were not facing a similar problem. Since it appears that the preceding period was optimal climatically over much of the continent, everyone would have eventually faced a relative decline in resources and peaceful emigration would have been an unlikely option. This model for prehistoric conflict in the Southwest essentially turns the more traditional formulations of war and peace upside down. It is not the warfare that needs explaining, but the extraordinary 250 years of peace that really begs for an explanation in the future.

Where To Go from Here

My intention was to make two points in this chapter. First, that archaeologists have regularly ignored evidence for prehistoric warfare, in spite of evidence that shows it was very common. This oversight has led to a serious lack of methods for recognizing warfare in the archaeological record. Second, there are several theories as to why there was warfare. I believe a good case can be made that the underlying causes for most prehistoric warfare were either material or ecological—competition over scarce resources. Simply put, population growth resulted in resource stress, and competition ensued. If ecological factors result in a decline in the amount of resources available, then competition will quickly intensify.

Chapter 2 is concerned with the nature of archaeological evidence for warfare in general and for the Southwest in particular. I argue that this evidence has more facets than have previously been generally investigated by archaeologists, and I go on to define further what some of the archaeological manifestations of warfare would be. I do not see this effort as being even remotely definitive, but simply one small step in developing a set of expectations and an interpretive framework.

In chapter 3, before reviewing the period-by-period evidence for the warfare model, I examine the evolution of Southwestern weapons and warfare technology. This further lays the groundwork for dealing with each time interval in detail. Then, the particular evidence for warfare is given for the three intervals—the Early, Middle, and Late Periods—in chapters 4, 5, and 6. And finally, a discussion of the consequences of warfare on other aspects of Southwestern societies is provided in chapter 7.

CHAPTER TWO

EVIDENCE FOR WARFARE

Just as the sky turned the colors of the yellow dawn, Ta'palo rose to his feet on the kiva roof. He waved his blanket in the air, whereupon the attackers climbed to the top of the mesa and began the assault. There were many of them, so many in fact that they filled the village of Awat'ovi. . . . Running from kiva to kiva, they found that the men were inside. Immediately, they pulled out the ladders, thereby depriving those inside of any chance to escape. Now all of them had come to Awat'ovi with finely shredded juniper bark and greasewood kindling. Upon removing the ladders, they lit the bark . . . they ignited the juniper bark and the greasewood kindling, which they hurled into the kivas. Next, they set the wood stacks on top of the kivas aflame and threw them down through the hatches. Then they shot their arrows down on the men. . . . Now the raiders stormed into all the houses. Wherever they came across a man, no matter whether young or old, they killed him. Some they simply grabbed and cast into a kiva. Not a single man or boy did they spare.

Bundles of dry chili were hanging on the walls . . . the attackers pulverized them . . . and scattered the powder into the kivas, right on top of the flames. Then they closed up the kiva hatches everywhere. As a result, the smoke could not escape. The chili caught fire, and mixed with the smoke, stung most painfully. There was crying, screaming, and coughing. After awhile the roof beams caught fire. As they flamed up, they began to collapse, one after the other. Finally, the screams died down and it became still. Eventually, the roofs caved in on the dead, burying them. Then there was just silence.

—Hopi oral tradition from "The Destruction of Awat'ovi,"
by Ekkehart Malotki (1993)

Along with wanting to dispel the myth that early warfare in the Southwest was insignificant, I also want to encourage readers to be open-minded in considering my interpretation of the *nature* of prehistoric war—an interpretation that can be accomplished with various classes of information. Some of this material—such as early historical and ethnographic accounts of Southwestern warfare—is taken into consideration both to refute the idea that conflict did not take place historically and to discover what patterns of behavior can be found in the archaeological record. Various aspects of warfare as seen in the archaeological record can be used to build a framework for viewing the evidence from the Southwest.

Evidence for prehistoric warfare comes from several different sources.

The clearest and strongest is from settlement-pattern data—specifically, defensive community configurations and the locations of sites. Independent from this data is more direct evidence of actual warfare, as seen in burned sites and bodies that were not formally buried. Also, early Spanish accounts and Puebloan ethnography provide further supporting evidence for significant warfare in the late prehistoric and early historic periods. Each of these topics is discussed in this chapter. Also, because much of the discussion assumes that warfare in the Southwest was interpueblo, this topic is considered as well.

Before continuing, I must make one note of caution. Employing ethnographic analogy can be a useful—but also a dangerous—exercise in archaeology. Although analogies can be extremely helpful, it is unjustifiable to assume that an archaeological find that is similar to the ethnographic analogy proves a similarity in behavior. Moreover, looking only for patterning that was first defined by ethnographic analysis eliminates the possibility of finding different patterns in the past. It is essential to tread carefully when employing these data, and I have attempted to do so.

EARLY HISTORIC AND ETHNOGRAPHIC ACCOUNTS RELATING TO SOUTHWESTERN WARFARE

The ethnohistorical literature is full of references to warfare throughout the Southwest. The references point to warfare as having been an extremely common activity; it was well planned; military leadership was important; and warfare had a major impact on the societies involved. It also resulted in burned communities, massacres, the rounding up of women and children as captives, and the taking of body parts as trophies.

Historical information relating to Puebloan warfare has recently been summarized by Haas and Creamer (1995, 1997) and need not be repeated in detail here. Their overview provides ample historical accounts, oral traditions, and information on the nature of institutions to show that warfare was very important in Pueblo society. Florence Ellis (1951, 1967) also presents considerably important discussions on this topic. The strength of her argument is that social aspects of warfare—from leadership roles to ceremonial practices—were so deeply embedded in the matrix of Pueblo life, that warfare could not have been just a recent phenomenon nor a trivial one.

Because interpueblo warfare began to decrease rapidly by the late 1600s and the Pueblo people began to ally themselves against the Athapaskans and Spaniards (discussed in chapter 6), many later historical accounts and oral traditions concerning warfare may not be fully relevant to understanding earlier behaviors. The accounts from the 1500s, however, would be quite relevant. Chronicles from the expeditions of Coronado (Hammond and Rey 1940; Winship 1896), Chamuscado, Espejo, Sosa, and the other late-1500s expeditions (Hammond and Rey 1966; Schroeder and Matson 1965) as well as those of Oñate (Hammond and Rey 1953) do provide some information concerning the nature of warfare and the weapon technology utilized during the 1500s. The information is quite scanty and it is sometimes contradictory, but it is still useful.

In general, these early accounts provide evidence not only for the existence of warfare but also for its nature. The Coronado-era chronicles report alleged warfare between Zuni and Acoma as well as between Zuni and Hopi (Hammond and Rey 1940). Similarly, when Espejo, in 1582, went from Zuni to Hopi, some eighty Zunis "armed with bows and arrows" accompanied him, allegedly to attack the Hopi (Hammond and Rey 1966:187).

Of particular interest are the battle tactics employed by the Zuni and the Hopi during their first encounters with the Spaniards. Both groups initially defended themselves against the invaders by coming out of the pueblos to fight on open ground in rather formal ways. They apparently "lined up by divisions," used trumpets to signal maneuvers, and may have used a winged attack plan at Hopi (Bolton 1964). (Incidentally, this behavior seems to represent tactics that had evolved in conflicts with other large groups of organized fighters, and not with small groups of "nomads" employing "hit-and-run" tactics.) For the Rio Grande area, the early Spanish accounts mention that some groups were at peace and stayed within their boundaries. Such statements make sense only in reference to interpueblo warfare.

T. J. Ferguson and Hart (1985) provide a summary list of historically recorded incidents of violence relating to Zuni. They mention three incidents of warfare with Hopi and Acoma between 1692 and 1706. These include instances of attacking and of being attacked. However, after 1705 or 1706, all remaining references to warfare are with Athapaskans. Although it is known that Zuni and other pueblos were attacked or harassed by Athapaskans from the mid-1600s on (Dozier 1954), prior to 1705–1706 interpueblo conflict still occurred and was significant enough to be recorded. After that date, all references change and focus on one opponent. Apparently, the Athapaskan threat became so severe that around 1700 previous hostile relationships were quickly converted into alliances by the Pueblo groups against the Athapaskans. (Incidentally, if the Athapaskans had always been the enemy, such a shift would not make sense.)

The historical record, however, is not without its difficulties. When Espejo traveled from Zuni to Hopi in 1582, eighty Zuni warriors accompanied him because they were apparently at war with the Hopi. En route they met a small party coming from Hopi that consisted of one man, three women, and three children. That is, they met a small, defenseless band of Hopis apparently casually going between the two areas. Such a trip would have been an extremely dangerous thing to do if serious warfare was in progress. But, such behavior is explainable given the conditions that, during a conflict, certain people were afforded neutral status—a pattern found elsewhere in the world (Hammond and Rey 1966:187).

In the Rio Grande Valley, defenders bolstered the defensive features of their pueblo after Coronado's advance party attacked it (Bolton 1964). Although this group had not seen fit to take such precautions against non-Spaniards, the people certainly knew how to improve their defenses—and the pueblos were very defensible, as the Spaniards repeatedly noted. The Spaniards did see a pueblo that had recently been attacked and destroyed in the Galisteo Basin (Hammond and Rey 1940; Bolton 1964). Whether this was at the hands of other Pueblo people or plains nomads is open to interpretation (Wilcox 1991). Nonetheless, everyone was well armed, enmities did exist between neighboring groups, and the Puebloans were ready to fight.

There is also some historical information on weapons. The Spaniards make repeated references to "Turkish bows" (Hammond and Rey 1966) and how effective they were (a topic considered in chapter 3). It was noted that in a particular Rio Grande pueblo at the time of his marriage a man was traditionally given a bow, shield, club, and spear with which to defend his family.[1]

Pueblo oral traditions contain additional information on interpueblo warfare. Malotki (1993) provides extensive narratives of Hopi oral traditions detailing the abandonment and destruction of seven villages. Six of these events involved attacks by people from other Hopi villages, or outside people, most of whom were also clearly living in farming villages. Most attacks resulted in the village being burned, and many involved killing men and boys, but taking women and girls captive. While none of these stories are couched in terms of resource competition or long-term intergroup warfare, they seem to describe the same type of destruction seen archaeologically as well as behaviors found in warfare of this type in other parts of the world. As is discussed in chapter 6, the period of destruction for these Hopi communities appears to have been the 1300s or later.

Cushing ([1896] 1988) provides a Zuni account describing a battle fought with allies of Acoma. After a long fight, the Zuni succeeded in killing the other group's leader, the opposition fled, and the Zuni entered their great town. Some survivors were then assimilated by the Zuni. The site involved is generally considered to be south of Zuni, possibly what is now called Fort Atarque (see in the Appendix, under the headings Colo-

---

1. This reference to the spear as a gift to the groom is perplexing (also discussed in chapter 3). Spears are noticeably rare in Southwestern paintings and rock art, and they are not recovered from caves (with one possible exception) or other sites. The Spanish do not mention them in their fighting the pueblo groups. They make no reference to anything but arrows and rocks as projectiles, and do not discuss clubs, shields, or spears (either thrusting or throwing) in battle descriptions. There is evidence that clubs and shields were in use and were important, so the reference to a spear is probably more a problem with the historical accounts than it is a description of reality.

rado Plateau Clusters, "The Techado and Jaralosa Draw Clusters"). That the nature of the alliance between these enemies was an important component of this account and that their ally was Acoma is of particular interest. And since there are also other historical accounts in which Puebloan resistance faltered when a leader was killed, it appears that these "military leaders" played a very important role in making war.

Oral accounts can also be interesting regarding prehistoric armaments. Narratives provided by Cushing (1988) describe the important Zuni gods known as the Warrior Twins:

> They were armed, as were the warriors of old, with long bows and black stone-tipped cane arrows carried in long-tailed catamount-skin quivers; with slings and death-dealing stones carried in fiber pockets, spear throwers, and blood drinking broad knives of gray stone in fur pouches with short face-pulping war clubs thrust aslant in their girdles. And shields of cotton plaited with yucca upon their backs. About their bodies they wore casings of scorched raw-hide, horn-like in hardness, while upon their heads were helmets like the neck-hide of the elks from which they came.

Clearly, this description of the gods' elaborate battle dress is far more extensive than what the usual armament of any single Zuni warrior would have been. But, it is interesting to note that black obsidian arrowpoints seem to be described, suggesting there was interest in the particular point types used for war. The spear-thrower is also of interest. Although it was early on a weapon of war, it seems to have dropped out of use well before the end of the first millennium. Hand-held weapons were extremely prominent in this description, as was armor. The apparent importance of the latter suggests that the archaeological record is deficient in this regard and that warfare was intense enough to have resulted in the development of armor.

Beaglehole (1935) notes that Hopi armament included the usual bow, arrows, and shield, and he describes throwing-sticks carried in the warriors' belts. He also discusses the importance of hand-held weapons, including the stone club, stone ax, and lance. The lance was rare and was used as a close-combat hand weapon. Beaglehole provides one account of the Hopi attacking a Navajo settlement at night or early dawn. Four Hopis swooped down on each hogan and killed and scalped many enemies. Another narrative describes how Navajos, Paiutes, and Mexicans joined with First Mesa Hopis to attack the Hopi town of Mishongnovi. During the ensuing fight, one defender with a shield and throwing-stick blocked the top of each trail to the village while others shot arrows from behind him. There was fighting in the village; houses were torn down, looted, and set on fire. First Mesa men looted many houses and ran off with all the buckskin and turquoise they could steal. The men from Mishongnovi counterattacked and killed many women and warriors in the First Mesa village in retaliation.

Also, Beaglehole reports that women were taken captive and sometimes married. Again, the above narrative provides evidence of alliances and the taking of goods and women as the spoils of war. It appears that part of the village was set on fire in the midst of battle, but that the entire community did not burn. Of note is that access to part of the village did not mean immediate victory—a pattern seen in Spanish attacks on pueblos, when, even after gaining access to some parts of the village, they had to fight "hand-to-hand" to fully subdue the remainder. This type of warfare seems to be reflected in the archaeological record.

There are several other historical or anthropological accounts relevant to a discussion of prehistoric warfare, specifically those of the Mohave people in the Colorado River area (at the present-day Arizona/California border) and the people of the Sonora area of northwestern Mexico. While these examples are not from the Pueblo area, they are geographically close enough to suggest that these people would not have fought in ways completely alien to their Pueblo neighbors.

In discussing Mohave warfare, Fathauer (1954) notes that spies (which probably also included what could be classified as scouts) were an important and valued class of men, implying that military intelligence was important and sought after. He goes on to note that there were different classes of fighters, some armed with bows and others with clubs and that tactics were designed to take advantage of these differences. He also notes that "A few young females were sometimes taken as prisoners. . . . [T]hey were given to old men to marry" (Fathauer 1954:99).

Fathauer reports a considerable amount of ritual behavior with respect to scalps. He provides clear evidence of alliances and military support among the entire Mohave tribe, with special means of communicating for help between separate communities in case of attack. There were also alliances with other polities, such as the Yuma—an association that chased the Halchidhoma and Kohuana out of the Lower Colorado River Valley. In summary, from the Mohave narratives the evidence points to special classes of fighting men, organized fighting, alliances, signaling for help, scalping, and the capture of women. I contend that all these behaviors were present prehistorically in the Southwest, as well.

Also of relevance are the historical accounts of warfare in Sonora and adjacent areas of northwestern Mexico. Wherever there is good, early information from this area, there is evidence for continuous warfare by rather large groups of well-organized men as well as the taking and displaying of trophy heads and other body parts.

These Sonoran "statelets" (Riley 1987)—which were like the alliance groups seen in the Southwest (discussed in chapter 7)—were contacted by the Spanish during the Ibarra expedition in 1565, and there are descriptions of them by Obregon (Hammond and Rey 1928) and Ruiz (Sauer

1932). Described in one instance is a fortress made of four houses (room blocks) built in the form of a square. It was large and strong, with stout walls and a large central patio. It also had a corner tower and a narrow entryway passage, and was protected on two or three sides by a deep gorge. This description is strikingly similar to late Pueblo III and Pueblo IV sites on the Colorado Plateau, in particular those in the El Morro Valley (discussed in chapter 6).

In one attack, the Spaniards were met by 400 warriors arranged in units, who fought with bows and arrows and spears, with some armed with clubs and shields. Apparently, another encounter involved 600 warriors. In this fight, resistance collapsed when the war leader was killed. A similar midconflict breakdown occurred under similar circumstances in a Rio Grande battle of the 1500s between Pueblo people and the Spaniards. Even if these numbers are exaggerated, the accounts represent large groups of quite well organized warriors.

There are also repeated references from the northwestern Mexico region to the taking of human trophies. One account of a Sonora group is particularly illustrative:

> Dead bodies, heads, arms, legs, tongues and ears were hanging in the streets and prominent places . . . The latter [their enemies] had assaulted a town, and when informed, they came out to meet them and routed them. They killed them and took away the loot, spoils, and slaves which they had taken, and as a sign of victory had hung up the limbs of their enemies. (Obregon in 1584 [Hammond and Rey 1928:175])

Obregon also noted that "They do not eat human flesh. However, they quarter those whom they kill in war and distribute and hang them in their houses and terraces as trophies (Hammond and Rey 1928:168).

Slightly farther south in Mexico, early accounts of the Yaqui of Sonora and the Acaxee and Xixime of Durango describe skulls and other bones of enemies that were hung as a display or used in ceremonies (Beals 1933). Beals (1932) also gives warfare-related information for northern Mexico and parts of the Southwest that was recorded before 1750. The taking of scalps was practiced by the Cocopa, Yuma, Mohave, Maricopa, Paiute, Yavapai, Havasupai, Navajo, Ute, Zuni, Apache, Pima, Opata, Tepahuane, and Sinaloa groups. (Incidentally, Beals notes that almost all of the Californian groups also took scalps.) Some warring groups took heads, including the Tarahumare, Yaqui, Tepahue, Acaxee, and Tepehuane. A few groups are recorded as preserving the skulls and bones of enemies, including the Acaxee, Xixime, Yaqui, and Tarahumare. Haas and Creamer (1997) discuss historical evidence for scalp taking in the Pueblo area.

Since ancestor worship could be one way to interpret the highly charged topic of human-body trophy taking, it is important to note that all the cited descriptions of scalping behavior and other trophy taking involved the scalps and body parts of enemies. Furthermore, there is no evidence of the skulls, other bones, or scalps of one's own people being used in public displays or as artifacts. While such intragroup behavior is known from other parts of the world, it is unlikely that archaeological finds of such items in the Southwest would be evidence of ancestor worship, the maintenance of charnel houses, or any other form of mass curation of ancestral bones. To propose for the Southwest a type of ancestor worship for interpreting this kind of remains would require considerable supporting evidence—especially since there is good evidence that the trophy taking of enemy body parts was a well-established practice in the region. The relevance of this argument to the Southwestern situation is discussed below.

The Sonoran accounts also touch on the topic of weapons: Beals notes that virtually every group is recorded as using clubs and shields. The Pima, Opata, Pima Bajo, people of the Fuerte River, Sinaloa groups, Acaxee, and Jumano were also recorded as using spears (not atlatl darts). Several groups are described as having organized formations, including the Pima Bajo, who used two squadrons; the Rio Fuerte, who deployed at least 1,000 men in four squadrons; and the Ocoroni, who had 400 to 500 men in three squadrons. While such lists are rather crude indicators of behavior, the overall pattern is clear. Warfare in the Sonoran area was very far from being occasional and irrelevant, and it was well organized.

The Spaniard Obregon observed that communication between groups was both fast and informative. In 1584 he saw in Sonora that "From this point they could perceive large numbers of smoky fires by means of which it is the custom and practice here to call and warn their friends to prepare for war. . . . By means of these fires they communicate with and understand one another easily" (Hammond and Rey 1928:155). The Sonoran accounts describe how these smoke signals effectively transmitted information concerning the activities of the Spaniards over large distances—apparently covering 450 kilometers within two days. Such signaling seems to have been employed prehistorically on the Colorado Plateau and adjacent areas as well.

Obregon also makes mention of settlement groupings and alliance building in the Sonoran accounts. He states that one political group comprised five communities, spaced 1 to 2 leagues (3 to 6 miles) apart—a pattern not unlike that seen in the Southwest (see chapter 6). There is also rather good evidence for alliance maintenance in the form of agreements between polities as to the number of men to supply and how the spoils would be divided for particular military campaigns. In general there is significant evidence in the early accounts that warfare in Sonora was endemic, organized, and large-scale.

Another account of warfare comes from even farther outside the Southwest, but it describes a form of fighting that is probably relevant to the Southwest. Secoy (1953) relates an eyewitness account of fighting between Shoshone and Blackfoot in the very early 1700s. No guns or horses were involved, but some arrows had iron tips. The number of men involved was large, with each group fielding more than 300 men. Quivers were said to have held fifty arrows, and knives and axes were considered valuable weapons. This firsthand account noted that

> both parties made a great show of their numbers. . . . They sat down on the ground, and placed their large shields before them, which covered them: We did the same, but our shields were not so many, and some of our shields had to shelter two men. . . . [Arrows were then shot at each other]. . . . On both sides several were wounded . . . [but none killed] . . . and in those days such was the result, unless one party was more numerous than the other. The great mischief of war then, was as now, by attacking and destroying small camps of 10 to 30 tents, which are obliged to separate for hunting.

This account points out the great value of shields and just how rare they could be. It is further evidence as to the relatively nonlethal aspect of arrows as well as to the importance of hand-held weapons. The account reads much like descriptions of a New Guinea formal battle, with prominent display by each side of their numbers—and few deaths. Also as in New Guinea, raiding and ambush were considered very deadly. However, destroying a camp of thirty tents, which would seem to result in a massacre of more than 100 people, could hardly be called a minor ambush. This account also shows how large a group could be assembled from among people who had no more complex organization, or even less complex, than did the Puebloans.

More recent historical accounts of actual warfare in the Southwest exist, but the introduction of metal weapons, horses, Europeans, and disease so complicated the situation that using them as models for the prehistoric period is of limited utility. But, a few examples are worthy of note. Apparently soon after the defeat and retreat of the Spaniards during the Pueblo Revolt of 1680, the Keres and Pecos Indians became actively hostile toward the Tewa and the Tano (Dozier 1954). Was this a return to earlier hostile relations and old alliances after a brief new alliance against the Spaniards? After the reconquest, some Tano with Tewa allies lived on the top of Black Mesa near San Ildefonso—raiding up to 16 miles away in Santa Fe—and held out against the Spaniards for nine months. It was part of this group that moved to Hopi, where they founded a village on First Mesa. The Hopi welcomed them as allies and a source of military strength (Dozier 1954).

Titiev (1944) noted that the chief weapons for the Hopi were bows and arrows, clubs, throwing-sticks, and spears. He also provided evidence that scalp taking was very important and quite ritualized. He relates one clan origin story that describes a battle, apparently with the Chemehuevi. Some form of distraction created by this clan gave them the opportunity to attack the Chemehuevi successfully, killing eighty men. Because of this success, the clan was given land at Hopi and allowed to join the community. Titiev also noted that while all Hopi men were considered warriors, those who had killed an enemy were called *real* warriors and had an obligation to fight in the vanguard. There is a clear indication that they gained stature and certain prerogatives as *real* warriors.

The historical account of the battle between the Quechan and Maricopa in the 1850s (Kroeber and Fontana 1986) was mentioned in the discussion on massacres in chapter 1. Of further note is that the attackers originally were part of an alliance that had disintegrated, which surely contributed to their defeat; it was the Maricopa's allies, the Pima, who eventually overwhelmed them. Also, the Quechan crossed over the territory of an intervening group to make the attack some 150 miles from their home territory. This instance points to the value of solid alliances and just how far people would go to attack other groups.

Who Was the Enemy?

One of the ongoing questions that arises when considering evidence for prehistoric Southwestern warfare is: "Who was fighting whom?" This is a critical issue because it has such an important impact on the understanding of the consequences of warfare in terms of intergroup relations. Since it is generally accepted that there was warfare during the Early Period and the Middle Period up to the late 1200s, it is reasonable to assume that any conflict would have been with two or more sedentary groups. However, since various new people who did not practice agriculture (at least initially) and who were derived from different linguistic groups entered the Southwest sometime after A.D. 1200 and before 1600, the question arises as to whether these groups were relevant to warfare after 1200. Of course, there were always hunter-gatherers on the peripheries of the Southwest who could have been in conflict with Southwestern farmers. The question is whether these people or people newly arrived in the area began to constitute a new and greater threat than had existed before.

In the past, most researchers who thought there was strong evidence for warfare in the late Prehistoric Period usually evoked non-Puebloan peoples—presumably nomadic nonagriculturists—as the enemy. For example, the old Point of Pines field-school song, "The Great Pueblo Fall," related to me by Point of Pines alumna (class of 1953) Patty Jo Watson, refers repeatedly to the "Athapaskan raiders." As Madsen (1994) has pointed out, Numic-speaking people—Utes and Southern Paiutes—who now occupy the former northern range of the Anasazi, would have been potential candidates for the role of non-Puebloan combatants. And a Hopi tradition, discussed by R. Lightfoot and Kuckelman (1995), related the destruction and abandonment of sites in the Four Corners area to non-Puebloan people. Of interest: The sites in that area were abandoned in the late 1200s.

One aspect surrounding this question of who was fighting the Puebloans is this: Just when did the Athapaskans (and the Numic speakers) enter the Southwest? This is a hotly debated topic. Some argue for dates as early as sometime in the 1400s (P. Reed and Horn 1990), while others (Wilcox 1981b, 1988) strongly disagree and see a date of after A.D. 1500 as more defensible. While an early date seems increasingly more likely, it would appear to be far later than the mid-1200s when increased evidence for warfare begins.

In addition to the issue of dating is the question of whether such groups were ever a military threat—assuming they did exist. There are several lines of evidence to suggest that non-Puebloans were not the primary enemy. The tactics employed by the Pueblo warriors during their first encounters with the Spanish—coming out of the pueblos, lining up by divisions and charging—were probably not what the Puebloans would have used against small groups of "nomads" with "hit-and-run" tactics. As mentioned before, early Spanish accounts for the Rio Grande area referring to some Pueblo groups as remaining—peaceably—within their boundaries further supports the evidence for interpueblo warfare.

It seems unlikely, as Linton (1944) and, subsequently, C. White (1976) point out, that non-Puebloan aggressors—again, nonfarming nomads—were a significant threat to many of the Pueblo III and Pueblo IV communities of the late 1200s to 1540s. It is difficult to see how such groups—without horses—could have fielded war parties of any significant size. Certainly, these potential attacking forces would hardly have been large enough to threaten the communities with populations of 1,000 or more people (such as Pueblo de Los Muertos in the El Morro Valley, W:10:50 at Point of Pines, or Kin Tiel) that existed at the time. Moreover, there is good evidence (discussed in chapter 6) that these large sites were clustered together in the form of alliances, further enhancing their military strength—and at least some of the alliances probably could easily have fielded more than 500 men. Small nomadic groups would have been helpless against Puebloan combatants intent on removing them as a threat.

Some of the most convincing evidence, both for warfare, and for its being interpueblo, is the distribution of sites and resulting "no-man's-lands." This evidence is discussed in great detail in chapter 6 and in the Appendix. But, briefly, the point here is that there were clusters of sites—usually three or more sites, but sometimes up to eighteen—separated from each other by about 20 miles. And the spacing between these clusters grew larger over time. Certainly, there can be no reason for such settlement patterns if the threat of conflict came from non-Puebloan nomadic groups. While it would make sense for settlements to cluster for mutual defense against nomads, why would these no-man's-lands grow up between clusters? The opposite response is more likely: clusters of clusters or long linear arrangements of settlements would have been a better response to the threat of non-Puebloan enemies for the mutual support they would provide. This, however, is in sharp contrast to the widely separated clusters that are found.

The final point in this discussion of who was fighting whom is, as Haas and Creamer (1995) demonstrate (and as discussed above), the early historical record is filled with accounts of Puebloan versus Puebloan warfare and enmity (see also Wilcox 1991).

Any conflicting evidence for inter-Puebloan and non-Puebloan warfare may simply be a reflection of the time intervals involved. By the mid-1600s, the Pueblo populations had been greatly reduced in numbers due to Spanish impact and the introduction of European diseases. Meanwhile, the Athapaskan population seems to have increased—and they had access to horses. Thus, Athapaskans would have become an increasing threat. As noted above, the historical accounts seem to show a shift in enemies and alliances at around 1700. It is more likely that prior to this time, any extant groups of hunter-gatherers would have affiliated themselves with appropriate Pueblo alliances and may have participated in inter-Puebloan conflicts in that capacity.

Until evidence is produced to the contrary, the conclusion that there was significant warfare between Puebloan groups seems justified. However, both the Numic expansion and the entry of the Athapaskans into the Southwest occur close to the time warfare increased in intensity—which is too coincidental for comfort. This issue should not be considered completely settled, and the possible role these groups played in the evolution of late Prehistoric Period warfare should continue to be evaluated in light of new data.

GENERAL ARCHAEOLOGICAL EVIDENCE FOR WARFARE

Delineating the archaeological signatures of warfare is always a serious exercise for scholars. Cordell (1989) recently argued, essentially, that the only convincing data is direct skeletal evidence in the form of trauma and embedded weapons. I single her out only because, to her credit, she is very clear on the subject. Many other archaeologists seem to hold the same sentiments, but they are so vague that it is hard to pin them down. Keeley, however, in *War before Civilization* (1996) presents good, convincing lines of evidence that do not involve skeletal remains, such as palisaded villages with concentrations of arrowheads near walls and, especially, around gates. Haas and Creamer's (1993) entire argument about Kayenta warfare is made without significant reference to skeletal data. Obviously, it is possible to find a number of independent lines of evidence for a serious exploration into the existence of prehistoric warfare. Certainly, skeletal data are an important and useful line of evidence in this search, but they are not essential—nor, in fact, do they provide much insight into the nature of warfare.

Because the archaeological evidence for prehistoric warfare can take many forms, a review of the nature of this evidence is important in order to put data from the Southwest into perspective. What follows is an expansion of the review by Wilcox and Haas (1994). Direct evidence for warfare is actually very limited. Of course, strong evidence can be found in bodies—whether formally or nonformally buried—showing evidence of violence that presumably lead to death, such as arrowheads embedded in vertebrae or depressed cranial vault fractures. Other strong evidence can be found, presumably, in trophies—including trophy heads and other bone trophies—and in indications of scalping in the form of cutting marks on the skull. Also, historical accounts of warfare are available that, in some instances, complement the archaeological record.

There are, however, other forms of archaeological evidence for prehistoric warfare that, although less direct, are potentially more useful. These include settlement patterns, site configurations, the locations of sites, site intervisibility, burned sites, and the remains of humans who died from violent causes. In chapter 3, I discuss the distribution of weapons and their production techniques as well as artistic representations of actual warfare, warriors, prisoners, etc.

It must be remembered that none of these lines of evidence should be considered in isolation—they are discussed individually here merely for convenience. What should be looked for are clusters of traits, traits that individually suggest warfare, but where their combined presence makes a much stronger case. What should also be looked for are changes in the frequency of occurrence and changes in the distribution of warfare-related behavior over time. Although it may be possible to find some slight evidence for warfare at almost any time in any region, this kind of evidence reveals next to nothing. It is the major increases or significant decreases of this evidence that can indicate how important warfare was at a particular time.

SETTLEMENT PATTERNS

Settlement data are one of the most obvious and most frequently mentioned types of archaeological evidence for Southwestern warfare. This large subject has a number of important aspects: specifically, four major issues—each of which has one or more additional facets.

1. Site configurations
    Evidence for sites being planned and laid out for defense
    Evidence for sites increasing in size over time

Evidence for smaller sites being abandoned before larger sites
Evidence for rapid construction of sites
2. Sites on defensible land forms
Evidence that smaller sites are on more defensible land forms than
larger sites
Evidence for sites located to provide secure domestic water supplies
3. Site distributions
Evidence for clustering with empty zones between clusters
The sequence of site abandonment within clusters
The sequence of cluster abandonment among clusters in a region
4. Sites located for line-of-sight communication
Evidence that line-of-sight links were bounded and so define site
alliances

All these classes of settlement evidence can be interpreted within a given
time frame, but they are more convincing if it can be shown there were
changes between periods in how common each of these settlement features was. And, again, evidence that these various factors co-occur is the
most powerful evidence for significant warfare.

Site Configurations

DEFENSIVE LAYOUTS

Perhaps one of the most obvious archaeological indicators of warfare is
the defensive site. High unbroken walls, dry moats, and hilltop locations
can all be evidence for defense. While it is true that palisades or fences can
be erected to keep animals in or out, that walls can be built to restrict
public access, that dry moats may have some other function, and that
hilltops can be occupied for various purposes, these interpretations relate
to unlikely or rare phenomena. When walls have redoubts, or bastions,
then there is no doubt they were for defense. And when dry moats are
associated with palisades, their function is clear. So, as always, single lines
of evidence are not as persuasive as multiple, converging lines of evidence.
Defensive sites frequently have more than one aspect to them; and when
such co-occurrences are found, it greatly reinforces the interpretation that
defense was the intent.

Furthermore, as discussed in chapter 1, defensive structures have worked
well enough to have been regularly used the world over, so they would
become an expected part of the scene if warfare intensified. Throughout
the millennia, from the time of prepottery Neolithic Jericho, but before
the aquisition of gunpowder, defensive structures relied upon not only
land forms but also walls, towers, and moats.

In Southwestern settlements, walls were the predominant defensive feature. They consisted of three different kinds: palisades, or stockades, made

FIGURE 2.1
The site of Kotyiti in the Rio Grande Valley has a typical inward-facing layout. In this case, however, it has two large central courtyards instead of one. Long, straight walls can be seen with the cross-walls clearly abutted to them. This is an excellent example of "ladder" construction. Photo ©Baker Aerial Archaeology, transparency 017397.

of logs; freestanding walls of adobe or stone; and walls actually composed of the outer walls of rooms. Palisades (rows of stakes or posts set into the ground) were an early form of defense in the Southwest and are discussed in detail in chapter 4. Often, they were circular and enclosed one or more structures. Freestanding adobe or stone walls were usually used to bridge the gap between rooms, and often the combination of room walls and freestanding walls would form a perimeter around a site. Because freestanding walls have a tendency to disintegrate and are not as stable as room walls—and are often not excavated—it is sometimes difficult to determine whether the combination of room walls and freestanding walls completely enclosed the perimeter of a settlement.

Building a site so the structures themselves form a defensible wall is another type of protective feature. This was the most widespread method of settlement defense in the Southwest; and often the walls of rooms formed an unbroken perimeter, accomplished by constructing massive blocks of rooms with no exterior doorways. Typically, the outer walls were two stories high, forming a very effective barrier. There were two different types of such settlements in the Southwest: those that had large central plazas (often referred to as inward-facing pueblos) and those that had more of a "honeycomb" layout. The central-plaza structure, which had antecedents in the Chaco architecture, came into common use in the late 1200s, as discussed in chapter 6. (See Figures 2.1 and 2.2.)

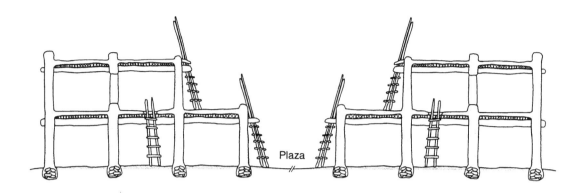

Plaza

FIGURE 2.2
A cross section of a
typical inward-facing
pueblo. The width of
the plaza has been
reduced for this
drawing.

Building the rooms to form an outer perimeter wall is a method of defense not restricted to the Southwest, and it is a particularly efficient way
to build defensively when wood for palisades is scarce. The famous
Neolithic site of Çatal Hüyük in Turkey was similarly constructed around
6,000 B.C. (Mellaart 1967). Closely related are sites constructed with groups
of rooms forming walls and spaces between the room blocks enclosed
with freestanding walls. So, there was a continuum of palisades encircling
all rooms inside a freestanding wall, a combination of rooms and freestanding walls forming a barrier, and, finally, just the rooms themselves
producing an enclosing defensive wall.

In the Southwest, there are very few examples of dry moats—or large
ditches running along an outside wall—that were defensive measures. The
most famous example is Crumbled House in the San Juan Basin (Marshall
et al. 1979).[2]

Although towers built into settlements were not widespread in the Southwest, they were common in the Mesa Verde region, including Hovenweep,
in the 1200s, the beginning of the time period in which warfare intensified
(Kenzle 1993). (See Figures 2.3a–d.) Other towers have been found in the

2. Dry moats usually serve to deny access to the base of the wall to attackers intent on
undermining it and to deny anyone a good platform from which to launch an attack on the
walls. For any group without metal tools, attempting to undermine the walls would not be
very practical, so there are only a few examples of dry moats in the Southwest. Employing
the strategy of constructing a tower in order to attack a settlement's walls usually required
wheels to move the tower into position. Given the lack of the wheel and the overall level of
technology at this time in the Southwest, such offensive structures were most likely impractical, and so dry moats would not have been necessary for this purpose. Another reason to
construct a dry moat would be, in effect, to heighten the defensive wall. In Europe, coastal
Peru, and the North American Midwest, ease of digging probably made dry moats more
practical. In the Southwest, however, it probably would have been easier to build a higher
wall than to dig a moat.

FIGURE 2.3a
A three-storied tower built against a large boulder at Site 1138, Mesa Verde National Park. (See also Hayes 1964:Figure 83.) Photo courtesy of Mesa Verde National Park; negative number 1103.

FIGURE 2.3b
Tower at Holly Group, Hovenweep National Monument. It was built on a freestanding boulder, which both increased its height and made it more inaccessible. Photo courtesy of Mesa Verde National Park; Jack Smith, photographer; negative number 01025.

FIGURE 2.3c
Twin Towers,
Hovenweep National
Monument. Two
towers are imme-
diately adjacent to
each other and a third
stands nearby. Only
one tower would have
been needed if
signaling was their
function. Photo
courtesy of Mesa
Verde National Park;
Leland Abel,
photographer;
negative number
4936.

FIGURE 2.3d
Tower in Navajo
Canyon, Mesa Verde
National Park. The
location on an isolated
mesa remnant greatly
increases the defensive
nature of this struc-
ture and renders it
very impractical for
purposes other than
defense. Photo
courtesy of Mesa
Verde National Park;
negative number
2457.

Gallinas area; there were some in the Zuni–Manuelito Canyon area; and a few were found elsewhere. Towers were also built into the room areas of some Chaco Great Houses, such as Kin Ya'a and Salmon Ruin. The presence of towers in Sonora was mentioned earlier. It would appear that once the technique of using multiple-storied rooms as a defensive outside wall was perfected, towers provided no additional benefit and they fell into disuse. (It should be noted that towers could have been used both for defense and as high platforms to signal allies.)

In the Northwest Coast area, the Tlingit built log palisades, but not all houses would necessarily have been located inside such defenses. These stockades had a sort of drawbridge-type of closeable entryway made of a log—which, archaeologically, would be seen only as a gap in the palisade. Thus, from an archaeological standpoint, defended entryways may not be apparent where there is evidence of a palisade. Also, a site with some suites of houses defended and not others would fit the Tlingit pattern. In the northern Southwest, sites were found where only a portion of the community was enclosed by a palisade, and which date to the Early Period. (See chapter 4.)

Safeguarded entryways were commonly associated with defensive sites. A classic example is the European method of building a passage leading to a gate that exposed an aggressor's nonshielded side to attack from above. Many large Southwestern pueblos had no entryways—just unbroken outer perimeters with all access via ladders. The pueblos that did have entryways may have had various means of defending them. There has been no systematic testing of the region's entryways to look for evidence of defensive features. In several cases, such as Grasshopper Pueblo, Pueblo de los Muertos, and Besh-Ba-Gowah, the entryway was roofed over and was, in effect, a long dark tunnel. These covered entrances were often defended by loopholes in the side walls and the roof, and it must have been very dangerous to enter the pueblo single file through them. That these pueblos generally had only one such entrance is good evidence of their defensive role. Surely it would have been more convenient to have many entrances to these large communities with hundreds of residents.

Other methods of furthering the defensive capability of a site were internal walls and features similar to a keep. In studying these archaeologically, there must certainly be considerations on whether these features were designed for restricted access or whether they had a social function. But, defense in warfare must be equally considered. Such internal strongholds may be indicators of alliances since one role of a keep was to enable the defenders to hold out until help arrives. There are only a few possible candidates of such structures in the Southwest. These include Mesa Verde's Balcony House, with not only strong external defenses but also an internal defensive-looking wall. Casa Grande could have been a keep structure within an outer defensive compound wall; and similar centrally placed high structures within outer compounds are seen in other Salado sites as well.

And, finally, tunnels can be a minor feature of settlement defense. The Mae Enga of New Guinea used tunnels as escape routes from the men's houses, and considerable effort was made to hide their existence. Such features are found in the Southwest, particularly in the Mesa Verde area where tunnels linked kivas, or pit structures, with towers. Pit structures and kivas were places where people could be trapped during an attack, whereas towers were the most defensible part of a site. Linking them together made perfect sense, especially when viewed from the perspective of what is known about New Guinea warfare.

INCREASING SITE SIZE

There are certainly some subtleties involved in community defense, but size alone can be beneficial. A community that is many times larger than any other may be immune from attack because it has so many defenders and, as a consequence, may not need to fortify. Or, an empire may be so large it can, essentially, relegate all warfare to its border areas, eliminating the need to fortify communities in the center. The Roman Empire is a classic example of this, but Moche in northern Peru is another good one, and it is possible that the Chaco interactive sphere functioned this way. There are repeated statements in ethnographic contexts that larger communities had significant military advantage over their smaller neighbors— a benefit that relates to site size. Even with alliances, a single very large site would have been safer than several smaller allied ones.

In the Southwest there was a clear trend in the Late Period for the sizes of sites to increase. This appears to have been accomplished by the combining of the population of separate communities into single or fewer large communities. This form of defense closely correlates with other trends in defensive behaviors. However, a diachronic view of site size can be important. When Teotihuacan was founded, it was much larger than any possible competitor, and it was not fortified. However, it was ultimately destroyed, most likely by an adjacent polity or alliance of polities. Similarly, Rome was ultimately not immune from attack. And Casas Grandes was much larger than any other contemporary site in its region, but it, too, was ultimately destroyed by attack (DiPeso 1974; Ravesloot and Spoerl 1989). Others of the large sites in their respective regions of the Southwest also were attacked and destroyed.

The ability to form alliances, which provided a larger population than that of a single big site, could thus have threatened even the largest community. As discussed in chapter 7, there were considerable disadvantages to living in very large communities. Certainly, there must have been trade-offs between the security a very large site provided and the high cost of living in one.

Scholars who argue that big sites in the Southwest were not organized for defense frequently note that large populations were necessary for ceremonial or other public activity purposes (e.g., Lekson and Cameron 1995). However, throughout the region during most time periods there were numerous examples of dispersed communities, from the distributed room groups in the Chaco time period to the Hohokam dispersed pit house clusters. Even in the presence of the largest canal systems or the elaboration of ball courts and great kivas, there were not large numbers of people living in the same immediate locality. On the contrary, when the big sites were found, there was less—not more—evidence of investment in facilities for public activities. Great kivas were no longer made; and while there were unroofed circular features probably used for public ceremonies, they represented very little labor investment.

SMALLER SITES ABANDONED AND REPLACED BY LARGER SITES

As soon as a portion of the population resided in large defensible settlements, it would have been almost impossible for small, homestead-like sites to be viable. Once the size of the attacking group grew large, compared with the number of defenders, the small sites had to be abandoned and the inhabitants had also to move into larger settlements. That is, warfare dictated the size range of viable settlements. Certainly, warfare was possible with everyone living in relatively small groups, as frequently was the case in New Guinea. However, once one group aggregated into a large site, it gained a military advantage over dispersed small sites, and the residents of the small sites would have been forced to either follow suit and join forces or flee. The evolution of numbers and size is the hardest of these site aspects to utilize archaeologically. Were smaller sites really contemporary with the larger ones? Were the smaller ones actually nondefensible or did they have palisades that have gone unrecognized? So, while a pattern of large sites found along with many small indefensible sites could indicate a lack of warfare, that conclusion should not be accepted too quickly.

RAPID CONSTRUCTION OF SITES

There are a number of instances in the Southwest where it appears dispersed communities were burned and abandoned and a large defensive site was built immediately thereafter (discussed in chapter 6). And, there is an indirect line of evidence that these new, larger settlements were built very quickly, using a technique particularly suited to rapid construction. I know of no other archaeological examples of techniques particularly suited to extremely rapid construction of defensive sites, but I suspect there are some.

The inward-facing communities built in the late 1200s and early 1300s

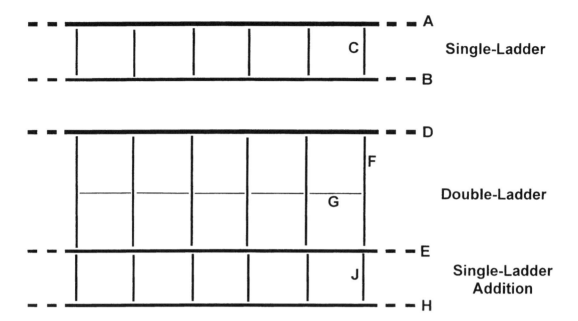

sometimes display a very distinctive building technique that seems associated only with large sites at this particular time interval. Termed "ladder" construction by Roney (1996c) and "spinal" by Dean (1996b), it was first noted by Mindeleff (1891) for Kin Tiel and Fire House (Eighteen Mile) ruins in the Hopi area. The details of this building method were also described by Watson et al. (1980) and S. LeBlanc (1989a) for the Atsinna and Pueblo de Los Muertos sites in the El Morro Valley near Zuni, but the practice also shows up over a considerable area in the Southwest.[3]

The ladder-type rapid construction technique is found in two versions that could be called "single-ladder" and "double-ladder" construction (Figure 2.4). Single-ladder construction consisted of building two long parallel walls, with cross walls abutting these to form the room cells. (The parallel walls constituted the "poles" of the "ladder," and the cross walls

3. Ladder-type rapid construction is seen, for example, at Wide Reed Ruin between Hopi and Zuni (Mount et al. 1993), in some Middle Rio Puerco sites near the Rio Grande (Roney 1995, 1996c), at Horse Camp Mill well to the south of Zuni (McGimsey 1980), possibly at Long House in the Kayenta area (Dean 1996b), and even in the circular structure at Mound 7 at Gran Quivira to the east of the Rio Grande Valley (Hayes 1981). Only in the Zuni area, however, has it been shown that the ladder technique was used to construct sites directly adjacent to previously occupied sites that were abandoned and robbed of building stones to construct the new ones. But the Zuni area is the only region from which there is any survey and excavation data gathered near the sites built with ladder construction. So, it is not possible to test whether there is always an association between ladder construction and the removal of stones from older pueblos for building materials.

were the "rungs.") The thickness of the cross walls was usually less than that of the long parallel walls, and the pueblo's outermost parallel wall was often thicker than the parallel wall to the inside.

In the "double-ladder" variant to this construction technique, the long parallel walls (the poles of the ladder) were built the equivalent of two rooms apart, with longer cross walls (rungs) added next, making cells that were doubly wide; still more cross walls were added to these cells, turning each of them into two rooms. An extreme form of this construction occurred at Pueblo de Los Muertos, where a double-ladder set of rooms was constructed around the perimeter, then a single-ladder set of rooms was added on the plaza side, resulting in three rows of rooms built as a single effort—in effect, a "triple-ladder."

What can be inferred from this construction technique? First, and possibly foremost, no one could move in until everyone moved in. This was group-effort construction. It also required fewer walls per room than the previously built, smaller, linear room blocks since more walls were shared between rooms.[4]

In the El Morro example, the later, large, inward-facing pueblo required half as many walls per room as did the earlier community with its small room blocks. It is a very efficient way to use existing stocks of wall stones. If most, but not all, of the existing stones could be salvaged from pueblos that were being abandoned, then the fastest way to build a new pueblo was to use less stone per room so no new stone need be quarried and shaped.

Ladder-type construction is also a very efficient way to build quickly. If no new stones must be quarried and any person could work on any section, with no idiosyncratic design allowed, then work could progress without interruption. For example, the initial construction of 630 rooms (including second-story rooms) at Pueblo de Los Muertos, built by stone-robbing the nearby Scribe S site, could have been carried out in five to seven days.[5]

These large sites, built using the ladder construction technique, may

4. Because rooms in room blocks share walls, the number of wall segments per room varies with the shape and size of a room block. For example, at Pueblo de Los Muertos the triple-ladder rows result in an average of 1.17 walls per room. A typical one-room-wide room block would have more than three walls per room. At the earlier Scribe S site, where room blocks were usually two rooms wide, a typical wall-per-room average is 2.5. So, the triple-wide room blocks built into a rectangle required less than half the number of walls the former, more typical, construction did. The walls in second stories are less efficiently constructed; an overall estimate of half the number of rooms as previously built below is about right. Formulas for the numbers of walls per room are: for one-row room blocks, total walls = 3 x rooms + 1; for double-row room blocks, it is 2.5 x rooms + 2; for triple-wide room blocks built into rectangles, it is 1.17 x rooms + 0.

5. This conclusion is based on the following reasonable assumptions: That there was one adult per room, that each room required one and a quarter walls to be built, and that building roofs was no more effort than building the walls. The final assumption is that the stone had to be moved on average less than one-half km.

well be monuments to an incredibly organized response to what must have appeared a crisis situation—and a need for a new, more defensive site to be built *posthaste*.

Sites on Defensible Land Forms

Establishing settlements on defensive locations is a worldwide phenomenon, and the tops of hills are the most frequently chosen positions. Hilltops bestow the obvious military advantage of height as well as provide an excellent view of anyone approaching. They can also ensure good line-of-sight communication with allied sites. In contrast, cave locations can present defensive possibilities, but they do not provide good views in all directions and can prove extremely difficult to enter and leave.

And humans do not—not without very good and compelling reasons—locate their communities in places that are difficult of access. Yet, sites are found that lacked easy access to water, fuel, and other necessities, that were dangerous (such as on hilltops in the Southwest and subject to lightning strikes), or that were generally unpleasant (i.e., exposed to cold wind). Nevertheless, despite the worldwide use of hilltops for defense—and their obvious social cost—archaeologists in the Southwest have repeatedly proposed other explanations for these seemingly illogically located sites. Among the antidefense explanations are that hilltop locations provided a nice view or were selected to conserve farmland, to get away from mosquitoes, or for religious reasons. These theories must be viewed with some caution, for they seldom withstand hard scrutiny. In the Southwest, in particular, these defensive locations were not used during all time periods. Their use closely correlates with other evidence of warfare. (See Figure 2.5.)

Again, as with defensive construction techniques, the combination of a site's defensive attributes increases confidence in this built-for-defense interpretation. For example, when hilltop sites have walls along the most accessible routes, such as the Promontory Site in the Pine Lawn area of the mountain Mogollon, or have defensive walls surrounding the hilltop, then the intent is clear. Overall, because defense is overwhelmingly the most likely reason why sites were placed on isolated hilltops of difficult access, any other proposed explanation must be defended with convincing evidence.

A more enigmatic case of settlements that were situated in hard-to-access locations is the placement of sites on the edge of a mesa or bordering other drop-offs (Figure 2.6). In the Southwest, the number of sites that were placed so as to restrict access on one or more sides is very high. In almost all cases, it would have been very easy to build the site even as little as 50 to 100 meters away from the edge. Such locations would have been more convenient in many ways—and safer for children. Admittedly, in some cases a spring existed at the foot of a mesa and the settlement location may have been selected to minimize the distance to water. And mesa

FIGURE 2.5 *(top)*
The site of Cerro
Colorado in the
Chama Valley in
northern New Mexico
is a classic hilltop
location with difficult
access on all sides.
Photo ©Baker Aerial
Archaeology,
transparency 20C909.

FIGURE 2.6
The site of Puye on
the Pajarito Plateau is
an example of a site
defensively located on
the edge of a mesa,
very near a significant
drop-off.

edges provided good viewpoints that may have had nonmilitary benefits. Nevertheless, there was a major tendency to place sites that were built in a defensive manner right on the edges of mesas and to put sites that were not built defensively farther away from the edges. These precarious mesa-top locations must have provided enough greater defense that they were worth the cost.

SMALL SITES ON MORE DEFENSIBLE LANDFORMS THAN LARGE SITES

Because, in general, smaller sites needed more defensive capabilities than larger sites, the size of sites found on defensible landforms can be used as a test for the functional reason for choosing such locations. Other proposed reasons (rather than defense) for sites being located on hilltops would apply equally well to large sites and to small sites. And, in that case, the expectation would be an equal frequency of all site sizes to be found on high landforms. However, if large size alone can provide adequate defense, then a hilltop location may not be needed. Given these situations, relatively more small sites should be found on hills rather than large sites. Now, it may be that defensive requirements dictated that all sites, regardless of size, be placed on defensible landforms wherever possible. If so, then the equal use of hilltops by sites of all sizes does not negate the role higher landforms played in defense. And, conversely, a disproportionate use of hilltops by smaller sites is evidence that hills provided a defensive advantage. Two examples can elucidate this distinction. During the Early Pithouse period in the Mogollon, virtually all sites, regardless of site size, were on hilltops (see chapter 4). However, none of the sites was very large, and apparently the hilltop advantage was useful to everyone. But, in the Late Prehistoric period there was a very strong pattern of relatively small sites being located on hilltops, while larger sites were rarely so situated. This pattern was so strong, there can be little question that the additional protection afforded by hilltops was critical to the survivability of small sites. Yet, the inhabitants of large sites did not find the additional protection of higher, more defensible landforms afforded enough advantage to be worth the cost.

SECURE DOMESTIC WATER SUPPLIES

Protected water supplies were another subtle factor of defense-related site locations. In the Southwest, there are a very large number of clear instances of "guarding" a water supply. Water sources tended to be springs, wells, or very small drainages, and the intent was clearly to protect water for domestic use and not for use in irrigating fields. Examples include building around canyon-head springs, as in the Mesa Verde–McElmo–Hovenweep area, or building directly on springs in other areas, damming small drainages right at the edge of sites, and the construction of walk-in wells in plaza areas of inward-facing pueblos. Examples of the latter type include the Cienega sites in the El Morro Valley, one at Horse Camp Mill, and even one at Casas Grandes.

Ethnographic accounts of warfare point to the very significant danger of ambush. Having a source where domestic water could be procured without fear of ambush would have been very valuable—and considerable effort was made to provide this security in some cases. It can be argued that close sources of domestic water were simply a convenience and that when sites were small the labor required to provide this convenience was not worth the effort, but when they were big it was. This argument, however, is not supported by the evidence. During the early periods, sites could have been placed very close to sources of water, but they were not. And especially during the Middle Period, the inhabitants of Chaco Great Houses were certainly capable of expending the effort to build walk-in wells and the like, but these activities were not undertaken. There was undoubtedly a good reason why people—if given a choice—would not choose to live right on top of their water sources because of potential contamination (see chapter 7). It's probable that when localized water sources were inferior, a short walk to cleaner water was the preferred solution. I suggest it was fear, not efficiency, that dictated the response to securing domestic water supplies—at the expense of water quality.

Site Distribution

Archaeological evidence of warfare in the form of settlement patterns is closely allied with site configurations, and there are several aspects to these patterns. The most important trend was the presence of site clusters, with adjacent empty spaces—no-man's-lands or buffer zones—forming between the clusters. This phenomenon occurred widely the world over, in many different times and places. It was particularly common throughout North America during certain periods, and it was seen on a very small scale in New Guinea. Another aspect to settlement patterns was the location of sites so they were mutually visible. And, the final aspect to these patterns in the Southwest was that during intervals of extreme warfare, small sites ceased to exist—that is, everyone resided in some form of a larger, fortified community.

CLUSTERING AND NO-MAN'S-LANDS

The long scholarly history of identifying no-man's-lands reflects their occurrence at various times in the past. That such areas existed is an extremely strong line of evidence for warfare, because it is unlikely that people would have given up their use of an area without a very good reason. The existence of these zones apparently dates back to Basketmaker and Pueblo I times in the northern Southwest (Steward 1941; Aikens 1966; Matson et al. 1988; Fairly 1989; Rohn 1989). However, survey data are much more difficult to evaluate for earlier times than for later periods, so it is difficult to say much more than that these buffer zones did exist in the Early Period. Their absence, or near absence, in the Middle Period is as important for understanding that time period as is their occurrence for other times.

The existence of no-man's-lands in the Late Period for the Anasazi area is noted most explicitly by Wilcox (1981a) and Upham (1982) as well as by Mera (1935, 1940), Jewett (1989), and Haas and Creamer (1993). Their presence is also recognized in the Hohokam area by Wilcox (1988b, 1989) as well as by P. Fish and Fish (1989), Debowski et al. (1976), Canouts (1975), Wilcox and Sternberg (1983), and Doelle and Wallace (1991). Empty zones of this time period are considered at length in chapter 6, but the evidence for their existence and evolution over time is very clear and compelling. At this point, suffice it to say that most of the entire Southwest consisted of site clusters, each surrounded by large empty zones.

It cannot be stressed too strongly that site clusters and associated empty zones are probably one of the most legible "signatures" of warfare. And the reason for this is clear: Such highly concentrated settlements were very inefficient. The clusters of communities distributed people unevenly over the landscape, causing overexploitation of immediately adjacent resources and underutilization of more distant ones (see Wilcox 1981a). Furthermore, this "clumping" tended to reduce the amount of environmental variability available to a community, increasing the likelihood that drought, flooding, insects, etc., would affect the entire, intensely utilized habitat. Such clustering would have been even more undesirable in the Southwest, where the optimum strategy appears to have been farming a number of diverse zones so that certain areas with lots of rainfall would do well, while others might barely get by with less rainfall. The overall idea, however, would have been to ensure that some of the fields would almost always be productive.

Collecting wood for fuel and wild plants also would have been negatively affected by the concentration of people in small areas. In many places, fuel and wild plants would soon have been expended, requiring the people to relocate altogether. Thus, under many—if not most—circumstances, such clustering of people was a nonoptimal strategy to be undertaken only by necessity. Certainly, people would have avoided forming such concentrated settlement clusters unless strongly compelled to do so.

The spacing between clumps of communities was also critical. Each had to be close enough to another to provide mutual defensive support. After all, aid must arrive in time for it to be useful. The longer a particular site could hold out against attack, the greater the spacing could be to the next settlement. European castles could be spaced quite far apart because of their ability to withstand attack. However, spacing sites a few miles apart seems to have been a likely expectation in nonstate situations—figuring that sites had to be situated close enough to provide prompt aid, combined with the ability to signal a need for support. This does not mean that sites located farther apart might not have also been part of an alliance, just that a community would have needed nearby help and that more distant help would have been of no use.

The various forms of defensive sites can be looked at from a military point of view. Military doctrine defines three types of defenses: refuges, strongholds, and strategic defenses, with increasing construction and maintenance effort required in moving from the simplest to the more complex of these types. This concept can help in the interpretation of the Southwestern data. There are a few sites that seem to fit within the concept of refuges. A refuge is a place where people can move when threatened. Small hilltop sites such as those in the Chevlon drainage (C. White 1976) and the Verde Valley (Pilles 1996; Schroeder 1947), as well as the Hohokam *trincheras* (Wilcox 1979), would seem to fit this model. These hilltop sites were so small and had so few associated artifacts that they were probably only occasionally used; many of the *trincheras* had villages at their base and may not have been the scene of daily life.

A number of other sites are harder to evaluate. They were somewhat larger, but still not very big, and were often on very high hills. Unless the group sizes were small and defense was extremely important, they may have been refuges and not full-time residences. Some along the Aqua Fria seem to fall into this category (Spoerl 1984), some in the Prescott area (Page 1970), and Wilcox discusses some located around the Flagstaff area (Wilcox and Haas 1994). In spite of their widespread distribution, refuges were always a minor form of defensive site.

Technically, strongholds are places were people can reside either permanently or for very long stretches, and are designed to withstand siege and concerted attack. With secure domestic water and stored food in case of crop failure, some Southwestern sites would likely have been able to withstand a siege, although it is unlikely the combatants would have been able to maintain one for a significant length of time. The vast majority of the Southwestern examples of defensive sites seems to have been strongholds, which are more accurately described as fortified towns or hamlets. They ranged from small palisaded hamlets to large towns holding more than 1,000 people, and appeared to be much more common than refuges. From this information, it is possible to conclude that when prehistoric people in the Southwest needed protection, they usually shored up their defenses where they lived rather than built a noninhabited safe refuge.

The site clusters can be thought of as strategic defenses, with the settlements geographically situated to be mutually supporting. Even such apparently linear defenses as Hadrian's Wall, the Great Wall of China, or the Maginot Line were actually a series of forts that supported each other, with walls or other lightly defended facilities located between them. In the Southwest, no such linking facilities existed, but the basic principle of mutually supporting "forts" seemed to be present.

SEQUENCE OF WHICH SITES WITHIN CLUSTERS WERE ABANDONED FIRST

In general, smaller sites are less defensible than larger sites. So, if warfare and population attrition is taking place, smaller sites should become undefendable more quickly than large sites. Abandonment of the smaller sites would be expected to occur first, with the surviving population relocating in larger communities. But the concept of "smallness" is relative, not absolute. If most sites were 500 rooms in size in a particular area, then sites of 100 rooms would be relatively undefendable and likely to be abandoned. However, if in another area, the largest sites were only 100 rooms, the smaller sites of perhaps 30 to 40 rooms would be the ones most likely abandoned. This process can be observed indirectly by seeing large sites grow at a rate that could not have been due to intrinsic population growth. The doubling in size of a site in a decade or two was surely the result of immigration. This influx of immigrants must mean that other sites were being abandoned. Almost invariably, under these circumstances it was the largest sites that grew, implying that the smaller sites were being abandoned.

SEQUENCE OF WHICH CLUSTERS WERE ABANDONED FIRST

The same reasoning applies to site clusters. The smallest clusters, in terms of overall population, would have been militarily the least viable and the most likely either to be annihilated or abandoned (and have their inhabitants move in with allies elsewhere). Smaller clusters would probably have been abandoned before larger clusters—even if, ultimately, most of the clusters were abandoned.

It should be noted that the exact opposite pattern would be expected if warfare was not the cause. The smaller clusters would most likely be in better ecological balance and would probably survive the longest if the factors causing abandonment were simply environmental/ecological, without social interaction being a causal variable.

Line-of-Sight Communication

Site intervisibility was closely related to the presence of site clusters. If sites were located to be mutually supporting, then they must be able to send for help during attack. While there were other means of asking for prompt assistance—and there were certainly site clusters that did not have intervisibility, in particular some of the cliff dwellings—signaling would have been one of the best and fastest ways. Site intervisibility has rarely been investigated, although there are some good examples from the Southwest. Determination of intervisibility is not trivial; several factors are crucial: that sites were contemporary and that the height of the point where signaling could have been executed is known, as well as the extent to which forest or other obstructions would have blocked the view in the past. In spite of these considerations, intervisibility is something that can be determined with minimal excavation, and its value is high for showing evidence of warfare and for defining boundaries of site-cluster alliances.

That intervisibility between settlements was intended to enable a group to watch its potential enemies, and was not for the purpose of signaling for defense, is a likely assumption. However, this does not seem to be the case. In the Southwest, most site clusters were too far away from each other for detailed observations of behavior—it was simply not possible to "keep an eye on the neighbors." Rather, the intervisibility that can be demonstrated involves communication, and the ethnographic explanation for such communication is defense (A. Ellis 1991).

There is some debate among scholars as to the distance that signaling is practical. However, signals can be very simple if mutual support is needed. Signals that work only at night would have their limitations, and sunlight-reflecting mirrors would not be useful in all circumstances either. Probably some combination of fire at night and smoke during the day would have been both practical and adequate for many parts of the world. Given that there is very good evidence from Sonora that such signaling did take place (Riley 1987), it could have worked elsewhere in the Southwest.

LINE-OF-SIGHT LINKS DEFINED ALLIANCE BOUNDARIES

As Haas and Creamer (1993) have elegantly shown, it's possible that clusters of sites belonging to the same alliance would have contained sites that were intervisible. However, it was important that allied sites not be intervisible with enemy clusters. That is, just as empty zones marked the boundaries of alliance clusters, so the lack of intervisibility between sites probably defined the alliance boundary if sites *within* the boundary were intervisible. If a number of sites are found that are intervisible, and then a gap is found where there is no intervisibility with another site cluster, it's probably evidence for an alliance boundary.

Summary

Evidence for warfare can be seen from various aspects of settlement data. These involve site configurations (including defensive layouts), an increase in size of site over time, rapid abandonment of small sites, and rapid construction of some sites. Site location—including sites (especially small ones) on defensible land forms and sites located to protect domestic water supplies—are also evidence for warfare. Further indicators of conflict are site spacing (including areas with empty zones), the early abandonment of small sites and clusters with few sites, and sites located for line-of-sight communication. Whenever several of these traits are found to occur simultaneously, the likelihood they were caused by some reason other than warfare becomes minuscule.

BURNED SITES

Burned sites, in general, are perhaps the most overlooked indicator of warfare—particularly in the Southwest. Because the presence of warfare has been so long ignored, the reasons why sites were burned has not been carefully examined. Certainly, accidental fires occurred and, obviously, are not relevant as evidence for hostile action. However, if fires were the result of warfare, then they become very relevant. And, again, close scrutiny of site burning in the future may not only provide evidence for the existence of intensive warfare but also hold clues as to its nature.

It must be noted that massively burned sites are frequently associated with the presence of bodies that were not formally buried. However, because the following section covers evidence of deaths from violent causes, the nonformally buried remains associated with burned sites will be discussed here only minimally.

Heavily or completely burned pueblos, as Wilcox and Haas (1994) point out, are an indication of warfare. And while they cite examples of burned pueblos, they do not address the issue of nonformally buried bodies. This line of evidence has received scant attention and, furthermore, is considered by some scholars to be nonexistent. The recent opinion by Cordell (1994:131) that "physical evidence of conflict, such as burned villages or skeletons bearing mortal wounds, is lacking" is simply not correct. Wilcox and Haas present a list of burned sites—small and incomplete though it is. There are a surprising number of burned sites in the Southwest from the time periods under consideration, as discussed in chapters 4 and 6 and in the Appendix, and even these accounts are probably far from a complete listing.

It is not necessary to find burned sites to demonstrate the existence of warfare. As noted, properly constructed defensive sites should have withstood most attacks, which was, of course, why they were built. Thus, burned sites may be evidence for warfare, but their absence does not mean there was no warfare.

Interpretation of burning found on sites in the Southwest is, in theory, rather straightforward. There should be only a few explanations for a site or a portion of a site to have burned. However, it quickly gets complicated because there appears to be a tradition of burning some types of structures deliberately, and this behavior may not relate to warfare. In general, the logical possibilities for burning sites or portions of sites are (1) accidental fires; (2) deliberate burning of sites that was not related to warfare; (3) deliberate burning of particular structures (such as kivas) while the community continued to be occupied—again, unrelated to warfare—(reasons for this burning might include ceremonial purposes, internal community violence, death of its inhabitants, or pest removal); and (4) burning of all or part of the community due to warfare—including the special case of burning by the resident group to deny the site to the enemy.

In the archaeological record of the Southwest there are certainly good examples of accidental burning, deliberate nonwarfare-related burning, as well as warfare-related conflagrations. Good examples for warfare-induced burning by the site's residents are, at this point, equivocal at best. While the determination of the cause of burning in any one case can be in error, it should be possible to characterize enough of these events accurately to find general patterns. Unfortunately, there has been a surprising lack of interest in determining how to differentiate among the types of burning. Each of the enumerated possibilities is discussed in turn, but it must be remembered that this is a rarely considered topic and the formulation may be somewhat primitive.

Accidental Fires

Accidental burning should be rather random in time, over a region, and within a site itself. It should also not be very common. While accidental fire is the usual explanation for burned structures in the Southwest, it has recently become clear that setting fire to either pit houses or pueblo rooms was rather difficult. This has been demonstrated by replicative experiments as noted by Glennie (1983) and Wilshusen (1986). Hopi oral history accounts describe attackers carrying pitch and other flammables in order to generate room fires (Malotki 1993). Furthermore, Anyon (1983) and Anyon and LeBlanc (1980) note that many apparently deliberately burned Mogollon Great Kivas had significant amounts of fuel added to them before they were set on fire. The obvious implication is that they would not have burned well without help.

Finally, to my knowledge, there is no case of a historical pueblo burning completely that was due to an accidental fire. And, there are no historical accounts of entire pueblos burning accidentally, despite a reasonably good record spanning hundreds of years and involving scores of pueblos. Thus, it appears that devastating accidental fires must have been exceedingly rare. If major fires due to accidental causes were historically as common as is the prehistoric evidence for burning—whatever the cause—there would be ample historical evidence of it. And, yet, there is not.

Instead, accidental fires—or the burning of a room when someone died or to rid the room of pests—should result in rather restricted amounts of burning. A single room or structure is the likely pattern. Even if repeated over time, the locations of such burned structures would have been intermittent and should not have resulted in large contiguous blocks of burning. So, the logical conclusion would be that accidental fires would not have burned contiguous sections of a community at the same time. Accidental burning would not have been massive—that is, involving many adjacent rooms. And multiple instances of accidental burning would have been random and relatively rare over a site. So, if discontinuous parts of a site were burned at the same time or if a large proportion of a site was burned, it follows that these instances are not likely to have been the result of accidental fire.

The site of Turkey Creek Pueblo, a 335-room site occupied in the late 1200s and early 1300s (Lowell 1991), seems to be a typical example of what would be found in cases of accidental burning. About 5 percent of the site had burned rooms. These rooms were in different places and they seem to represent at least a half-dozen different fires—which would suggest that fires did not usually get out of control and consume an entire pueblo. In this case, in six out of six instances of fire outbreaks, the entire pueblo—or even a substantial portion of it—did not burn. Accidental fire could conceivably consume an entire pueblo, but this apparently happened very rarely.

The Deliberate Burning of Sites—Not Related to Warfare

Deliberate burning—but not warfare related—of all or most of a site could have several causes and several signatures. In any case, the expectation is for the burning to have been controlled. It is unlikely that a room would be set on fire that had a reasonable chance of setting other rooms on fire. Thus, isolated rooms would have been the logical focus of such fires. This seems to be the case: Almost, if not all, cases of proposed deliberate burning of structures involved pit houses, kivas, or great kivas—and not rooms within room blocks. The act of burning these types of structures would reasonably be expected to have reduced the risk of setting other portions of the community on fire.

Burning most of the community on abandonment without the presence of an enemy threat might have taken place when the community moved to a new location and, for ritual reasons, burned the old community. The presumption here is that the group was permanently abandoning the village and did not plan to return. And, their new location was too far away for it to be feasible to salvage valuable materials—such as timbers—from the old pueblo. So why destroy it? In the absence of hostile groups, it would have made more sense to leave the site intact, particularly if the relocation was close enough so that the surrounding area was still within their own territory. That is, an abandoned pueblo with wood, and at least partial shelter, would have been useful as a camp for hunting-gathering groups on a temporary basis. The value of the structures as a temporary camp would have mitigated against this strategy of wholesale destruction, unless no such trips were planned—or the benefit of denying the structures to the enemy was higher than any potential future reuse. The early historical record is filled with accounts of pueblos that were temporarily abandoned to avoid the Spaniards and of abandoned sites that were not burned. In the Rio Grande cases, the inhabitants usually did return to the abandoned pueblos, so abandonment without burning was clearly a common practice.[6]

It is unlikely that small, easily transported high-production-cost items would be left behind if burning was planned. For this type of deliberate burning of an entire community, the prior removal of very valuable items is expected. Metates would have been left, but not axes, or stone effigies, turquoise, or the like. So, in situ remains of a full complement of artifacts in association with burning was not likely the result of "burning upon abandonment." Neither was the presence of unburied bodies associated with burning the likely result of "burning upon abandonment." Nor was the presence of large amounts of burned foodstuffs.

There is no firm evidence from the Southwest that ritual burning of abandoned sites was the norm or even common. Many sites were abandoned without burning, and those that were burned rarely show the pattern just described for deliberate abandonment burning. When a site was totally burned, valuables were usually left behind, and frequently there were unburied bodies. Thus, if any sites were deliberately burned by their owners, they were most likely burned to deny their use to the enemy, and really represent another form of warfare-related burning.

Deliberate Burning of Particular Structures

A very different situation that needs to be discussed is the deliberate burning of particular structures within a large community, when the rest of the community was not burned or abandoned. In the Southwest, almost all examples of such burning involved the apparently deliberate destruction of ceremonial structures. While it is possible that some pit houses or other structures were burned to rid the area of pests—especially insects—there is little evidence to suggest this was actually ever done.

Rather, proto-kivas and kivas, both large and small, were burned, and there is no evidence for significant burning of nearby room blocks. As noted, a history of burning kivas on abandonment of their use can certainly be demonstrated. In some cases, this may have occurred when one ceremonial structure was replaced by another. In the Mogollon region (Anyon 1983; Anyon and LeBlanc 1980), there is a long sequence of evidence for Great Kivas being abandoned and burned, with new ones built on the same site over the span of many centuries. Structural burning of this type should also show evidence of any special preparation of the structure. This might include the placement of additional fuel, removal of valuable items, or demolition of portions of the structure (e.g., deconsecration

6. As Wilshusen (1986) has noted, large, primary roof timbers were a very valuable item in the Southwest and were frequently scavenged from old constructions to be used in new constructions. It seems unlikely these large wooden beams would be destroyed, unless the new community was so far away that transporting them was impractical. Therefore, determining whether timbers were salvaged before burning or not seems useful information.

by means other than fire, as well as fire). Such would especially be the case if the burning was to rid the area of insects or other pests. Everything salvageable would have been taken out first. This is just what is found in the Mogollon area: Kivas were regularly cleared of items, and often fuel was added to the floor before the fire was set. There is no instance of unburied bodies associated with these burnings.

The burned kivas in the Anasazi area present significant interpretive problems because they often contained unburied bodies or parts of bodies—some of which showed evidence of very violent deaths. Numerous examples of such events go back to Basketmaker III times, and they were particularly common in late Pueblo III and Pueblo IV times. Two instances of this type of deliberate burning bear describing.

Around 1890 Richard Wetherill found a body in Ruin 16 (near Long House at Mesa Verde): "It had not been buried, but lay in an estufa [kiva], half within the [ventilator]. . . . It was the body of a man, probably one of the ancient inhabitants of the cliff-dwelling who had fallen in defense of his hearth and home. The position seemed to indicate that he had tried to escape from the [kiva] by the said passage" (Nordenskiold [1893] 1973:35).

An even more poignant, but strikingly similar event was revealed in kiva 704 at the Homolovi II site: "The roof of the kiva had been burned down over an adult male between 30 and 40 years of age. Several projectile points lay near the skeleton; one rested in what would have been the soft tissue of the lower back. This was not a traditional burial, for it appears that this individual had been killed at the time the kiva was destroyed. . . . The position of the body suggests that the individual was attempting to get fresh air from the ventilator while the fire burned. He lay with his head extended into the vent tunnel" (W. Walker 1995:92–93). The fragmentary remains of three other individuals were found in the fill of this same kiva, but pothunters had disturbed the context, so it could not be determined whether their deposition was part of the same event.

Several possible explanations present themselves for instances of structural burning: (1) ritual destruction of the kiva related to witchcraft, which included killing the witch or witches and leaving them in the kiva; (2) ritual destruction of the kiva, which also involved human sacrifice (presumably of enemies); (3) use of a kiva as a tomb, presumably for the burial of an important individual; (4) the special case of using kivas as a depository for cannibalized human remains; and (5) use of kivas as refuges during an attack, with the burning of the kiva by the attackers to kill or drive out the people inside.

BURNING KIVAS ASSOCIATED WITH WITCHCRAFT

The witchcraft explanation for burning kivas has received the most attention. Darling (1995) and W. Walker (1995) present this argument in great detail, and Walker lists a number of possible examples. In short, the argument is that there was a strong historical concern (continuing to the present) for witches among Pueblo people; and social deviance was equated with witchcraft. There is no doubt that witches were killed in the historical period, up to this century. There is also reason to believe that the deaths could be quite violent and that bodies were treated badly after death. Moreover, a few cases appear to consist of killing multiple witches at the same time (Darling 1995). There is, however, no evidence that the bodies of witches were placed in functioning kivas that were then burned down. While it is possible that an entire political group (e.g., a clan) with a kiva could be accused of witchcraft and the group and its kiva disposed of, such a scenario was not particularly likely.

Why destroy a structure in order to kill a captured and defenseless enemy or a suspected social deviant? Such an explanation does not account for the placement of nonhumans—such as dogs—in kivas before they were burned (see W. Walker 1995). Billman (1997) discusses problems with this kind of explanation and points out how witchcraft cannot account for many of the cases of proposed cannibalism (covered in chapter 5).

RITUAL DESTRUCTION ASSOCIATED WITH SACRIFICE

The ritual destruction of the kiva that also involved human sacrifice has received scant attention up to now, but it seems to be a possible explanation for a number of cases. And if this theory proves accurate, then the humans found in these kivas are far more likely to have been captured enemies than social deviants. Let us assume that for some reason it is appropriate to "deconsecrate" and then burn a kiva. We might mount a raiding party, capture one or more enemies, and throw them into the kiva before igniting it. Or, if a raid is not possible or is unsuccessful, we might substitute an animal instead. There are a number of cases in which animals were treated much like these "sacrificial" human victims: They were deposited in kivas or pit structures and then the structure was abandoned. W. Walker (1995) reports on thirty-four different kivas or pit structures that contained dogs—several dogs in some instances—treated in this manner. He also reports finding a handful of birds, mostly raptors, and a few mammals other than dogs in similar circumstances. In about half the cases, the structure was burned (data are lacking in a number of examples). Dogs were by far the most common animal present in these situations. Were they sacrifices? If so, in some cases the sacrifice could have been of a dog or a turkey; in others, of a human. Other ritual behavior could leave other types of ritual material in the same kiva, which was often the case. This "ritual sacrifice" scenario makes far more sense than most other cases for bodies found in burned kivas. There is some historic evidence of transferring treatment intended for a person to an animal as a substitute. Killing a dog and referring to it as an enemy instead of killing an actual enemy was recorded by Cushing, but not in the context of kivas or sacrifices (Hinsley and Wilcox 1996:84).

Possibly a related behavior was placing human heads, or animals, in the ventilator shaft of a kiva, but not setting it on fire. The case reported by Fewkes (1909:24) of skulls in the ventilator shafts of four kivas at Spruce Tree House is illustrative. This could represent the sacrificial deconsecration of these kivas with the heads of enemies when the site was abandoned. Or, it could have been the enemy placing the heads of four defenders of the site in the kivas when it was attacked and destroyed. There is no strong evidence that Spruce Tree House was ever conquered, so the first explanation would seem more likely. But the possibility of desecrating an enemy's kiva is not without precedent, as noted in chapters 5 and 6. It is also difficult to find an explanation for such behavior by witchcraft or when such behavior involved treating the heads of individuals from one's own community in this way—especially since the Spruce Tree House community probably did not have more than a total of forty adults. A number of other instances of isolated skulls in kivas are also known, and are discussed in subsequent chapters.

The cases that fit this description of kiva-sacrifice behavior are far more common when there is other evidence for relatively more warfare than when it appears less intense. Also, there are records of ethnographic behavior found throughout the Americas in which enemies were sacrificed—from the Pawnee, to the Iroquois, to the Aztecs and Maya. (The special case involving possible cannibalism is considered in chapter 5.) However, the main difficulty with this kiva-sacrifice interpretation is that there is no historical or ethnographic evidence for ritual kiva destruction—much less one that involved sacrifices of any kind.

BURNED KIVAS AS A TOMB

The use of kivas as tombs is rarely proposed as an explanation for the deliberate destruction of kivas with bodies present, because, except for a few instances, the bodies do not seem to have been buried with respect, much less with the large number of grave goods expected in a formal burial. While using ceremonial structures as tombs may have taken place on occasion (Weiner-Stodder 1985), it seems so rare that it can be ignored from a general perspective.

BURNED KIVAS AS ACTS OF WARFARE

There are a number of cases involving people trapped, or otherwise contained, in a kiva and then the structure being set on fire that can only be explained by warfare. Certainly, the burning of the Salmon Ruin kiva with more than thirty children in it appears to be a case of individuals seeking refuge in the kiva, and then its subsequent destruction by enemies. Other cases are similar, including the tower (which may have served some of the functions of a kiva) at the Charnel House site, which was burned and contained unburied bodies. In most of these cases, there were so many bodies in the structures that it is almost impossible to see this as sacrificial behavior—much less as witchcraft related. Another example is the site of Te-ewi in the Rio Grande Valley, where the kiva was burned and had at least thirty bodies in it; the rest of the site suffered massive burning at the same time. At the Hopi site of Awatovi, a kiva was burned with at least one body in it, and it is known from historical accounts that this site was attacked and people were deliberately trapped in kivas, which were then set on fire. Thus, good, clear examples exist of individuals either being caught in kivas during a surprise attack or taking refuge in kivas during an attack. There is no question these are warfare-related events.

A number of other situations of deliberate structural burning are very hard to place, even tentatively, in any explanatory category. The burning of early pit structures with and without bodies in them has been noted for the late Pueblo I time period. A large sample of these structures was analyzed by Wilshusen (1986). And, because the structures may be considered proto-kivas, or at least structures that had some kiva-like functions, these instances might well represent the same phenomenon. Although there are earlier examples of burned pit structures, the pattern of burned kivas with unburied bodies in them is very restricted in time, occurring with any frequency only in sites from the late Pueblo I time period and the late Pueblo III to early Pueblo IV time periods. That this pattern strongly associates with time periods when there is plenty of other evidence for warfare makes the witchcraft or tomb explanations unlikely.

Burning Due to Warfare

Warfare-related burning should be characterized by entire sites, or at least suites of rooms, being burned, with assemblages in place. However, burning an entire pueblo would not have been easy during a battle, and it is not clear whether it would always have been advantageous. This is a topic for comparative ethnographic research. To burn a pueblo, it would, presumably, have to be captured first. Shooting "fire arrows" into a stone and earth pueblo hoping to set the roofs on fire is the stuff of Hollywood. It seems more likely that it would be necessary to gain nearly complete access to a pueblo to burn it thoroughly. As mentioned earlier, Hopi oral tradition features men using pitch they brought along expressly to start fires when they destroyed a pueblo (Malotki 1993).

Why would wholesale burning be desirable? There are several possibilities. Presumably, one purpose of warfare was to displace the inhabitants, either by killing them or forcing them to migrate. A possible motive for burning was to kill combatants who had hidden in the pueblo and who might retaliate if not killed. Defenders could be forced into pueblo rooms, and then the whole structure burned.

Also, a burned pueblo left the defenders with the problem of surviving after their homes and resources were destroyed, instead of being free to follow and attack the retiring victors, who were probably laden with their spoils. This latter point is important in understanding partially burned pueblos. If access was gained to only a portion of a pueblo, but the remainder was too well defended to capture entirely, the attackers could burn the section they controlled and then withdraw. This would weaken the defenders in the long run and help cover the withdrawal of the attackers, since the defenders would be busy dealing with the fire and its aftermath.

A number of these burned pueblos contained substantial amounts of corn that burned. Why wasn't this grain salvaged before the pueblo was destroyed if warfare was the reason for the burning? Perhaps the explanation is that the attackers were able to carry only part of the stored corn because any surviving defenders still posed a threat to the retreating and laden attackers. And, if the burning was for the above reason—killing or incapacitating the defenders—the enemy might have had to set fire to a pueblo, corn and all, even though saving the grain would have been desirable to the attackers.

In conclusion, burned kivas represent a particularly difficult interpretive problem. They definitely were a dangerous place to be caught in unawares and they were a focus of enemy attack. Stories of the sacking of Awatovi mention how the attackers deliberately caught people in their kivas. The massive number of people trapped in the kiva at Te-ewi seems to have been a similar situation. The presence of tunnels connecting kivas to surface rooms and towers—and possibly hidden rooms in kivas—reinforces the notion that getting trapped in a kiva was a real enough worry that an exit plan became a priority in some cases. The military strategy of attackers focusing on kivas is reminiscent of the Mae Enga method of attacking the men's houses. Here again, the plan was to set the structures on fire and kill as many men as possible as they came out. The Mae Enga countered this threat by building escape tunnels from the men's houses.

Interpretation of Evidence for Burning

As discussed, massive burning of all, or major sections, of communities was most likely due to warfare. Burned kivas with large numbers of bodies in them—especially when they included women and children—also represent warfare in most cases. However, kivas burned without the rest of the site being burned—with or without bodies—present a difficult interpretive problem. One difficulty arises when only kivas have been excavated on a site or the sample from elsewhere on the site is very low. It is difficult then to differentiate between warfare burning of kivas and their destruction by the community.

If there is information on the amount of burning from an entire community, it seems likely that a clear understanding of the reason behind it is reachable. The problem really comes from working with small samples or inadequately recorded excavations. For example, the random and limited burning of rooms at Turkey Creek Ruin, combined with the absence of unburied bodies and the lack of in situ remains, suggests multiple accidental fires. And, the burning of all of Site 616 (Horse Camp Mill) (McGimsey 1980), with in situ remains (including unburied bodies), strongly suggests warfare as the cause. Similarly, but with less evidence, Wide Reed Ruin shows the apparently simultaneous burning of a section of the room block and the central-plaza kivas, suggesting warfare. However, the sample is too small to use the other criteria, such as in situ remains or unburied bodies, for interpretation. Also, the burned tower kiva containing some thirty or more individuals at Salmon Ruin points to warfare as the cause.

To summarize, in some cases the cause of burning seems to be clear, in others it is much more problematic. However, the sum of the cases is of particular interest. There are very few cases of burned sites during Pueblo II and early Pueblo III times. There are very few, if any, cases of burned kivas in the Anasazi area during the same interval of time. Conversely, during late Pueblo III and early Pueblo IV periods, burned sites, burned kivas, unburied bodies, and unburied bodies in burned kivas, are all common. It is hard to explain this overall change in pattern except by warfare.[7]

DEATHS FROM VIOLENT CAUSES

The presence of burials of individuals who died from violent causes is another line of evidence for warfare. And a similar, but more indirect, form of this type of information is found in nonformally buried bodies. This category of evidence is somewhat intertwined with burned sites and

7. It is this last point that presents the conundrum and, again, leads us to ask, "Who was fighting whom?" If the attackers were efficient parasitic raiders, such as the Apache, their goal would have been to obtain resources. They would not want to get killed themselves, and they would want to leave enough people alive to produce more resources for subsequent raids. Under these circumstances, burning a pueblo to the ground would not be a good idea. In essence: Don't destroy your future producers, and don't so anger the remaining host population that they come after you in force. The goal of parasitic raiders would be to have a minimal effect on the host system and keep its response as low as possible.

However, if the only way to make a "clean getaway" effectively was to kill or completely incapacitate the defenders by burning the pueblo, then the archaeological consequences of nomadic raiding would look just like deliberate burning by a sedentary rival group trying to eliminate their victims as competitors. Either group might burn pueblos—but for different reasons. While massively burned pueblos are more likely to indicate peer groups trying to remove competitors, a pattern of burned pueblos is actually only evidence for the existence of warfare, not its type. Unfortunately, burning doesn't provide as much evidence about the nature of the conflict as we might hope.

structures, but can logically be considered as a separate topic with many facets, including traumatic deaths, unburied bodies, skewed sex ratios among the deceased, human body parts used as trophies, human sacrifices, and disarticulated bodies and possible evidence of cannibalism.

TRAUMATIC DEATH

In examining archaeological information found in the form of humans who died from violent causes, it is again necessary to assess what the likely evidence should be. First, in tribal warfare, most deaths are due to ambushes and not formal fights (see chapter 1). In addition, many deaths occur after battles from wounds received, rather than on the battleground from fatal wounds suffered in the fight. In these cases, the expectation is either a formal burial (although maybe of a special form) or, if never brought back for burial, for the body to remain beyond the community and unburied. Hence, many lethal wounds would not result in archaeologically visible evidence. Arrows removed from a body either before death or before burial would not leave arrowheads in place. Death from infection of war wounds would also not leave evidence. Because arrows are not as lethal as often imagined, most deaths would likely have been a result of clubbing, or other close-contact fighting, rather than arrow wounds. Expected would be broken skulls, smashed jaws, and the like as much more likely causes of death than arrowpoints in bodies. Such evidence is often ignored by archaeologists, with little effort to differentiate between skeletal damage resulting from perimortem causes (which occurred near the time of death) and that resulting from postmortem causes. Given all these factors, direct skeletal evidence for conflict is probably very rare, even if warfare was common. And, not surprisingly, such evidence is indeed relatively rare.

In the Southwest, a number of broken skulls have been uncovered, and projectile points found within the body cavity have been recorded for all periods (Wilcox and Haas 1994), with particular examples reported by Guernsey and Kidder (1921), Judd (1954), McGimsey (1980), McKenna (1984), Earl Morris (1919, 1939), Roberts (1940), Shutler (1961), W. Walker (1995), Wiseman (1982), and Wormington (1947, 1955). However, direct skeletal evidence of violent death is not common, representing certainly well under 1 percent of all burials—even including those cases where violent death is indicated from other evidence. This is in contrast to some time periods in the eastern United States and California where such indications of violent death represent 20 percent or more of the recovered bodies in some periods (Lambert 1997b)—suggesting that close combat and ambush were relatively more common in the East and Far West than in the Southwest. In particular, the many cases of crushed skulls reported by archaeologists in the Southwest without further confirmation that the crushing took place at the time of death and not later, are a major source of potentially useful—but, at this stage, practically useless—information. So, even though there are numerous statements that such skull damage existed, I have discounted much of them due to lack of verification.

Unburied Bodies

The presence of bodies that were never formally buried is surprisingly common in the Southwest, and unburied or hastily buried bodies are, in most instances, a good signature of warfare. However, the number of unburied bodies recovered by scientific methods would be smaller than the number of those actually killed and left unburied at the time of the original event. For example, a body left on the surface of a destroyed pueblo after a conflict would have been consumed or scattered by scavengers and would leave no archeological trace. Only those bodies of victims that were originally in structures which then collapsed over them and preserved the remains would be recognized archaeologically. Rapid interment by the survivors could leave remains that would, archaeologically, appear similar.

In appearance, nonformally buried bodies were dramatically different from what was seen in formal burials. Formal burials in the Southwest were just that: highly standardized and formal. Although such burials were treated in different ways at different times and places, there is always a recognizable pattern. Conversely, unburied bodies were usually found in haphazard positions. They lacked grave furniture, although they may have retained artifacts of apparel. These bodies were not found in prepared graves, but on the floors or in the fill of structures. They frequently occurred in groups—and sometimes were missing body parts, such as heads and hands.

While it is possible that a contagious epidemic could have been so virulent that a site was abandoned and the dead left unburied, such an event must have been extremely rare. Except for cases of new diseases for which there was no immunity—the bubonic plague in Europe or European diseases in the Americas—most populations would have had adequate resistance to disease in times of epidemic to maintain enough survivors to bury the dead—or at least to remove the corpses from the habitation area.

There are other possible explanations for these nonformal burials. Accidental fires could overtake and mortally burn some people before they could escape. Rooms could collapse, burying individuals. Social deviants might have been buried without the usual formalities. However, the simultaneous occurrence of massive burning and nonburied bodies would be extremely rare, unless caused by warfare. It is the occasional unburied body in the absence of massive burning that is difficult to interpret. However, these instances should be fairly random, both spacially *and* temporally. But if they are found in high frequency in only a few places and at a few times, then they are probably not the product of accidents or deviant behavior, but represent violent deaths most likely caused by enemies.

What do these instances of massive burning coupled with the presence of nonburied bodies reveal about the nature of warfare in the Southwest? First of all, the pattern doesn't seem to fit with raiding in the traditional sense, and the goal, apparently, was not just to kill someone in revenge for a previous death. The risk to the attackers in actually storming and holding a pueblo long enough to set it on fire would have been much greater than in just attacking people who were outside the settlement. Typical "hit-and-run" raiding occurred in the historic period; for example, the Hopi would attack Zuni—and two or three people would be killed—but they never tried to storm the pueblo (T. Ferguson and Hart 1985). Conversely, the massive killing of dozens of people—and, on occasion, the entire population of the community—was more than revenge killing. Rather, killing as many of the population as possible and then burning the community as completely as possible seems to have been the goal. This fits with conflict directed at eliminating competing groups. Intense warfare may have devolved into revenge raiding by the historic period, but initially it must have been much more than that.

In general, large numbers of unburied bodies—especially when accompanied by site abandonment and, perhaps, burning—are very hard to reconcile with any behavior except warfare. This does not mean it could not have happened. Rather, in any statistical sampling of cases, the overwhelming majority of instances must represent warfare and not pestilence or other such factors. One such case that may or may not represent warfare is a room in Wupatki that had the remains of individuals that exhibit rodent gnawing. These individuals apparently lay unburied for some time before the remains were collected and placed in the room. It is not possible at this point to determine the cause of death of these people.

Sex Ratios of the Deceased

If warfare is taking place, the sex of deceased individuals should reflect events relating to one of two different scenarios involving this kind of indirect skeletal evidence. For example, if a community is successfully attacked, then a likely outcome is for significant numbers of adolescent and adult males to be killed and some of the women and children to be taken captive. Thus, a higher number of military-age males and a lower number of women and children would be represented in the burial population. However, if the males were engaging in combat far afield, it is unlikely that those killed in battle would be buried in the usual fashion at their home settlement. Therefore, if a significant number of men die in this fashion the fighting-age males should be underrepresented in the burial population.

At first glance, it might appear that these two expectations would be of no utility archaeologically, since either a deficit or surplus of males or females could be explained by warfare. Thus, any deviation from equal numbers could be attributed to the same cause, and would not be convincing. However, this is the case only if there is no other warfare-related information to be found on the site and in the nature of the remains. If the site does not appear to have been destroyed during the time the burials were made, then the expectation would be for men killed in battle—and buried—away from the site, and only a deficit of male burials would be an indicator of warfare. Conversely, if the site was destroyed and, in particular, if the bodies seemed to be unburied or hastily buried, the expection should be a deficit of females. So, in a larger context and with a good understanding of the site-abandonment process, the sex ratio of the burial population should provide a useful piece of evidence.

Artifacts of Human Bone

A related piece of evidence for warfare is the presence of artifacts made from human bone. These turn up around the world, and can logically be made from the bones of one's own people or one's enemies. In North America, human-bone artifacts are relatively common in California, but they also show up in the Midwest (Owsley et al. 1994) and elsewhere, including the Southwest.

Such artifacts are not very common in the Southwest, but many probably have not been recognized. Examples of human-bone artifacts recovered in this region include bowls made from skull parts (Ezell and Olson 1955), inlaid skulls (Kidder 1932:270), a perforated tarsal (P. Martin et al. 1949:176), a flesher made from a femur (Reiter 1938:85), a Basketmaker III pendant made from human cranial bone (Peckham 1963), and a few others.

Wright (1979) mentions that Hopi bow guards were sometimes made of human scapulae taken from enemies. At Casas Grandes, DiPeso (1974) found human-bone wands, dishes, and pendants as well as a decorated mandible, a finger-bone necklace, and rasps. Artifacts of human bone were also found in the Anasazi area—the Colorado Plateau and Rio Grande areas—and the Mogollon region, and were not confined to a single period.

Trophy skulls and other bone pieces used as trophies represent the same basic activity: removal and curation of parts of a slain enemy. They also are found all over the world. This behavior has a particularly long time depth in the eastern United States, where it dates as early as 5000 B.C. (Mensforth 1996). Trophy bones may be drilled for mounting or hanging, but not otherwise modified. The well-known skulls from Casas Grandes (DiPeso 1974) with holes drilled in the tops for suspension are good examples. These are in turn similar to the massive numbers of skulls found farther south in Mexico at Alta Vista, representing at least twenty-one individuals (E. Kelley 1978; Pickering 1974), and at La Quemada, representing at least eleven individuals (Nelson et al. 1992), where long bones also seem to have been used as trophies. At both these sites, when the sex of the individuals could be determined, the bones were from males.

I know of no other drilled skulls from the Southwest, but there have been suggestions of long-bone trophies at Babocomari Village (DiPeso 1951) and in the Tonto Basin (Hohmann 1985a). It also should be noted that, while there is little evidence of fighting portrayed in the Mimbres bowl images, at least three decapitation scenes (Figure 2.7) and various severed heads are depicted (for example, Brody et al. 1983:colorplates 35 and 42).

To be noted for the Southwest, however, is that skeletal remains of bodies without heads and heads without bodies are far more common than human-bone artifacts. They occur from Basketmaker II times onward (see, for example, Haury 1936; Gladwin 1945; Rohn 1977; Turner and Turner 1990). That is, although evidence for the formal display of skulls is rare from the Southwest proper, there is evidence for "trophy" heads in all periods.

Another form of trophy taking is the removal of scalps. A careful analysis of a skull for cut-marks will often reveal evidence for this practice. Again, such analysis has not been routinely undertaken for the Southwest, so evidence for scalping is underrepresented in the literature. However, its presence is noted from Basketmaker II times onward (W. Allen et al. 1985; Howard and Janetski 1992). The nineteenth-century Papago took only long temple hairs, not full scalps, which would not have left skeletal traces (Underhill 1979).

How should the artifacts of human bone be interpreted? While it is possible that these objects were made from the bones of members of the same community that owned them, it is more likely they were fashioned from the bones of enemies. It has been argued that the "trophy" heads and long bones found at Alta Vista and La Quemada were used in some form of ancestor worship and that these deposits were charnel houses or some other form of mass curation of ancestral bones (Nelson et al. 1992). However, such an interpretation seems insupportable, as has been noted by Lincoln-Babb (1994). Had these human-bone artifacts been a form of ancestor worship, they would have been much more common and dealt with in more standard fashions—as is noted for the Natufian skulls from the Near East (Kuijt 1996). Moreover, as mentioned above, there is no historical tradition of curating human bones—including skulls—of one's ancestors in the greater Southwest; rather, virtually every early historical account mentions the display of human war trophies. Also, as Owsley et al. (1994) point out, ancestor worship would involve the remains of people of all ages, especially the elderly, and would most likely include both sexes. This is not what was found for Alta Vista and La Quemada, where the skulls were overwhelmingly from young adult males of fighting age.

FIGURE 2.7

Three Mimbres Black-on-white bowls showing decapitation scenes, around A.D. 1000–1130. A is shown before restoration (C. Davis 1995:146, 180). Both seem to depict ritual events with the decapitator wearing a horned serpent-head costume of some type. In each case he is seated and does not seem to be engaged in warfare. It has been suggested (M. Thompson 1994) that the scene involves the twin war gods who trick their adversaries into being decapitated. The third image, C (drawn from a photo, bowl unprovenienced), is different. The man is carrying a decapitated head and is also wearing a type of horned serpent-head costume. He is carrying a set of arrows that appears to be stuck into something like a pincushion. This is similar to other bowl depictions in which the man is hunting with a bow and arrows and the arrows are carried this same way (see Anyon and LeBlanc 1984:plate 83E). While this image is not clear evidence for warfare, it is more suggestive of it than the other two. There are other Mimbres bowls that just show decapitated heads, so some form of beheadings was a relatively common Mimbres motif.

A

B

C

Human Sacrifice

> In the days of long ago [before the Spanish entrada] all the Pueblos, Moquis [Hopi], Zuni, Acoma, Laguna, Jemez, and others had the religion of human sacrifice at the time of the Feast of the Fire, when the days are shortest. The victim has his throat cut and his breast opened, and his heart taken out by one of the priests; this was their religion, their method of asking good fortune. (As told by a Zuni to John Bourke 1884:196)

Certainly, another form of traumatic death is human sacrifice, which has taken many forms in many places. Individuals can be killed in a religious or ceremonial setting for a variety of cultural reasons. Classic examples of when human sacrifices occur are at the death of a leader, in times of extreme stress, or at the dedication of important buildings. (The only unequivocal case of human sacrifice in the Southwest was one undertaken as part of a building dedication. The skeleton of a child was found wrapped around the base of a post in the House of the Well at Casas Grandes [DiPeso 1974]). Such sacrifices may be regular—as on an annual cycle—or irregular, and may involve a single individual or thousands of people. Of particular relevance to this discussion is the question, "Who were the victims?" In many ethnographic and historical examples, the sacrificial victims were captives. That is, they were captured in war and later sacrificed. Victims may have been captured for that purpose or they may have been captured and enslaved, then later selected to be sacrificed. Nevertheless, warfare was a part of the process. It could also happen that individuals would be sacrificed by their own community, with no warfare involved. Archaeologically, it is very hard to differentiate between these two situations.

In general, when the number of sacrificed individuals is large when compared with the size of the group, the victims are more likely to be captives. But there does not seem to be a consensus on this. Nevertheless, when such sacrifices are found, it should not be assumed that the individuals were from their own group; archeologists must be open to the probability that warfare was involved and be prepared to find evidence for it. In particular, some human sacrifices in the Southwest have been identified, and a number of other interments have been proposed as, or considered candidates for, instances of human sacrifice (See Wilcox 1991). A likely, if not most likely, explanation for these cases is that they involved warfare.

Disarticulated Bodies and Cannibalism

Any issue as emotionally charged as cannibalism should be addressed very carefully. It must be addressed here, however, because evidence for cannibalism may be evidence for warfare, since it is unlikely that members of a group would consume other members. As it turns out, there is considerable proposed evidence for cannibalism in the prehistoric Southwest, although just how to interpret this material is far from clear. However, except for a couple of possible exceptions, this evidence dates to the Middle Period and, to avoid repetition, is discussed in chapter 5.

CONCLUSION

Based on the evidence, it is clear that the Southwest has a long history of warfare. Virtually all the types of evidence archaeologists would expect to find are present. There are historical and ethnographic accounts. There are the remnants of warfare behavior in the social and ceremonial aspects of Pueblo life. There is archaeological evidence in the form of burned sites, defensive sites, unburied bodies, and individuals who died from violence. Some of this evidence is sketchy, but much of the deficiency may be due to the lack of interest in looking for such information.

Obviously, warfare was far more common and more important in prehistoric times than has been generally recognized, and there are definite archaeological manifestations of it. This evidence, to be sure, is not clear-cut—but neither are other categories of archaeological information. The evidential data must be carefully analyzed, and excavators should make every effort to determine why sites burned, why bodies were unburied, etc. Also, settlement pattern analysis will remain incomplete if it is not examined for boundaries that may indicate the existence of alliances.

However, looking for these aspects of human behavior individually misses the point. It is their co-occurrence that enables the researcher to overcome the limitations of inference based on any one line of evidence. This is, of course, in keeping with basic scientific method. In the chapters that follow, I use the various lines of evidence, models, and assumptions presented here and set about to determine the level of intensity of warfare in the Southwest as well as the implications of its structure and consequences.

I conclude this chapter much as I began: The question is not whether warfare or its threat existed, but the extent to which social behavior was significantly modified with respect to warfare. In particular, were settlement patterns, community configurations, and intergroup relations significantly modified? If so, how and by how much?

CHAPTER THREE

THE EVOLUTION OF SOUTHWESTERN WARFARE TECHNOLOGY

In addition to the spies, the Mohave were divided into a large number of bowmen and clubbers. The latter were the braves, equipped with great war clubs which they used to smash heads or faces of the enemy. The clubbers formed the center of the Mohave line. The bowmen . . . laid down a barrage of arrows from the flanks while the clubbers advanced upon the enemy. . . . [T]he clubbers did most of the obvious damage since several arrow wounds were usually required to kill a person.
—as told to George Fathauer (1954:99)

In spite of more than a century of archaeological work in the Southwest, the serious study of the region's prehistoric weaponry is still in its infancy. This dearth of information is due, in part, to the lack of interest in and recognition of warfare in the Southwest. But it is also because some implements—such as knives, bows and arrows, and spears—had dual hunting and fighting roles, thus making their study more difficult. Regardless of this limitation, there is a lot that can be said about weapons, although with a greater degree of speculation than might be desired.

While warfare technology is just a small component of the model and the understanding of warfare as a whole, it is an important piece of the puzzle. In particular, scholars need to integrate changes in weapon technology into the overall models of Southwestern prehistory. While Judd (1954) argued that the prehistoric Pueblo people used only bows and arrows, clubs, and rocks as weapons, recovered remains showing evidence of violent deaths demonstrate that this is not correct. Knives and daggers were employed in warfare at least some of the time in the Southwest.

On a worldwide basis, it is easy to recognize the weapons used exclusively for war—helmets, shields, and chariots—while other weapons are more ambiguous. Bows and arrows, axes, and atlatls (spear-throwers) are the most obvious items for which dual purposes can exist. However, there are ways of differentiating how these implements were employed. For example, weapons should be constructed more carefully than hunting tools.

Referred to as "overbuilding," this ensures against catastrophic failure. An ax that breaks while being used to chop down a tree is not a disaster, but one that fails in the heat of battle is likely to cause the death of its wielder. Obviously, it behooves a warrior to go to great lengths to ensure that his weapons hold up in a life-and-death situation. Also, there may be differences in design between common tools and the tools of war. An "ax" or "maul" used for warfare is more likely to be better balanced and have a different weight from one used for chopping wood. Arrowpoints may also display nuances in design. For example, arrowpoints intended as weapons of war may be hard to remove (i.e., shaped with barbed edges or tangs) or could even be designed to separate from the shaft entirely to remain embedded in the wound when pulled out.

It is also much more likely that weapons, rather than hunting tools, would be stockpiled. Just how many arrows does a hunter need? The discovery of caches of arrows is far more likely to be evidence for warfare than for fanatical advance planning by hunters. For example, the bundle of eighty-one arrows found in room 32 at Pueblo Bonito (Pepper 1920) does not seem to represent a stockpile for hunting purposes. All of the methods for differentiating tools and weapons require very careful analysis. Unfortunately, little effort has ever been given to this type of archaeological research.

Although some implements are very likely to be weapons, they can't be cataloged definitively as such. Certainly, dagger-like implements have little, if any, role in hunting or butchering. The only possible role for a dagger—a short, pointed blade used for stabbing—is in hand-to-hand combat between humans. Admittedly, such an implement may not be a dagger at all, but an awl, a weaving tool, a hairpin, or some other pointed tool instead. However, a large, sharp, pointed implement may not be an awl or hairpin any more than it's a dagger. There must be a concerted effort to determine the object's actual function before coming to any conclusions.

Spears present a similar problem in differentiation. Once atlatls or bows were available, spears had few uses for hunting (although spears were used in mounted pursuit of buffalo) and were almost always a weapon. But, when is a "projectile" point too large for an arrow or atlatl dart and instead is either a knife or a spearhead? When is a very well made knife blade intended for warfare or for butchering? Very seldom does lithic analysis address these issues. In time, further study most likely will determine that these implements are weapons in most cases, so they should not be routinely interpreted as part of a hunting-tool assemblage. So-called effigy weapons also add to this interpretive problem. While particular examples of such effigies may have been for display purposes only, they surely did not exist in the absence of similar items intended for actual use. The idea that someone would go to considerable effort to fashion effigy axes after an implement used for the everyday job of chopping wood seems unlikely. Consequently, it is surely more accurate to describe the effigy axes of the

Mississippian period in the eastern United States as effigy *battle*-axes.

More easily interpreted are tools whose sole purpose, universally, was for making war. Various types of protective or defensive gear—from helmets and body armor to shields and atlatl "fending sticks"—are indisputably weapons of war. Researchers should be able to use an item's size, construction, and design in determining the nature of the warfare in which it was employed, as well as the role its user played. While many of these implements are perishable, this is no more the case than it is for several other classes of archaeological objects. Prehistoric weapons of war should be studied for what they are, not ignored or assumed to be something else.

Weapon Roles and Uses

Most prehistoric people, in particular those who were not organized into states, used similar weapons. And they almost always were implements that could have been—and were—used in other capacities. Specialized weapons, such as clubs, axes, daggers, and knives, were universally used in prehistoric times and were far more important than is easy to conceptualize today. For the most part, bows and arrows, atlatls, spears, and slings are not as accurate or deadly as is currently supposed. The perfectly shot arrow piercing the heart of the driver of a fast-moving stagecoach occurs only in novels or Hollywood Westerns. In real life, most arrow wounds were not instantly fatal; often the arrow was removed and the injured individual continued to fight. When seriously wounded, the victims of bowmen would either be rescued by their compatriots or dispatched by the enemy with hand-held weapons. Many groups made a special effort to create arrowheads that were hard to remove, or contaminated the points to increase the likelihood of infection, or used poisoned arrows. Such concerted efforts to increase the lethality of arrows would have only been necessary if they were intrinsically not very deadly.

Because these long-distance weapons had no guarantee of military advantage, weapons designed for close-combat fighting took on an enormous importance in prehistoric warfare. For example, European groups of people known as the Franks, Saxons, and Lombards were named after their favorite types of hand-held weapons: a small battle-ax, a machete-like sword, and a long battle-ax, respectively (Oakeshott [1960] 1994). And of these hand-held weapons, clubs of some type—including axes—seem to have been the dominant weapon used over much of the world. Knives and daggers appear to have been less important, overall, than war clubs. (This scenario may have changed with the development of metal swords, but because they are irrelevant to the Southwestern case, I do not consider them further.)

Clubs and battle-axes are extremely effective—and significant—early weapons of war. The famous Narmer palette of Egypt shows the pharaoh clubbing his victim as a sign of victory. The Mae Enga men of highland

New Guinea all carried stone axes in their belts, and were quite uncomfortable going anywhere without one. They used only a few other weapons—no knives, daggers, or clubs—although other New Guinea groups did. The primary use of stone axes in many parts of the world was as a weapon and not as a woodworking tool. But, if a serious effort to look for them is not made, this class of weapon is easily missed. Clubs can be made of wood and not preserve archaeologically, and stone ax- or club-heads can be misclassified as woodworking axes or mauls.

Bows and arrows and atlatls, primary weapons of war in the past, present few problems of interpretation and are considered in detail below. Spears, however, create some difficulty in interpretation and discovery because there are several types. Short, thrusting spears are really another form of hand weapon and are rare around the world, except those tipped with metal, as found in Africa. And very long spears, or pikes, were not thrown, but used defensively against warriors on horseback, just as lances were used from horseback. So, not unexpectedly, there is virtually no evidence of these kinds of spears in the prehistoric Southwest.[1]

Throwing-spears—or javelins—were widely used prehistorically around the world, but were not typically a primary weapon. While many societies employed javelins, they were used by relatively few individuals or were a minor part of a group's arsenal. Realistically, a warrior can carry only one javelin—which limits its utility. Mae Enga men may have gone into battle carrying a throwing-spear and bow and arrows. They would quickly hurl the spear and then use the bow and arrows. Only a small number of the men (about 10 percent) used spears and shields as their primary weapons. Spears were also employed as stabbing weapons in ambushes. And, generally, Mae Enga men using bows and arrows did not carry shields. The Southwestern usage of such weapons would probably have been similar. One military scenario was to throw and impale the spear on an enemy's shield, hoping to drag the shield down, render the holder temporarily defenseless and strike a quick blow. Such tactics are known historically for the Southwest, but it is unclear whether this behavior was common.

Southwestern Weaponry and Its Evolution

There appears to have been a fairly well developed weapon technology in the Southwest from the Basketmaker II time period onward. The number of weapons recovered from early time periods is as great, or greater, than from later periods. Beyond a simple noting that these weapons existed, it is possible to develop an evolutionary scenario for them. Although the timeline is highly speculative, it should be testable.

Briefly summarized, the initial atlatl-dart technology included carrying "fending sticks" (Heizer 1942), which allowed the user to hold a dart and

1. Beaglehole (1935) believed thrusting spears were used by the Hopi.

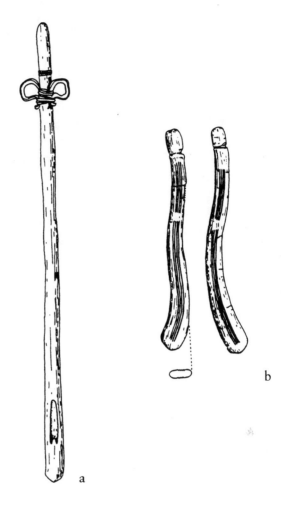

FIGURE 3.1
The atlatl or spear-
thrower (a) was both
a hunting tool and
weapon. It was
superseded by the self-
bow between A.D. 200
and A.D. 500 in the
Southwest. Fending
sticks (b) were used as
a form of shield when
the atlatl was in use.

atlatl in one hand while fending off thrown darts with the other (Figure
3.1). (Atlatls, or spear-throwers, were used to launch spears, known as
"darts.") With the adoption of the simplest form of bow (or self-bow), a
fending stick became impractical for warding off the much swifter, smaller
arrows, especially if shot from fairly close range. Also, a "loaded" atlatl
can be held in one hand leaving the other free to hold the fending stick, but
a bow with the arrow nocked requires both hands at the ready. After the
introduction of the self-bow, the atlatl and associated fending stick disappeared, and there was apparently no widespread use of shields during the
A.D. 550–1100 interval.

Sometime, probably toward the end of this 600-year interval, a type of
wooden sword began to be used in the Southwest (Lutonsky 1992). At
first, these swords may have been two-handed types, and then were probably superseded by one-handed swords used with large wicker shields.
The sword and wicker-shield innovation seems to have been well in place

by the mid- to late 1200s. Finally, the sinew-backed recurved bow came into general use after A.D. 1300 in the Southwest, along with arrow shafts made from solid wood. Based on the reports by Spaniards and others about the incredible penetration capability of arrows shot from sinew-backed bows, including penetrating hide armor and pinning a rider to his horse, I believe solid-wood main-shaft arrows shot from sinew-backed, recurved bows would have penetrated basketry shields. Better, stronger shields were subsequently developed and became a necessary part of weaponry. Although animal-hide shields replaced the wicker models, the tradition of large body-shields continued. This may be the weapons complex seen in the Pueblo IV kiva murals and encountered by the Spaniards.

Thus, a possible technological sequence would be warriors in the Southwest initially using atlatls with fending sticks (substituting for shields); then using self-bows along with two-handed swords (again, the swords substituting for shields); followed by a complex of self-bows, one-handed swords, and wicker shields; and finally, sinew-backed, recurved bows and hide shields.

The consequences of this progression in technology may have been profound. As the new weapons became increasingly more effective, they would have required increasing costs in terms of production effort and access to materials, such as buffalo hides for the shields. The wooden-sword/wicker-shield complex may have been part of a heroic or champion fighting tradition, with warrior specialists—or at least some extra strong, very competent warriors playing a leading role in the conflicts. Social structures must have developed to train, equip, and manage the champion fighters. So, there may have been an evolution from nonspecialist, low-intensity fighting in the 500s to the 900s to more specialized, almost champion-style fighting by the 1300s. However, the rate of change seemed to pick up as the sinew-backed, recurved bow appeared: Warfare rapidly became even more dangerous and more effective.

Along with these changes in weapons technology may have come a new set of battleground tactics and associated behaviors. As noted previously, when Coronado attacked the Zuni settlement of Hawikuh, rather than remain in the pueblo and defend it from the roofs, the Zuni sent out a contingent of warriors to meet the Spaniards on open ground in front of the pueblo. Was this tactic a continuation of the then-prevalent shield-oriented open-ground fighting? Once the Puebloans learned that such tactics were not effective against the Spaniards, they quickly abandoned them. But the description of this first battle is very instructive. (The Hopi apparently used the same open-ground tactics when Coronado's contingent first got to the Hopi mesas at Kawaika-a.)

Thus, it is obvious that weapons and tactics are intertwined for deployment in warfare, but the progression in the technology must be seen as dynamically evolving and not simply as a static list of weapons. To continue the examination of prehistoric weaponry, I next consider the evolution of the atlatl, to the self-bow, to the recurved bow. Then shield technology, which is closely related, is reviewed. And, finally, other types of weapons are considered.

Bow and Arrow Technology

While many may consider the bow one of the mainstays of the prehistoric arsenal, this technology was introduced into the Southwest only 1,300 years before European Contact; and while in its earliest form it may have been more effective than the atlatl, the bow did not seem to be a particularly potent weapon. Much of the following brief description of bow and arrow technology is presented in more detail in Bergman and McEwen (nd), McEwen et al. (1991), and Pope (1923).

Atlatl is the Aztec word for spear-thrower, and this short, notched stick is used to propel a light spear (or dart) with much greater speed and force than can be achieved if hand-thrown (see Figure 3.1a). Atlatls were used all over the Americas from Paleo-Indian times onward, and were still in use in Mesoamerica and the Andes at Contact. A self-bow is any bow made from a single material. Self-bows were most often fashioned from a stave of wood that was tapered at each end but was not itself formed with any curvature. It was basically a single piece of wood, close to being perfectly straight before being strung. In order to provide good draw lengths and to reduce the chance of breakage, a self-bow should be long. However, Southwestern self-bows were not particularly long and were probably quite weak.

The sinew-reinforced or sinew-backed bow is a wooden self-bow with sinew glued to its back (see Figure 3.2a). A bow reinforced with sinew has an extended draw length, which means it can shoot an arrow with a faster and longer flight. The performance of a bow can also be improved by changing the shape of the original stave, so that, for example, when the bow is unstrung the tips bend forward, away from the shooter—referred to as a recurved bow. When strung, the recurved bow has a distinctive shape that can be seen, even in sketchy drawings (Figure 3.2b). This shape is sometimes referred to as a "cupid's bow" shape. While it is possible to make a recurved bow that is not sinew backed as well as a sinew-backed bow that is not recurved, in the Southwest the two technologies almost always co-occur: Bows are either self-bows or recurved and sinew-backed. (Thus, I refer to the sinew-backed, recurved bow as either recurved or sinew-backed.) Although these bows could be made of bone or horn and not just of wood, in the Southwest they appear to have all been wooden.

There are considerable differences in the performances of these weapons. An arrow shot from a self-bow flies more than 50 percent faster than a dart thrown from an atlatl. An arrow shot from a typical Southwestern sinew-backed, recurved bow flies about 25 percent faster than one shot from a self-bow. These measurements were taken with ethnographically

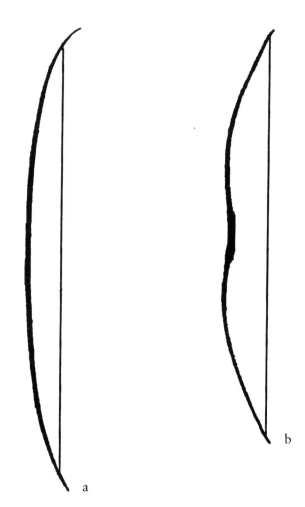

FIGURE 3.2
Self-bow (a); recurved
bow (b).

collected weapons at a time when bow technology was declining. In other parts of the world, an arrow shot from a recurved bow flies twice as fast as one shot from a self-bow (see S. LeBlanc 1997 for greater detail). Therefore, it can be surmised that, in the Southwest, the self-bow was a potentially more dangerous weapon than the atlatl and that the recurved bow would have been more effective as a weapon than a self-bow, a finding supported by early Spanish accounts.[2]

Of note is the change in the type of point appropriate for each weapon. It has long been known that atlatl dart points were larger than arrowpoints (Thomas 1978; see Holmer 1986 for a summary discussion). Differences

2. An atlatl can propel a dart around 21 meters per second (MPS). An African self-bow (much better made than the Southwestern self-bows) shot arrows at a speed of 35 MPS, a dramatic increase. A replica of an Apache sinew-backed, recurved bow shot arrows at 43 MPS—a 23 percent increase over the self-bow. Composite bows from other parts of the world produced much higher figures, in the 50 to 60 MPS range (Bergman et al. 1988; Pope 1923; Raymond 1986).

between arrowpoints for self- and recurved bows are harder to discern. It stands to reason that for the arrow to fly faster, the point should be smaller. Obviously, an arrow's fast flight and penetration capability would be important, both to hit a moving human target capable of defensive action and to pierce any body armor or a shield the enemy might be carrying. There is no clear evidence that arrowpoints got smaller after the introduction of the recurved bow, although the widespread appearance of the Desert Side-notched point, or its equivalents, may be related to it. There may have been a tendency to use obsidian to make points in the Late Period, which may be related to the new bow technology.

The Introduction of the New Bow Technologies

Bow and arrow technology underwent significant change from Basketmaker II times up to the historic period. During the Basketmaker II time period, the atlatl and short spear, or dart, were used for both hunting and warfare. Then, around A.D. 200, the self-bow was introduced into the Southwest. Some 1,000 years later, between A.D. 1100 and the mid-1400s, the sinew-backed or recurved bow was introduced into the Southwest. Both the self-bow and, later, the recurved bow were introduced from farther north, and in time spread over the entire Southwest region.

It has long been known that there was a shift from atlatls in the Early Pithouse period and Basketmaker II times to bows and arrows at around A.D. 200–700 (Lipe 1978; E. A. Morris 1980; S. LeBlanc 1989a; Geib and Bungart 1989). Although there is some difference in opinion as to when the bow first arrived in the Southwest (Blitz 1988; Geib and Bungart 1989), it is generally agreed that it reached the northern Southwest first, having been introduced from Asia. Recently, it has been proposed that the bow was in North America much earlier than has been generally accepted (Bradbury 1997). However, earlier dates are not supported by Southwestern data.

In North America, the sinew-backed, recurved bow was widely distributed from at least the Arctic to the Plains at the time of European contact. The strong similarity between the recurved bows of Asia and those of California and the Northwest Coast suggests that the recurved bow was introduced from Asia into the Americas (Robert Bettinger, personal communication 1996). This supposition has the recurved bow entering the Southwest from the north, but I know of no direct evidence for this.

The most likely scenario is that the self-bow reached the northern Southwest in the A.D. 200–300 range, and took several centuries to reach the southern Southwest. In the Mogollon area, there seems to have been a shift away from habitations on hilltops at about the same time self-bows and arrows reached the area (discussed in chapter 4). It may be that hilltop locations lost some of their advantage with the advent of the bow and arrow, and were no longer worth the cost of using. Occupying the high

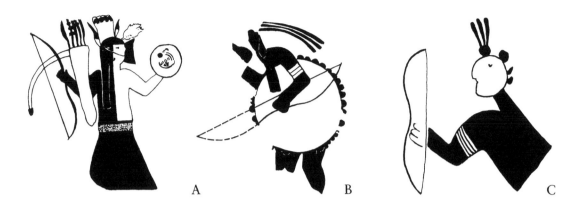

A   B   C

FIGURE 3.3
Depictions of re-
curved bows from
kiva murals at Pottery
Mound. A from
Hibben (1975:Figure
49); B from Crotty
(1995:Figure 44); C
from field drawing,
Kiva 10, Layer 23
(Maxwell Museum
76.70.9).

ground almost always imparts a military advantage and would have remained so when bows were in use. However, it is extremely difficult to
throw an atatl dart while moving uphill; it is much more difficult than
shooting an arrow uphill. So, the advantage of living on high locations to
resist attack by bow users may have been much less than the benefit gained
by forcing atlatl users to release their darts up a steep slope when attacking a hilltop site. No one has suggested any change in settlement patterns
or settlement layouts associated with the introduction of the bow in the
Anasazi or Hohokam areas. However, palisaded villages became common
at this time in the Anasazi area (see chapter 4).

It is possible that the appearance of the recurved bow in the Great Basin
area of Utah and Nevada sometime after A.D. 1150 is reflected in the appearance of Desert Side-notched arrowpoints and is related to the so-called
Numic expansion (Holmer and Weder 1980). But this is no more than a
suspicion for now. Alternatively, there could have been a High Plains route
(along the eastern slope of the Rocky Mountains) for the introduction of
the recurved bow via Athapaskans farther to the east (Wilcox 1981b,
1988a). This explanation was proposed by Downs (1972) and is favored
by S. Baldwin (1997), but the arrival of the Athapaskans appears to have
been too late for them to be vectors. Moreover, such an explanation fails
to account for the widespread distribution of the recurved bow over the
entire western United States.

The really important piece of evidence for determining the earliest appearance of the recurved bow in the Southwest comes from kiva murals.
There are several examples of recurved bows from the Hopi site of Awatovi
(Farmer 1955; Smith 1952b, especially Figure 61b) and from Pottery
Mound (Hibben 1975). Crotty (1995) has recently analyzed these kiva
murals and assigns a 1400s date for the recurved-bow depictions. (Some
examples are shown in Figure 3.3) And, in the early Spanish chronicles are
numerous statements referring to "Turkish bows [that are] all reinforced,
and very strong" (see in particular Hammond and Rey 1966:73, 102, 160).
Clearly, these are references to recurved bows. Turkey was a major center

FIGURE 3.4
Mimbres Black-on-white bowls depicting self-bows, dating to A.D. 1000–1130. From C. Davis (1995:172 [man with bird], 179 [men around blanket]).

for the production of very high quality composite bows at that time, and the description seems to be an attempt to differentiate Southwestern bows from the well-known English longbow style of self-bow. Since only self-bows have been found in caves dating up to the late 1200s, and are the only bows depicted in the Mimbres bowl images of the early 1100s, the adoption of the sinew-backed, recurved bow dates to somewhere between A.D. 1200 and A.D. 1450 (Figure 3.4).

Arrows and Arrow-Shaft Straighteners

There was also a change in arrow technology that correlates with the introduction of the recurved bow. Virtually all prehistoric arrows from the Southwest were made of cane (*Phragmites*), with short wooden foreshafts Yet, many ethnographically collected arrows from the same area had shafts of solid wood. Nothing in the literature, nor any opinions by archery experts (Charles Grayson, personal communication 1995; Christopher Bergman, personal communication 1995), indicate that the shift to solid-wood arrows was a requirement that accompanied the shift to recurved bows. Nevertheless, the solid-wood arrow came into widespread use at some point. One possibility is that the adoption of the new arrow was related to the increased warfare which occurred after A.D. 1300. From early historical accounts of how deeply arrows penetrated Spanish leather armor, solid-wood arrows were probably already present by the 1500s.

I doubt that the large diameter of a cane arrow's main shaft would have penetrated a wicker shield or a hide shield. However, I believe that solid-wood arrows shot from recurved bows would have penetrated wicker shields, rendering them obsolete. The Lower Colorado River Yumans saw the need to hold a shield away from the body so if an arrow penetrated the shield it would not injure the person behind the shield. The primary role for these solid-wood arrows may have been for warfare.

Potentially related to the use of arrows and warfare are arrow-shaft straighteners. These pieces of soft stone with grooves cut into them probably had a variety of uses (Woodbury 1954), but the making of arrows was certainly one of them. (The stones were probably heated and the arrow shaft rubbed back and forth along the groove in order to smooth and straighten the wood.) Of interest is that arrow-shaft straighteners became much more common after A.D. 1300. This is noted by a number of scholars, including Toulouse (1939), Woodbury (1954), and R. Lange (1992) (see also S. LeBlanc 1997). It is difficult to quantify the occurrence of this item, but I chose to compare the frequency of arrow-shaft straighteners with stone axes, which are roughly the same in size, durability, and likelihood of being curated. Samples from the 1200s have ratios of twenty-five or more axes to one arrow-shaft straightener. But, the 1300s sampling often yielded as many shaft straighteners as axes (S. LeBlanc 1997).

To explain this rather dramatic increase in the number of arrow-shaft straighteners, indicating they had rapidly become much more common, two possibilities present themselves. First, the number of shaft straighteners began generally to increase at the same time the recurved bow made its appearance. Also, they became more common at a time when warfare became much more intense. It is possible—but not demonstrable—that the sudden increase in these tools relates to a change in arrow production. Adding to the quandary, Cosner (1951), in a series of replicative experiments, showed that stones with smooth grooves are useful for both straightening and removing the joints in *cane* shafts. And, furthermore, arrow "wrenches" (pieces of bone or antler with a hole in the shaft through which arrows were passed and "tweaked" to straighten them), such as ethnographic specimens made from horn or wood (Wright 1979), were used for straightening *solid-wood* arrow shafts. So, it does not appear that arrow-shaft straighteners were associated solely with solid-wood arrows. Consequently, at this point there is no way to determine whether they were associated with the recurved bow, or increased warfare, or both.

Sword-Like Weapons

There may be a class of weapons in the Southwest that has long gone unrecognized: so-called swords. Although the study of this possible weapon is still in its infancy, it is worth reviewing. Anthony Lutonsky (1992) has recognized this category of potential weapons, and he argues that these wooden sword-like tools—which have been previously classified as "digging sticks"—were very specialized weapons, made and used by specialists.

The "swords" were very carefully made from oak (see Figure 3.5). Based on replicative experiments Lutonsky believes that the stave would have

FIGURE 3.5
Curt Schaafsma
holding up a cache of
"swords" found near
Grants, New Mexico.

been dried for a year or more before it was shaped; the final product was apparently coated with some form of sealant. The swords come in several lengths, but typically more than 1 meter to 1 1/2 meters long, and are extremely standardized in their shape and finish. They show no evidence of use as digging sticks, in contrast with other wooden implements that do show such use. What is so surprising is that more than 100 examples of these highly perishable items have been recovered (Anthony Lutonsky, personal communication 1995), which must mean that they were very widely used.

The argument for these items being weapons is not without its problems. Some "swords" have been found in association with digging sticks. Also, there are no unequivocal historical descriptions of their use as weapons, although there are accounts of Yuman groups fighting with "staves" (Kroeber and Fontana 1986), which may represent a similar weapon technology. Finally, the depiction of these implements on kiva murals (see below) is tenuous. Nevertheless, at this juncture the argument that they were weapons is stronger than that of their being digging sticks. Not until Lutonsky publishes the full corpus of his information can its validity be examined, but, in the meantime, a serious consideration of the possible role of these artifacts as weapons is warranted.

Lutonsky suggests that two-handled "swords" also occurred in the developmental weapons sequence during the time self-bows were used. They would have been used without shields, and could have been employed as striking weapons as well as for fending off arrows shot from self-bows. However, these long "swords" were either replaced by, or were contemporaneous with, shorter swords that were used with large basketry shields, a topic considered below.

Shields and Fending Sticks

During most of the prehistoric sequence, the people of the Southwest employed some form of shield technology in warfare. But it changed significantly over time. The earliest "shield" was actually the fending stick, and was first recognized as such from Basketmaker II contexts by Guernsey and Kidder (1921). This tool is a short stick, often slightly curved, and equipped with a thong to hold a wrist strap (see Figure 3.1b). Heizer (1942) provides an excellent summary of the distribution of fending sticks throughout the western United States. They were found in Archaic and Basketmaker II contexts and in direct association with altatls. Although these sticks look somewhat like boomerangs or rabbit sticks, Heizer makes a convincing argument that they are a very different implement (see also Geib 1990). These weapons are known from Mesoamerica, and statues at the Temple of the Warriors at Chichen Itza are sculpted with the figures carrying atlatls and fending sticks (E. H. Morris and Burgh 1931).

One battleground scenario might be that the warrior would let the fending stick hang free on its thong while using two hands to load an atlatl with a dart. Once fully "armed," he would then grasp the fending stick and use it to bat approaching atlatl darts out of the way. Given an atlatl dart's relatively slow speed, this seems feasible.

Of particular note is that fending sticks frequently have sets of long parallel grooves carved into their flat sides. These grooves were purely decorative. Such standardization of form may imply that the sticks were common, and an important enough item to receive stylized treatment. At least one atlatl has been found that was curved much like a fending stick. It, too, had grooves along its flat surface, and may represent a variation in design whereby the atlatl also served as a fending stick (Kidder and Guernsey 1919).

With the introduction of the self-bow, the fending stick seems to disappear in the Southwest (but not in Mesoamerica). It, apparently, was first replaced by a basketry or wicker shield. Only three basketry or wicker shields have been found and recognized as such from the Southwest (E. H. Morris and Burgh 1941). However, there are numerous fragments of "baskets" that may have been shields, but are too incomplete for such a determination. The known examples of wicker shields all seem to date to Pueblo III times, and are about 90 cm (36 inches) in diameter. The specimen from Aztec Ruin (E. H. Morris 1924) in northwest New Mexico is the best preserved. Some shields were painted with bold designs, including the use of selenite paint, which would have sparkled in the sun.

Apparently there is almost no archeological evidence for shields prior to these basketry examples. The one possible depiction of a shield on a Mimbres bowl is discussed below; and shields shown in rock art are difficult to date, but all seem to be compatible with a date of Pueblo III or later. As noted, fending sticks have been recovered from the same period as atlatl use (Heizer 1942; Geib 1990), as well as quite a bit of dry cave material from later periods—yet, no shields or even possible remnants. If shields were a common item, there should have been found, in addition to the three mentioned above, at least a few examples from this span of 800 years—especially since their functional equivalent (the fending stick) is known from an even earlier period.

Sometime after A.D. 1300, a major change in shield technology took place: Wicker shields were replaced by animal-hide shields. No hide shields are known from Pueblo III times or earlier. However, by the historic period, they were made of hide (Hammond and Rey 1966:73, 221; Wright 1976). There are no historical accounts of wicker shields, so sometime in the late Prehistoric Period they were replaced by hide shields. Apparently, only buffalo hides were acceptable for these new shields, and, at least in some cases, the hides were doubled (Wright 1976). The hides had to be heated, pounded, and shaped to produce a tough shield, and it's unclear whether these production techniques would have required the skills of specialists. But, if every adult male needed such a shield, then the consequences for exchange with the Plains people in order to obtain buffalo hides must have been significant.

Even a casual review of rock art (e.g., Castleton 1987; Schaafsma 1972, 1980, 1994) shows how widespread and common are the depictions of men carrying shields (Figure 3.6). Such images of shield bearers are also extremely common in the kiva murals mentioned above and summarized by Crotty (1995). A set of three shields is known from the Fremont River area in Utah (Morss 1931; see also McCoy 1984). Known as the Pectol Shields, they are made of buffalo hide, have maximum diameters of 95.2 cm (37.5 inches), 87.6 cm (34.5 inches) and 78.7 cm (31 inches), and are dated to around A.D. 1500 by Loendorf and Conner (1993). The cultural affiliation of the Pectol Shields is unclear, but they closely resemble shields depicted in rock art and kiva art, both in size and in their bold, eye-catching designs. They provide good examples of what prehistoric Puebloan

FIGURE 3.6
Rock art showing
shield bearers from
the Galisteo Basin,
New Mexico.

shields were probably like, but, unfortunately, do not help with dating the use of such shields.

Shield bearers depicted in kiva murals (and many examples in rock art) are usually shown with the shield covering the holder's torso from neck to crotch, or slightly below the crotch (Figure 3.7). Estimates from the kiva murals and rock art result in shield diameters of 28 to 37 inches (70 to 93 cm). (This calculation is based on an assumed height of the shield bearer at about 5 feet 6 inches [1.65 m], S. LeBlanc [1997].) Thus, the prehistoric hide shields seen in kiva murals and in rock art were quite large, and appear to match the Pectol Shields as well as those used in the Shoshone-Blackfoot battle described in chapter 2.

Although there is good evidence for fending sticks (used as a "shield") in the Early Period and ample evidence for the existence of large, buffalo-hide shields in the Late Period, there is a dearth of evidence for shields from the Middle Period. This absence, or rarity, of shields from about A.D. 500 to almost A.D. 1300 is intriguing. Perhaps warriors could easily dodge arrows shot from a self-bow. For example, it is known that Yuman boys shot blunt arrows at each other in order to practice dodging arrows in anticipation of actual warfare (Kroeber and Fontana 1986). Or, per-haps more simply made shields would have provided adequate defense, and would not have preserved or even been recognized as shields. Although

FIGURE 3.7
Kiva murals of shield
bearers. The shields
are large and each has
a unique, distinctive
design. After Hibben
(1975:Figure 4.9).

it seems unlikely, shields from this time period could have been made of wicker and not survived the ravages of time.

Images from the Mimbres bowls provide some information, although interpretations of what the images represent differ. The bowl images date from the late 900s to the mid-1100s, and there is a noticeable absence of shield depictions, especially given the number of bows depicted. The one possible image of a shield, found in the Swarts Ruin (Cosgrove and Cosgrove 1932:Plate 227e), shows a man carrying a quiver of arrows and what appears to be a shield on one of his arms. However, this is interpreted by Brody (1977) as some form of banner and not as a war shield. Clearly, the association of this object with someone carrying a quiver of arrows cannot be ignored. Yet, it is not the large, round body shield of the type depicted later in kiva murals and rock art. Even if this is an image of a shield, such depictions are rare. Given the very large number of painted Mimbres bowls, especially in comparison with the number of kiva murals, the lack of depictions of shields—or anything that even remotely looks like a shield—is striking.

As discussed in chapter 1, there is little evidence for warfare throughout the Southwest during the interval from A.D. 900 to nearly 1200. The time interval for which there is a lack of shields—as well as a dearth of shield depictions—very closely correlates with our Middle Period and a striking decrease in warfare. So, this absence of evidence for shields may be no accident of preservation.

In summary, there was the early tradition of fending sticks (used in conjunction with atlatls), which were supplanted by basketry shields, which were, in turn, replaced by hide shields. These later shields were body shields, providing protection from the neck to mid-thigh. They were equipped with carrying straps, and would have been heavy. Thus, shield technology was well developed and underwent repeated evolution, presumably in response to changes in warfare overall. The shift to hide shields took place, in broad

FIGURE 3.8
Historical nineteenth-
century shield from
Tesuque Pueblo, New
Mexico. This shield is
smaller (diameter 52
cm, 20.5 inches) than
prehistoric Pueblo
shields, but the design
concepts relate to the
prehistoric depictions
on kiva murals and
rock art.

terms, about the same time as the shift to recurved bows. The emphasis on shields in the rock and kiva art correlates closely with depictions of recurved bows and the increased warfare in evidence at that time. That is, a well-developed shield tradition occurred late—at the time of increased warfare—and is possibly linked to the introduction of the recurved bow.

Shield Imagery and Champion Fighting?

The imagery depicted on the big shields of the Late Period is noteworthy and needs more careful analysis. A cursory review shows that historical shields, especially those from the same pueblo, were decorated with similar imagery. The horned-figure motif found on the Jemez shields is the clearest example (Wright 1976) (Figure 3.8). Lutonsky (1992) very interestingly points out that the imagery on prehistoric shields is extremely bold and eye-catching. He also suggests that, since these shield designs are very individualistic, the bearers could have been recognized and identified by the shields they carried. Are the kiva murals depicting particular individuals famous for their wartime prowess? A Pima informant explained that the designs on shields were deliberately eye-catching so that the sudden movement of a shield might draw an adversary's attention to one side, providing an opportunity to strike a blow (Woodward 1933).

This concept of individuals carrying distinctively designed or decorated shields conjures up scenes similar to those in *The Iliad* in which champions or heroes contended for the honor of their communities. Hector, for example, did not hide behind the walls of Troy, but came out with his army to fight on the plains. Such fighting is described as one-on-one, with individual fighters known and clearly recognizable by their armor. Another similarity between the Aegean and the Southwestern pattern of warfare can be found on Greek vases, which depict warriors with very large body shields. There is at least one example of champion-type combat in the Southwest from the historic period: In a battle between Jocomes-Apaches and Sobaipuris in southern Arizona, the total number of combatants was several hundred, but the initial fighting was conducted by ten men from each side (Spicer 1962:127).

It's worth noting that a similar description of such fighting for the Eastern Shoshone in 1735 is given by David Thompson (1916:327–32; related by Shimkin [1986:323]):

> The Shoshone assembled over 300 warriors, conducting formal battle with champions backed by a line of shield-bearing warriors armed with sinew-backed bows, obsidian-tipped arrows, and short clubs.

This description provides a good model for the Puebloan fighting that occurred several centuries earlier during the 1300s. It is easy to envision a few particularly large and strong Pueblo warriors, with three-foot shields, leading fighting men from a village. Every warrior on both sides would know each leader's reputation as a fighter and could identify them as the sun glistened off the selenite designs on their shields. Given the highly standardized swords and shields that have been found—plus Coronado's account of how he was engaged at Hawikuh—such a model seems quite plausible.

In addition to the evidence for champion fighting, there are indications that war leaders once played a very important role in prehistoric society. Todd Howell (1996) found that an extremely clear set of status-differentiation items at Hawikuh, from the very late Prehistoric Period, was war related. Thus, overall status and war leadership may have been closely related. The image of this pattern of behavior does not fit in with the pervasive contemporary Puebloan pattern of self-effacement by the leadership. In modern times, the acceptable pattern is not to brag and boast or differentiate oneself by fancy or distinctive adornment. The vain and uncooperative Achilles would not have fit in at all in contemporary Puebloan society.

However, the heroic tradition could have been on the wane by the time the Spaniards arrived, an event that would have struck the final blow to a diminishing tradition of champion fighters. It has been almost 500 years since the heroic tradition could have died out, and its diminishment could have occurred because it was no longer appropriate. Such roles could have been co-opted into practices of mutually beneficial activities and behavior that were eventually dictated by the kachina cult and much of the contemporary religious tradition. Perhaps bow priests—the Zuni religious leaders who played very important sociopolitical roles—were much evolved descendants of champion-warrior leaders.

Shields, shield-bearer depictions, and shield imagery have not been incorporated into the overall understanding of late prehistoric military or social behavior. Yet, these data are complementary to traditional archaeological information, and deserve closer examination.

Clubs and Other Hand-Held Weapons

In addition to the warfare-related tools and objects already mentioned, there are several classes of implements that have been very minimally studied and, unfortunately, about which little can be said. There is, as noted, considerable evidence for hand-to-hand fighting weapons being used in prehistoric warfare, and this evidence is in the form of recovered remains with broken facial bones, missing front teeth, and contusions of the skull. These injuries appear to have been caused by blows from clubs.

Clubs

Clubs made of wood or antlers have been found archaeologically. Both types have been found in Bullet Canyon, White Canyon, and Allen Canyon in southeastern Utah. From that area, the Hyde Exploring Expedition of 1893–94 recovered a pair of war clubs, one like a baseball bat and the other like a policeman's billy fashioned of elk horn (Wetherill 1984b; see also Hurst and Turner 1993). One of these clubs had a thong hole on the small end, and the other was found in association with a hafted ax (therefore Puebloan), which may also have been a weapon. The club found at White Canyon is made of oak, is 25 inches long, and has a knob on the small end to prevent it from slipping from the hand. It appears to be Basketmaker II in age. Judd (1952) also found a club like a policeman's billy that was from a Pueblo III context; it was 29 inches long. Judd (1954) claims that wooden clubs have been found in sites throughout the Pueblo area, but few have been reported. Two, heavy elk-antler clubs were found in Pueblo Bonito (Pepper 1920), one of which contained a hole for a thong, as did the club just described from Utah. The Tonto Cliff Dwellings have also yielded wooden clubs.

Kiva murals feature images of what seem to be clubs (Crotty 1995). Hurst and Pachak (1989:19) describe rock art at Defiance House in Glen Canyon that may show fighting with clubs. And, finally, is the account by Cushing ([1896] 1988) of a Zuni oral tradition of the heavily armed, mythical warrior twins that noted the atlatl and a "face-pulping" war club.

FIGURE 3.9
A double-bitted ax.
These axes seem to
be more carefully
made and do not
show the wear of
single-bitted axes.
They were probably
weapons and not tools
for chopping wood.

AXES

Scholars in the Southwest have repeatedly mentioned that small, symmetrically made "mauls" and double-bitted "axes" from a variety of sites do not show evidence of wear (e.g., Cummings 1940; Woodbury 1954). Or, as Rohn (1971:248) notes, such an implement "has some feature that disqualifies it as a wood-chopping tool." Eleven such items were found in Mug House, and Rohn felt that "club head" was as good an explanation for them as any other. (This contrasts with seventy-seven axheads recovered from the same site.) Also, two of only six axes found at nearby Big Juniper House (Swannack 1969) do not seem to be wood-chopping tools. Jeançon (1923) notes that the Tewa had a special term for double-bitted axes and claimed they were used only for war, as Cushing claimed for the Zuni. The burial that contained the shield from Aztec Ruin, described above (E. H. Morris 1924), also contained two axes, which most likely were weapons (Figure 3.9).

DAGGERS

Hurst and Turner (1993) report direct, unequivocal evidence for bone daggers being used as weapons in Cave 7 in southeastern Utah. And, as they note, they would have been called "awls" in any archaeological report. Thus, some of the so-called awls found in the region are probably daggers. It appears that such a weapon would need to be at least 20 cm long in order to be useful. "Long awls" do exist, for they were found, for example, at Big Juniper House (Swannack 1969). Now, many awls are clearly not daggers, and some long pointed objects made of bone are hairpins (see Tanner 1976; Olsen 1979). The objects identified as hairpins are often very blunt, or have two fragile points, and look like big, old-fashioned clothes pins. Other objects, however, are large and pointed, and may well be daggers. There are male burials with weapons and "hair pins" in association. While some men did wear hairpins, it may be that some of the "hairpins" found buried with men were daggers they carried.

However, trying to sort out which awls may have been daggers is difficult. For example, Mug House burial M31 was a male between forty and fifty years old. He was buried with two large bone awls, which may well have been daggers. However, they were in direct association with five smaller awls that do not seem to have been weapons; they could have been weaving tools since weaving was probably a male activity. Why would there be this association if the larger items were daggers? Also, early Spanish accounts do not mention daggers in any context. Clearly, this is a subject for further research.

KNIVES

Similarly, large stone knives were shown by Hurst and Turner (1993) to be weapons and not just utensils. Stone knives are not very common in the Southwest, yet twenty-nine were found in Mug House (Rohn 1971) that varied in both size and haft notching. Other recovered knives include those found by Guernsey and Kidder (1921), and several large, very well made ones from Chaco contexts. One of these was buried with what appears to be a warrior and a shield at Aztec Ruin (E. H. Morris 1924), and two were recovered in a cache at Pueblo Bonito (Judd 1954). Some of the knives are very large and particularly well made. They appear much too well made for simply skinning animals, and are likely to have been weapons or possibly utensils for use in human sacrifice. Florence Hawley Ellis (1951) makes clear how important large knives were in Puebloan ideology, and Cushing (1970) also describes the role of large knives in war-related ceremonies at Zuni. And, again, as with many other classes of tools, the warfare implications of these knives has generally gone unrecognized.

SPEARS

Spears represent an even greater interpretive problem. There is only one possible prehistoric spear recovered from the Southwest. It is 4 feet long, with a large and well-made chert point, and was recovered from a cave in Lake Canyon, Utah. There are, however, Mimbres bowl images of men holding spears and kiva murals showing men holding spears (Hibben 1975). There are also historical mentions, one given previously, of the use of spears, and there are Pima accounts of how someone fights using a spear. Given all this secondary evidence, where are the actual spears and

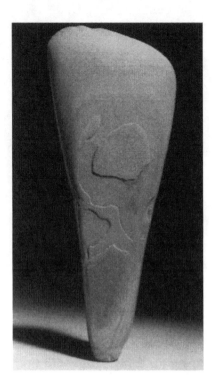

FIGURE 3.10
Tchamahias are made
of soft stone and
often have asymetric
sides. They have been
proposed as tips for
hand-held weapons,
but it is difficult to
reconcile the soft
stone they are made of
with such a function.

were they ever common? Spears are known ethnographically from such groups as the Yanomamö and prehistorically and historically from the Old World, including Paleolithic examples. However, most of the Old World contexts of spears involve warfare and horses; and spears were, indeed, a good defensive weapon against mounted warriors. As mentioned, in a nonequestrian context, spears can be embedded in the shield of an adversary, rendering it useless. Sometimes a warrior would pierce the shield with the spear, embedding it, then step on it, pulling the shield down and exposing the bearer to be struck by a sword or a club. Given the presence of shields, as discussed above, spears would not have been out of place. Nevertheless, the lack of their recognized archaeological presence is intriguing.

TCHAMAHIAS

Another possible class of weapons are *tchamahias*, celt-shaped, ground stone objects. They seem to have been produced in the Four Corners area. They are made of soft stone, and can vary in length, but 20 to 25 cm is typical (Figure 3.10). Again, as with the swords described above, these objects have generally been considered farming implements (i.e., tips of digging sticks). It is clear that they were hafted (E. H. Morris 1939), and a case can be made that they were the stone tips of some type of weapon (Larralde 1992; Larralde and Schlanger 1994). They seem to have been hafted lengthwise onto a handle (in other parts of the world, similar implements—such as a tomahawk—were hafted sideways). Larralde does note that, historically, *tchamahias* presumably recovered from prehistoric contexts were used by Pueblo people in ritual contexts, and these contexts had some relationship to warfare (See also F. Ellis 1967). However, the case as to how and why they were used as weapons is not particularly convincing. *Tchamahias* were often made of soft stone—in particular horn-stone—seemingly the exact opposite kind of stone that would be used for a weapon. But, Rohn (1971) makes a good case that the argument for their use as digging implements is also weak.

While *tchamahias* are generally found in Pueblo II and Pueblo III sites in the Four Corners area, they are not found throughout the Southwest. And, they don't appear to be found in special contexts, nor are they particularly used as burial goods. Thus, evidence is lacking that they had a prehistoric ceremonial function or that they were farming tools. If weapons, *tchamahias* might possibly provide some further support for Lutonsky's argument that very specialized weapons were being produced prehistori-cally. But because these objects are from a very small area (near the Four Corners), they do not represent a widely used weapon if they ever were one. The case for *tchamahias* being weapons is much weaker than that for swords. However, as with swords, additional work is certainly needed to clarify the situation.

In summary, since there are a number of implements that were most likely used as hand-held weapons for close fighting and since hand-to-hand combat would have been very prevalent in most prehistoric warfare, these weapons are of considerable interest.

Kiva Murals and Rock Art

Artistic images and depictions of warfare have been given little scholarly consideration as useful archaeological information. Such imagery has been noted worldwide, from hunter and gatherer rock art (Keeley 1996), to Mayan paintings (as at Bonampak), to the Egyptian Narmer and other late prehistoric palettes (Aldred 1984). However, few scholars have fo-cused on this class of information to determine what weapons were in use at the time or to discover who was fighting whom or what tactics were being employed. There are a few exceptions to this lack of focus on pre-historic art: Oakeshott ([1960] 1994) uses Greek vase paintings and other artistic renderings to understand more about the use and construction of various weapons, from shields to chariots; and, as previously discussed, Farmer (1955) uses kiva art to show the existence of the recurved bow in the prehistoric arsenal.

Much can be learned by closely examining this artwork. Kiva murals have been observed to change through time in their frequency of depic-tions of fighting and weapon orientation. And the widespread occurrence of images of men with large shields (shield bearers) in both kiva murals and rock art can be correlated with other evidence for increased warfare.

Warriors and weapons are commonly depicted on kiva murals (e.g., Smith 1952b:Figure 61b; Hibben 1975:Figures 32, 49, 58). Also featured are images of shields, bows, arrows, clubs, and spears. The number of kiva murals alone can be instructive: There are some 375 painted panels at Pottery Mound and 134 at Awatovi. Since many of these panels are very fragmentary and essentially unreadable, any estimate of the frequency of weaponry is surely an underestimate. Nevertheless, Crotty's very detailed synthesis (1995:Tables B.1–5) indicates that about 20 percent of all the panels at each site have some form of weaponry depicted. This is not an occasional image of war, but indicates almost a preoccupation with images of weapons and war.

Rock art imagery also contributes to the warfare model proposed here, for there are a number of depictions of shield bearers and, possibly, just shields. Cole (1990) believes that the shield-bearer motif dates to late Pueblo II and Pueblo III, but in the Rio Grande area it seems to be late Pueblo III and primarily Pueblo IV. It's difficult to determine if a decorated circle represents a shield in the absence of a person carrying it, and there has been little effort spent to see whether there is spatial patterning to particular forms of shield-bearer motifs. Nevertheless, the shield bearer becomes a very common motif in rock art, and generally occurs late—just how late is debatable, but is certainly before the end of Pueblo III. The increase in the number of shield-bearer images in the artwork does broadly correlate with the increase in warfare during the Late Period, and probably relates to the development of the buffalo-hide shield, although the rock art could be depicting either basketry or hide shields.

There are a few rock art scenes that appear to show actual warfare. One well-known example is found at Castle Rock, where the site was attacked and destroyed. Cole (1993) makes a good argument that a pictograph from Grand Gulch, Utah, depicts a trophy skin taken from a human head that looks much like an actual trophy skin found in a Basketmaker cave in the same area (described in more detail in chapter 4). However, except for the understudied shield-bearer images, rock art in general provides little information about Southwestern warfare.

Summary

While there is considerable evidence for weapons of war from the Southwest, at this point, only the evolution of the atlatl–bow–recurved-bow technology and the associated shield evolution goes beyond the simple statement that weapons did exist. Yet, the bow and shield information has broad implications: Each projectile technology was more deadly than its predecessor. The self-bow was more of a threat than the atlatl, and the sinew-backed, recurved bow had the potential for being much more deadly than the previous self-bow. Each new technology could have considerably increased the intensity and consequences of warfare. Moreover, the presence of the self-bow and then the sinew-backed, recurved bow probably sparked changes that influenced arrow technology, shield evolution, and perhaps initiated and instigated the development of other weapons and tactics as well.

Certainly, making a sinew-backed, recurved bow cannot have been a trivial process. What glues were used? How many layers of sinew were applied? How long should each layer dry? Not all groups necessarily obtained this technology at the same time, and such differential availability of critical information could have been extremely destabilizing. If the new bow technology was available to some groups before others, it could have upset the fragile relationships previously worked out between communities and rapidly altered the balance of power.

New weapons technology could have played a role in changing the structure of trade, producing new sets of relationships and alliances. The change in technology from wicker to hide shields would have required buffalo skins—and possibly buffalo sinew for the recurved bows—necessitating access to these materials. As discussed in chapter 7, a new east/west dynamic in trade appears to have replaced the previously dominant north/south-oriented system when the desire for new raw materials combined with the change to a colder climate in the Southwest. The climatic change appears to have brought the buffalo into the southern plains in close proximity to some Puebloan groups and increased the need for hide robes as well.

Clearly, these new weapons did not cause warfare in the Southwest, but their introduction could have had a major impact on the war-making potential and the nature of alliances. So, these evolutions and changes may be more important to the overall cultural systems than just technical improvements in a weapon class. There is an unutilized potential for further study of this class of data, and much of it should be reexamined not simply to find evidence of warfare but to learn something about its nature.

CHAPTER FOUR

ENDEMIC WARFARE
IN THE EARLY PERIOD
The Basketmaker and Pueblo I Periods

Ninety-seven skeletons were taken from this cave. Many of the men showed evidence of having been killed, as spearpoints were found between the ribs and arrowpoints in the backbones. . . . The number of skeletons found at one level and in one place would suggest a sudden and violent destruction of a community by battle or massacre. Many of the skulls are broken, as well as the ribs, and the bones of the arms and legs.

> —From accounts by Richard Wetherill of Basketmaker finds from Cave 7, southeastern Utah

The time of the first significant use of corn and the first settled hamlets is a fascinating period in the prehistoric Southwest. Although the people did not develop agriculture independently, the area is still quite relevant to understanding the processes by which agriculture became adopted over much of the world. In theory, such a time would be one of a rapidly increasing carrying capacity as domesticates were being selected for local conditions and as techniques for planting, processing, and storing crops were being perfected. All of these events would have led to increased yields. Thus, of all times, the expectation for this period should be one of little conflict. The low absolute population numbers should reinforce such an expectation, since there would exist a classic band-type organization with broad mate-exchange–based social networks providing the social "glue" to resolve conflicts peaceably.

So much for educated guesses. Regardless of the expectations, the reality of the situation was far different: The introduction and adoption of agriculture in the Southwest was not a peaceful process. The amount of evidence for warfare found during the Early Period—from weapons, defensive sites, burned sites, and the recovered remains of massacred individuals—comes as something of a shock. There is no escaping the conclusion that the introduction and acceptance of agriculture was associated with warfare. This by no means suggests that agriculture caused the warfare, just that the adoption and ever-increasing importance of agriculture was accompanied by—and did not eliminate—warfare.

And, there is good reason to believe that warfare was endemic and not just restricted to a few times and places. This suggestion is not original; over the last decade there has been increasing recognition of the possible importance of warfare in the Early Period time range. In particular, Kane (1989) and Orcutt et al. (1990) point to evidence for significant warfare during the latter part of the Pueblo I Period, when there is particularly strong evidence for the burning of sites and the formation of empty zones between settlements.

The earliest time span yielding enough information for examining the nature and level of warfare for the Southwest is the late Archaic and the first evidence of pottery use. Taken together, this Early Period consists of the last few centuries B.C. up to around A.D. 900. In the Anasazi area, there are useful data from Basketmaker II (800 B.C.–A.D. 500), Basketmaker III (A.D. 500–800), and Pueblo I (800–900).

In the Mogollon area, the Early Period consists of the San Pedro (or related cultures) stage (the first millennium B.C. to A.D. 200) and is followed by the Early Pithouse period (A.D. 200–550), including the Pine Lawn phase of the Reserve area and contemporary equivalents over the rest of the Mogollon range. This interval actually provides most of the earliest warfare-related evidence.

In the Hohokam, my Early Period includes the late Archaic, Red Mountain, and Vahki phases. Information is also included from the subsequent Late Pithouse period of the Mogollon and the Colonial period of the Hohokam, from A.D. 500–600 up to about 900.

Although the entire Early Period has a very long time span, which I have divided into temporal segments, so much of the data is skimpy and imprecise that there is little benefit at this point in trying to refine it for the purpose of warfare analysis. I simply treat it as a long "early" period. Because the beginning of the Early Period has such sparse evidence for behavior of any kind, it is impossible to discuss warfare at all. So, although the Basketmaker II period starts early in the first millennium B.C., almost all of its relevant data dates from the end of the period—probably around A.D. 0 or later. Consequently, my discussion starts at what is not a very significant point, but simply one with adequate data. The end of the Early Period is far more culturally significant and can be more meaningfully interpreted. In other words, if the Early Period were a play written in three acts, we would be coming in on the second or third act.

There are two watershed events in this time period: agriculture and ceramics. Following the introduction of agriculture, which began before 1000 B.C., is what appears to have been a major population increase and the utilization of areas that were previously very sparsely inhabited. Evidence for this larger population is discernible at around A.D. 0, or even a few centuries before, especially in the Hohokam area. Then, during the interval between A.D. 200 and 500, there is another major change in life-style over the entire Southwest: the adoption of ceramics, ground stone axes, trough metates, much larger and more substantial houses, and the bow and arrow. (Some tools seemed to arrive from the north—such as the bow and arrow—some from the south—such as pottery—and some perhaps were locally developed.) At this point, the population grew again—or at least became much more visible—with a tendency to live in larger communities. Also, the initial evidence of pottery use vastly improved the potential for more meaningful archaeological interpretations. The origins and dating of agriculture in the Southwest are summarized in Minnis (1992), Huckell (1995), Matson (1991), and Wills (1988) (see also M. Berry [1982] for issues involved in dating).

Evidence for warfare or its absence during the Early Period is far more fragmentary than for later periods, so my purpose is to paint a general picture. I intend for this "sketch" to stimulate further investigation into the nature of warfare during this early time period rather than have it provide a detailed picture. The lack of details is due in part to a poor understanding of the period as a whole—an understanding, however, that is rapidly improving, especially in the Tucson basin. People at this time lived in subterranean structures—pit houses—rather than the masonry structures that are found later. These open, or noncave, sites tend to be buried, making it difficult to estimate population sizes or even the number of contemporary structures in a settlement. Even site boundaries are hard to determine. Consequently, sites are not as obvious as they are for later periods, so there is only a small sample of Early Period sites. And, the ability to find site clusters or cluster boundaries (if they existed) is limited. This rather "foggy" picture of the Early Period is in sharp contrast to later time periods, when a majority of the large sites have been studied and are better understood.

The realistic model of warfare in nonstratified societies presented in chapter 1 and the nature of human population growth and carrying capacities make the significant evidence for warfare during the Early Period more explainable. According to the model, the expection would be for warfare to have declined due to increased carrying capacity and the reduced resource stress provided by agriculture. Warfare would be expected to have flared up again when the population once more came close to the carrying capacity. The problem at this stage is that there is very little evidence relevant to warfare—either for its existence or its absence—until the size of the population had grown considerably. So, it is very hard to test this proposition for the Early Period at the present time. Despite these limitations, in this chapter I summarize the evidence for warfare during the entire period, and then give my interpretations of the evidence in light of the model.

EVIDENCE FOR WARFARE

During the Early Period, evidence for warfare comes from several sources: locations of sites, defensive constructions at sites, and burned sites. There is also direct evidence of war in the form of the unburied remains of victims of traumatic death. Analysis of the weapons used at this time is also enlightening. Further evidence for war-related behavior exists in the form of scalp-taking, but there does not seem to be any convincing evidence for warfare-related cannibalism during this time. All of the evidence for warfare in the Early Period comes from the Anasazi and Mogollon areas. The Hohokam and its unique history is considered separately.

Wetherill's Cave 7

During the 1890s the Wetherills excavated a number of caves in southeastern Utah. It was at this time that they first discovered the Basketmaker culture that underlay the late Pueblo deposits. Their finds are now classified as belonging to Basketmaker II, from a time prior to pottery production. This material and the Wetherills' work have recently been studied by the Wetherill–Grand Gulch Project (Atkins 1993). The finds in several of these caves are relevant to warfare and are discussed in appropriate sections below. However, the material from one cave, Cave 7, is so important that it needs particular consideration. The remains have been reassessed by Hurst and Turner (1993), and what follows is a summary of their work, with additional interpretations.

Cave 7 is a relatively small cave situated in a minor tributary in the upper end of Cottonwood Wash. There are various accounts of the find by the Wetherills, including letters and magazine articles. They describe the recovery of ninety-seven Basketmaker "burials" that seem to have been placed in the cave at one time. Many of the individuals showed signs of traumatic death. Various excerpts from the Wetherills' accounts are relevant:

> Six of the bodies had stone spear heads in them . . . in one joint of the backbone of Skeleton 103 a spear point of stone sticking into the bone at least one inch. The same thing occurs with Skeleton 128. . . . [There are] several breast bones shot through with arrows and many broken heads and arms.

Only two of the burials had any associated artifacts, except for those items that might have been worn at the time of death. That is, only two individuals were found with anything that might be considered grave goods. In the case of the two burials with grave goods, both were males and both "are characterized by inordinate numbers of bifacial blades arrayed around or next to their bodies." Fourteen of the burials—some clearly, and others probably—had bifacially flaked stone blades or bone "awls" in the bodies. And nine more had stone or bone blades or bone "awls" associated with them in unspecified locations. As Hurst and Turner state (1993:159), "the entire assemblage can be plausibly accounted for by the violent destruction of a group and perhaps the formal burial of two individuals whose associated goods reflect a strong association with weapons."

The authors next analyzed the stone and bone weapons found in association with the bodies. First, in spite of the Wetherills' use of the term "arrow," it appears that all points found in or associated with the bodies were from atlatl darts or knives.[1] There is the possibility that a spear was used, but it is not very strong evidence. There is, however, definite evidence of the use of bone "daggers" as weapons. Hurst and Turner illustrate two examples of daggers that are 21 to 23 cm in length, which in any other context would have been described as large bone awls. Many of the skulls and mandibles found in the cave show evidence of bludgeoning, but no clubs were recovered.

It is not possible to determine the number of people in Cave 7 that died by each weapon, because the associations given in the Wetherills' notes are not entirely clear. In any case, it is more likely that a knife or dagger, rather than an atlatl point in a foreshaft, would have been used and then removed from the victim's body to be used again. It is also probable that clubs and spears would have been recovered by their users and not left with a victim.

Not all the remains in Cave 7 were saved, and not all the saved remains have survived. But Turner, in a nice job of sleuthing, found and studied sixty-one skeletons (1983; Hurst and Turner 1993). Just as the Wetherills had claimed, Hurst and Turner confirmed that there was evidence of fatal blows with clubs or the equivalent, projectile points in bodies, and the possible taking of scalps, ears, and heads, judging from cut marks. Turner was drawn to examine the skeletal material as part of his massive study of Southwestern cannibalism. While he found evidence for human-induced trauma on two-thirds of the individuals examined, he found no evidence for cannibalism. He was able to determine the sex of fifty-five of the adults. Of these, forty were male, fifteen were female, and six were adults of unknown sex. Of the sixty-one individuals Turner examined, only nine were subadult. Given the accuracy of the Wetherills' interpretations, their count of ninety-seven individuals must be given serious consideration. It is also unlikely that they disproportionally saved male skulls, so Turner's sex ratio is probably valid.

How do we interpret these findings? First, the remains from Cave 7

1. According to the Wetherills, the Basketmaker II tool kit contained very large, diagonally notched bifaces that were hafted knives and smaller points with horizontal side notches that were dart points, although there were some diagonally notched points that were also dart points.

look like a classic example of a tribal-level massacre. Individuals of both sexes and all ages were killed, and individuals were shot with atlatl darts, stabbed, and bludgeoned, suggesting that fighting was at close quarters and not the result of a formal battle. As Hurst and Turner note (1993:186), the sex ratios imply that far more men were killed than women and children: "It can be hypothesized that some women and children were taken captive." It is possible, of course, that some of the attackers were killed and buried with the victims. The two males buried with large numbers of points could have been fallen attackers. However, the general lack of formal burial of almost all of the individuals in Cave 7 suggests that even if some of the dead were attackers, the vast majority must have been the remains of victims.

It is also possible that the remains in Cave 7 represent the burial of individuals killed in warfare from many different events over time. However, I know of no ethnographic cases of victims of warfare of all ages and sexes being interred in places separate from the rest of a community's dead, nor is there any evidence of such behavior in other places and times in the Southwest. So while this is a theoretical possibility, it is very unlikely to be the explanation for these bodies; and even if the case, it still demonstrates a very high level of warfare.

Adjusting for the missing women and children, Hurst and Turner (1993) estimate that the original group consisted of about 150 individuals. However, the exact number is unimportant. The important point is that this was a large social group, probably larger than what most estimates would have been for that time. Moreover, the group that successfully massacred them would, presumably, have been at least as large, if not larger. This is more than minor skirmishing, and the social and demographic consequences of such a massacre would have been profound. Cave 7 is discussed later, for determining the implications of this find in an analysis of weapons, tactics, and social groups.

Weapons

The general nature of the development of weapons in the Southwest was discussed in chapter 3. However, there are additional details in the evidence for actual specialized weapons during this time interval of particular interest. Heizer (1942) demonstrated, in a wonderfully synthesized article—now generally overlooked by most Southwestern archaeologists—that there is a class of tool which is warfare-related: the fending stick. He shows that these implements were in use from the Great Basin to Texas. (I briefly described fending sticks and the related atlatl in chapter 3. See Figure 3.1.)

Fending sticks are almost always decorated with sets of parallel grooves along their flat faces. The highly stylized form of these fending sticks suggests that they may have been used in formal warfare of the kind known from New Guinea or Australia, where warring groups met in formal settings as opposed to engaging in ambushes and raids. In these formal battle situations, demonstration of individual prowess and skill is important and behaviors may have become stylized and formalized over time. Thus, the parallel grooves may have been a standardized form, as was their curved shape. This is not unlike the decorating of war shields, whose painted designs fall within prescribed cannons that have nothing to do with their efficiency as shields. In a simpler form, this is perhaps what was happening with the standardization of fending sticks. If correct, this could mean that fairly large groups of warriors met in prearranged places for formal conflicts, suggesting that warfare at this time had become well incorporated into a social context.

As discussed for Cave 7, there is clear evidence in the Early Period for the use of atlatls as weapons as well as for bone daggers (usually labeled "awls"), knives, and clubs. Both bone and wood clubs—including some that are like a baseball bat and a policeman's billy—have been found in this time range, but evidence for spears is equivocal. Thus, the standard Southwestern repertoire of weapons was available in the Early Period. Over time, the bow replaced the atlatl, and the shield replaced the fending stick—and for a time a wooden sword may have been used. Other than that, the Early Period weapon assemblage is little different from the one Coronado encountered, and close hand-to-hand fighting was apparently important at all times.

Site Location and Configuration Information

Some of the best evidence for Southwestern warfare in the Early Period comes from defensive sites found in the Anasazi and Mogollon areas—not only in the location of the sites but also in how they were constructed.

STOCKADED VILLAGES

In the Anasazi area there are numerous examples of fortified farmsteads, also known as stockades, palisades or, simply, sites with enclosing fences. These include the Paine site and the Gillian site, both near Yellow Jacket, Colorado (Rohn 1974, 1975), and the Basketmaker III sites of Knobby Knee Stockade (site 5MT2525) (Fuller and Morris 1991), Cloud Blower Stockade (5DL121B) (McNamee 1992), Vinegar Hamlet (5DL1138) (McNamee and Hammack 1992), and Palote Azul Stockade (5DL112) (McNamee et al. 1992) in the same general area (Figures 4.1a, b, and c). There are also several palisaded sites in the Gobernador area of New Mexico (E. T. Hall 1944). In the Piedra phase (A.D. 850–950), the Bancos Village site had stockaded units, and the Sanchez site (LA 4086) had a

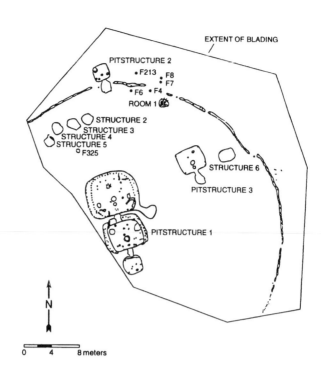

EXTENT OF BLADING

PITSTRUCTURE 2

• F213   • F8
            • F7
• F6 • F4
ROOM 1

STRUCTURE 2
STRUCTURE 3
STRUCTURE 4
STRUCTURE 5
○ F325

STRUCTURE 6

PITSTRUCTURE 3

PITSTRUCTURE 1

N

0   4   8 meters

FIGURE 4.1a
Site plan of Pallote
Azul, a Basketmaker
village with a palisade.
After McNamee et al.
(1992).

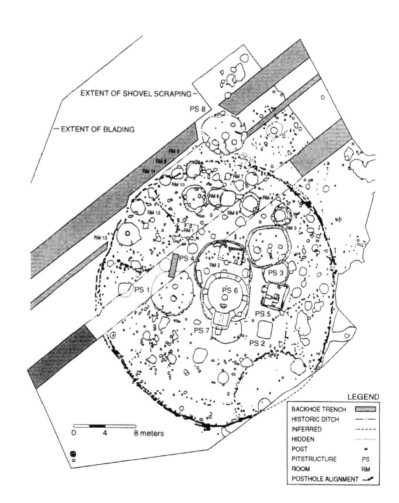

EXTENT OF SHOVEL SCRAPING

PS 8

EXTENT OF BLADING

RM 5
RM 9
RM 11
RM 10   RM 7
RM 12   RM 8
                    RM 6
RM 1
RM 13
                    RM 3
                    PS 4
                    RM 2
                    PS 3
PS 1
            PS 6
                    PS 5
            PS 7
                    PS 2

LEGEND
BACKHOE TRENCH
HISTORIC DITCH
INFERRED
HIDDEN
POST   •
PITSTRUCTURE   PS
ROOM   RM
POSTHOLE ALIGNMENT

0   4   8 meters

FIGURE 4.1b
Site plan of Knobby
Knee, a Basketmaker
village with palisades.
After Fuller and
Morris (1991).

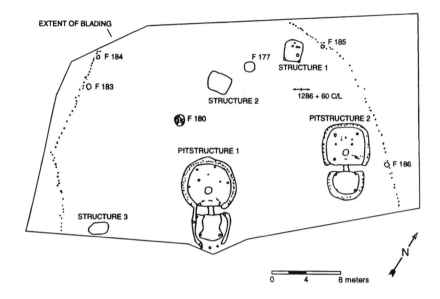

FIGURE 4.1C
Site plan of
Cloud Blower, a
Basketmaker village
with a palisade. After
McNamee (1992).

post stockade. Earl Morris found some stockaded houses on the Animas River near Durango, Colorado (Carlson 1963). All these examples are Basketmaker III to Pueblo I in time. Examples of the Pueblo II fortified sites have been found in the Kayenta area (Black Mesa and Glen Canyon areas), the Gallina area (Lindsay 1969; see also Wilcox and Haas 1994), and southwestern Colorado at the Dripping Springs and Roundtree Pueblo sites (J. Morris 1991).

At around the same time in the southern Southwest, the Convento site (Viejo period, Convento phase, site Chih:D:9:13) at Casas Grandes, which dates to around A.D. 700, had a stockade, as did the Tres Alamos (Tuthill 1947) and Bidegain (DiPeso 1958) sites in southern Arizona, which date in the 800s. Art Rohn (1975) makes a good case that stockaded farmsteads were likely to have been more common than recorded because most excavators did not surface strip far enough away from pit houses to find evidence for the fortifications.

Stockades were usually made with fairly large wooden posts, and the construction effort in some cases would have been quite significant. For example, the stockade around the Knobby Knee site was more than thirty meters in diameter and made from about 500 substantial posts. (Incidentally, most of the pit and surface structures contemporary with the stockade at Knobby Knee were burned, as well as possibly part of the stockade.) These stockades did not seem to have complexly designed, defensible entryways. As noted in chapter 2, it is unlikely that closeable entryways would leave archaeological evidence. Moreover, at least at some of these

FIGURE 4.2
An Early Pithouse
village is located on
top of the high hill in
the distance in the
Mimbres Valley, New
Mexico.

sites not all the houses were enclosed within a palisade. While the outer
structures may not have been contemporary with the palisade, it is known
from some ethnographic examples that only part of a community might be
defended by a wall. Thus, none of these factors precluded these stockades
from being erected for defense.

While researchers rarely address the issue, the location of fortified sites
with respect to more defensible locations is very important. I would pre-
dict that building a stockade was an alternative to selecting a hilltop location. Was there a nearby hilltop available? In some cases—for example,
the sites near Yellow Jacket and the Convento site along the Casas Grandes
River—the answer is "no." There was no elevated landform nearby on
which to place a village, so building a "fort" was the only choice if people
wanted to live in that location and in a defendable community.

It is difficult to find any other reasonable explanation for stockades
except warfare (Wilcox and Haas 1994). If they represented such things as
fences to protect children and control animals—a proposed explanation—
stockades should be common in all time periods since these needs would
not change. This is not the case. Stockades and palisades seem not to have
been used after the early 900s. Also, these "forts" represent a considerable
labor investment: Trees had to be cut and hauled to the site. Certainly, an
ordinary brush fence would be more than adequate to constrain children
or animals. And, finally, the stockades found in the Southwest are strikingly similar to the fences the Mae Enga put around their men's houses—
similar as to size of area enclosed, level of construction effort involved,
and general locations. The Mae Enga fences were erected as protection
against night raids.

FIGURE 4.3
View of a typical
hilltop location for
early Mogollon pit
house villages; the
MacAnally site is on
top of the hill.

DEFENSIVE SITE LOCATIONS

There are three very different types of site locations that were selected for
defensive purposes in the Early Period: hilltops, cliff overhangs or caves,
and *trincheras*. The most striking examples of the three styles can be found
in the southern Southwest: The Mogollon and the southernmost Anasazi
areas have an overwhelmingly clear pattern of Early Period sites with hilltop locations. These include sites for the Mimbres area (Blake et al. 1986),
where almost all Early Pithouse period sites dating between A.D. 200 and
550 were located on high, isolated hilltops. This type of location subsequently ceased to be used for habitation sites in the Mimbres. A similar
pattern holds for the Blue River area of Arizona (Rice 1974, 1975). Also,
Bluhm (1960:540) noted that in the Pine Lawn Valley area of New Mexico
the early villages "were scattered on high mesas or ridges." Danson's survey (1957) of the Upper Gila Plateau and surrounding area also found
early sites "on high mesas or bluffs." And Wendorf's survey (1956) in the
nearby Tularosa Valley found that "there was a tendency for [early] villages to be located in defensive positions, on high, almost inaccessible
mesas." Longacre (1962, 1964) found the same pattern for the Vernon–
Upper Little Colorado River area of eastern Arizona. Accola (1981) found
that all the early pit house villages were on high, isolated landforms in the
lower San Francisco River area and that these locations were not used
later (Figures 4.2, 4.3, 4.4).

Particular examples of hilltop sites include the Promontory site in the
Pine Lawn Valley area (P. Martin et al. 1949); Mogollon Village (Haury
1936); the McAnally and Thompson sites in the Mimbres (Diehl and

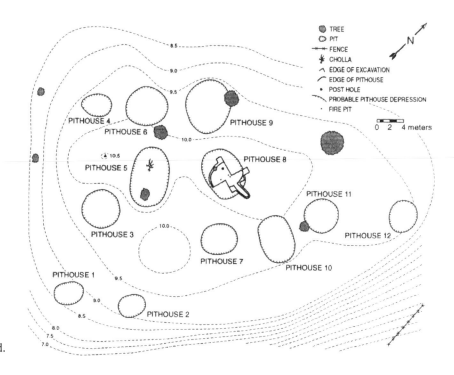

FIGURE 4.4
Plan of the
McAnally site, an
early Mogollon pit
house village, show-
ing the extent of the
hilltop used for pit
houses, only some of
which were excavated.

LeBlanc, in press); the Mesa Top (Berman 1978) and Duncan sites
(Lightfoot 1984a) in southeastern Arizona; the Cerro Colorado site on the
Upper Gila Plateau (Bullard 1962); the Flattop (Wendorf 1953) and
Sivu'uvi (Burton 1991) sites in the Petrified Forest area; and the Bluff site
(Haury and Sayles 1947) in eastern Arizona—where two more early sites
were also situated on nearby high landforms. This list is far from exhaustive, but is indicative of the pattern. Almost all known Mogollon sites
from the early pottery-producing period in this large region are on high
ground. This use of hilltops is probably one of the most clear-cut and
prevalent settlement patterns found for the entire history of the Southwest. The exceptions are possibly the earliest occupations of some sites in
the San Simon area, including the San Simon Village and Cave Creek sites,
which are both located on low-lying landforms (Sayles 1945).

This hilltop selection for sites requires some discussion. Not all of the
chosen hilltops are extremely high or difficult to access. While some sites
in the Mimbres Valley are 850 feet (275 m) above the first terrace (see
Figure 4.2), other sites, like the McAnally, that are 200 feet (65 m) above
the terrace are quite typical (Diehl and LeBlanc, in press) (see Figure 4.3),
others are simply on the most elevated landform around. That is the case
for the relatively indefensible Mesa Top site, but it is on the most defendable locality available in the area. The Cerro Colorado site is in a similar
situation. It is located in the caldera of a small, extinct volcanic cone—
and not a particularly high cone either, but it is the only such feature in

FIGURE 4.5
View of the Cerro
Colorado site. This
Early Period village is
located in front of and
inside the caldera of a
small extinct volcanic
cone.

an otherwise flat landscape (see Figure 4.5). That is, the site is situated in
the best defensive location available in that locality. Some of the pit houses
were located in the flat area below the volcanic cone, but a number
were situated right in the cone itself, along with a number of storage
structures.

The Early Period is the only time these elevated locations were utilized.
Hilltops were not used later in the Mimbres, Blue River, Pine Lawn Valley,
Petrified Forest, or the Upper Gila Plateau areas, except in a few instances
during the Late Period (see chapter 6) when they were again chosen for
defensive purposes. Early preceramic sites, such as Hay Hollow or the
County Road site in the Vernon area, were not defensively located. However, Hay Hollow was extensively burned. This strong tendency for sites
to shift away from hilltop locations beginning in the A.D. 500s was noted
by the authors cited above as well as by Stewart (1980) and Haury (1985).

There are also hilltop defensive sites from the Anasazi area that date to
this same general time range. The Rock Island site in southeastern Utah is
a good example (Matson 1994). This Basketmaker II site contained at
least five pit houses and was situated on an isolated butte with only one
access point—which may have had a protecting wall. However, the topography in the northern Southwest does not have many isolated hilltops, so
this type of location was not widely used. Also, there was a tendency in
later periods in at least part of the area to move off of these high landforms (Irwin-Williams 1973).

CLIFF OVERHANGS OR CAVES

A different form of defensive location is found in the northern mesa country. Here, cliff overhangs—such as those occupied at Mesa Verde on a grand scale at a later time—were also used for habitation during Basketmaker II and into Basketmaker III. Examples include rock-shelters in the Prayer Rock District of northern Arizona (E. A. Morris 1980). The caves of the Grand Gulch area mentioned above and those in the Kayenta region and at Canyon de Chelly are also well known (Kidder and Guernsey 1919; E. H. Morris 1938).

The same cliff overhangs and caves were occupied again only during the late Pueblo III Period, when (as argued in chapter 6) they were used as defensive habitations and storage facilities. During the intervening period, cliff overhangs were rarely used for permanent habitations. Many of the later cliff dwellings were designed to be particularly well defended, but this does not seem to have been the case for the Early Period sites. However, these locations did provide considerable protection from attack: There was only one direction of approach and an attacker would have to advance uphill. Since the occupation of the cave or overhang sites was before the introduction of the bow and arrow, the topography would have provided the defenders with a major advantage. Moreover, if the inhabitants' goal was protection against minor raids when they were sleeping, such sites may have provided adequate protection without extensive construction efforts.

TRINCHERAS

The most dramatic defensive setting, a *trinchera*, is found in the southern Southwest. A *trinchera* is a hill site with numerous low stone walls. Sometimes the walls were concentric, encircling the hill completely, and sometimes there were shorter walls that covered only part of the hill. A *trinchera* might have had dozens—or hundreds—of walls. These terraced sites were common in the Late Period in Sonora and southern Arizona (considered further in chapter 6) (Figure 4.6).

However, such sites recently found in Chihuahua give every indication of being preceramic and would then date to before A.D. 200. Several good examples have been found and mapped. The hilltops on which the sites are located are up to 425 feet (140 m) high. Series of low walls have been built on the flanks of the hills. The sites are adjacent to river floodplains near good farmland. The argument (e.g., P. Fish and Fish 1989) that later Southwestern *trincheras* were built not for defense but for agricultural purposes is considered in chapter 6. But, that they existed correlates very well with other evidence for warfare, and they are hard to explain any other way. Similarly, the early *trincheras* occur at a time when there is other Early Period evidence for defensive site postures, and they don't

FIGURE 4.6
The preceramic
trinchera site of
Cerro Juanaquena,
Chihuahua, Mexico.
Since there was ample
good farmland at the
foot of the hill, the
people were probably
living on the fortified
hill and farming below
(Roney 1966a).
Photo ©Baker
Aerial Archaeology,
transparency
19MX97.

occur when the other evidence is not found. Presumably, these *trincheras* were built when the region had a fairly low population, so there is an appropriate question: Why would extensive agricultural features be constructed into a hillside near an area with lots of good farmland below the hill? (The same argument is considered by Sauer and Brand [1931].) It makes far more sense to see *trincheras* as protecting the people who claimed these prime farming areas as well as safeguarding their stored harvests.

OTHER SITE SETTINGS AND FEATURES

In addition to the distinctive and clearly defensive locations mentioned thus far, there are other intriguing sites that don't quite fit the pattern. These sites have some defensive attributes, but they are not clearly defensive in nature. For example, in the middle Southwest, between the hilltop sites of the Mogollon and the stockaded sites of the greater Mesa Verde region, are sites such as Shabik'eschee (Roberts 1929) and its counterpart at the other end of Chaco Canyon, 29SJ423 (Wills and Windes 1989). These two sites are situated on mesa tops, yet their settings are not quite as defensive as the previous examples. Mesa tops provide a good view of the surrounding terrain, and most approaches could be defended; but because they are so broad, they would have been difficult to defend simultaneously on all sides. Some of the sites are the largest of the Basketmaker

III settlements in the Southwest. Shabik'eschee had sixty-eight pit houses (Wills and Windes 1989), although not all were contemporary, but site 29SJ423 had no more than twenty-four structures. In contrast, Broken Flute Cave, one of the largest of the Basketmaker III sites, had no more than ten structures, not counting storage cists (E. A. Morris 1980). So, sites like Shabik'eschee that were much larger than most other contemporary sites probably needed to be only moderately defensive given their population size. Interestingly, the relatively much smaller Broken Flute Cave was a defensive site.

Other sites, such as the Basketmaker II site of Ignacio (Fenega and Wendorf 1956), are also enigmatic. This site is on a mesa spur, but is marginally defensive at best. The Talus Village site is on a steep slope, but it is not clear whether this was a defendable location, although a deliberately deposited isolated skull was found there and at least the largest house was burned (E. H. Morris and Burgh 1954). Other sites do not seem to be defensively located at all, or are so marginally defendable that to classify them as such would obscure the difference between their setting and those in well-chosen, defensive locations. These sites include such examples as the Pia Mesa site at Zuni (Varien 1990)—which, incidentally, was burned—and a variety of early sites from the Rio Grande to Black Mesa areas summarized by Matson (1991). Farther south, the early Cave Creek site in the San Simon area (Sayles 1945) as well as the early Hohokam Vahki-phase sites—for example Snaketown (Gladwin et al. 1937; Haury 1976)—do not seem to be defensively located.

Perhaps the presence of nondefensive sites at roughly the same time as defensive sites is less significant than it appears. The details of the local sequences may not be sufficiently worked out in some cases to make clear what was taking place. Where there is a good understanding of the local sequence, there does sometimes seem to be a discernible pattern to the temporal events. A particularly interesting case is the change in site locations in the Little Colorado area near Vernon, Arizona. In this area, there are several late preceramic sites that are not located defensively. The Hay Hollow site is on a gently sloping terrace thirty feet above the valley floor. It had three clusters of structures, each with one to three houses. All were burned (P. Martin 1967). Not far away, the preceramic Tumbleweed Site is on a mesa, with apparent rock walls at all accessible points (P. Martin et al. 1962). All three of its structures were burned. The roughly contemporary County Road site is also not defensively situated. Then, in the immediately following period in this area (the initial ceramic period), larger, deep pit houses appear, and the settlement pattern shifts to defensively located sites on hilltops. An unavoidable impression is that low-lying locations were deemed adequate by the inhabitants until some sites were attacked and the structures burned, and then the site locations were switched to hilltops.

A final thought on defensive aspects of these early sites concerns underground storage facilities or cists. Gilman (1987) notes that one of the obvious advantages of underground storage is that it is hidden. She was considering the benefit of hiding food from those who might demand some of it based on kinship ties or other reasons. However, a more important role may have been protection from raiders. While, of course, underground cists could have been found by successful attackers, it would have taken considerable time, as well as effort, to find and empty them. In a situation where the attackers had to retreat quickly because of the threat of a counterattack or the arrival of the defenders' allies, then there would not have been time to locate and empty the cists. This fluid and often inconclusive type of warfare is very much like that seen in New Guinea (e.g., Meggitt 1977) and, there, "hidden" cists would have been very advantageous.

Site Size

The Early Period sites in the Anasazi area vary greatly in size. Just as there is considerable variability in the use of defensive locations in the Early Period, there is also considerable variability in the number of structures at these sites. Because the pottery is not very time sensitive and the houses are spaced apart so there is no superposition of structures or wall bonding and abutting, the number of contemporary structures at these sites is difficult to determine, and any estimates of their population size at any given moment in time are subject to error. However, the difficulty in making such a determination is probably at an acceptable level. Some of the very early Anasazi sites possibly had as many as twenty contemporary pit houses, such as the Basketmaker II site of Talus Village (E. H. Morris and Burgh 1954), the Field Camp site (LA2605) near Ignacio, Colorado (Fenega and Wendorf 1956), and the Arizona site D:7:3133 on Black Mesa (Leonard et al. 1984). Both the Black Mesa site and a site with fourteen pit houses on Cedar Mesa (Dohm 1994) consisted of several clusters of three to five pit houses. Whether they represented a single hamlet or small village is open to interpretation. Many, if not most, other apparently contemporary sites had only a pit house or two. (Later Anasazi sites, including Shabik'eschee, were much larger than the earlier ones, with maybe twice as many contemporary structures.) In addition to these (for the times) large sites, there are also numerous small habitation sites, often consisting of a single structure.

So, in both Basketmaker II and Basketmaker III times, there is a broad range of site sizes, from very small to reasonably large. Apparently, the relatively big sites represent the end of a continuum—in contrast to the Late Period when all sites were large. As noted previously, some of the smaller sites were stockaded; there is no evidence that all of them were fortified. Some of the larger sites appeared to have pit houses in clumps of about four houses, and these clusters were often aggregated into what have been termed "neighborhoods." So, for the Anasazi, there seems to have been a range of defensibility in the sites, from small ones that were highly defensive to small ones that may not have been defensive at all and from large sites that may have had locations with some defensive advantage to large sites that, because of their population size, may not have needed a defensive location. Because not all the examples date from the same time period—and this is a large geographic area—defensive needs may have varied. Up until the mid-700s few, if any, sites contained more than 200 individuals, and most were much smaller. Thus, compared with later Southwestern communities, all these sites were small. Actually, it may be more appropriate to refer to them as hamlets rather than villages. However, after A.D. 800 some sites very quickly became very much larger. These large Pueblo I sites are discussed below.

There appears to be an obvious difference between the Mogollon and Anasazi areas—not necessarily in terms of site size, but in defensive locations. Although numerous Mogollon sites had twenty-five or more pit houses, it is not clear how many of them were contemporary. Some sites had only a few pit houses; but there seems to be a complete range from a few to many. In spite of the size differences, unlike the Anasazi situation, virtually all Mogollon sites were defensively located. There was a time (around A.D. 200–550) when the overwhelming majority of Mogollon sites were defensive. And, they almost all had the same kind of location: hilltops. In the Anasazi, there are numerous examples of defensive locations, but they vary from rock-shelters to hilltops and stockades. Also, there are, apparently, examples of nondefensive sites that were contemporaneous with defended ones. I have no explanation for these differences.

In the Hohokam area, the sites were similar in size to Mogollon sites, with few prior to A.D. 700 containing more than 200 individuals. Many smaller habitation sites also existed. Again, the difference between the Hohokam and other areas is that, at this point, there is no evidence for defensive features or locations for any of the Hohokam sites.

Burned Sites

Burned sites are quite common during the Early Period, as has been known for a long time. Earl Morris (1939) in particular noted that there was widespread burning in Basketmaker III and Pueblo I times, as did Roberts (1930) before him. More than fifty years later, after considerably more excavation, the same opinion holds. As Wilshusen (1995) notes: "The fiery destruction of late [Pueblo I] structures is common in the area." Because sites in this early time frame tended to have separate structures and to engage in significant rebuilding of existing structures, it is hard to determine whether burned structures were truly contemporary with each other. It is much more difficult to determine whether multiple, single structures were burned at the same time in these Early Period villages than it is for the late Pueblo III and Pueblo IV sites, where the rooms were contiguous.

Most excavators have not focused on this issue, which makes it almost impossible for anyone to draw such conclusions based on the evidence. My technique has been to look for sites where most of the structures were burned, or where pit houses and aboveground (often jacal) units were also burned. This approach generally rules out accidental fires and ritual burning (discussed in chapter 2). It does not, however, differentiate between burning at the hands of an enemy and burning when a site is abandoned.

In some cases the burned community under consideration is small, such as the Twin Trees late Basketmaker III site on Mesa Verde (Lancaster et al. 1954). Here, the pit house was burned while in use, but because the site is so small, it's difficult to determine whether the fire was accidental or deliberate. Nearby, at Site 16, the late Pueblo I or early Pueblo II (about A.D. 900) component was burned, but not the later Pueblo II components. Interestingly, the burned component at Site 16 consisted of surface jacal rooms, instead of the more commonly found (at this time) burned pit structures. The burning of the early component and not the later ones is typical and seems to be symptomatic of the change in the nature and intensity of warfare that took place during the Middle Period (discussed in chapter 5).

At the Basketmaker III Stevenson site (5MT-1) near Yellow Jacket, an extra-large kiva as well as others were burned, suggesting that most of the community burned. At nearby 5MT-3, some burned structures were full of corn (Lange et al. 1988). A series of Basketmaker III sites near Durango, Colorado, was reported by Carlson (1963). It was not determined whether these sites were all contemporary, but they were situated on small ridges and virtually all the sites had burned. (One site, Ign 7:22, contained an unburied body, which is considered below.) That these structures were located on ridges, and presumably attacked and burned, strongly suggests that the rings of stones surrounding these sites were in some way related to defense, but exactly just how this would have worked is not clear. At the Field Camp site (LA2605), near Ignacio, Colorado, all twenty structures were burned.

Another Anasazi area with considerable evidence of site burning is the Prayer Rock District (E. A. Morris 1980) in northeastern Arizona, where a number of cliff overhangs (considered caves) contained Basketmaker III pit structures. At Broken Flute Cave, all but one of the large dwelling chambers had burned. Some of the sites seem to have been abandoned before burning, but others were clearly in use when burned—and contained large quantities of food and artifacts. One adult male had been "killed by a heavy blow on the upper side of the head" (E. A. Morris 1980:51). Morris suggested that this death as well as the burned pit houses may have been the result of a successful raid. In nearby Cave 1, two of three pit houses had burned while occupied. Cave 2 contained at least three of four pit houses that burned while in use, and Pocket Cave had two of four pit houses burned, also apparently while in use. Finally, Cave

8 contained four pit houses, and all had burned while occupied. This Prayer Rock District example is one of the clearest patterns of burned structures found in the entire Anasazi area.

As widespread as the Basketmaker III burning is, the amount of burning during Pueblo I at the end of our Early Period is massive. Evidence for this exists for Burnt Mesa (Bunker and Dykeman 1991), Blue Mesa and the Durango area in Colorado (Fuller 1988; Carlson 1963), and the Gobernador region in New Mexico (Cater and Shields 1992). The Duckfoot site, near Cortez, Colorado, is significantly burned (R. Lightfoot and Etzkorn 1993), and the overall evidence for warfare found there is quite great. All three of the inhabited pit structures, six of seven front-row surface rooms, and one of ten back storage rooms were burned. Seven unburied bodies were found in a pit structure. An estimate of the site's population at the time of the burning is about twenty to twenty-five individuals. So, apparently one-third of the population died when the site burned. Another case is the very extensive burning at the Grass Mesa Village in the Dolores area (Lipe et al. 1988). At this Pueblo I site, almost all of the pit structures were burned and the site was then abandoned. Nearby, McPhee Village (Kane and Robinson 1988) also experienced major burning. Roberts (1930) noted that at the Stollsteimer sites in southwestern Colorado most structures were destroyed by fire, as were most of the nearby Pine River Valley houses. He also found a tunnel from a proto-kiva to a surface room in B-village.

The famous Site 13 at Alkali Ridge (Brew 1946) had the aboveground storage rooms and habitation rooms almost entirely destroyed by fire. The site dates to the late 700s, the middle of the Pueblo I Period. Since the site consisted of multiple rows of rooms, it does not seem possible that an accidental blaze could have set them all on fire. There was a "burial" on the floor of proto-kiva D, placed there possibly at abandonment or later. Incidentially, the site was on high ground with good visibility, but it was not protected by steep slopes. Defense would have been dependent on its size.

All of these examples of burned sites are in contrast to other Pueblo I sites Wilshusen (1991) describes in which some pit houses were burned, but not the sites as a whole. While I am not completely willing to rule out warfare at these sites, clearly something different was going on in these instances, as considered below.

Eddy (1972) found 80 percent of all surface structures burned in the Navajo Reservoir area in New Mexico. The sites seem to be primarily Pueblo I in time. The large Bancos Village and the Sanchez site (LA4086) experienced significant burning and both had post stockades. (Bancos Village is discussed below.) At the Sanchez site, most structures outside the stockade were burned, including both pit houses and surface rooms. Inside the stockade, the one pit house and at least two of the four contemporary surface rooms were heavily burned and contained in situ deposits.

Farther south, at the early site K3:201 on Pia Mesa, south of Zuni Pueblo, all three excavated pit structures had burned, and there is no evidence of reoccupation (Varien 1990). However, the extent of the community is unknown, so the relative amount of burning cannot be ascertained. The site appears to date in the A.D. 400s, about the time of the Flattop site in the Petrified Forest area. It is one of the most southerly sites of this era that is not defensively located (as, not too far to the south, were the hilltop Mogollon sites). The Hay Hollow site, temporally equivalent to Basketmaker II, occupied a nondefensive location and was burned. In the same general area, but dating later—to around A.D. 700–800—Roberts (1939) found a number of burned structures near Whitewater in eastern Arizona; he also found projectile points embedded in bodies and burned bodies.

In the Mogollon area (or the boundary area between the Anasazi and the Mogollon), the Petrified Forest sites are somewhat enigmatic. At the Flat Top site, some structures had burned, but apparently not all of them. At nearby Sivu'uvi, also located on a very defendable mesa top, essentially all tested structures had burned (Burton 1991). Most of the structures at the Cerro Colorado site had also burned, including all within the volcanic cone. It is apparent that twelve out of a total of fourteen excavated Basketmaker III structures were burned. One intensely burned structure at Cerro Colorado—No. 405—had six unburied bodies on the floor, including three adults and one subadult. (Incidentally, this site dates later in time than the early Mogollon defensive sites discussed above. However, defensive sites and evidence for warfare extend later in time, from south to north, so the setting for this site and the burning of structure 405 fits the overall pattern.)

One particularly anomalous case is the Turkey Foot Ridge village site in the Pine Lawn Valley area (P. Martin and Rinaldo 1950). This mesa-top site consisted of about sixteen pit houses, all apparently built soon after A.D. 780. Although the site setting was defensive, most Mogollon sites at this time were not defensively located, and there is little evidence for significant warfare at this time in this area (although it was significant farther north). However, fifteen pit houses were excavated at Turkey Foot Ridge; and, of these, there is some question whether thirteen of them burned. There is no question that eleven structures did burn. A reasonable amount of in situ material was recovered. One pit house contained an unburied body whose bones were scattered over part of the area. While the evidence is not overwhelming, it certainly suggests that the site was abandoned after a successful attack.

In conclusion, there are good examples of burned sites from much of the Anasazi area during Basketmaker II, Basketmaker III, and Pueblo I, my Early Period. However, this is a large area with a long time interval—more than half of the Southwest and representing almost 1,000 years—and the overall evidence does not suggest that most communities were destroyed by fire. Yet, the above discussion clearly covers more than a few isolated instances. Obviously, destruction of sites by burning was a relatively common phenomenon in the Anasazi area during the Early Period. There is less evidence for burned sites in the Mogollon area, but perhaps the practice of settling on hilltops provided adequate protection, and, thus, fewer successful attacks occurred.

Unburied Bodies, Violent Deaths, and Scalping

Along with numerous burned sites, a reasonably large number of un-buried bodies, or remains showing evidence of violent death, have been found in Early Period sites. A few were mentioned previously, and a number of them are listed in Table 4.1—but it is by no means a definitive list. Only particular examples are discussed here. One of the biggest difficulties with the early Anasazi data is that most of the information about the Basketmaker II people comes from the excavations of cave deposits. While it is not the case that caves were exclusively utilized as habitation sites during this time period, most fieldwork has been conducted in cave sites because of the high level of preservation and ease of discovery. Most of the fieldwork, however, was done very early in the history of Southwestern archaeology. For example, a great deal of the work was undertaken by the Wetherills in the 1890s and represents the very beginning of archaeological work in the Southwest. The quality of the early work suffers by comparison with that of the work done by today's standards, and many of the field notes and recovered specimens are no longer available for restudy. Thus, this early, very tantalizing evidence has not been replicated by modern work and must be interpreted with caution on the one hand and by extrapolation on the other.

Some of the first archaeological work in the Southwest completed by Richard Wetherill and, later, by Earl Morris found very significant evidence for major acts of warfare. The most dramatic and well known of these is Wetherill's finding the burial of at least ninety-two individuals dating from the Basketmaker II time period in Cave 7 (previously discussed). Wetherill made two other Basketmaker finds in southeastern Utah with recovered remains exhibiting evidence of violent death. These remains have been tracked down by the Turners. Adults from the Green Mask Cave and nearby Red Canyon had wounds to the head, apparently resulting in their deaths (Christy Turner, personal communication). In 1894, the Wetherills' Grand Gulch expedition "found remains of arms and hands from elbows, and legs and feet from knees, showing evidence of having been cut off before burial" in Cut-In-Two Cave (Cave 19) (Blackburn and Williamson 1997). The Green Mask Cave is of particular interest because there is a Basketmaker II–style pictograph that Cole (1993) convincingly argues portrays the flayed and painted skin from a human head. It is a depiction of a trophy head skin like that found by Kidder and Guernsey

(1919) in the Kayenta area mentioned in chapter 3 and discussed below.

Another clear example of evidence for violent deaths comes from Battle Cave in Canyon del Muerto (Canyon de Chelly). Earl Morris named this cave for the Basketmaker II remains of thirteen individuals found in a storage cist, along with a mummified body with an embedded foreshaft, most likely from an atlatl dart (A. Morris 1933; McDonald 1976:37). According to Ann Axtell Morris (1933:217):

> we [the Morrises] found clear evidence of a dreadful prehistoric massacre. There were a large number of broken and cracked skulls. The nature of the fractures showed them to have been made with heavy stone axes—even children and babies had not been spared this brutality. There was one old lady who had been done to death in this summary fashion in the final hand-to-hand stage of the fighting who had in the preliminaries been shot with an arrow.

Apparently, thirteen individuals were killed: three children, one adolescent (probably a male), three adult males, and three adults of undetermined sex (probably males), two adult females (one old and one with the embedded foreshaft), and one old adult of unknown sex. Once again, represented are individuals of all ages and both sexes, but few children and women. The question, again, is: Do the bodies represent a single episode of deposition or repeated use of the cist as a burial location? Since the presence of multiple burials in abandoned storage cists was known in other contexts (e.g., in the Kayenta caves [Kidder and Guernsey 1919]), Earl Morris was surely aware of these prior finds and this possibility, so his assessment that it was a single episode carries considerable weight.

Battle Cave has the expected signature of a massacre in which all the defenders were killed, except reproductive-age females, who were presumably taken away by the victors. The possibility that the placement of the bodies in a cist was precursory behavior to the later tendency to place bodies of victims in kivas is worth considering. Both caves and kivas are already underground chambers, so excavation of a pit for burial purposes wouldn't have been required.

Other examples of evidence for violence recovered from these early cave deposits include Kidder and Guernsey's find (1919) of a curated scalp buried with another individual in a cave in the Kayenta area and the twenty burials of both male and female individuals of all ages, all of them missing skulls, found in nearby Woodchuck Cave (Lockett and Hargrave 1953). Also, work at Tseahatso Cave recovered the remains of eighteen children in a cist (A. Morris 1933:200). The likelihood that this was the result of an epidemic, as Ann Morris proposed, can be discounted, given the number of individuals and the small sizes of groups at the time. While the Tseahatso Cave example could have represented repeated use of the cist as a burial chamber, the theory that the remains were the result of another massacre must be equally considered. Guernsey and Kidder (1921) discuss

TABLE 4.1.
Anasazi Sites with Unburied Bodies or Evidence of Violent Deaths from the Basketmaker II, Basketmaker III, and Pueblo I Periods.

Site	Period	Unburied Bodies	Notes	Reference
North Shelter	BMII	skull		E.H.Morris and Burgh 1954:35, Fig.71
Shabik'eschee	BMIII	2 individuals	Pit Structures B and F-1	Roberts 1929:17, 32
Kinboko Cave I	BMII	scalp		Kidder and Guernsey 1919:81
Ignacio 7:22, Colorado	BMIII	1 individual	virtually all structures burned	Carlson 1963
Cerro Colorado	BMIII	6 individuals		Bullard 1962:40
Broken Flute Cave	BMIII	2 scalps		E.A.Morris 1980:35
Battle Cave	BMII	10 or 11 individuals	most in storage cist	A.Morris 1933
Dead Horse	BMIII	1 individual		Adams 1973:40
AZ D:7:262	PI	2 disarticulated individuals		Sink et al. 1982:99–100
Duckfoot	PI	8+ individuals		R.Lightfoot et al. 1993
AZ D:11:2023	PI	1 individual	Pit Structure 1	Olszewski 1984:186
AZ D:11:2062B	PI	4 individuals	Pit Structures 4 and 8	Sink et al. 1984:270
Kiatuthlanna	PI	5 individuals, 1 skull	Pit Structures A(2+skull), C(2), D(1)	Roberts 1931:23-24.
Site 1676	PI	1 individual	House 1, Structure 13?	Hayes and Landcaster 1975:57
Whitewater, part I	PI	1 individual, 1 fragmentary individual	Pit Structure A, extramural	Roberts 1939:184–86
Whitewater, part II		2 individuals	dropped in hole and covered over	Roberts 1940
ZNP-21	PI	2 fragmentary individuals	Structure 1	Schroeder 1955:85
Bancos Village	PI or PII?	4 disarticulated individuals	Pit Structure	Eddy 1974:81

Site	Period	Unburied Bodies	Notes	Reference
Sambrito Village	PI or PII?	15 individuals (?)	Pit Structures 6 and 15	Eddy 1966:247–48
C-Village Unit 3	PI	1 individual	Pit Structure A tunnel from A to surface room	Roberts 1930:59
Artificial Leg	BMIII or PI	1 adult male	with artifacts, floor of pit structure, deliberately burned	Frisbie 1967:52–54.
Turkey Foot Ridge	A.D.780	1 individual (age, sex?)	scattered in pit house, burned	P.Martin and Rinaldo 1950
Ruin 6		5 (?) individuals in kiva		E.H.Morris 1939:42
Animas Valley		3 individuals		Morris 1939
Grass Mesa		3 fragmentary individuals	Structure 13(2) and Pit Structure 153(1); major burning	Lipe et al. 1988
Stevenson Site 5MT-1.	BMIII	1 female (unburied?)	extra large BMIII pit house and 2 others burned	F.Lange et al. 1988
Site 13, Alkali Ridge	PI	1 individual	floor of protokiva at abandonment	Brew 1946
Stollsteimer— C village	PI	1 individual unburied, 2 isolated skulls	in burned Pit House A	Roberts 1930
Woodchuck Cave	BMII	20 individuals without skulls	both adults and children, some missing first two vertebra.	Lockett and Hargrave 1953
Tseahatso Cave	BMII	18 children in cist	no direct evidence of violence	A.Morris 1933:200
Green Mask	BMII	1 individual	pictoglyph of trophy head	Cole 1993; Turner, personal communication
Cut-In-Two Cave	BMII	? individuals	leg and arm remains	Blackburn and Williamson 1997

several other Basketmaker II burials of apparent victims of violence and trophy head-taking. In Broken Flute Cave, as mentioned previously, an adult male had been killed by a heavy blow to the head (E. A. Morris 1980:51). Howard and Janetski (1992) describe at least six scalps and basketry scalp stretchers from Utah. Based on one C14 determination and the method of construction of the basketry, these seem to date to Basketmaker times, although where they were found would appear to be farther north than the generally accepted Basketmaker area. The basketry scalp stretchers are quite similar to and seem to represent what is considered a rather standard artifact used for this one purpose. It is, therefore, reasonable to assume that scalp-taking was common during this period of time and that the associated behaviors were quite codified—similar to the standardized behaviors relating to atlatls and fending sticks. This again suggests that warfare had long been common in the northern Southwest.

In summary, given the limited amount of excavation that has taken place in these rock-shelter sites and how early much of the work was undertaken, the number of unburied bodies and other evidence for violent death found in caves is substantial.

Noncave deposits from the Early Period have also yielded significant direct evidence of violent death. In the Navajo Reservoir area, it was noted that sites such as Bancos Village (A.D. 850–950) had stockaded units and a great many burned structures, both pit houses and surface rooms. Projectile points were especially common finds (Eddy 1966, 1977). Seven individuals, including four adults, two children, and one adolescent, were found unburied in two different pit houses. Only two formal burials were found at the entire site. The overall pattern at Bancos Village strongly suggests a major act of warfare.

At nearby Sambrito Village, at least fifteen individuals were found in one location; none had been formally buried. While Eddy suggests that the remains represent an act of cannibalism, which is not currently supported, they definitely are indications of warfare. There may be at least twenty-nine additional individuals who were not formally buried at this site; some of the burials may have been the result of prehistoric disturbance of formal burials, but this is not definite (Eddy 1966). The forty-four nonformal burials contrast sharply with the twenty-five formal burials recovered at the site. Given the size of the site (thirty-eight pit houses and twenty-five surface structures, but perhaps not all contemporary), this is an extremely large number of unburied individuals, and may represent evidence of a massacre or at least major fighting.

At the previously mentioned Stollsteimer sites, Roberts (1930) found at least one unburied body in a structure and two male crania and a few cervical vertebrae with four bowls in a pit in the refuse mound. There are also a number of unburied bodies from the Dolores area (Wilshusen 1991), which were not previously discussed or listed in Table 4.1. They were found in what seem to be proto-kivas, and they often occurred as multiple burials. While there is no clear evidence that these remains represent warfare, they could represent the practice of killing captives taken in warfare, as discussed in chapter 2.

As also noted in chapter 2, in cases where warfare was involved, the sex ratio of recovered remains should deviate from 50-50. The Dolores Project found the remains of fifty-three adults: eighteen males, twenty-four females, and eleven of indeterminate sex (Weiner-Stodder 1985). Based on ratios alone, these numbers would be consistent with a population in which the males were being killed elsewhere about 25 percent of the time. However, the small sample size combined with the large number of individuals whose sex could not be determined preclude drawing much of a conclusion from these numbers.

As mentioned, the Duckfoot site near Cortez contained seven unburied bodies. Given that the site would have had a population of twenty-five people or less (R. Lightfoot and Etzkorn 1993), the remains represent about one-third of the total site population, a significant number. In contrast, the Cerro Colorado site, as previously mentioned, had six unburied bodies. It is hard to determine the number of contemporary pit houses on this site, but it seems to have been several times larger than the Duckfoot site. So, the Cerro Colorado site does not have the same earmarks of a massacre as does the Duckfoot Site.

In summary, in the Anasazi area there are a very large number of instances of unburied bodies or individuals who died violently in the Early Period. These include clear instances of massacres, and are evidence for much more than the occasional ambush. Such evidence is lacking in the Mogollon area, except for the previously mentioned Turkey Foot Ridge site with one unburied individual.

Intensification of Warfare in Late Pueblo I Period

There is some evidence that there may have been an increase in the level of warfare during the late Pueblo I period—in the late 700s and 800s. As previously mentioned, the number of burned sites is particularly high for this time range. There is also evidence for the existence of much larger sites than earlier, suggesting that there may have been an aggregation of people for defensive purposes. If this was the case, then empty zones should have been forming between major groups of sites. While the information at present is too spotty to determine this directly, there are repeated observations about areas that contained Pueblo I occupations and then were abandoned (e.g., Kane 1989; Orcutt et al. 1990; and Wilshusen 1986, 1991, 1995). The question arises as to whether the areas that seem to be uninhabited, or lightly inhabited, were actually completely empty, contained only a few small sites, or are simply due to inadequate site surveys. It is also not clear whether such empty areas lay between clusters of communities; that is, were they buffer zones between large population aggregations or just areas that were not occupied perhaps for some environmental reason?

The large size of some of these late Early Period sites is particularly noteworthy. The sites consisted of suites of pit houses situated in front of a row of aboveground rooms. The suites, in turn, were clustered together into room blocks of varying lengths, each of which may have held anywhere from five to ten families. These family groupings, or room blocks, were scattered over an area as large as 1 km or more. The largest sites, such as Blue Mesa, had as many as sixty of these room-block clusters, and would have housed a total population of more than 1,000 people. A number of other sites from this period, such as Morris 23, May Canyon, Cline Crest, and Cedar Hill, accommodated 400 or more people (see Wilshusen 1991, 1995). Just in southwestern Colorado, there were about twenty communities that had populations of more than 200 people. The Cedar Hill site in Colorado is an example. It consisted of about seventy-six household units in about forty different room blocks. The room blocks were not contiguous, but were spread out over an area of about 6 km. Wilshusen estimates that at least two-thirds of the seventy-six household units at the Cedar Hill site were burned at the time of abandonment.

This site and most of the others listed do not have particularly defensive arrangements, when compared with later population aggregates. But they are unlike anything that preceded them. A number of the sites were as densely populated as any that ever existed in the northern Anasazi area, containing as many people as did the large defensive sites of the Late Period. These large groups of people may have provided a form of defense by their sheer size alone, as discussed in chapter 2. They may also represent a social compromise between living in dispersed communities scattered over the landscape and the later solution of living in a compact pueblo.

There are smaller sites from this time period that were not part of such massive groupings. Did these sites have palisades? Tentatively, this seemed to be the case. Could perhaps Pueblo II sites (my Middle Period) with palisades be a continuation into the 900s of the warfare intensification taking place in the northernmost periphery of the Southwest? In spite of their large size—and the fact that their builders may have sought safety in large numbers—late Early Period communities were not effective when it came to defense. Most were massively burned. So—in spite of the limitations of the current information—there is good reason to suspect that a period of more intense warfare began to unfold in the late part of the Early Period (Pueblo I), given the large population aggregations, the probable existence of buffer zones, and the intense burning found on most of the sites. This period of intensifying warfare did not last long; it did not cover the entire Southwest; and was eventually superseded by the Middle Period *Pax* Chaco. It is unclear, at this point, why the rate of warfare intensified at that time or why it was so abruptly terminated.

The Hohokam

Up to this point all evidence indicating warfare in the Southwest during the Early Period comes from the Anasazi and Mogollon areas. The Hohokam were living in villages that were at least as large as those found in the other two areas, and they had built extensive irrigation canals at least by the end of this time period. Is there evidence for warfare in the Hohokam, as well? "Little, if any evidence," is the answer at this point, which is surprising because there is ample evidence of warfare in the Hohokam region in later time periods.

There are some possible reasons why Early Period warfare might have been present in the Hohokam area and yet go unseen. Most habitations at that time were found on low ground along major river drainages. Later, when there is evidence for warfare, these same low locations were still being used. The Hohokam people did not move to hilltop settlements some distance away from the rivers at later times when it is known that warfare *did* exist, so they may not have moved if there was warfare in earlier periods. Also, Hohokam houses were shallow and simply built. They would have been easy to escape from, and, therefore, finding unburied bodies in them as a consequence of attack would be highly unlikely. Also, the Hohokam practiced cremation of the dead, so evidence of violent deaths would be almost impossible to recognize. And, as discussed in chapter 5, there were very few burned houses in the Hohokam area until the 1100s.

However, there are some hints of possible Early Period warfare in the Hohokam area. Projectile points found in this area are the most standardized in the Southwest. And, a significant number of them are serrated, which some scholars believe indicate their use as weapons. Also, some very long "awls" and small stone axes and mauls have been found that might be weapons and not utilitarian tools. There are other subtle indications of warfare in the area, including burials at Los Hornos and Pueblo Grande of individuals without heads, although these may have occurred later in time (see Wilcox and Haas 1994). Beyond these few hints, there is a significant lack of evidence for Early Period warfare in the Hohokam. I can offer no explanation of why warfare would be absent there and so common in the rest of the Southwest at this time. However, David Wilcox (personnal communication) feels that by Gila Butte times (A.D. 700s) there were large villages about 3 miles apart that were integrated by ball-game rituals, which served to regulate conflict among neighboring villages, resulting in a Pax Hohokam.

Possible Alternative Explanations of Site Locations

Possible alternative explanations of evidence for warfare were considered in chapter 1. However, several of the defensive features previously described for the Early Period have been the subject of particular alternative explanations that need brief mention. A number have been offered for the presence of the early Mogollon hilltop sites. The original suggestion of defense as an explanation was made by Haury (1936). Other explanations for these sites on high landforms include moderate temperatures, good drainage (Wheat 1955; Woodbury and Zubrow 1979), good view (Bluhm 1960; P. Martin and Rinaldo 1947; Woodbury and Zubrow 1979), protection from floods (Wheat 1955), and avoidance of insects from nearby water sources (Bussey cited in Berman 1978). Diehl (1994) suggested that living on hilltops would enable the inhabitants to see visitors approaching, giving them enough time to make preparations; and Rice (1975) suggested that high sites would have been convenient for exploiting plants found on and near them. Rice (personal communication) no longer holds this view and supports a defensive explanation. Similar nonwarfare explanations have been offered for palisades, including keeping animals out of the village and the children in.

However, all these alternative explanations fail to account for the temporal changes in patterns or the association of patterns with each other. Why should we find them so patterned, if the above explanations are correct? We get palisades when we get hilltop sites. We do not find them later. We get burned sites at the same time we find unburied bodies, and so on. I think the time has come for those who propose alternative explanations for the various features and events to propose independent lines of evidence to support their explanations and to explain the general correlations between these factors by some other means.

In my opinion, the only explanation that accounts for all the described cases and lines of evidence is that they were for defense and warfare. It is no longer acceptable to reject this explanation without providing a valid, reasonable alternative. The evidence for warfare cannot be wished away.

INTERPRETATION

For Early Period warfare, all the expected elements are found. There is evidence for raiding or ambush-like behavior, as in those instances where only a few dead were found and where there were defensive sites that appeared to be specifically designed to survive raiding. Villages with partial defenses (wall palisades only around certain portions) or sites that were only slightly defensively located may indicate a pattern of ambushes and raids. At the same time, there is also strong evidence for massacres in the Early Period. As seen in chapters 1 and 2, such evidence should be uncommon because massacres should be rare. Most warfare deaths at this time should be due to raiding, so the number of instances in which a significant number of inhabitants were killed and the site destroyed is rather surprising. Evidence exists that large groups were involved in the fighting, larger than expected at this time. Even some large sites were built to be defended, which is further evidence that the competing groups were large. There is also evidence for special weapons of war as well as rather standardized weapons. The conventional design of fending sticks suggests that perhaps formal battles took place. The act of scalp-taking existed, and was probably integrated into the socioceremonial milieu.

Cave 7 is worth special consideration for what these finds imply about the nature of Early Period warfare. The most reasonable Cave 7 model is that this was some form of catastrophic massacre. Either by ambush, ruse, or the fortunes of war, one group completely, or almost completely, killed off another. Estimating that five to seven people occupied one pit house, the Cave 7 population would have occupied between fifteen and thirty pit houses, which would have been as large a community as is known for this time and area. If the attacking group was at least as large, then the evidence for group sizes goes beyond what is found archaeologically in terms of villages of contemporarily occupied pit houses. One explanation to resolve the differences in concepts of site size might be that the massacre took place at a time of year when small groups gathered together for ceremonies or trade, thus creating an unusually large—and a differently constituted—group. Yet, in terms of military strategy, such a large group would be considered the least vulnerable to attack. To attack small groups separately and at different times would make more sense. All in all, warfare in the Early Period seems to have been more sophisticated than expected, given what is usually assumed about the size and social complexity of people in the Southwest at this time.

It is indeed tempting to search for and interpret changes in the intensity of warfare in the Early Period. There is ample evidence for warfare beginning around A.D. 0 on up to around A.D. 900 in various parts of the Southwest. Acts of war occurred after the introduction of agriculture and before and after the introduction of pottery, trough metates, stone axes, and the bow and arrow. This elementary statement does not provide much help in reaching an understanding of the processes involved. But, it is difficult to refine the statement. Was the intensity of warfare constant, or did it change over time? Because the nature of the data changes over this interval, it is very difficult to make this comparison. For the Anasazi, the impression is for more warfare in the late Basketmaker II (A.D. 0–500) period than in Basketmaker III (A.D. 500–750) period, then another increase in warfare for Pueblo I (A.D. 750–900), in particular around 850 to 900. For the Mogollon, there was minor warfare from A.D. 0–200, increased warfare from A.D. 200–500, then a decline. The patterns, if correct, do not match between the two areas. However, the technological innovations did not reach all areas at the same time; different areas may have been more or less adaptable to agriculture, for example. It does not seem practical to overanalyze the data at present.

Another difficulty with interpreting data is defining exactly what is meant by "relatively little" or "more intense" warfare. Neither the massacre of more than 100 individuals in Cave 7 nor the burning of Grass Mesa Village was a minor event. Nevertheless, in contrast to events that took place in the Late Period, there is a difference. In the Early Period, warfare did not become more intense over time, sites did not become increasingly defensive, a regular pattern of no-man's-lands did not develop, and major abandonments did not take place on the scale of what is seen later. However, a major empty zone separating the greater Mesa Verde area from the Kayenta area had developed by Pueblo I times. Whether this represented the same type of empty zone that was common later or a different cultural phenomenon is not clear. Viewed subjectively, as significant as the warfare of the Early Period probably was, it was nothing like that of later times. An overall inability at this point to judge accurately the relative amount of warfare that took place during the Early Period undoubtedly affects how researchers interpret these events.

Warfare and Carrying Capacity

If there is Early Period evidence that points to fairly significant levels of warfare, why would it occur at this time? As argued in chapter 1, it is the *absence* of warfare that should be surprising, not its presence. However, one expectation might be that the presence of new cultigens and new technologies, such as the bow and arrow and the ground stone ax, would have raised the carrying capacity rather significantly, making warfare unlikely, at least during the Basketmaker III and the early pit house periods.

Prior to corn becoming important in the Southwestern subsistence strategy, hunters and gatherers were probably close to their carrying capacity, with typical band-level warfare the norm. Once agriculture took hold, the carrying capacity would have been raised sufficiently via greater yield per person, so that it might have taken several hundred years for the population to grow sufficiently to once again press against the carrying capacity. Is this what is seen? Did agriculture become important beginning around 1000 B.C., allowing the population to grow for hundreds of years, and then, around the first centuries A.D., was the carrying capacity once more under stress so that warfare rapidly increased?

While this may be a reasonable model, new technology, such as ceramics, trough metates, and ground stone axes, became available between A.D. 200 and 500. It would be reasonable to assume that these additions would have raised the carrying capacity once more and that warfare would have again diminished. This, however, does not seem to have been the case. There is, in the Anasazi area, evidence for warfare both just prior to and after the introduction of these improvements in technology. Moreover, it is at this time that warfare seemed to intensify in the Mogollon (although the presence of the preceramic *trincheras* indicates that warfare already existed). The Hohokam area would seem to fit such a model better. There, during the first centuries A.D., the large river valleys were farmed probably with small-scale irrigation systems, greatly increasing the carrying capacity. Around A.D. 700 the use of large-scale irrigation would have once again raised the carrying capacity. The Pax Hohokam concept fits well with this long-term rise in carrying capacity.

Obviously, a model based solely on carrying capacity and ignoring other changes in technology and social structure as well as the complexity and variability in the overall environment is overly simplistic. The bow and arrow may have increased the carrying capacity by making hunting more efficient, but may also have had an effect on warfare. The introduction of this weapon may have coincided with Basketmaker III in the Anasazi area and reached the southern Mogollon area in the 500s. Is it possible that differential access to this technology and its ability to upset prior offense/defense relationships may have led to warfare, in spite of the lower population to carrying-capacity levels?

While the shift to a mix of more farming and less wild-food collecting would have increased the carrying capacity overall, it would not necessarily have done so uniformly. Some bands' territories might not have included good farmable land, or not very much of it. The new strategy may have required a completely different use of space, with different zones needed in proportions different from before. This would have required a new allocation of territories, if that was possible. However, such shifting may only have been possible by means of encroachment on the territories of others and the use of warfare or its threat.

SUMMARY

The Early Period in the Southwest seems to begin with evidence for typical hunter-gatherer carrying-capacity–constrained warfare, dating from the last centuries B.C. or very early A.D. As substantial villages began to be built, the pattern continued by establishing them in defensive settings or configurations. Over time, up to around A.D. 900 to 950, the evidence continues for warfare, with site burnings, defensive site settings and configurations, and unburied bodies. This was a long interval, spanning almost a millennium. There is evidence for a growing population, and continued development of technology. In spite of changes in resource base, technology, and population size, there is evidence for warfare throughout the interval, especially in the northern Southwest later on in the the Early Period.

The lack of evidence for Early Period warfare in the Hohokam area is quite surprising, given its presence elsewhere. Either everyone is failing to see it, or something very different is happening in the low desert as compared to the rest of the Southwest. Perhaps the carrying capacity in the Hohokam area grew so rapidly with irrigated agriculture that it took a very long time for the population to catch up.

The Early Period model for Southwestern warfare acquires an interesting aspect when seen from a worldwide perspective on warfare as it relates to hunters and gatherers and the shift to agriculture. The prevalence of such warfare elsewhere in the world is generally unrecognized and is very poorly studied (discussed in chapter 1). There has been very little discussion of the theoretical likelihood and the actual presence of warfare during the shift to agriculture throughout the world. So, it is probably both unexpected and of some interest that it can be said, with certainty, that in the Southwest the introduction and adoption of agriculture was not peaceful. The intensity of warfare did vary over time and space and also from areas and times where it seems to have been essentially nonexistent to times and places where it was pervasive; but it is difficult to draw many more conclusions that are supportable. This chapter does not do the Early Period justice; but before a better treatment is possible, it is going to take many years of reanalyzing existing data as well as a careful assessment of the defensive nature of sites to find the means and reasons for burnings and to achieve a better understanding of the role and importance of early agriculture in this time range. Only then will it be possible to assess the nature of Early Period warfare with greater sophistication and insight.

CHAPTER FIVE

PAX WITH A TWIST

Warfare in the Middle Period—Pueblo II and Early Pueblo III Times

A number of the skulls had small, circular broken areas that apparently were produced by means of a comparatively sharp-pointed instrument. Others had larger more irregular places where the bone was crushed in but not pushed out, wounds undoubtedly produced by a blunt object such as a maul or club. . . . Projectile points were associated with skeletons in several instances in positions suggesting they had been in the body of the person when it was interred. . . . [A]n adult, probably male . . . was peculiar in that the body had been placed front down with the face turned to one side. The legs were tightly flexed. The left arm extended along the side and the right was crossed over the back. The positions of the arm bones suggested that person had been bound, his hands tied behind his back. The individual appeared to have been dumped on the floor and then covered with refuse. . . . [T]he fact that there were no accompanying mortuary offerings and that the individual apparently was tied suggests a captive or prisoner of war. . . . One other skeleton exhibiting a similar position, sprawled face down with the arms crossed over the back and the left foot drawn up as though tied to the lashing that held the wrists, was uncovered in a shallow pit . . . [in the fill of Kiva A]. . . . A portion of skull rested on the bench. The remaining bones were just below that level and somewhat scattered.

—Frank Roberts (1939:204, 1940:136), Whitewater District

The Middle Period, from A.D. 900–1150, represents a considerable change from the preceding Early Period. Suddenly, there is a no ticeable lack of evidence for warfare throughout the Southwest. While this does not mean there was no warfare, certainly something had changed radically. The following 100 years—from about A.D. 1150 to 1250—are particularly difficult to characterize in terms of warfare, but there are the beginning signs of conflict once again. This hundred years can be seen as either the final aspect of the Middle Period pattern or the precursor to what takes place in the Late Period. The lack of warfare in the Middle Period is of considerable interest in its own right, but what follows is so major and so dramatic that it provides the base line to understanding the Late Period.

My Middle Period coincides in general with the Pueblo II Period (which includes the Chaco-related sites) of the Anasazi area, the latter part of the Late Pithouse and the Classic periods (and equivalents) in the Mogollon, and the Colonial period and Sacaton phase in the Hohokam area. As a whole, in each of these areas there is less evidence for warfare during this time than for any other time period in the Southwest. Stephen Lekson has termed this interval in the Anasazi area "*Pax* Chaco." However, it is clear that, although the nature of warfare and violence changed during the Middle Period, war was not totally absent.

When looked at in the overall temporal scheme for the entire Southwest, this 200-year Middle Period stands out for its almost total disregard for defense in site location, in site size, and in site configuration. There are fewer burned structures and the instances of nonformally buried bodies do not seem to be associated with warfare. However, there are a few defensively located and configured sites, a few cases of burning, a number of unburied bodies, and—unlike other periods—the possible evidence of cannibalism on a major scale. Because of the increased amount of archaeological information available for the Middle Period, compared to what there is for the Early Period, it is appropriate to consider each of these geographical areas in turn.

ANASAZI A.D. 900–1150

The most interesting information relating to warfare—or its absence—during the Middle Period comes from the Anasazi area, in particular within the so-called Chaco Interaction Sphere. This is a broad concept that involves most of the eastern Anasazi area (it does not extend into the western Anasazi area). The Chaco Interaction Sphere has been discussed by a large number of scholars, and the papers in Crown and Judge (1991) provide both a summary and a good entrée to this literature. The concept of this "sphere" involves an increase in commonality among areas that were previously more distinct, with New Mexico's Chaco Canyon as the model influencing the spread of similarities over the surrounding areas. The similarities are seen in community plans that consisted of a Great House surrounded by numerous small room blocks of a very different architectural style. Great Houses usually contained one or more Great Kivas. Great Kivas had existed before (although were constructed differently), but the pattern of a Great House, a Great Kiva, and surrounding room blocks was new. Also associated with the Chaco Interaction Sphere are roads that, for the most part, radiated outward from Chaco Canyon, where the greatest density and largest of the Great Houses were located. The roads did not link all Great Houses, but their presence suggests some form of integrated communities. Much of what is seen today, as well as the evidence supporting the concept of the Interaction Sphere, is relatively late, dating to the latter part of the 1000s and the early 1100s.

After A.D. 1150, few new Great Houses were constructed and Great Kivas almost all reverted to being unroofed shallow structures. Construction of roads also ceased. Although the Chaco Interaction Sphere represents a unique constellation of architectural and community layout traits, it is much more than this. The Great Houses, Great Kivas, and roads indicate construction efforts on a much more massive scale than anything ever before undertaken in the Anasazi area. Also, the amount of turquoise recovered during this time period is many times greater than for any other time or place (most having been found in Chaco Canyon itself). Clearly, something different was going on during this Chaco period of influence, although there is a vigorous debate over what these differences mean. However, there does seem to be a greater degree of social integration than witnessed at other times, and most likely there was a greater degree of social complexity.

About half of the Anasazi area is in some way related to the Chaco Interaction Sphere during the Middle Period. The Great Houses are of particular interest, with distinctive masonry and rooms that were much larger than those at other sites. Kivas were built within the room blocks instead of in front of them, greatly restricting kiva access. Most Great Houses had sections that were multistoried. This combination of multistories and large rooms prompted scholars to call them "Great Houses." The large structures are in sharp contrast to the much smaller, single-storied, small-roomed buildings that housed most of the population. There were probably between 100 and 200 Great Houses, whereas the smaller room blocks numbered in the thousands. It appears that Great Houses were first built in Chaco Canyon, then their construction spread. By the 1100s, they were present over much of the eastern Anasazi area, but did not extend into the Rio Grande area or the western portion of the Anasazi range.

The question remains as to what extent the Great Houses represent a single polity or simply the adoption of an architectural style by autonomous groups. For my purposes here, the Chaco Interaction Sphere is simply a reference to that portion of the Anasazi area that contained Great Houses at any time. Some scholars extend the Chaco Interaction Sphere beyond A.D. 1150, with Wilcox (1993a, 1995, 1996) making the most convincing case for such continuity. Certainly, continuities existed, but there were also enough changes to suggest that the A.D. 1150 date represents some important systemic change. Without becoming involved in that argument, I see evidence for increasing warfare after this time, so I treat the A.D. 1150 date as a useful terminal point for discussions of this period.

Site Location

In general, the Middle Period in the Anasazi area is characterized by nondefensively located communities—in some cases, extraordinarily so. The communities often consisted of a Great House surrounded by a number of small room blocks that typically ranged in size from six to perhaps twenty or so rooms. Frequently, there was a kiva or two in front of the room block. Room blocks usually were concentrated near the Great House, but they tended to decrease in number the farther away from the Great House they were built. Room blocks were sometimes located a couple of miles from the Great House. Since the Great Houses were sometimes only 8 miles or so apart, in certain areas there was almost a continuous distribution of habitations over the landscape. The saying that "Pueblo II is everywhere" has some validity. (This settlement pattern is remarkably similar to that found for the Mogollon area, as discussed below.) Generally, in the Chaco Interaction Sphere, each Great House and each room block is given a separate site designation by archaeologists. For other time periods, a designated site and a distinct community are usually considered a single unit and given its own site number. But for the Middle Period in the eastern Anasazi area, an individual site is rarely in and of itself a distinct community and is not treated as such.

In almost all cases, Chaco-era sites, both large and small, were usually situated in low places near water, farmland, or similar resources. High, defensive localities were rarely used. Communities almost always were to some degree spread out; there were no defensive walls or palisades, nor were room blocks arranged into a defensible perimeter. There are exceptions to this general pattern of "defenselessness," the most notable being a few of the Chaco Great Houses. Located on the eastern and northeastern margin of the Chaco Interaction Sphere, the Chaco-style Great Houses of Guadalupe Ruin in New Mexico (Pippen 1987) and, in Colorado, those of Chimney Rock Mesa (Eddy 1977) and, to a lesser extent, Escalante Ruins (Hallasi 1979) were on high points and well situated for defense. A few other sites were similarly defensively located, such as Bis sa'ani, near Chaco Canyon (Breternitz et al. 1982). Other sites, such as Kin Hocho'i, at the mouth of Manuelito Canyon (Fowler et al. 1987), Allentown (Roberts 1939), Chambers, Cottonwood, and Navajo Springs, were on ridges or hilltops, but not nearly as defensively situated as Guadalupe Ruin or Bis sa'ani. (These Chaco Great Houses are considered in detail below.) Ridge Ruin, near Flagstaff, is not a Chaco Great House, but it is one of the larger western Anasazi sites. Its location is somewhat defensive, with steep access on some sides but not all (Figures 5.1, 5.2, and 5.3).

Site Configurations

In some respects, the configuration of a typical Chaco Interaction Sphere community might be described as being very similar to a medieval community: a castle surrounded by undefended homes. The vast majority of all Chaco sites in the Middle Period were not constructed with defense in mind, and were primarily single-story room blocks, without enclosing walls. When there were multiple room blocks, they were not arranged to provide a good defensive capability. There were no keep-like towers, or

FIGURE 5.1
Plans of Chaco
Great Houses: (A)
Pueblo Pintado and
(B) Peñasco Blanco,
showing how final
building episodes
consisted of arcs of
rooms that formed
enclosing walls. After
Morgan, 1994.
*Ancient Architecture
of the Southwest.*
University of Texas
Press.

A.

B.

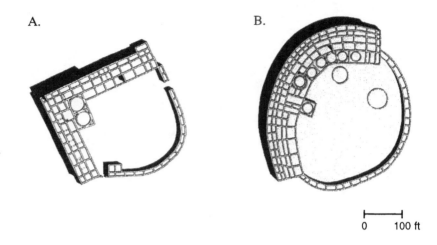

0   100 ft

FIGURE 5.2
The Guadalupe Ruin
Chaco Great House,
on the exteme eastern
edge of the Chaco
Interaction Sphere,
was on a very
defensive butte. While
some other Chaco
Great Houses were in
defensible localities,
most were not.
Photo ©Baker Aerial
Archaeology,
transparency H70591.

FIGURE 5.3
The Village of
the Great Kivas
consists of a Chaco
Great House (people
standing on it) and an
immediately adjacent
Great Kiva. Another
Great Kiva depression
and additional small
room blocks lie in the
distance. The site was
in a very exposed
location, situated at
the foot of a mesa.
Finding Chaco Great
Houses in such
locations argues
against significant
warfare at this time.

other such features, except as part of Great Houses themselves. These sites
or room blocks represent the vast majority of all habitations found in the
Chaco Interaction Sphere (Figures 5.4 and 5.5).

The major exceptions to the above description are the Great Houses
themselves. They have two characteristics that might be interpreted as
defensive. First, they were generally multistoried, or at least partially so.
Kivas were located within the structure, and could have been entered only
after gaining access to the roof level. So, the Great House structure itself
usually presented unbroken outside walls. Second, most of the structures
had a back row (or rows) of multistoried rooms and a front row (or rows)
of single-storied rooms. So, part of the Great House would have presented
a high outer wall, but other equally extensive exterior parts of the structures would have been only one story high and easily accessible.

Many Great Houses had a plazalike space that was walled in; this enclosing wall is probably a late phenomenon. A few sites, such as Kin Ya'a,
Salmon Ruin, La Ventana, and Chetro Ketl, had multistoried towers in the
center of the room space, which are often termed "tower kivas." While
most Great Houses were not massive forts, they could have been defended
better than the small room blocks that surrounded them. However useful,
this discussion fails to make the obvious point: If all of the rooms in the
room blocks surrounding the Great Houses had been combined into a

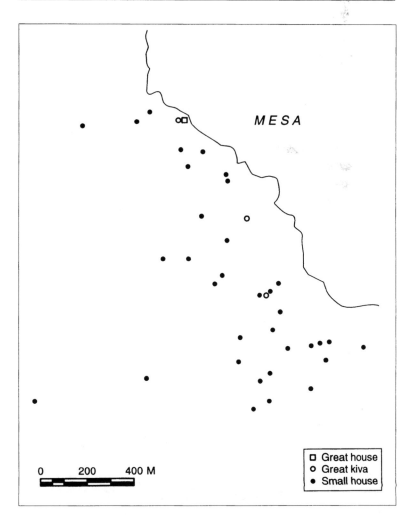

FIGURE 5.4
Bee Burrow Chacoan community. Small room blocks were dispersed over a distance of almost 3 miles. Note that only sites within the survey boundaries were recorded; additional sites may lie outside the survey area. After Powers et al. (1983).

■ Great house
● Small house
▬ Prehistoric road
– – Survey boundary

0   1 km
0   1 mile

MESA

FIGURE 5.5
Andrews Great House Chaco community. Sites were widely dispersed and may have extended beyond the mapped area. After Van Dyke (1997).

□ Great house
○ Great kiva
● Small house

0   200   400 M

single, large structure and if more of the structure had been two-storied, then the overall community would have been much more defensible. Thus, it's possible to suggest that there was absolutely no attempt at making the entire community defensible. The residents of the Great Houses did, however, afford themselves some protection. Wilcox and Haas (1994) hypothesize that the earthen berms that surround some of the Great Houses may be the bases of palisades (Figure 5.6). Fowler and Stein (1992, Stein and Fowler 1996) see these features as space-defining architecture. No one has ever shown the berms to be defensive, although—to be fair—there has been scant excavation of any of them. The configurations of these berms do not particularly suggest a defensive purpose. They frequently do not appear to be continuous, and sometimes enclose very large areas or spaces that otherwise would probably have been hard to defend. The proposition that they are part of a palisade is testable, but until such testing is accomplished, it should be considered only a speculation.[1]

There is one clearly important change in the Great House over time. Many of the largest ones have a set or arc of rooms enclosing a plazalike space that previously would have been more readily accessible to inhabitants. The added rooms were usually very small, in contrast to the large

1. The Chaco-style Great Houses are known for their very large rooms, including large storage rooms. If Great Houses stored food for the entire community, then there would have been a community-wide defensive aspect to the structures. However, no one has ever demonstrated that such was the case.

FIGURE 5.6
This Chaco Great House near Ganado, Arizona, has a very large, circular, earthen berm in front of it. The berm was discovered by Tom Baker from the air—a good demonstration of the utility of aerial reconnaissance for archaeology. It is not clear whether the berm forms a complete circle; but, even if it does, it would seem to provide evidence against the hypothesis that berms were the bases of defensive palisades. In this case, the palisade would need to have been over 200 meters in length. To construct and defend it would probably not have been a practical undertaking given the size of the community. For defensive purposes, a palisade with a circumference a quarter of this length would have been more than adequate. Photo ©Baker Aerial Archaeology transparency 28FC1420.

rooms of the Great Houses, and they were often more poorly constructed than the rest of the site. They appear more like a barrier than a set of rooms that was important or needed for space. Creating a "barricade" out of rooms had an important advantage: Their roofs provided a platform for defenders, something a freestanding wall would not. In order to increase the defensive capabilities of the Great House structures once the need arose, erecting arcs of enclosing rooms would have been an obvious action to undertake.

Great Houses that have added, enclosing rooms include Pueblo Bonito, Una Vida, Peñasco Blanco, Hungo Pavi, Chetro Ketl, Pueblo Alto, Pueblo del Arroyo, and Tsin Kletzin in the immediate Chaco Canyon area; and those outside it include Standing Rock, Wallace, Aztec, Site 41, Haystack, Navajo Springs, Pueblo Pintado, Red Willow, Figueredo, Kin Hocho'I, and Cox Ranch. It is apparent that almost all the larger Chaco-style Great Houses had these enclosing structures by the mid-1100s. A major exception is Salmon Ruin. However, it is not clear that the excavations undertaken on the site would have revealed an enclosing room arc even if it had existed (David Wilcox, personal communication).

Of importance, the enclosing walls seem to have been added to the Great Houses very late in the history of the Chaco Interaction Sphere. Lekson (1986) places each reasonably well-dated example in the last or almost last building episode for each structure, and they seem to be generally datable to the first couple of decades of the 1100s. Since construction on the Great Houses was begun much earlier—some as early as the 900s, but most by the mid-1000s—the enclosing walls of rooms represent an activity that took place several, if not many, generations after the major construction of these sites. Certainly, over time the Great Houses became more defensive.

Among the defensively placed Chaco Great Houses, mentioned above, a number of the big, canyon-area Chaco sites could be considered the most defensible within the entire Anasazi region. Peñasco Blanco and Tsin Kletzin, with their Great Houses and enclosing arcs of rooms, are on high mesa localities within the canyon area. They have terrific views in all directions. Tsin Kletzin, at least, is not located with respect to any particularly good farmland, and both sites—along with Bis sa'ani Ruin at the northeast end of the Chaco central area—have the look and feel of fortresses or guard-like sites.

There are, however, a number of factors that mitigate against adopting such a simple model for the increased defensive nature of the Great Houses. There are Chaco Great Houses that are anything but defensive: White House in Canyon de Chelly and Village of the Great Kivas are notable examples. Also, a number of the Great Houses located on high places are arguably there to function as nodes in a signaling system. Moreover, some Great Houses, as mentioned, do not have the added row of rooms that enclose the plaza, which have been described as defensve measures—for example, Judd's assessment (1959) of the enclosing arc at Pueblo del Arroyo. And, finally, the enclosing plaza spaces in the large sites may be related to a change in social access. That is, the added arcs of room may have been architectural elements defining space and access, not designed for defense. David Wilcox (personnal communication) points out that some of the sites, like White House, that do not appear defensive date to the mid-1000s, whereas some of the obviously defensive sites, such as Bis sa'ani, date in the 1100s. To the extent that this pattern may prove valid, it points to an increase in defensive characteristics in late Chaco times, as do other lines of evidence.

In sum, the case for the Chaco Great Houses being defensible is spotty at best. On the one hand, there is no consistent and pervasive defensive characteristic to them. On the other, there is far more evidence that some of these structure were built with defense in mind than for any other sites in the entire Southwest at this time. And the defensiblity of a number of the Great Houses was greatly enhanced toward the very end of the Middle Period, right after which the evidence for warfare and many more defensive sites in general appears again in earnest.

The small room blocks not linked to Great Houses show virtually no evidence for defensive considerations. They are not clumped together or arranged for defense, nor are they located on high points for good views or defensive purposes. In general, there is no evidence for palisades around them, although exceptions include a few palisaded small sites at the extreme northern edge of the Anasazi area in southwestern Colorado. As always, palisades can be overlooked if excavations concentrate on the buildings themselves. But so many of these small house sites have been excavated that if palisades were a pan-Anasazi pattern, other examples would most likely have been encountered. Moreover, the small sites near the Great Houses are dispersed. Each would have required its own palisade. It seems logical, therefore, to assume that if defense had been important, the groups of rooms would have been very tightly clustered in order to share a common defensive palisade or wall.[2]

Nonformally Buried Bodies and Badly Treated Individuals

There are a number of instances of unburied bodies—or parts of bodies—present in Middle Period sites. And, these sites are virtually all located within the boundaries of the Chaco Interaction Sphere. While some of the sites in question had rooms burned, very few sites were completely burned.

2. The palisaded sites tended to have several components; and they do seem to be Pueblo II in time, such as Dripping Springs Stockade (J. Morris 1991) and two others (Kuckelman and Morris 1988). The stockades at these sites appear to be anomalous. If they were truly common and the evidence missed, then this will require considerable rethinking of the Middle Period. If they were restricted to the northern limit of the Anasazi, then this may help us understand the nature of that boundary.

Almost invariably, bodies and body parts were very concentrated within the overall confines of the site. This is in sharp contrast to the pervasive burning found in sites of the Early Period, and differs dramatically from sites of the Late Period, which have both extensive burning and numerous unburied bodies widely distributed over the entire site. That is, even though unburied bodies and some burned rooms are found during the Middle Period, the pattern they present is unlike what preceded or followed. Moreover, the pattern does not look like one caused by warfare, at least not warfare in the form proposed here. Instead, the presence of bodies and body parts seems to be part of an overall pattern of badly treating some individuals at the time of death. Many seem to have been killed violently and their bodies not formally buried; and in some cases bodies were actually deliberately "mangled."[3]

Many examples of Middle Period unburied bodies have been ferreted out and examined by the Turners in their extensive search for Southwestern cannibalism. Without their intense effort, most of the data used in the following examples of violent deaths would not have existed. These examples, however, are not evidence for cannibalism. That evidence is considered in the next section.

One of the first examples of violent treatment at the time of death for this period was excavated by Richard Wetherill (1894a). It was found at the site of Snider's Well, which is part of the Yucca House, a late Chaco Great House complex in southwestern Colorado. The find was discovered in a 3 m deep kiva with painted walls. Decorated kiva walls are relatively common in the Chaco time period, a feature that supports such a date for the structure. There were at least twenty-five individuals found within the structure, based on a count of skulls with perimortem damage. Wetherill mentions finding fifty individuals, and Turner believes up to ninety individuals are possible (Turner and Turner 1995). Wetherill determined these individuals had a different form of cranial deformation than was found for formally buried individuals recovered at the site. Some of the bones were articulated, so the bodies were apparently just thrown in the structure. Also, the remains do not appear to be skeletal material that was later dug up and redeposited. There seems to be no information on the age and sex of these individuals. Since the excavations were undertaken years ago, it is not clear whether this find is really Chacoan in time or a later occupation of a Chaco community, which was a common occurence. So, while this is strong evidence for some form of violence, it is not necessarily associated with Pueblo II times. However, the Grinnell site, which has good evidence for cannibalism, is definitely Pueblo II and is also near Yucca House.

3. Somewhat complicating the interpretation of Great House sites is that many—if not most—were either continuously occupied or reoccupied much later than 1150. Most of the occupation debris is from the later occupations, and apparently most of the evidence for burning also is from the Late Period (these instances are discussed in chapter 6). Consequently, the evidence of burning that took place prior to A.D. 1150 is quite small.

Snider's Well, in seeming to represent a large number of "buried" individuals from the Chaco time period, is the exception to the general evidence for a paucity of burials from this time interval, particularly from Great Houses. Moreover, the few burials that are recovered are often of infants. So, in particular, adult burials are very rare. The vast majority of burials from Great Houses are from later reoccupations. For example, at Aztec Ruin, there were only six or eight Chaco-time "burials" and more than 150 burials dating to the later so-called reoccupation. The Chaco-time burials included two infant burials and a skull found on the floor of a kiva. Thus, there were only three to five adult burials from the entire Chaco occupation of Aztec Ruin and one badly treated body. Such rarity and ratios of formal burials to fragmentary remains is typical. The paucity of burials and the high proportion of bones from badly treated individuals from the Chaco sites are unlike anything found at any other time or place in the Southwest. I believe this difference from other periods lends credence to the interpretation that the fragmentary remains also represent acts of violence or nonformal treatment of the dead.

Pueblo Bonito's well-known (Pepper 1909) and repeatedly analyzed burials in Room 33 are of particular interest (e.g., Frisbee 1978; Reyman 1978; Wilcox 1993a). Described are two "high status" individuals who were interred on a specially prepared bed of sand sealed by a planked lid. In other words, a formal burial vault. Above the planking, deposited in some fashion, were the skeletons of twelve other individuals. The burial-vault area contained 30,000 beads made of turquoise and other materials, dozens of vessels, and other rare items. One individual was buried with several thousand beads, but the other had the bulk of the turquoise and other items, which Pepper interpreted as an elite burial. Of interest is that this burial, a male, had a bashed-in skull (Pepper 1909). One suggestion is that the twelve individuals were sacrificial victims placed there at the time the two elite individuals were interred, even though they were above the two elites in the fill. The skeletons of the twelve individuals were partially disarticulated, which lends credence to this interpretation. As mentioned, like most Chaco Great House sites there are few formal burials from Pueblo Bonito, and the likelihood that fourteen individuals just happened to die simultaneously and be buried together—when there are so few burials overall—is remote.[4]

---

4. Whether the Pueblo Bonito find of fourteen bodies included the formal burials of a pair of "elite" individuals is questionable. What is the likelihood that two members of the elite would die at the same time—essentially the only elite burials in the site—and that one of them would die violently? Wilcox (1994) suggests that if there was dual leadership and one leader died, the other might have been ceremonially killed. Both were high-status individuals, because they had considerable turquoise buried with them. However, that one of them received the bulk of the funerary deposits, that their bodies were not laid out in the same orientation, and that the one with the fewest goods was at a higher level than the other suggests they were not of equal rank. I still consider it unlikely that these were two simultaneous elite burials. Instead, there may have been only one very high status individual involved.

Something very different is going on in this Pueblo Bonito example. If these two formally buried individuals were both elite, then they most likely were killed in some violent way, possibly in warfare, and then interred together. At least eighty-one arrows tied in bundles were found in adjacent Room 32, further suggesting a military aspect to this area of the site; large bundles of arrows are unlikely to relate to hunting (see chapter 3). The twelve individuals buried above them may have died in the same event (either as enemies or allies), or they could have been sacrificed. Wilcox (1993a) argues that these and other burials at the site were sacrifices and were not contemporary, but represented a ceremonial act repeated many times. Regardless of whether they represent a single event or repeated events, the suggestion that many of the bodies at Pueblo Bonito were sacrifical victims is the critical one.

Human sacrifices as part of a death ritual are unknown archaeologically from the Southwest except for Casas Grandes at a later time. If such a sacrifice did take place at Pueblo Bonito, it is an anomaly. But, as Lekson (1996) has pointed out, Pueblo Bonito and Casas Grandes are both unique sites. To further complicate things, Pepper (1920) believed that two other rooms in Pueblo Bonito held the remains of acts of cannibalism. And, except for a handful of child burials, almost all the other "burials" at the site came from a few rooms that had multiple individuals in them, most of whom had been "disturbed." For example, in Room 330 Judd (1954) found the remains of more than twenty individuals, disarticulated and scattered, one with an arrowhead in a vertebra. Essentially, there are no "normal" burials from the site. Whatever the case, Pueblo Bonito, in the Chaco time period, seems to be an example of abnormal burial practices and to yield evidence of possible violence and the very careless handling of the remains of some individuals.[5]

Unfortunately, the previous examples are difficult to interpret, but other examples of individuals apparently badly treated at death are more straightforward. An unburied adult in a kiva at Site 499 on Mesa Verde was found with "a small bone awl . . . in the chest cavity, suggesting that the person had been stabbed. The individual's back was bent backward and the neck so twisted that the head faced to the rear" (R. Lister 1964:79). This site is part of the Far View group, which seems to include a Chaco-like Great House and a number of smaller sites. This is, incidentally, another example (see "Wetherill's Cave 7" in chapter 4) that further supports the idea that some bone "awls" are really daggers. These single, unburied individuals, as noted in chapter 2, present the greatest interpretive problem. The Site

---

5. Pepper (1920) found fourteen parrots in Room 38 which is not far from Room 33 containing the fourteen burials. It appears that two parrots had been given special treatment and the other twelve had not. Thus, there is the interesting correlation of two (elites?) plus twelve (sacrifices?) humans buried in one location and not far away two (special?) plus twelve (nonspecial?) parrots buried in another location. This reinforces the idea that neither the humans nor the parrots died natural deaths over any extended period of time.

499 instance could easily be a case of internal community violence. However, nearby Site 866, also part of the Far View group, had evidence of violent deaths (R. Lister 1966).

Two small sites in Chaco Canyon that date to the Chaco time period also had evidence of violence. In Site 1360, there were six individuals (two adults) plus two dogs found in a pit structure that was purposely destroyed while in use (but not burned). At least one of the adults had two projectile points in the body cavity (McKenna 1984). No attempt to bury these individuals had been made, and they appear to have been deposited in the kiva and left for carnivores to consume. (Or they were left outside, carnivores chewed on them, and then they were thrown in the pit house.) In the Bc 51 Site, not far from Casa Rinconada, Kluckhohn (1939) found scattered bones throughout the site, usually in the fill. Five of the six kivas had human bone in them, including a skull (with possible scalping cuts) on the floor of one and a mandible on the floor of another. The bones were those of infants as well as adults. Also in Chaco Canyon, the major Great House site of Chetro Ketl, in spite of very extensive excavations, yielded only one burial: the formal burial of an adult male with a projectile point in his ribs.

At a small site located near the Teec Nos Pos Great House, an adult and a child were found on the floor of a burned room. They were not intentionally buried; body parts were missing, and the adult had two bone awls next to the body. Turner (1989) considers this a case of cannibalism, a topic considered below. Minor examples of unburied bodies include Sites LA 2699 and LA 2675. These small Chaco time-period sites, located near Gallup, date to A.D. 1000–1075. LA 2699 had six rooms and a kiva, and the site was not burned. In the hearth of the kiva, a human parietal fragment was found along with the burned section of a human mandible. The LA2675 site had isolated bones and disarticulated skulls (Olson and Wasley 1956).

The implications of the previous examples of harshly treated bodies are fairly clear. For the most part, it is not reasonable to interpret them simply as redeposited formal burials. Although a large number of examples of recovered body parts not found in burial situations have often been assumed to be the result of postdepositional disturbance, the remains are difficult to interpret because of their fragmentary nature and have, for the most part, been ignored by excavators or later interpreters of the sites where they were found. However, as individual examples they are not very convincing as instances of deliberate acts, but they become interpretable as part of a much larger pattern. Included are cases from Great Houses as well as from small room blocks nearby. Bones of individuals were found in the fill of rooms, on the floors of rooms, and in trash. The bones were neither smashed as from a violent act nor burned. Superficially, the bones appeared to be from disturbed burials and, in most other contexts, that would be the likely explanation. The problem is these Chaco-time sites yield few, if any, burials, so there would be even fewer to have been disturbed. These unusual instances of human bone finds are far better interpreted as part of the overall phenomenon: individuals that were not afforded a formal burial.

A few of these examples bear describing. At sites next to or near the Sanders Great House in Arizona, of twelve recovered "burials," six were anomalous. Some consisted of only a few bones. Two skeletons were missing mandibles; a skull was found in a ventilator shaft (Fletcher 1994). Peckham et al. (1956) made a somewhat similar find along Apache Creek in New Mexico: a decapitated head in an abandoned pit house, dating to late Pueblo II or early Pueblo III. No other burials were found. As is typical for this time period, the structure was not burned. It was unclear whether the structure should be considered a kiva.

Another example is the "burial" of an adult in a bell-shaped pit in the Great House at the Village of the Great Kivas (Roberts 1932). This pit, located in the plaza in front of the Great House, had an opening diameter of about twenty-one inches. Stuffed into it was the body of an adult, found without grave goods. Given that a typical adult has a shoulder span of about twenty-one inches, it would have been necessary to practically force this individual into the pit. This was not a formal Anasazi burial. (See Table 5.2 for a more inclusive list of nonformal burials.)

Other marginally interesting skeletal information came from burials at Chaco-related sites around Houck, Arizona. The sites appear to date to this general time interval and are geographically within the Chaco Interaction Sphere. Of the individuals buried, 54 percent were males. Although the total sample was not particularly large, the male to female ratio was not 50-50; women were perhaps being extracted from the population, but the evidence for this is not very strong or convincing. Similarly, the burials from Chaco Canyon itself were evenly divided with 48.5 percent males.

Another comparison of males and females in the burial populations reveals an interesting phenomenon that has not received much attention: the much higher percentages of burials of young women in contrast to that of young men. This ratio can be computed for both examples from Houck and from Chaco Canyon (Akins 1986). Of the Houck burials that could be aged and sexed, only 17.5 percent of the males were under the age of thirty, whereas 43 percent of the females were under thirty (D. Berry 1983). This same pattern may hold for Chaco Canyon proper. Akins (1986) divided the skeletal sample into several time periods. In her Gallup Period—mid-Chaco in time—the ratio was about 50 percent for both adult males and females under thirty, while in her later McElmo Period sample—late Chaco—only 10 percent of the adult males were under thirty, with 80 percent of the females under thirty. It should be noted that the overall sample was not very large and a fairly high number of individuals could not be both sexed and aged accurately enough to compare with the Houck sample. Also, some interpretation was needed to classify the age groups. In the remainder of the Chaco Canyon samples from all other time intervals about half of the males were under the age of thirty, while about two-thirds of the females were under the age of thirty. But so many different time periods were involved that interpretation was not feasible.

It may be no accident that a similar difference occurs at Casas Grandes, the one site in the Late Period that is most unusual and in many ways most like Pueblo Bonito. Here, of formally buried bodies that could be classified as young, middle-aged, or old adults, 41 percent of adult men were counted as young, while 58 percent of adult women were young. What could this difference between males and females represent? A high incidence of young female deaths may be women dying in childbirth, but the ratio seems rather extreme even for those cases. Or, were the communities sampled simply composed of many young women and many old men? Whatever the explanation, it appears anomalous and needs further study.

Another indicator of the nature of the poor treatment many Chaco-time individuals received is the number of scattered human bones that show evidence of being gnawed by carnivores. These bones cannot be the result of disturbance and reburial long after the original burial; the bones would no longer have had nutritional value. So, they must represent bone that was exposed at the time of, or soon after, burial (or nonburial). The frequency of gnawed bones was recorded for recent excavations at seven sites in Chaco Canyon (Akins 1986). Of the 100 or so individual bones that were found, 22 percent had been gnawed. From these seven Chaco sites, there were no more than fifteen formal burials recovered. Even if some of the scattered bones from these sites represent the same individual, there is no escaping the conclusion that more people in these seven sites were carelessly or informally buried than were interred according to normal procedures.[6]

It is possible that many of these bones simply represent shallow burials that were disturbed by carnivores soon after interment. Why, only at this time in the Southwest, would a community's inhabitants place their dead in such shallow graves and not care when the bodies were exhumed and eaten by carivores? Evidence of carivores gnawing on the bones of the dead is rare both before and after this time. It seems unlikely that the people of the Chaco Interaction Sphere would suddenly lose interest in careful burial of their dead and then regain an interest in "proper" burials just when the period ended and at the same time that other forms of harsh treatment of individuals emerged.

One aspect of this continuum of the mistreatment of individuals at the time of death is recovered human bone that was broken, burned, or other-

6. An additional sixty-four individual bones were recovered from two other sites which date early enough that they may have preceded the dates of the Chaco Interaction Sphere, and thus are excluded.

wise very badly "mangled." This is the Turners' cannibalism evidence. Before interpreting these various cases of harmful and callous treatment of individuals, I must address the topic of cannibalism.

Processed Human Bone—Cannibalism

As George Pepper (1920:223, 267) found at Pueblo Bonito,

> most of the specimens found in this room were in the debris covering the floor; fragments of a human skull, scattered about in the southwest corner; pieces of a jaw with teeth and fragments of the cranium, blackened and charred to such an extent that it seems hardly possible that it could have been accidental . . . the pieces of skull lay as if they had been scattered by hand [Room 61]. . . . [A] number of human bones were found. They were scattered throughout the debris and had evidently fallen from one of the upper rooms. These bones show evidences of having been burned and they were broken [Room 80].

And, at Canyon Butte, Ruin 3, Walter Hough (1930:901) reported:

> In the cemetery . . . was uncovered a heap of broken human bones belonging to three individuals. It was evident that the shattered bones had been clean when they were placed in the ground, and some fragments showed scorching by fire. The marks of the implements used in cracking the bones were still traceable. Without doubt this ossuary is the record of a cannibal feast.

Perhaps one of the most unexpected and perplexing revelations that have recently come to light is the prevalence of evidence for cannibalism in the Middle Period. Christy and Jacqueline Turner, in a long and difficult effort, discovered a surprising number of instances of what they believe can only be interpreted as cannibalism (Turner 1983, 1988, 1989, 1993; Turner and Turner 1990, 1992, 1995, 1999). The Turners' work has been augmented by other endeavors (Dice 1993a, 1993b, 1993c; Lambert 1997a), in particular by the carefully detailed analysis of T. White (1992). In total, there is a very substantial body of data that demonstrates evidence for cannibalism. An incomplete and very synoptic list of cases is given in Table 5.1. This list includes the clearest cases, and those where the published data are reasonably available. Turner and Turner (1995, 1999) provide a more extensive list. Of primary interest is the number of individuals involved and their ages.

The evidence for cannibalism consists of broken and burned bones; cut marks on the bone; bones broken for the marrow; bones broken to a length that would fit into a cooking jar—such bones have actually been found in jars (e.g., the Grinnell Site [Luebben 1983; Luebben and Nickens 1982])—and polish on the tips of bones from rubbing against the interior of a

TABLE 5.1.
Sites with multiple Individuals Represented in Single Events of Processed Human Remains.

Site	Individuals	Reference	Notes
La Plata 23	5 individuals: 2 adults, 2 subadults, 1 infant	E.H.Morris 1939; Turner and Turner 1995	
Morris 41	6 individuals: 4 adults, 1 adolescent, 1 child	E.H.Morris 1939; T.White 1992	Seems to be Chaco in time; in or near the Great House
Mancos 5MTUMR-2346	29–33 individuals; full age spectrum	Nickens 1975; T.White 1992	Not a single concentration
Rattlesnake 42SA18434	20 individuals	Baker 1990	Chaco or slightly later
Sambrito Village	11 individuals	Dittert et al. 1966; Turner 1983; Turner et al. 1993	A.D. 950?
Cowboy Wash Sites	24 individuals	Billman 1997; Lambert 1997a; B.Leonard 1997	Chaco; in rooms and kivas
Aztec Wash Sites	13 individuals: 4 adults in one site; 2 individuals in nearby site	Errikson 1994; Dice 1993b	Late Chaco; kiva floor and two rooms, one of which then burned. Possibly single episode
House of Tragedy	4 individuals	Smith 1952a; Turner and Turner 1990	A.D. 1100–1200
Ram Mesa Kiva	12 individuals: 5 adults, 2 subadults	Herrmann et al. 1993	Single episode, Chaco
Small House	8 individuals	Turner 1993	900s or later
Hansen Pueblo	3 individuals in kiva: 2 adults, 1 subadult	Dice 1993b	Chaco A.D. 1134, tried to burn roof
La Plata highway, LA 37592	7 individuals: 3 adults	Turner et al. 1993	Chaco, pit house floor; single event

Site	Individuals	Reference	Notes
La Plata highway, LA 37593	5 individuals: 3 adults	Turner et al. 1993	Chaco, pit house floor; single event; some question
La Plata highway, LA 65030	6 individuals: 3 adults	Turner et al. 1993	Chaco or a bit later, Pithouse 8 trash; some question
Yellow Jacket Site 5MT-1	4 individuals: 1 adult	Malville 1989	Chaco time, storage pit in a house
Yellow Jacket Site 5MT-3	10 individuals: 5 adults.	Malville 1989	Chaco time, kiva; individuals were processed in it
Peñasco Blanco	2 individuals	Pepper 1920; Turner and Turner 1995	Probably Chaco time
Canyon Butte 3	4 individuals	Hough 1903; Turner and Turner 1992	1000–1200
Grinnell	7 individuals: 4 adults, 2 children	Luebben and Nickens 1982	Chaco time; only a possible case
Marshview Hamlet	20 individuals: 8 adults, 4 adolescents	Turner 1988; Weiner-Stodder 1988	ca. 1150
Cotton Wood Wash	4 individuals: 2 adults	T.White 1988, 1992	900s
Blackrock Project, LA12842	Total unknown; from 8 different features	Wiseman 1977	1100–1175
Burnt Mesa	11 individuals: 7 adults.	Flinn et al. 1976	900s
Leroux Wash	At least 35 individuals in 2 charnel pits: 9 age 12 or under; 5 subadult; 21 adults, both young and old	Dice 1993a; Fay and Klein, 1988	1060—1200

vessel during the boiling process, known as "pot-polish." Human heads seem also to have been processed in a particular way. The overall pattern of bone modification during this time period is very consistent, and it seems to have paralleled the methods used to process large game. That is, human bones and animals bones were treated in the same way. Or, probably more correctly, the bodies of humans were treated the same as the carcasses of animals.

The major exception to the above statement is that human bones were not deposited in the same manner as those of animals. While there are cases of human bones that appear to have been processed for meat and that were found in trash deposits, these cases are rare. The prevailing pattern is for the human bones to have been deposited in a structure—particularly, but not limited to, a kiva—and then the structure abandoned and sometimes burned. Obviously, this act is very different from eating animals and discarding the remains.

One issue that arises is whether finds with this kind of evidence do indeed represent cannibalism. That these instances represent the treatment of witches has been proposed by Darling (1995). Without dealing at length with this argument, I find it not convincing for a variety of reasons. First, there is no ethnographic evidence showing that witches were ever dealt with so closely parallel to animal processing. Also, in many instances there were too many individuals to be reasonably interpreted as witches killed at one time. And, finally, this behavior of treating humans and animals similarly is so restricted in space and time that to relate it to the general pervasive Southwestern fear of witches is simply too weak an argument. The arguments put forth by Bullock (1991, 1992) and Dongoske (1997) are based on little more than their opinions that they do not believe cannibalism could have taken place; and no matter what the evidence for it might be, they will not change their minds.

So, while there are doubters, in my opinion the data are overwhelming that sometimes bodies were prepared to be eaten and that the residue was often disposed of in a special way. The bodies were very deliberately, almost publicly, treated like animals. There is, of course, no obvious way to demonstrate that the meat was actually consumed—and there are some interesting reasons to think it was not—but whether it was eaten is almost immaterial. I think it is reasonable to believe that this was not starvation-based cannibalism; hence, if the meat *was* being eaten, it was not for nourishment. Because the word "cannibalism" is so emotionally charged, using a more neutral term, such as "processed human remains" or "disarticulated human remains," would have its advantages. However, the literature is filled with the term "cannibalism" for these cases, and it cannot be erased. In spite of this, because I see these instances as closely related to the mistreatment of individuals, the term "processed human remains" best describes the similarity and is my term of choice. I am not suggesting that there was no cannibalism, but I am leaving the consumption aspect of the act open to further analysis.

Christy Turner (with assistance from David Wilcox) was the first to point out that there is a very strong correlation between the episodes of processed human remains and the area of the Chaco Interaction Sphere, both in time and space. There is some legitimate question as to whether almost all reported cases of processed human bone are Chaco-related, however. Some are certainly earlier than anyone would accept for a "Chaco System" or "Interaction Sphere" time frame, and at least one case seems to be later. In addition, some cases dating broadly to the Chaco time range are well outside what is considered by most—but not all (see Wilcox 1995)—the area of the Chaco Interaction Sphere (e.g., from House of Tragedy near Wupatki [Smith 1952a; Turner and Turner 1990, 1999]). At this time, however, the best model is that the majority of these cases of processed human remains are somehow related to the Chaco Interaction Sphere in its broadest sense and to the Chaco time frame in its broadest sense. This volume is not the place to debate the issue of exact contexts and temporal placements of these cases because much of the data are currently unpublished and have not been closely scrutinized as to dating. A few dating errors and some differences of opinion about the actual edge of the Chaco Interaction Sphere will not obscure the broad patterns I am looking for, however.

In order to interpret this information, it is necessary to address two additional aspects of this phenomenon of processing human remains. First, the events almost always involve several individuals, and the number of cases is impressive, as can be seen in Table 5.1.[7] The table lists twenty-four instances of a number of individuals being processed in some way, whereas Turner and Turner (1995) report thirty-two sites, regardless of the number of individuals involved, that fit their criteria for cannibalism. Billman (1997) believes there are twenty-four well-documented cases (involving a number of individuals) in the Four Corners area alone. The difficulty with these numbers involves determining what constitutes "good evidence" as well as a "site." Determining the degree of evidence present for cannibalism (regardless of the number of individuals involved) can result in the inclusion or exclusion of possible cases, but the determination must be free of bias. Then, because communities of the Chaco time period were spread out, in several instances (as previously mentioned), each room block in what probably should have been considered one community was assigned a different site number. That excavators did this is not surprising, but it hampers accurate enumeration.

Cowboy Wash is a particularly illustrative case of violence done to

7. There may be some bias in that the condition of the remains of a single individual would less likely be recognized by the excavators as a case of cannibalism and more likely be attributed to other causes.

humans (Billman 1997; Lambert 1997a; B. Leonard 1997). The processed remains of at least twenty-four individuals were found in four room clusters (designated as four sites) that existed along with five other unexcavated room clusters, all of which constituted the community. There is a larger site nearby, but not one usually considered a Great House. A known Great House, Aztec Springs, is not far away (5 miles or 8 km), but there seems to be some debate on its date. Based on the number of rooms in the four excavated sites at Cowboy Wash, Billman estimates the total population of those rooms would have been 35 people, so the 24 individuals who were killed and processed represent about two-thirds of the population. If the same ratio held for the unexcavated portion of the community, then the total population of the community would have been between 60 and 100 individuals, with the estimated number of processed individuals between 40 and 65. It is possible that these processed individuals may have been brought to the site from elsewhere, and were not the residents. However, Cowboy Wash was abandoned at the end of this episode, which argues against this possibility. Also of note is that the site was not looted, and valuable items such as *tchamahias* were left on floors. These sites were not burned, and one individual apparently defecated in the hearth of one of the kivas at the time of abandonment (the excavators were convinced the excrement was human and not animal). Since the excrement most likely was left by one of the perpetrators of these acts of human defilement, it would appear to have been the ultimate insult.

Table 5.1 summarizes a number of cases of processed human remains, and the vast majority represent single episodes of bone processing. The number of individuals involved in these single events range from one to thirty-five individuals. Most events involved four or more individuals, and at least ten of them involved ten or more individuals. It appears that six to seven individuals was a typical number of people being killed and processed, but the Turners estimate the average number of "victims" at more than nine per site. Almost all examples have a full age spectrum represented, with generally about half of the individuals being adults. Due to the fragmentary nature of the recovered remains, it has not generally been possible to sex the individuals.

As for evidence relating these cases to warfare, the number of individuals involved—and their ages—strongly suggests groups of individuals who died in raids. The examples do not look like ambushes, where one or two individuals are killed away from the community. Instead, they look very much like small communities that were attacked, and where everyone, or almost everyone, was killed and their remains processed. Whether some women and children were spared cannot be determined. The evidence definitely does not indicate that the remains represented captives from battles, which would have been primarily adult men. As mentioned, it also does not indicate examples of witchcraft. In the case

of witchcraft, the vast majority of the cases would have been single individuals, or only a couple of people; also children would have been very
underrepresented.

There is another level of analysis that can be directed at the data on
processed human bones. It is not a particularly pleasant topic to consider,
but it is enlightening. If the bones were processed to extract all of the
possible calories—as would appear to be the case if they were broken to
extract marrow, or were boiled in pots, or if individuals' heads were
cooked—then just how much food would be produced? A typical processing event involving three adults, two subadults, and a child might result in
seventy-five pounds of meat each from the adults, forty pounds each from
the subadults, and probably insignificant meat from the child. Such an
event would result in more than 300 pounds of meat. Notice in Table 5.1
that many events would have produced substantially much more meat.
The amount of meat represented in the Cowboy Wash case alone is stag-
gering, more than 1,200 pounds, and would have been from roughly half
of the community, the half that was excavated.

There is potentially a lot of food available to the sites listed in Table
5.1. And, as these appear to be single events, the meat would have been
consumed in a very short period of time. Even at consumption rates of
two or three pounds of meat per person per day, a typical event would
have fed 100 to 150 participants in the event, and several of these events
would have fed twice to four times that number. The few scenarios that
might make sense out of these numbers are not very good. It is possible
that the occasion was similar to a (noncannibalistic) Polynesian feast, in
which the food is cooked and displayed, but the participants eat only a
small portion and take the rest home to be distributed to nonparticipants.
However, it is something else if it means having to carry marrow and stew
home. In a warfare model, the alternative to the concept of a shared feast
is that the group which perpetrated the attack would be very large. The
implication that 150 men would engage in attacking a small hamlet hous-
ing ten people seems unlikely, however, and even more unlikely is the
probability of the 400 or more men taking part in the attack that the
larger episodes of processed human remains would call for. For Cowboy
Wash, even if seventy-nine people were killed (an estimate of the total
community population based on the portion excavated), there would have
been about eighteen fighting-age men to defend the community (based on
the estimate of 23 percent of a population being fighting-age males discussed previously [see C. Lange 1978]). An attacking force even five times
larger would have represented less than 100 attackers, far too few to have
consumed this much meat.

It might be argued that such quantities of human meat would not have
been unlike that procured when an elk or buffalo was killed. Or, as is
more relevant to the Southwest, when an entire herd of antelope was killed

in some form of drive. However, the usual method of processing game animals in these circumstances was to cut the carcasses into manageable portions, which would include some bone, and then carry them to where they would be consumed or set aside for later consumption. If this pattern of behavior is applied to instances of processing human remains, then the individuals would be cut up and the portions widely spread throughout the "participating" community. But there is no evidence supporting this scenario. Why would the human bone wind up in piles in a few structures rather than randomly scattered? And why would the site be immediately abandoned? Why would the bone be left on the floors of rooms rather than discarded in trash deposits?

Consuming the individuals in the hamlet where they were presumably killed, consuming so much meat at once, and consuming it in localized places within the communities does not make sense from the standpoint of efficient caloric consumption. If calories were the goal in a time of food crisis, why not consume the individuals with that goal in mind? It would make far more sense for a small group to attack and kill a few individuals in another group, then consume them over a span of time. Why go to such lengths to extract the marrow and break and boil the bones if all of the meat was not needed right away? In short, no scenario seems to make much sense. There is simply too much meat being produced at one time for it to be considered a nutritionally rational activity. These cases of processing human remains do not seem to have been responses to threats of starvation or even preparations for feasts.

Just as interpreting the act of processing human remains is difficult, so is attempting to interpret the cases simply as evidence for violence among human beings. There has been almost no serious attempt at dealing with the issue. No one has made the effort to characterize the sites involved. What are their dates? Where did they fit into the overall regional community structure? Were the people impoverished?

In summary, the Middle Period evidence that large numbers of individuals were being killed and their bodies processed as if they were animals is overwhelming. However, the evidence for consumption of the meat—especially if considered starvation-driven—is weak or not convincing. It appears something else was going on.

Locations of Badly Treated Bodies

Examining spatial distribution of the cases of badly treated bodies—nonformally buried bodies, fragmented burials, and processed human remains—should lead to an understanding of how they fit into the puzzle of social behavior among the Middle Period Anasazi. Thus far, scholars have taken only a cursory look at the location of the instances involving processed human remains. For example, one suggestion is that the processing took place on small sites that were neither close to nor under the political control of communities that included a Great House. Although the Turners proposed such a "rural" aspect to these cases, they believe this practice also showed up in the Great Houses themselves (Turner and Turner 1995). They and T. White (1992) believe there is evidence for cannibalism in Peñasco Blanco in Chaco Canyon. Pepper (1920) and the Turners also think there is evidence of it in Pueblo Bonito (Turner and Turner 1995). Earl Morris (1939) argued for evidence of cannibalism at the La Plata River Great House called Morris 41, and he reported scattered human remains at the "Old Fort" site near Farmington. The Old Fort site was definitely occupied during late Pueblo III occupation, but the presence of a Great Kiva suggests a Chaco time-period component as well (Stein and McKenna 1988).

While the distribution of processed human remains alone does not provide a distinct pattern, if all of the evidence for badly treated individuals is taken into account, then a Middle Period pattern for the Chaco Interaction Sphere becomes clear. Examples from the existing evidence of mistreatment include the fairly complete remains of individuals that were not formally buried; fragmentary remains, such as caches of skulls, that appear to have been deliberately placed in a nonburial context; bodies that may not have been placed in an enclosed space at death or were buried very shallowly so that the bones became scattered over time; and the remains of processed human bodies. In all these cases, human bodies were treated as if the bodies were those of animals or subhumans. At times, corpses were discarded as the body of a dead dog might be. At other timess, human bodies were systematically processed for consumption, as a deer would be.

A clear pattern emerges when all cases of mistreatment of human bodies are combined. If communities can be defined as consisting of Great Houses and the small sites immediately adjacent to them, then this question can be asked: "How often did this broadly defined behavior happen in a community that included a Great House?" The numbers that emerge in answering this question are overwhelming. Without exhaustively seeking out all possible examples, I have complied a partial listing of such cases in Table 5.2. (This is not a complete list of all cases of badly treated bodies; it includes only those cases where the remains were found in or near a Great House. It includes processed human bodies, so some cases overlap with those in Table 5.1.)

There are more than twenty different Great House communities that had examples of badly treated individuals. It must be remembered that most Great House sites have not been excavated, and those that have been excavated were often only partially sampled. The surrounding smaller room blocks in the communities have received even less attention and smaller samplings were taken. Moreover, much of the skeletal material

TABLE 5.2.

Chaco Communities with Great Houses that Have Evidence for Disrespectful Treatment of Human Remains. ("Neighborhood" refers to the small room blocks in an area somewhat removed from a Great House. PHR = Processed Human Remains.)

Site	Site Type	Evidence of Violence	Reference	Notes
Pueblo Bonito, Bc 51, site 1360	Great House, neighborhood	P.Bonito: disarticulated bodies; neighborhood: PHR, disarticulated bodies	Turner and Turner 1995, McKenna 1984	
Peñasco Blanco	Great House	PHR	Pepper 1920	
Aztec Ruin	Great House	Skull on floor of kiva	E.H.Morris 1919	
Guadalupe Ruin	Great House	Disarticulated bodies	Pippen 1987	
Far View Sites 449, 866, and 875	Neighborhood	Unburied bodies, violent deaths	Lister 1964, 1965, 1966	
Morris 41, La Plata Highway	Neighborhood	PHR	E.H.Morris 1939; T.White 1992; Turner 1993	
Morris 33, La Plata Highway	Great House	Smashed skull nonburial in kiva, possibly 4 more	E.H.Morris 1939; Turner 1993	
Yucca House, Grinnell, Snider's Well	Neighborhood	See text; disarticulated, PHR	Luebben and Nickens 1982; Turner and Turner 1995	
Village of the Great Kivas	Neighborhood	See text	Roberts 1932	
Yellow Jacket, 5MT-1, 5MT-3	Neighborhood	Disarticulated bodies, PHR	F.Lange et al. 1988; Malville 1989	
Canyon Butte 3	Neighborhood	Disarticulated bodies	Hough 1903; Turner and Turner 1992	
Teec Nos Pos	Neighborhood	Disarticulated, PHR?	Turner 1989	
Houck K	Great House	PHR	Turner and Turner 1995	
Allentown (Whitewater)	neighborhood	Violent deaths, burnt bodies	Roberts 1939	May be pre-Chaco

Site	Site Type	Evidence of Violence	Reference	Notes
Sanders	neighborhood	Cranium in vent, skeleton missing mandible, etc. 6 anomalous	Fletcher 1994	
Pueblo Alto	Great House	10–20 individuals represented in fill deposits; weak evidence	Akins 1987	
Pueblo del Arroyo	Great House	Disarticulated, violent deaths	Turner and Turner 1995	
Wupatki, House of Tragedy	Great House, neighborhood	Disarticulated, missing crania	Turner and Turner 1990; Smith 1952a	Post-A.D. 1130
Salmon Ruin	Great House	2 processed individuals	Shipman 1983	May be post-A.D. 1130
Wallace Ruin	Great House	Burned and broken bone,	Bruce Bradley, personal communication	May be post-Chaco
Ida Jean	Great House	Skull in kiva	Joel Brisbane, personal communication	May be post-Chaco
Cottonwood Wash	Neighborhood	PHR	T.White 1988, 1992	
Lowry, Site 3	Neighborhood	Some disarticulated remains	P.Martin and Rinaldo 1939	Not too near Great House; information vague
Gallup dump	neighborhood	Fragmentary remains	Olson and Wasley 1956	
Apache Creek	neighborhood	Decapitated head	Peckham et al. 1956	Presence of nearby Great House questionable
Old Fort Site, Farmington	Great House	Disarticulated remains	E.H.Morris 1939	Chaco time?

has never been properly studied. Because there are probably less than forty such communities from which even a minor excavation sample is available to consider, the phenomenon of mistreatment of human bodies in or around Great Houses must have been very common. Over half of all communities in which there was even a minor amount of excavation work done have shown evidence for badly treated human remains.[8]

The Chaco System and Warfare

Overall, as indicated earlier, there is very little evidence for warfare within the Chaco Interaction Sphere. Most sites were undefended; there are very few cases of massive burning, and these are restricted to very small sites. However, quite apart from the badly treated bodies, there are some tantalizing pieces of evidence that belie a fully peaceful society. There are two aspects of Chaco Canyon architecture that bear scrutiny. First, the canyon is ringed with four sites that are on high points with exceptional visibility. By the end of their occupation, the sites had a functional defensive configuration (see the above discussion, "Site Configurations"), and they were all visible to each other. The sites are Peñasco Blanco, Tsin Kletzin, Pueblo Alto, and Bis sa'ani, which are roughly situated, respectively, at the western, southern, northern, and northeastern edges of the canyon complex. (Pueblo Pintado, located slightly farther to the east, may have been another site of this type.) Directly north of Pueblo Alto, along the great northern road, is Pierre's Site. The Great Houses at this site, Units A and B, are located on a very defensive butte, and could represent a further component in a ring of defensive sites around Chaco Canyon.

As Lekson (1986:231) notes, "The unusual location of Tsin Kletzin appears to have been fixed by the intersections of several lines-of-sight. . . . [S]ix other major buildings are visible: Pueblo Alto, Penasco Blanco, Kin Kletso, Kin Klizhin, Bis sa'ani and Kin Ya'a. A shift of 10 meters in any direction would have made these multiple views impossible." A good description of the Chaco Canyon settlement layout would be "a central place, ringed by forts, which could signal each other for help." Moreover, the signaling system is known to extend far outside of Chaco Canyon. As noted for Sonora and the historical Rio Grande area, long-distance signaling is associated with warfare.

The second point about Chaco architecture is that, again as noted ear-

---

8. Table 5.2 includes some cases of mistreatment in or around Great Houses that are difficult to interpret. For example, the Cowboy Wash community may be considered by some scholars to be part of a Great House community, and not by others. Conversely, the remains of a seven-year-old child that had cut marks and burned parts were found at PM 205 in the McKinley Mine area near Gallup (Allen and Nelson 1982), which is about 5 miles from the Hunters Point Great House. Is this find part of the Great House community or not? (The case was not included in Table 5.2.) In spite of a few ambiguities, mistreatment of bodies was not a "rural" phenomenon. Whatever was happening, it happened in Great House communities with considerable regularity.

lier, many Great Houses underwent modification late in their history. The change was always the same: a row of rooms added to the southern portion of the site so that the plaza was enclosed, making the site much more defensible as a result. All of the alterations date rather late—some may date just after A.D. 1075, but most seem to be after A.D. 1105–1110.

Other Chaco sites, mentioned earlier, were also built in very defensive locations, for example, Guadalupe Ruin, Chimney Rock, and Escalante Ruin. In the case of these three defensively located sites, they are the last sites on the outer edge of the distribution of Great Houses. In other words, they define the edge of the Chaco Interaction Sphere in their respective areas. However, this pattern of "defining-edge" defensive sites does not continue around the entire circumference of the Chaco Interaction Sphere. Continuing along the northern edge of the Chaco sphere, some defining-edge sites, such as Cottonwood Wash, have a sharp drop-off in one direction and are on a hill, and can be considered moderately defensive. But, others, such as Cajone, are not the slightest bit defensively located. Farther to the east and south of Guadalupe Ruin, the next candidates for defining-edge sites include LA51,967, Salado Community Great House, and possibly La Mesita (John Roney, personal communication), none of which can be described as defensively located. And, this lack of defensively located defining-edge outlyers continues to the south and west. It may be possible that the few Chaco sites considered to be defensive were to guard particular sections of the frontier against some form of hostility, but the threat was not present at all locations around the periphery.

David Wilcox (1995, 1996) suggests there may have been competing polities within the overall Chaco Interaction Sphere. He bases this idea on the observation that there is no falloff in the size of the Great Houses as construction of sites moved away from Chaco Canyon. He notes that the sites do get smaller in general and that there are occasional large ones, which he interprets as regional centers. He sees boundaries between the Chaco core and a group of Great Houses centered on Allentown, another boundary between the core and a group centered on San Mateo, and other boundaries as well. He points out that the roads radiating from Chaco Canyon seemed to end at sites, such as Kin Ya'a, Peach Springs, and Skunk Springs, that he describes as fortresslike.

In spite of repeated attempts to do so, I am unable to find convincing evidence for these boundaries. While this theory may be correct, and certainly deserves further testing, the stronger pattern seems to be that the locations of sites within the whole Chaco sphere are quite continuous. Although the gaps, both large and small, are few and there are a few distantly situated sites (such as, incidentally, two of the most defensive ones—Chimney Rock and Guadalupe Ruin), the distribution of Great House communities is rather consistently spaced. I believe the Chaco Interaction Sphere looks far more like a dendritic system than a group of independent and competing polities. If it is a set of competing polities, I can find no boundaries based on no-man's-lands or defended borders. There are a few other Great Houses, such as the Twin Angels site, that are located on hilltops in addition to the ones surrounding Chaco Canyon and along the outer boundary. Other Great Houses, such as Peach Springs and Skunk Springs, are situated on high ground with good views, but I don't believe they can be classified as defensively located. Taken together, these sites do not seem to define internal buffer zones. I think a different model for the Chaco Interaction Sphere may be worth considering.

Models of Chacoan Violence

It is simply not practical to review here the numerous models that have been proposed over the years to explain the Chaco Interaction Sphere (but see Crown and Judge 1991; Doyel 1992). However, one thing about the Chaco Interaction Sphere is remarkably clear: This is the only time in the entire Anasazi sequence when there is striking evidence for distinct classes of people. The people who lived in Great Houses inhabited structures very different from the rest of the population. Great House rooms were several times larger and taller than those in the surrounding room blocks. Great Houses were high and massive, whereas the room blocks were low and small. Anywhere else in the world, such a dichotomy of living arrangements would be seen as an elite/nonelite duality. These differences did not occur earlier in the Southwest, and they were gone by the beginning of the 1200s. Incidentally, this habitation dichotomy has not been found outside the Chaco Interaction Sphere—not in the Rio Grande area or farther afield in the Mogollon. (However, such differences may have existed in the Hohokam area at a later time.)

Now, it seems unlikely that this very distinct social differentiation would exist and not be somehow related to either the lack of evidence for warfare or the presence of numerous examples of badly treated bodies. Based on this as a possible interpretation, there are several models that can be proposed, but there is insufficient information that makes one more valid than another.

These models have to take into consideration that there is no evidence of actual warfare between politically independent polities. Few, if any, of the Chaco-sphere sites appear to have been sacked, burned, and abandoned at the time of the mangled burials. Many of the bodies were deposited in rooms and other features in sites that continued to be occupied. In the few cases, such as Cowboy Wash, where the sites were abandoned, there was no massive burning or any evidence of defensive preparations. This is in sharp contrast to what is found later, where there is a strong correlation between unburied bodies, burned sites, and abandonment with in situ deposits. Certainly, there is no evidence of wars of attrition that occurred later. That is, there does not seem to have been warfare between fairly equally matched independent polities. So, these Middle Period examples of scattered, disarticulated, processed, fragmentary, and nonformally buried humans contrast sharply with the massive numbers of complete and articulated unburied bodies often found in the intensely burned sites of the subsequent Late Period (discussed in chapter 6). While in both periods bodies were not formally buried, what was taking place in the Middle Period was completely different from the situation in the Late Period.

If equally matched interpolity warfare seems not to fit the observed patterns, the model for Chacoan violence that I think best fits the currently available data is a "central hegemony model." In this model, the sites in Chaco Canyon would have been occupied by a dominant elite that was expanding its territory and progressively taking over previously independent communities. Great Houses in outlying areas were the residences of the local elite. Adequate resources were extracted from the populace, in terms of food and labor, but on occasion people had to be coerced into meeting demands. However, because of the good climatic conditions, the system was generally capable of providing for the demands of the elite. Nonetheless, the elite used terrorism to enforce their demands, and entire communities were killed for noncompliance. Such terrorism included some form of processing the bodies of individuals, or sacrifice, or other forms of violence. One or more forces of highly trained and organized warriors—a standing miniarmy—were used to put down defiance and to incorporate new communities into the polity.

Toward the end of the Middle Period, political hegemony was waning and sites became more and more defensive. There were increased incidents of violence late in the period, as the elite tried to maintain its role. The system disintegrated, people were again independent, and soon a more traditional pattern of intercommunity warfare began.

An alternative model consists of "multiple competing groups." In many ways this model is similar to the one above, but there would have been no single central polity (i.e., separate polities were each doing much the same thing within their own spheres of influence.) Both these models are combinations and variants of those proposed by Wilcox (1993a, 1994) and the Turners (1995), although Wilcox sees the details rather differently. And, they are markedly at odds with previous models that have Chaco Canyon an empty religious center and other similar models that do not recognize the strong evidence for violence and make no effort to account for it or for the degree of social differentiation seen over the entire Chaco Interaction Sphere.

The two models proposed here are based on an overarching model of social integration. Their supposition is that the entire Chaco Interaction Sphere, or major areas within the overall sphere, was organized into polities with possible competition between polities. Most communities, small or large, were politically integrated at some level into one or more polities, or the polities were attempting to incorporate small autonomous communities into their spheres. If the central organizations were extracting, or were expecting to extract, labor or goods from the smaller or outlying sites, then failure to comply was dealt with by killing and processing the members, or some members, of the offending group as a lesson to any neighboring group. Some individuals might have been brought back to the centers where they were killed—perhaps sacrificed or processed in some manner to further demonstrate the lesson—or made into slaves. Such a system may have operated fairly smoothly with little resistance until it began to unravel in the early 1100s. Wilcox sees the overall system breaking up, with peripheral polities gaining power. Regardless of the reasons, a case can be made that failure to comply with the demands of the elite became more prevalent and that terrorism and violence increased as a response. Such models would account for the presence of badly treated bodies in the Great Houses, in Great House communities, and, possibly, in communities not part of Great House communities.

An interesting alternative to the above scenario is a "peaceful until near the end" model. This model theorizes that the Chaco system was participatory without coercion. The populace willingly provided labor and resources for maintaining the centers, roads, and other labor-intensive facilities. The optimal climate facilitated this, and real or perceived gains from participation were great enough to guarantee cooperation. Then, sometime in the early 1100s, the system began to break down. Perhaps climate deterioration made it more "expensive" than the people could handle, and the elite then began coercing them to participate. Violence and defensive moves occurred for a brief interval at the end of the period. This model has a good deal to recommend it, but it would require evidence for violence to appear only late in the interval, a possible, but as yet undemonstrated fact.

Another theory for Chacoan violence to be considered is a "ritual, participatory" model. This model is much like the above, only mistreatment of bodies was part of ritual behavior accepted by all, and labor was not coerced. The defensive measures seen late in the period could be explained as due to outside threats. This model relates to one proposed by Wilcox (1994), but again differs considerably in detail.

There are various problems with all of these models. For example, the multiple competing polities would be expected to have fought with one another, yet there are no defended sites on the borders and no burned sites. It is also extremely difficult to reconcile the large number of individuals killed in some instances of processed human remains with the peaceful acceptance of this as ritual behavior affecting members of the community. There simply is no ethnographic parallel to people deciding to grab and kill members—sometimes as many as ten to thirty-five individuals—of their own community and mistreat the bodies as part of ritual behavior. This model also fails to account for the very interesting evidence that some individuals—particularly women—appear to have been treated as inferiors, almost as slaves. The evidence comes from sites, in the Chaco time-span, along the La Plata River in northern New Mexico (D. Martin et al., n.d.). A number of individuals had suffered from broken bones and other evidence of violence, but had not died from their injuries. A disproportionate number of these individuals were women. The implication is that these women were physically abused on a regular basis and that the nature of their injuries—as well as their survival—does not suggest warfare as the cause. Thus, these individuals were apparently treated badly in life just as many of the people from the same area and time period were treated badly at death.

Surely, it's far too simplistic to suggest that communities in which all individuals were social equals would then, for some reason, make the wholesale decision to kill and mangle—if not cannibalize—some subset. If the argument is that, yes, there were slave-like individuals in these communities, for whatever reason, and on occasion they were killed and their bodies mistreated, then the usual interpretation would be that these were the poorest individuals. However, the finds at Cowboy Wash do not support this. The artifact assemblages appear to be complete and not impoverished; nor were the sites where the mistreated bodies were found described as having small rooms, poor masonry, or similar indications of destitution. Perhaps the entire community was made up of slaves. Such a model is compelling because it would explain the victimizing phenomenon as a social-control mechanism. The public killing, and perhaps cannibalizing, of a group of oppressed individuals would certainly be a strong lesson for others in like situations.

If the "central hegemony" model is accepted, how did such a social system develop? There seems to have been no gradual evolution of elites, of human sacrifice or mangling bodies, or of military specialists. In addition, the "forced participation" and "central authority" models can explain the lack of warfare in the Chaco areas, but there is the same lack of warfare elsewhere in the Southwest where there is no evidence for elite, central authority figures and where there are only a few instances of mangled bodies.

None of these models involve clear evidence of Chacoan warfare. They all represent behavior within a polity, violent though it may have been. If these acts were generally part of a pattern of warfare, there would be defensive sites, as well as evidence for alliances that would come to the aid of the attacked. To casually kill and process the victims in their own communities, and not bother to burn the village down or even loot it, smacks of a demonstration of authority, not warfare. In each of the above models, most of these abhorrent acts would be considered violence within the bounds of the community, and only in some cases would they be seen as between independent political groups.

Certainly, it is difficult not to see warfare associated with the proposed cannibalism. And, if the Chaco slave model has any validity, then where did the slaves come from, if not through warfare? However, at present, the conclusion must be that this violent behavior—as repugnant as it appears—is probably not good evidence for warfare for the time period. If readers have trouble accepting any of these models as having any degree of validity, they are not alone. The Chaco Interaction Sphere has always been the most enigmatic interval of time in the entire Southwestern sequence; and the evidence for possible cannibalism, the large numbers of mangled and otherwise mistreated bodies, and the lack of evidence for warfare only make it more so.

MOGOLLON

Like the Anasazi, there is a lack of strong evidence of warfare for the Mogollon during the Middle Period (A.D. 900–1150), and what little there is tends to be from the Mimbres area. The Mogollon region as a whole had large sites, often spaced very regularly along watercourses. And, small sites were found in more marginal locations, usually consisting of ten rooms or less, with "field houses" of one to three "rooms" located near any arable land. Like the Anasazi area, the distribution of Mogollon sites included almost all suitable locations. Sites, both large and small, were almost invariably located near farmable land, without being placed in defensive locations (Figure 5.7).

There are, however, a few exceptions to this pattern. Some sites, for example, were on elevated locations. In the Mimbres area, the Three Circle, Montezuma-Beauregard, and Wind Canyon sites were situated on elevated locations. And the defensively located Mogollon Village, initially occupied earlier, continued to be inhabited for part of this period. Nonetheless, the majority of the Mogollon sites on elevated landforms were not nearly as difficult to approach as were those for the Early Pithouse sites in the Early Period. Some of the elevated, but easily accessible sites can be explained by the lack of any other good building sites in the immediate area. But far more importantly, they are a small fraction of all the sites. For every Mogollon site that could be considered even remotely defensively located, there are ten to twenty contemporary settlements that were low-lying, often immediately adjacent to the floodplain, or actually in it.

Neither is there evidence of palisades or freestanding walls at any of these sites; where there were multiple room blocks, they did not form enclosed spaces. Although the larger Mogollon sites, in particular those in the Mimbres area, often consisted of multiple room blocks, they were loosely spaced and did not enclose spaces or form defensive perimeters. Also, they were not multistoried, which might have provided some defense. While it is possible that evidence of palisades has been missed, the chance of this happening throughout the years of excavations in the area is practically nil. Moreover, where multiple room blocks were arranged

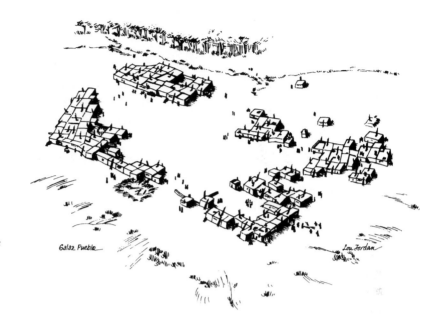

Galaz Pueblo   Lou Jordan

FIGURE 5.7
The Galaz site, a
typical Mimbres
pueblo of the Middle
Period with its
nondefensive layout.
From Anyon and
LeBlanc (1984).

very loosely, the effort of building a palisade around them would have
been substantial. If palisades had been planned, the room blocks would
have been arranged more efficiently to facilitate the effort.

There were burned rooms throughout the Mogollon area and throughout this time interval. There is some evidence for deliberate burning, such
as the burning of abandoned Great Kivas (Anyon 1983; Anyon and LeBlanc
1980). Also, there appeared to be, in general, more burned rooms than
could be considered the consequence of accidental fires alone. However,
there are virtually no examples of entire villages—or even major sections
of villages—that were burned with in situ deposits. And, with a couple of
possible exceptions, there were no unburied bodies on these sites. One
apparent exception is the very late occupation (during the Classic Mimbres
period) at the NAN Ranch Ruin in the middle Mimbres Valley. In Room
84, there was an unburied and slightly burned body, probably female
(Shafer 1991). A similar find from the late occupation at the Swarts Ruin
came from a burned room—another unburied individual may have been
present—but the discussion is unclear (Cosgrove and Cosgrove 1932:25).[9]
The burned room at the Swarts Ruin is near another late-occupation burned
room. So, while the overall frequency of burned rooms in the Mimbres, or
even the entire Mogollon area, is unclear, it does not seem to be large.
These examples would date to around A.D. 1130, at the same time there is
not only the first evidence of possible warfare in the Hohokam area but

9. This unburied individual, found at Swarts Ruin, is incorrectly listed by Wilcox and
Haas (1994) as having an arrow embedded in it.

also evidence for its beginning in the Anasazi area. A few cremations in the Mimbres area had arrows associated with the charred bones, but it is not clear whether they were in the body or were offerings (Creel 1989).

In spite of the general paucity of evidence for warfare in the Middle Period Mogollon, there are a few subtle indications that things might not be this simple. For example, there are finds of heads without bodies. A number of such examples are from the Galaz Ruin and elsewhere (Anyon and LeBlanc 1984). Because of the intensity of looting by modern-day pothunters over the years and the Mimbres propensity to bury individuals under the floors of rooms or just outside rooms, many of the Mimbres examples of disassociated heads are surely due to postdepositional distur-bance from pot-hunting or prehistoric remodeling that disturbed the body. However, it appears that not all such remains can be explained this way (See Wilcox and Haas 1994). Moreover, there are also Mimbres bowl de-pictions of decapitation scenes (C. Davis 1995) (see Figure 2.7) and im-ages of heads not in association with bodies (Brody et al. 1983). In addi-tion, a portion of a Mimbres bowl found in the Mattocks Ruin depicted what appears to be an individual shot with an arrow (Jelinek 1961). In some ways the decapitation bowl scenes, as well as recovered remains with disassociated heads, are reminiscent of what was happening in the Chaco area at the same time. In each case, people were being killed and the bod-ies not treated very well. Again, although this is the only time period for which evidence for this type of behavior is found with any frequency in both regions, it does not necessarily mean it was warfare related.

No other bowl images can be read as depicting warfare, although there are numerous examples of Mimbres bowls showing men hunting and en-gaged in other peaceful pursuits. As mentioned previously, Mimbres de-pictions of shields are rare to nonexistent, with only one possible example. This is not a large set of possible war-related images, given the more than 1,000 figurative images on the corpus of Mimbres bowls. The infrequency of anything that might be related to warfare in bowl decoration is dra-matically different from what is depicted in kiva murals from the four-teenth century in the Anasazi area, where such battle imagery is common.

Moreover, no one has ever reported evidence of scalping in the Mogollon area in general. And, projectile points from the region do not appear to be very standardized, nothing like those seen in the Hohokam area, for ex-ample. A couple of small symmetric "mauls" were recovered from the Swarts Ruin that the excavators thought were club heads, and similar ones were found at Mattocks Ruin (Nesbitt 1931) and Cameron Creek Village (Bradfield 1931). A double-bitted "axhead" recovered from the Galaz Ruin may really have been a club head (Anyon and LeBlanc 1984). There are few examples of large stone knife blades, however, and none of the awls look particularly long enough to be considered daggers. In all, there is not much evidence for serious weaponry in the Mogollon.

In sum, there is little evidence for warfare during my Middle Period (the late Pithouse and Mimbres Classic periods) in either the Mimbres area, in particular, or the Mogollon area, in general. This determination is based on such elements as settlement patterns, site configurations, burned rooms, and dismembered bodies. The Mimbres bowl imagery doesn't focus on warfare, nor is there specific evidence of weaponry in the region as a whole. This is a dramatic change from the preceding time period, where the settlement pattern information strongly suggests warfare up to the mid-500s. It is also relevant that at around A.D. 500 (as mentioned in chapter 3) the bow was introduced in the Mogollon area, replacing the atlatl. Yet, its presence did not lead to an increase in warfare in the area.

It certainly appears that as the Mogollon population grew in size, more and more effort was expended to increase the farm yield. There is good evidence for irrigation at this time in the Mimbres area (Minnis 1985; Herrington 1979) and for the building of check dams or other water-retaining devices to increase production (Sandor 1990). Settlement pattern data (Blake et al. 1986) show the location of sites spreading into ever more marginal areas and a considerable population growth. This situation could have been ripe for warfare as competition for the better agricultural land increased. There was undoubtedly some low-level warfare of the sort expected in most tribal settings in the Mogollon, but, be that as it may, it would have been unlike anything seen in the late 1200s and beyond—that is, the Late Period.

THE HOHOKAM AREA

The Middle Period in the Hohokam area seems to repeat the findings in the Mogollon area. Again, sites were widely spread and not situated in defensive locations. No one has found palisades or defensive walls on sites dating to before the 1100s. On large sites, structures were not clustered—that is, they were not closely packed together—and were not laid out defensively. Many small sites also existed, especially along minor drainages.

What *is* unique about the Hohokam is that the lack of defensiblity extends back to the Early Period, as discussed in chapter 4. The open settlement pattern dates back to A.D. 200 with essentially no change. The lack of evidence for warfare during the entire 950-year time range has been discussed by P. Fish and Fish (1989). However, because there is plenty of evidence for warfare later in time in the greater Hohokam area, its apparent absence could simply be based on excavators not recognizing it.

There is ample evidence for agricultural intensification in the Hohokam, particularly in the form of long irrigation canals to divert water from the Salt and Gila Rivers as well as minor water-control works on even very small watercourses. So, the same argument made for the Mogollon area can be repeated—even more emphatically—for the Hohokam area: Given 900 years of population growth and an ever increasing use of more marginal areas, the expected resource stress should have resulted in conflict at some point in this time span. Moreover, because not all locations were favorable for placing canal heads along the rivers, some areas would have been exceptionally valuable in that regard. The lack of competition for choice localities is remarkable. (This topic is considered further in chapter 7.)

All, however, was not completely peaceful in the Middle Period Hohokam. For centuries, there is little evidence for warfare in the region; then around A.D. 1150 and shortly thereafter, evidence of conflict becomes much more common. The site of Snaketown, south of modern-day Phoenix, is particularly revealing. Wilcox et al. (1981) point out that Snaketown, one of the largest Hohokam sites, was occupied for around 800 years (Gladwin et al. 1937; Haury 1976). More than 150 pit houses were excavated from all time periods, and 28 of them had been burned. Of the 28 houses, 23 were burned at the end of the Sedentary period (about A.D. 1100) at the time the site was abandoned. Although the 23 houses do not represent all the houses of the final period of occupation, in the case of some of the house clusters that appeared to be contemporary, all or most of the houses had burned. Wilcox et al. (1981) argue the burning was deliberate and the abandonment was rapid. After the abandonment of the site, an unoccupied zone opened up between other sites to the north and south, a precursor of the no-man's-lands of the Late Period.

At almost the exact same time, there appears evidence for burning at the site of Los Hornos, located along the Salt River close to Phoenix (Wilcox et al. 1990). The site has four excavated pit houses from the early Classic period or Santan phase, which would date it to just after the abandonment of Snaketown, a very poorly known time in the Hohokam. So the Los Hornos evidence provides welcome data from its sample of houses. All four pit houses had burned; a couple had in situ deposits; and none of them showed evidence of abandonment before they were burned.

There are several points to be made about the evidence for burning in the Hohokam area. Of all the structures in the Southwest, the Hohokam pit houses could have been the easiest to burn. They were made with a lot of small pieces of wood and grasses and with relatively small amounts of adobe, and were essentially aboveground. In the Snaketown example, if the 23 houses that burned in the final episode are excluded, then only 5 houses burned out of more than 125 over a span of hundreds of years. In other words, there were very few accidental fires at Snaketown. Also, Snaketown was one of the largest, if not *the* largest site in the area, which would suggest that some form of alliance between other sites in the region, such as those from the Salt River Valley, was created to destroy Snaketown.

An alternative explanation is that the site was destroyed for ritual reasons. But this seems unlikely, given the complete lack of evidence for such behavior in the preceding centuries and the site's destruction occurring at the same time as increased evidence of warfare elsewhere in the Southwest (see below). A more likely alternative explanation is that Snaketown was destroyed by its own inhabitants to deny the site's facilities to the enemies who had caused them to flee. But this is actually destruction due to warfare in another form. The evidence from Los Hornos reinforces the pattern of significant burning around the mid-1100s. For the reasons just given, it is extremely unlikely that four out of four pit houses would burn accidentally.

THE FREMONT AND OTHER PERIPHERAL AREAS

There is somewhat more evidence for warfare in the Middle Period along the peripheries of the Southwest than in the center. A difficulty here is that the dating of the periphery sites is somewhat inexact; and with the increased evidence for warfare throughout the Southwest, beginning around A.D. 1150, it becomes a question of how well the periphery sites fit the overall pattern of warfare. Are the examples of periphery sites that show more evidence for warfare just part of the same phenomenon of a panregional increase in conflict, but with dates that are less precise? Perhaps. However, several cases of warfare in the peripheries are worth mentioning.

On the far western edge of the Southwest, Mesa House, near Las Vegas, Nevada, is on the rim of a mesa, as its name implies. It was constructed to form a circle of rooms, so both its setting and configuration were at least mildly defensive. Many of the rooms were small, but a few were extra large. Two of the large rooms had burned as well as several others, including additional habitation rooms, but the entire site did not burn. One of the large rooms was apparently ceremonially burned with bodies in it. The excavator claimed that a possible woman and small child had been placed in the room in a pit dug slightly into the floor and the room deliberately set on fire. The quality of the excavation work at Mesa House was not very good, so the skeletal remains were never properly analyzed; from its photo the body of the adult might be identified as either sex. The individual was buried with a hafted knife, two antler clubs (19 1/2 inches and 16 inches in length) both with holes for thongs, and twenty-four very similar arrowpoints. This sounds like a male burial, and the site overall is perhaps evidence for warfare. Mesa House probably dates to the 1100s, somewhere toward the end of the Middle Period (Hayden 1930; Schellback 1926; Lyneis 1992).

Utah's Fremont area, located beyond the northern edge of the Anasazi, also begins to show signs of warfare sometime after 1150. The evidence points to a consistent defensive setting to many of the sites, such as Fort Bottom Ruin, SR 8-5 on Woodruff Bottoms, Nordell's Fort, Pinnacle Rock, ET 6-7, and PR 4-25, which are all on high locations with a difficult approach as well as other defensive features. Sites LS 13-2 and 13-5 seemed to have towers and enclosed spaces that also looked defensive, but were not as convincing as the other examples (Gunnerson 1969). Taken as a whole, these and other sites in the Fremont area show a marked increase of defensive measures when compared with earlier (pre-1100s) sites. While these are late sites for the area, it's unclear whether they date to the early 1100s or the following century. The Coombs Village site is unique and interesting, but probably not typical of the overall area. It was catastrophically burned at the end of its occupation, with twenty-five of thirty-five storage rooms, thirty-four out of thirty-seven jacal structures, and seven out of ten pit houses burned. Coombs Village is considered to be contemporary with Chaco, and was perhaps an Anasazi outpost in the Fremont area. Of interest in this regard is a "burial" in a ventilator shaft and occasional disarticulated bones (including an isolated head) from test trenches and the fill of structures (Lister et al. 1959–61).

There is some lack of clarity as to when the Fremont area was abandoned, or at least when the population ceased living in a semi-Anasazi mode. Some data suggest that soon after the sites became defensive, the area was abandoned in a fashion much like that in the northern Anasazi area, except that the transition apparently happened earlier in the Fremont area. Just how much earlier is not clear, although occupation probably lasted until the early 1200s. The presence of defensive sites in the Fremont area to the north of the Chaco Interaction Sphere that may initially date to the mid-1100s could be relevant to understanding the Chaco situation. At the extreme northern edge of the Anasazi area, just south of the Fremont Culture area, there were clearly defensive sites during Pueblo II times. It is feasible that there was conflict in the region between the Chaco-related Anasazi and the Fremont, which could explain the possible defensive sites both north and south of the border between these two areas. If this was the case, it would probably have been at the very end of the Middle Period.

For the eastern periphery of the Southwest—the Rio Grande, southeastern New Mexico, and the Largo-Gallina areas—there is little convincing evidence of warfare. Although there is evidence for conflict in the Largo-Gallina area—some of the strongest evidence actually—warfare does not appear to have begun prior to 1150.

THE IMMEDIATE POST-CHACO TIME SPAN—
A.D. 1150–1250

There are several lines of evidence indicating an increase or resumption of warfare beginning around A.D. 1150 throughout the Southwest. For the next 100 years, there is evidence for a much greater concern for site defense than existed earlier. Towers began to appear in the Four Corners area. Sites, such as Wupatki and the nearby Citadel, were more defensive than their predecessors. Similarly, sites such as the highly defensive Tom's

Rock, south of Cebolleta Mesa (west of Acoma), apparently date to this time (Fowler et al. 1987). The very defensively located sites of the Fremont area may first date to this period, or they may even have begun to show up slightly earlier, as discussed. Either way, these sites were certainly in existence by this time. The clear evidence for significant warfare from the Gallina area appears initially to date to the early 1200s. Some additional cases of bodies that were not burned also apparently date to this 100-year period.

The cluster of sites at Wupatki, with its Great House–like main structure, Great Kiva, and surrounding small sites, had many Chaco attributes, but was well outside the generally accepted geographical boundaries of the Chaco sphere. Wilcox (1995) describes the site as emulating the Chaco system, which he sees as continuing after A.D. 1130. I see it as a local attempt at copying the Chaco system after its demise. But the distinction is not important for this discussion. There was a population concentration in the Wupatki area between A.D. 1150 and the mid-1200s. Not necessarily initially, but soon, sites were defensively situated, in particular the Citadel, Tower House, and Lomaki. Wupatki is on a small knoll, but was not oriented as defensively as the others. There may have been three clusters of sites in this area (which included the above sites) that were close enough to each other to have provided mutual support. The clusters were about 5 to 6 miles apart and may have been located to facilitate signaling between them. However, this has not been carefully explored (B. Anderson 1990). Of particular note is that one room in the approximately eighty-room Wupatki Pueblo had the remains of at least nineteen individuals who had been dumped in the room after being exposed to carnivores. The remains included postcranial elements and jaws, but only two crania. In addition, other remains from Wupatki that do not seem to be formal burials—some with perimortem cuts and damage—have also been recovered (Turner and Turner 1990). Given the size of the site, this is a significant number of individuals.

In the nearby House of Tragedy, Smith (1952a) found two bodies on a kiva floor, an additional body on a room floor and two fragmentary skeletons in an exterior storage pit. This was only a four-room, one-kiva site with, presumably, a population of no more than ten people. So, the number of nonformally buried individuals represents at least 50 percent of the total number of people in the site. If Wilcox (1995) is correct, then this is one more example of the Chaco Interaction Sphere having an effect on the mistreatment of individuals. If my interpretation is more accurate, then the example indicates that Chaco-style behavior continued in this location after the collapse of the overall system.

There is additional evidence of increasing conflict elsewhere in the Southwest during this 100-year period. In the general Flagstaff area, an increase in warfare is seen at the defensive sites of New Caves Hill (NA486),

Crack-in-Rock Pueblo (NA537), Turkey Tanks Fort (NA113), and Medicine Fort (NA862). The Medicine Fort site had burned, with considerable food still in storerooms. The small NA408 site had one of two pit houses burned (the other was earlier in time), with in situ deposits. Also, one interment had five points next to it, suggesting they had been in a quiver. All these examples date to between A.D. 1050 and the early 1200s, with most appearing to be post-A.D. 1150 (Colton 1946, 1960).

Sites of this time period in the Jones Ranch Road area to the north of Zuni had both significant burning and disarticulated bodies. The sites were essentially hamlets—small isolated settlements—with pit houses, probably a continuation of the Chaco-type settlement pattern, and were occupied in the late 1100s and early 1200s. Site 108 had at least two nonformally buried individuals in the fill of one pit house and fragmentary remains in eight other structures, almost all of the buildings in the site (Anyon et al. 1983:757). Because of the extensive burning at Site 108, this case appears to be more like the warfare-related finds of the subsequent Late Period rather than the Chaco-style mistreatment of individuals. Incidentally, in the Zuni area these hamlets were replaced by more nucleal and slightly defensively located sites by the mid-1200s, and, finally, by the end of the century, the truly defensive large pueblos appeared. The Dobell Site, near the Petrified Forest, which seems to date to the same 100-year interval, also had pit houses, one of which contained two unburied bodies that were missing extremeties, which could have been taken as possible trophy parts (Harrill 1973).

Sometime during the 100-year interval—certainly after A.D. 1200—in the Largo-Gallina area of northern New Mexico, towers began to appear, and there is increased evidence of burning and unburied bodies (discussed further in chapter 6). One site, Rattlesnake Ruin, had the remains of ten adults (all with fractures and four with arrowpoints in them) heaped into a pile in a pit house; the bones of an infant were found in the air shaft. Although good tree-ring cutting dates in the A.D. 1220s are available from this site, the pit house could not be accurately dated (Baker 1990). The community consisted of a second pit house, a tower, and a surface room. The total population of Rattlesnake Ruin would probably have been no more than twenty people, and there would have been as many children as adults in all likelihood. So, this find represents a massacre of the entire adult population, with the possibility that the children were taken captive. The date of the massacre was not determined, but presumably it was after A.D. 1220. Many other indications of warfare in the Gallina area are considered in the next chapter, but it is interesting to note that they begin to show up first during this interval.

There are other, more subtle pieces of evidence for a change in defensive needs during the A.D. 1150 to 1250 time period. The change in building pattern between that of Carter Ranch and that of the nearby Broken K

Pueblo in the Upper Little Colorado River area is indicative. Carter Ranch dates to the early mid-1100s and seems to have no defensive features (Longacre 1970; P. Martin et al. 1964). Broken K dates to the early 1200s and has an almost completely enclosed plaza, created by the configuration of the room blocks (Hill 1970; P. Martin et al. 1967). Broken K may not appear very defensive in terms of later standards, but it seems to have been a step in that direction.

The transitional period between A.D. 1150 and 1250 is perhaps best characterized as a case of the Southwestern people simply reverting to a standard tribal level of warfare. Whatever social mechanism or other phenomenon that discouraged warfare during the Chacoan era seems to have ended—or at least been reduced—during this time. There was now evidence of some warfare, some defensive placement of sites, and some restricted, but significant, outbreaks of war in areas such as the Gallina. It is as if the situation had returned to the more expected state of affairs, given the type of social complexity. Perhaps the level of warfare—present, but barely visible in the archaeological record—that occurred in this transitional period is the middle ground between the invisible or nonexistent warfare of Chacoan time and the intensive, virulent warfare of the very late 1200s and early 1300s.

SUMMARY

The Middle Period (A.D. 900–1150) coincides with an interval of worldwide warming (described in chapter 1), a climatic change that affected the Southwest in expected ways. The distribution of sites indicates that a very wide range of habitats could have been farmed throughout the region. Consequently, this was a time of a raised carrying capacity and of population growth; and all archaeological evidence confirms this expectation. Until population growth caught up with carrying capacity, there would have been little stress on resources and little incentive or need for warfare. This, too, is supported archaeologically. Whatever the cause for the cultural changes that took place around A.D. 1150—the collapse of the Chaco Interaction Sphere, the end of the Classic Mimbres, and the abrupt change in the long-standing Hohokam cultural tradition—they seem to be associated with a return to a visible level of warfare.

However, it is wrong to view this peaceful Middle Period as the norm for the Southwest. It was exceptional, and should be understood as such. This period is reminiscent of other times and places when there appears to have been widespread cultural interaction, new forms of expression, and little evidence for warfare. Such eras might include the Hopewell period in the Eastern United States, the Chavin and Olmec periods in Mesoamerica and Peru, and early Teotihuacan in Mexico. These eras were not totally free of warfare, but when it did occur it was much less intense than what followed. Relative peace seemed always to end with what is often described as a "florescent" period, followed by increased warfare. Perhaps this interval in the Southwest is another example of a peaceful period of florescence, terminated with increased conflict. In any case, we should not attempt so much to understand *why* there was warfare preceding the Middle Period, but figure out why there was *so little* during it.

CHAPTER SIX

CRISIS AND CATASTROPHE

Warfare during the Late Pueblo III and Pueblo IV Periods

Early in the morning, on the day of the communal harvest party, the warriors from Qootsaptuvela set out. Upon reaching the vicinity of Sikyatki, they waited. When everybody [in Sikyatki] who was going to participate in the harvest party had descended to the field, they [the warriors] rushed the village. In no time they were inside. Quickly they pulled the ladders out from the houses where the women and children were. Having accomplished that, they set everything on fire. Some of the warriors had come with pitch they had gathered. This they smeared on the walls of the houses; as a result they quickly caught fire.

The men who were harvesting at the field spotted smoke. They saw that it was coming from the village. Thinking that something had happened, they ran back, one after the other. When the warriors who had set the fire saw them, they fell upon them. As soon as a man reached them, he was dispatched. Since the Sikyatki men had no weapons with which to resist, they died without being able to fight back. They were all killed, poor things.

—From "The Demise of Sikyatki" as told to Ekkehart Malotki (1993)

Following a period of unprecedented peacefulness, suddenly the Southwest was engulfed in warfare. Vast areas soon were abandoned, massacres transpired, and the survivors moved into increasingly larger defensive sites for safety. In my Late Period—from around A.D. 1250 to Spanish contact—things drastically changed and there is very good evidence for intense warfare. The entire concept of the Pueblo people—large numbers living in compact communities—derives directly from the several hundred years of warfare that began around 1300.

Virtually every class of archaeological data that could reflect increased evidence for warfare has it beginning in the late 1200s. Clearly, prehistoric warfare in the Southwest was as deadly—if not more so—than Lawrence Keeley (1996) suggests it would have been. War was having a major impact on the lives of the Southwest people in the Late Period. Of equal importance during this interval is that settlements, the way people were organized, and the way they made war changed dramatically from the preceding centuries.

The sudden increase in conflict is seen most dramatically in the Late Period settlement patterns and site configurations. Throughout the Southwest, large compact settlements and settlement clusters rapidly evolved. These communities required not only considerable energy for construction and maintenance needs but also strong leadership for proper organization. By the early 1300s, almost the entire population of the Colorado Plateau was living in about 120 large, compact, defensive pueblos, clustered into about twenty-seven distinct settlement groups. And similar, although less clear, settlement clustering seems to have taken place off the Plateau as well. There is further ample evidence for Late Period warfare from the incidences of burning and unburied bodies. Also, a significant number of massacres are recognizable. In addition, prehistoric art reflects an increase in conflict. All this evidence both corroborates and complements the settlement pattern information.

The archaeology of the Late Period is enough well known that considerable detail about warfare can be inferred. Much of the information is in the Appendix, enabling the reader to follow the general trends without having to wade through the details. However, these critical data provide the basis for the intrepretations made here.

Beginning with some background, I then examine, generally, the evidence for warfare in the Late Period—architectural and settlement patterns, burned sites, unburied bodies, etc. Next, I take a geographical tour of the Late Period Southwest, specifically scrutinizing the evidence from north to south—Mesa Verde to Chihuahua. And, finally, I synthesize all the information into an overall picture of Late Period warfare.

THE CLIMATE AND CULTURAL BACKGROUND

There is good evidence, as discussed in chapter 1, that the climate in the Southwest had begun to deteriorate by the mid-1200s. Because of an increasingly colder climate, some areas of the region may have become too marginal for agriculture, while others may have experienced added seasonal variability that resulted in more crop failures and lower yields. Some areas, however, such as the Rio Grande, may have enjoyed an improved agricultural potential that included the possibility of increased year-to-year variability. While these changes in productivity were not without precedent, they were probably greater than what had transpired earlier in the agricultural era. Furthermore, the population of the Southwest had grown significantly over the preceding 400 years, probably due both to the favorable weather conditions of the Medieval Warm Period and to the level of peace that had prevailed for a few centuries.

By the 1200s, the distribution of sites in the Southwest was not as widespread as it had been in the previous Middle Period, but settlements were not markedly clumped, either. The vast majority of people in the Anasazi and Mogollon areas were living in aboveground masonry or adobe structures, usually with multiple rooms combined into room blocks of varying sizes. Typical room blocks were not very large, with perhaps twenty to thirty rooms being the norm, and were frequently clustered into communities. Room blocks were also more compact than those in the Middle Period, but were still separated from each other. Smaller sites, of one or a few room blocks, were still to be found over much of the area. Sites were not consistently defensively designed, nor were they usually situated in defensive locations. There are a few candidates for Great House–like buildings with surrounding communities, but there were only a few of them in existence after A.D. 1200.

There seemed to be a greater level of group autonomy by the early 1200s than had existed previously. The architectural differences seen in the Great House/small room blocks dichotomy disappeared. Major centers like Chaco Canyon disappeared (with the exception of Casas Grandes and the Salt River Valley). In spite of the changes that took place during and after the Chaco phenomenon, there apparently was little population movement over any extended distances in the Anasazi area. Similarly, at the end of the Mimbres Classic period, a few areas were abandoned and there was a definite realignment of the population over the landscape. But there is no evidence of mass migrations to new areas. Most regions of the Southwest were still inhabited in the 1200s.

The same general conditions apply to the Hohokam area (although patterns are less distinct), with two exceptions. Pit houses continued to be an important Hohokam dwelling in the mid-1200s. And, more importantly, there is evidence of social inequality, as seen in the presence of houses located within compounds and structures situated on top of platform mounds, while other people were living in spread-out pit houses.

But, within a span of fifty years there was a pan-Southwest change. Sites became much larger, more defensive, and distinctly clumped on the landscape. Enormous areas began to be abandoned, and major movements of people began. Intertwined with these changes, and intimately related to them, was an era of very intense warfare, the Late Period.

EVIDENCE FOR LATE PERIOD WARFARE

The most compelling evidence for this period of increasing conflict comes in the form of settlement patterns and site configurations as seen in the Colorado Plateau and the White Mountains. Similar trends in the rest of the Southwest were also present, but they are not as clear-cut. There is also good information about Late Period warfare in the form of burned sites, unburied bodies, and prehistoric art.

Settlement Patterns

The most dramatic change that took place in the Late Period was a rapid movement of the population into large communities. Previously, in the Middle Period there had been many small communities; and, even when large, the settlements were made up of noncontiguous room blocks. By the Late Period, they were universally replaced by sites with hundreds of rooms, with the rooms linked together in massive blocks.

The settlement data consists of three components. First, there is evidence for a major shift in settlement locations and configurations; second, there is a rapid shift toward settlement clusters; and third, there is an evolution of the clusters over time. When taken together, these three trends provide strong evidence for warfare as well as its nature. (A detailed discussion of each of the settlement clusters is given in the Appendix and outlined in Tables 6.1 and 6.2; changes in the settlement clusters over time are shown in Figures 6.1 through 6.4.)

The list of these Late Period settlement clusters is probably very close to being complete. Everything suggests that all or almost all of the relevant sites for this period have been discovered and recorded. For example, repeated surveys of the Zuni area spanning almost a century after Spier's initial work have yielded only one or two new sites (Kintigh 1985). While there may be another one or two, it is very unlikely that there are many more undiscovered sites. Similarly, vast amounts of federal and reservation land have been surveyed in the last two decades, but few new Late Period sites have been discovered, and these have tended to be small sites that date toward the beginning of the Late Period. These newfound examples probably represent sites occupied during the transition to large defensive sites, and omitting a few of them does not alter the overall pattern of Late Period settlement changes.

The dating of sites in the list of settlement clusters is broadly secure, because the pottery sequences are generally well understood. However, the subtle particulars of the occupation span of each site are a very different matter. The temporal spans shown in Figures 6.1 through 6.4 and used in the discussions in the Appendix are a combination of tree-ring dates, dates of ceramics, and impressions of how long sites were occupied based on amounts of trash deposition. These estimates are certainly subject to considerable revision, but I think it unlikely that any changes will affect the overall patterns presented here, given the pervasiveness of the patterns.

Settlement Pattern Evolution

Throughout the Southwest, the movement into large, defensive settlements took several forms, but there was one guiding principle: For a village to be defensive, it must be very large or situated in a defensive location. This pattern resulted in small sites being situated on high, relatively inaccessible

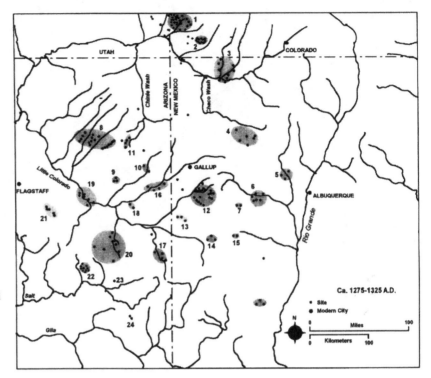

FIGURE 6.1
Sites and site clusters in the Colorado Plateau and White Mountains areas dating to A.D. 1275–A.D. 1325. Numbers refer to clusters named and described in Table 6.1. The founding of new sites in the Zuni area in the 1300s is not depicted.

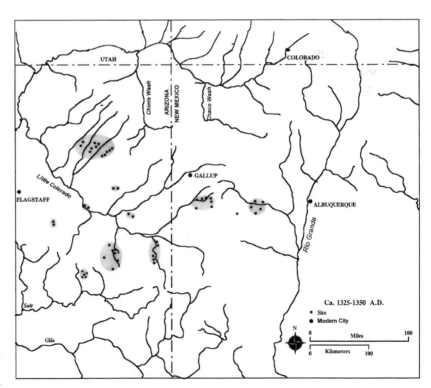

FIGURE 6.2
Sites and site clusters in the Colorado Plateau and White Mountains areas dating to A.D. 1325–1350. The site clusters are named and described in Table 6.1.

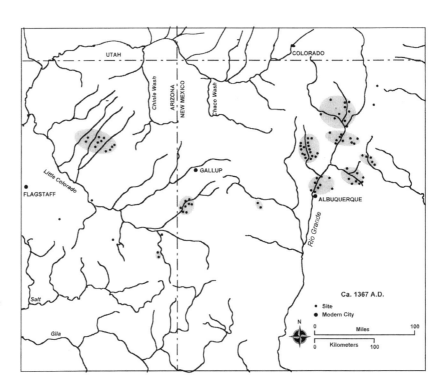

FIGURE 6.3
Sites and site clusters in the Colorado Plateau and White Mountains areas at around A.D. 1350–1375. Included are sites in the northern Rio Grande area, modified from Haas and Creamer (1992); excluded are possible ancestral Keres sites. Cluster spacing is quite clear when the Keres sites are not shown.

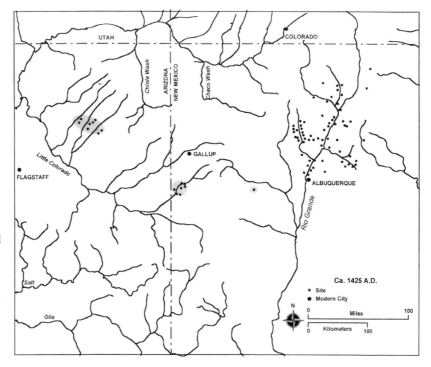

FIGURE 6.4
Sites and site clusters in the Colorado Plateau area at around A.D. 1400–1425. Included are sites in the northern Rio Grande area, modified from Haas and Creamer (1992), as well as possible ancestral Keres sites.

locations. If a site had to be small, then it was built with a defensive configuration and landforms were used to further protect it. This usually involved placing the site on a hilltop or building a cliff dwelling (see Figure 6.30).

However, if a site could be made large enough and if it had a defensive configuration, then a protected location was not necessary. What was neccesary was a secure domestic water supply. Large sites were commonly built next to springs or small drainages or had reservoirs or cisterns for water storage located close to the pueblo (a topic considered below).

Although some large Late Period sites were located in high, defensive settings, for example, Atsinna on El Morro, the Chavez Pass sites, or Acoma, most were commonly situated in low places. In either case, they were built to form an unbroken, or nearly unbroken, outer perimeter. In many instances, the outer perimeter was two stories tall and was usually made up of rooms that produced a *de facto* perimeter wall. Very rarely, as at the AZ W:10:50 site at Point of Pines (Lindsay 1987) and Sand Canyon Pueblo (Bradley 1992), there was a freestanding outer wall around all, or part, of the site. Freestanding walls were common in the Mesa Verde region in the late Pueblo III Period (Kenzle 1993), but it was not a general Colorado Plateau pattern. Freestanding wall segments were used south of the Plateau, however, especially in the Tonto Basin and with the Salado sites (Figure 6.5).

The site configuration change—from small to large, dispersed to compact—is quite dramatic. Most of the large sites were quite big—many times larger than previous villages—with 500 or more rooms common. Also, prior to this time (with the exception of a few Chaco sites), regardless of how big the communities were, they were not built very compactly. Furthermore, there were virtually no small habitation sites after A.D. 1300. By that time, a site of even 200 rooms was small compared with most of the sites on the Colorado Plateau. For the first time, in the Late Period, the entire Puebloan population was living in very large compact communities. Some plans of late period sites are shown in Figure 6.6.

Staged Aggregation

Increased population aggregation is an obvious aspect of the settlement pattern changes that took place during the Late Period. Actually, the trend toward "clustering" began during the early 1200s, and it seemed to take place in steps.

The first step in the aggregation process was room block (or small-site) clustering. Initially, sites or room groups began to be built more closely together than was the previous norm, but with little evidence of community integration (as was the case for Chacoan communities, for example). Very frequently, one of the sites in a cluster was either located on a relatively high place that provided a good view or was somewhat defensively

TABLE 6.1.
Late Period Site Clusters in the Colorado Plateau and White Mountains Areas.

(Map numbers refer to numbers on Figures 6.1–6.4; The number of sites represents a best-guess estimate of the largest number of sites that were contemporarily occupied in a cluster, usually at a time soon after the formation of the cluster. These counts do not correspond exactly with the number of sites listed for each cluster in Table 6.2 because that list includes some sites that were abandoned before some clusters reached their peak size.)

Map Number	Cluster Name	# Sites	Latest Existence of Cluster	Burned Sites in Cluster
1	McElmo	15	A.D. 1280s	Yes
2	Mesa Verde	12	1280s	No
3	Totah	13	1280s	Yes
4	Chacra Mesa	6	ca. 1300	No data
5	Rainbow Plateau	7	Late 1200s	No
6	Long House–Tsegi– Kayenta	15	Late 1200s	No
7	Klethla Valley	4	Late 1200s	No
8	Hopi Mesas	18	Post Contact	Yes
9	Steamboat Canyon	4	ca. 1300	No data
10	Hopi Buttes	3	ca. 1350	None
11	Wide Ruin	2	ca. 1300	Yes
12	Petrified Forest	2	ca. 1350	Yes
13	Upper Puerco, West	4	ca. 1300	No data
14	Jaralosa Draw	3	ca. 1325	No data
15	Zuni Area	18	Post- Contact	Yes
16	Cebolleta Mesa	2	ca. 1325	None
17	Greater Acoma	7	Post Contact	No data
18	Rio Puerco, east	3	ca. 1300	No data
19	Middle Little Colorado	7	Late 1300s	Yes
20	Anderson Mesa	5	Late 1300s	Yes
21	Silver Creek	7	Late 1300s	Yes
22	Grasshopper Group	1–2 big, 9 small	ca. 1350	Yes
23	Kinishba Group	4?	Late 1300s	?
24	Upper Little Colorado	7	Late 1300s	Yes
25	Techado	3	ca. 1325	Yes
26	Newton-Rattail	2	ca. 1325	Yes
27	Point of Pines	2	Late 1300s	Yes

TABLE 6.2.

Cluster and Site Details Dating between A.D. 1275 and the Early 1400s in the Colorado Plateau and Adjacent Areas.

(Terminology: very extensive = essentially the entire pueblo based on extensive excavations; extensive = most or all of a large section of rooms; significant = enough evidence to suggest nonaccidental fire; some = burned rooms present, inadequate data to determine how significant or extensive.) (Most of the sites listed in this table can be found plotted and described in Adler [1996]. The various areas discussed are individually synthesized in E. Adams [1996], Crown et al. [1996], Dean [1996b], Fowler et al. [1987], Gilpin [1989, 1995], Kintigh [1996], Pilles [1996], Reid et al. [1996], Roney [1996c], Spielmann [1996], Stein and Fowler [1996], and Varien et al. [1996].)

Cluster - Site (with Map Reference Number)	Evidence for Burning	Unburied Bodies - Number	Reference
McElmo - 1			Varien et al. 1996
Castle Rock - 5MT1825	extensive	22	R.Lightfoot and Kuckelman 1995
Hovenweep Square Tower			
Goodman Point - 5MT1604			
Miller Pueblo - 5MT1875			
Yellow Jacket - 5MT5			
Hedley	some: predefensive village		Richard Wilshusen, personal communcation
5MT1647			
Big Spring Ruin - 5MT17088			
Woods Canyon - 5MT11842			
Easter Ruin - 5MT3793			
Hibbetts - 5MT7656			
Seven Towers - 5MT1000			
Hovenweep Horseshoe–Hackberry			
Cannonball - 5MT338			
Mitchell Springs			
Morley-Kidder 1917			
Yucca House - 5MT4359			
Moqui Spring - 5MT4474			
Cowboy Wash - 5MT7740			
Brewer Pueblo			
Berkley Bryant			
Coalbed Village - 42SA920			
Landcaster - 5MT4803			

TABLE 6.2. (continued)

Cluster - Site (with Map Reference Number)	Evidence for Burning	Unburied Bodies - Number	Reference
Little Cow Canyon - 5MT1834–5			
Cottonwood			
Papoose Canyon			
Ruin Canyon Rim Pueblo - 5MT10438			
Cow Mesa 40			
Spook Point			
Pedro Point - 5MT4575			
Nancy Patterson Village			
5MT6359			
Sand Canyon - 5MT765	kivas	40	R.Lightfoot and Kuckelman 1995
Ruin Spring			
Radon Spring			
Herren			E.H.Morris 1929
Charnel House	tower burned, probably entire site	11 adults (3 isolated skulls) 3 infants in tower	E.H.Morris 1929
Mesa Verde - 2			Varien et al. 1996
Cliff Palace - 5MV635		burned body?	Fewkes 1911:77
Balcony House			
Long House - 5MV1200	burned kiva	4 (plus isolated bones in kiva fill, skulls without bodies, bodies without skulls)	Cattanach 1980:145,146
Bowman's			
Spring House - 5MV1406			
Ruin 16 - 5MV1241			
Oak Tree House - 5MV523			
Step House		burned body?	Nordenskiold [1893] 1979:49
Spruce Tree House - 5MV640		6?	Fewkes 1909:24
Site 20 1/2 - 5MT1449			
Kodak House - 5MV1212			
Double House - 5MV1385			

Cluster - Site (with Map Reference Number)	Evidence for Burning	Unburied Bodies - Number	Reference
Square Tower House - 5MV650		1?	Fewkes 1922:57
Mug House - 5MV1229			Rohn 1971
Totah - 3			Stein and Fowler 1996
Morris 41 - ENMU 5098	burned	charred skeletons	E.H.Morris 1939
Morris 39 - LA1897			
Twin Towers - NM-A-1-45			
Tse Taak'a			
LA2513			
Shannon Bluff - LA8619			
Tonache Tower - NA-A-1-8			
Old Fort - ENMU 5033		scattered human remains	E.H.Morris 1939
Aztec Ruin - LA45	significant: East Ruin, Great Kiva, upper floors West Ruin	burned bodies	E.H.Morris 1929; F.Lister and Lister 1987
Flora Vista - LA2314			
Salmon Ruin - LA8846	significant: late occupation	burned tower kiva with 33 bodies	Irwin-Williams and Sheley 1983; Shipman 1983
Chacra Mesa - 4			Roney 1996c
Paul Longsden - LA50055			
Kin Nazhin			
El Castillejo - LA51145			
Raton Well - LA14354			
Reservoir - LA15278			
Mesa Tierra			
Rainbow Plateau - 5			Dean 1996b
Yellow House			
Red House			
Upper Desha			
Pottery Pueblo			
Segazlin Mesa			

TABLE 6.2. (continued)

Cluster - Site (with Map Reference Number)	Evidence for Burning	Unburied Bodies - Number	Reference
AD D:2:236			
AZ D:2:1			
Long House - Tsegi - Kayenta - 6			Dean 1996b
Kiet Siel			
Twin Caves			
Batwoman House			
Six Foot Ruin			
Betatakin	1 male in kiva		Judd 1931
NA11958			
NA11980			
Tower House			
Pottery Hill			
NA12230			
Long House			
Brown Star Site	male with missing skull, and embedded arrowpoint		Haas and Creamer 1993
Kin Po			
RB568			
Moki Rock			
Parrish Creek			
Klethla Valley - 7			Haas and Creamer 1993
Little Thief Rock			
Kin Klethla	female skull in room fill	burned rooms	Haas and Creamer 1993
Thief Site		burned rooms	Haas and Creamer 1993
Valley View			
Hopi Mesas - 8			E.Adams 1996; Gilpin 1989
ORABI SUBGROUP			
Huckovi - NA872			

Cluster - Site (with Map Reference Number)	Evidence for Burning	Unburied Bodies - Number	Reference
Kwaituki - NA489			
Hoyapi - NA837			
Orabi - NA828			
MIDDLE CLUSTER SUBGROUP			
Chumalisko - NA1163			
Chukovi - NA1132 (Tsukuvi, Pumpkin Point)			
Sikyatki - NA814	significant		Fewkes 1898a; S.LeBlanc, personal observation
Kuchaptevela - NA1699			
Lamehva - NA1707			
Old Mishongnovi - NA871			
Old Shunopavi - NA868			
ANTELOPE MESA SUBGROUP			
Kawaika-a - NA1001	some		S.LeBlanc, personal observation
Kokopnyama - NA1019			
Nesuftanga - NA1048			
Awatovi - NA820	burned kiva	1 in kiva	Fewkes 1898a
Lululongturqui - NA1056			ends at 1300
Pink Arrow - J:4:1			
Eighteen Mile			
Chakpahu - NA1039			
Steamboat Canyon - 9			Gilpin 1989; Stein and Fowler 1996
Eagle Crag			
Hogay			
Bear Springs North			
Hopi Buttes - 10			Gilpin 1988
Bidahochi - NA1054			
Bidahochi Southeast - NA1052			
Bidahochi Southwest - P-48-a			

TABLE 6.2. (continued)

Cluster - Site (with Map Reference Number)	Evidence for Burning	Unburied Bodies - Number	Reference
Wide Ruin - 11			
Wide Reed	some: rooms and kivas		Mount et al. 1993
Klagetoh			
Kin Tiel	2 of 2 kivas excavated	5 in one kiva	Haury and Hargrave 1931; Hargrave 1931
Petrified Forest - 12			
Puerco Ruin - AZ Q:1:22	south, southeast sectors		Burton 1990
AZ Q:2:22			
AZ Q:1:275			
Adamana - Spier 206			
Stone Axe - AZ Q:1:199, NA1022			
Wallace Tank - AZ Q:2:21			
Upper Puerco, West - 13			
Isham -			
Sanders/Rocky Point - K:15:2			this is a questionable member of cluster
Emigrant Springs			
Taylor Springs			
Jaralosa Draw - 14			Fowler et al. 1987
Fort Atarque - LA55637			
Ojo Bonito - LA11433			
Spier 170			
Zuni Area - 15			Kintigh 1985, 1996
EL MORRO SUBCLUSTER			
Scribe S Community - NM 12:G3:4	extensive		Watson et al. 1980
Pueblo de los Muertos - LA1585			
Mirabal - LA426			
Cienega - LA425			
Hole-in-the-rock (Lookout) - LA1551			
Kluckholn Ruin - LA424			

Cluster - Site (with Map Reference Number)	Evidence for Burning	Unburied Bodies - Number	Reference
Spier 142 -			
Tinaja - LA427			
Pettit Site - LA1571			Saitta 1991
North Atsinna - LA430			
Atsinna - LA99			
HESHOTAUTHLA SUBGROUP			
Heshotauthla - LA5605			
Yellow House - NM G:14:2			
LA11530 Community (next to Heshotauthla)	significant: Scribe S phase		Zier 1976
SHOEMAKER CANYON SUBGROUP			
Jack's Lake - NM 12:13:29			
Archeotekopta II - NM 13:D:103			
Ojo Pueblo - LA27612			
Fort Site - NM 13:D:101			
Shoemaker Ranch - NM M:2:1	(Scribe S phase)		
Miller Ranch - NM 13:D:41	(Scribe S phase)		
PESCADO SUBGROUP			
Lower Pescado Village - NM 12:13:109			
Pescado West - NM 12:13:4			
Lower Pescado - NM 12:13:6			
Upper Pescado - LA9108			
RAMAH SUBGROUP			
Ramah School - NM 12:A3:17			
Lower Deracho - NM 12:13:110			
Day Ranch - NM 12:Z2:82			
LOWER ZUNI RIVER LATE GROUP			
Chalowe - AZ 15:H17			
Hawikuh - LA37			
Kechipauan - NM 13:A:3			
Pinnawa - NM 12:			

TABLE 6.2. (continued)

Cluster - Site (with Map Reference Number)	Evidence for Burning	Unburied Bodies - Number	Reference
Halona North - NM 12:k3:1			
Hampassawa - NM 12:L3:38			
Matsaki - NM 12:K3:62			
Kyakkima - NM 12:K:10			
Kwakina - LA1053			
Ah:kya:ya - LA49261			Anyon 1992
OTHER ZUNI			
Kay Chee - NM 12:13:29			
Cebolleta Mesa - 16			Roney 1996c
Ranger Station			
Calabash - LA1331			
Penole - LA11677			
Kowina - LA1334			
Greater Acoma - 17			Roney 1996c
Keashkawa			Upham 1982
Shumatzutstya - LA413			
La Mesita Redonda			
Flour Butte (Mesa)			
Cubero - LA494			
Bug Mesa			
Rabbit Butte			
Casa Blanca			Upham 1982
Tsiama			Upham 1982
Locomotive Rock			Upham 1982
Acoma - LA112			
Rio Puerco East - 18			Roney 1996c
AS-8 - LA13197	? maybe early		
Headcut Reservoir - LA59019			
Mesa Portales - LA4568			
Miller Pueblo - LA98366			

Cluster - Site (with Map Reference Number)	Evidence for Burning	Unburied Bodies - Number	Reference
Mesa Verde Butte - LA57614			
Loma Fria			
Cuervo - LA10505			
Coot Ridge - LA10405			
Middle Little Colorado - 19 (Homolovi group)			
Homolovi I - NA468 or NA952		1 adult, child	Fewkes 1898b; E.Adams 1996
Homolovi II - NA953	some: burned kivas, at least 1 room	3 adults in kivas, child	W.Walker 1996
Homolovi III - NA4089			
Homolovi IV - NA2212			
Chevelon - NA1026, P:2:3	significant burning, burned corn		Andrews 1982; Dennis Gilpin, personnal communication
Cottonwood Creek - NA1026			
Jackrabbit - P:3:23			
Anderson Mesa - 20			
Kinnikinnick - NA1629	2 adjacent rooms out of 2 excavated		Conner 1943
Grapevine - NA2803			
Pollock - NA43170			
Chavez Pass North - NA658	3 rooms out of 3 in 3 different areas		G.Brown 1982
Chavez Pass South - East and West Pueblos - NA659	W block, Great Kiva, adjacent room, upper floor of room in highest area	incidents of scalping, unburied bodies	G.Brown 1982; W.Allen et al. 1985
Silver Creek - 21			
Showlow - AZ P:12:2	22 of 29 rooms, "all late rooms"		Haury and Hargrave 1931
Flake - AZ P:8:1			
Fourmile - AZ P:12:4			
Shumway - AZ P:12:6			
Pinedale - AZ P:12:2			

TABLE 6.2. (continued)

Cluster - Site (with Map Reference Number)	Evidence for Burning	Unburied Bodies - Number	Reference
Tundastusa - AZ P:16:3			
Bailey - AZ P:11:1			
Grasshopper Group - 22			
Chodistass	extensive		Reid et al. 1996
Grasshopper Spring	significant		Reid et al. 1996
Glennbikii	significant		Reid et al. 1996
Grasshopper Ruin - AZ P:14:1	minor	incidents of scalping	W. Allen et al. 1985
Brush Mountain - AZ P:14:13			
Red Canyon Tank - AZ P:14:25			
Oak Creek Ranch - AZ P:14:15			
Hilltop - AZ P:14:12			
Cibecue Creek Ruin - AZ P:15:15			
Blue House - AZ V:2:13			
Canyon Butte - AZ V:2:49			
Black Mountain - GFS 86-3			
Spotted Mountain - AZ V:2:3			
Ruin Tank - AZ V:2:7			
Red Rock House - AZ P:14:14			
Q Ranch - AZ P:13:13	1 of 2 room blocks		John Hohmann, personal communication
Kinishba Group - 23			
AZ P:15:4 - Spier 264			
Stage Canyon Ruin - Spier 229			
G Wash Pueblo - Spier 250 (2 sites)			
R14 Pueblo - Spier 251			
Spier 249			
NA14,368? - Spier 238			
Kinishba - AZ V:4:1	some	20	Cummings 1940
Upper Little Colorado - 24			
Casa Malpais - AZ Q:15:3			
Oscar's			

Cluster - Site (with Map Reference Number)	Evidence for Burning	Unburied Bodies - Number	Reference
Baca - AZ Q:11:74	significant		Andrew Duff and Keith Kintigh, personal communication
Danson Site - 146			
Hooper Ranch - AZ Q:15:6			
Raven (Schuster) - AZ Q:11:48	1 section		S.LeBlanc, personal observation
Spier's 175 - AZ Q:7:7			
Spier's 176			
Table Rock - AZ Q:7:5			
Rattlesnake Point - AZ Q:11:118	very extensive	some?	Duff 1995
Techado - 25			
Veteado Pueblo - LA44918			Fowler et al. 1987
Techado Spring - LA6010	some, details unknown	"large number"	Fowler et al. 1987; pothunter informants
Horse Camp Mill - LA10983 - McGimsey 616	very extensive	2	McGimsey 1980
Newton-Rattail - 26			
Rattail - 68112			
Newton - LA13422	some, details unknown	1 child skull in "special" room	Frisbie 1973; Roney 1996c
Point of Pines - 27			
Point of Pines - AZ W:10:50	large room group		Lindsay 1987
Turkey Creek - AZ W:9:123	a few scattered rooms		Lowell 1991
NOT PART OF DEFINED SETTLEMENT CLUSTER			
Box S - LA5538			
Gallinas Springs		skeletons with trauma, disarticulated bones	Bertram et al. 1990
Many Farms - Hopi area			
Beautiful Mountain - Chuska Mountains			
Mummy Cave - PIII occupation		skeletons with trauma	E.H.Morris 1938
To Dil Hil Dry Lake - LA7575 Chuskas			
Crumbled House - LA7070–7080 Chuskas			

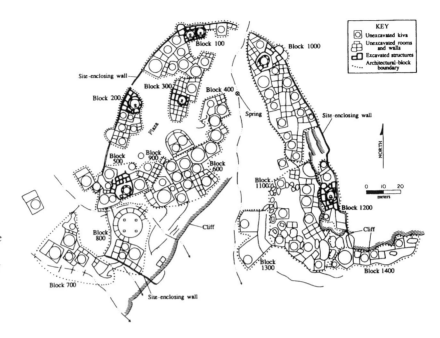

FIGURE 6.5
The plan of Sand
Canyon Pueblo
showing the defensive
wall and the pro-
tected spring. ©Crow
Canyon Archaeo-
logical Center;
reprinted with
permission.

FIGURE 6.6 *(right)*
Plans of Late Period
sites with defensive
layouts, all drawn
to the same scale.
The Fort site (A);
Turkey Creek (B);
Kuaua (C); Besh-Ba-
Gowah (D); Chavez
South, west pueblo
(Nuvaqueotaka) (E);
Awatovi (F). A, E,
and F are good
examples of inward-
facing layouts; B and
D are honeycomb
layouts. After
Morgan, 1994.
*Ancient Architecture
of the Southwest,*
University of Texas
Press.

constructed. It appears the concern for defense was strong enough to result in settlement relocation—and for sites to be inefficiently located with
respect to fields and some resources—but there were no major investments
in defensive measures.

The room-block–cluster sites seemed to be very short lived. It appears
that the threat to security was greater than first assumed, and more effective defensive solutions were sought. This resulted in a second level of
aggregation, in which, typically, the clusters of small, adjacent room block
groups or communities coalesced into single large sites. These large sites
could take the form of cliff dwellings, mesa-top "forts," inward-facing
plaza communities (walled towns), or massive room groups. As people
coalesced into the big sites, no more inhabitants than the combined numbers found in the prior loose clusters were necessarily involved. That is,
the actual "community" size might not be much larger than it was previously, but the area over which the settlement spread was greatly reduced.

Apparently, once one group in an area moved from loose clusters of
room blocks to a big defensive site, then all other groups in the general
area followed suit. Where the data are sufficiently detailed, they indicate
that large defensive sites and small nondefensive sites were not inhabited
at the same time. This is especially strong evidence for warfare, because,
earlier, there had been a range of community sizes. One aspect of the aggregation process was that building stones from the earlier, small sites

A.

B.

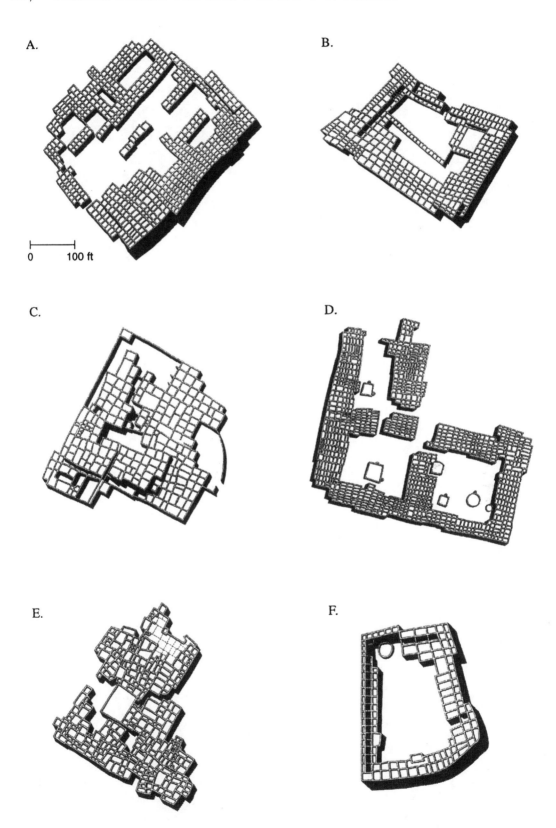

0   100 ft

C.

D.

E.

F.

FIGURE 6.7
A view of the back of
the outermost room
group at Acoma
Pueblo. Taken around
the turn of the
century. The high un-
broken wall formed
by the rooms is an
excellent analogy for
the exteriors of the
prehistoric inward-
facing pueblos.
Photo courtesy of
the Southwest
Museum, Los Angeles;
photographer
unknown, possibly
George Warton James;
photo number P7503.

were often taken to construct the later, large sites. So, the earlier sites are
particularly difficult to find and to understand unless there is intensive
survey (see e.g., Watson et al. 1980).

The process was repeated over a very wide area—most of the northern
Southwest—and during a very short period of time, in fifty to seventy-five
years. If it had been the result of responding to local environmental factors, then there would not be such a clear pattern. The same pattern is seen
at high elevations; in low areas near rivers, and away from them; in areas
to the north; and in the White Mountains to the south.

A second minor aspect to this settlement clustering that perhaps provides further insight into the process was juxtaposing some of the large
communities into pairs. Paired examples of Late Period sites are the Cienega
and Mirabal sites, the North Atsinna and Atsinna pair in the El Morro
Valley (see Figure 6.16), and the Chavez Pass sites. In these cases, very
large sites were located within a few hundred meters of each other. Sometimes, two large groups of rooms that on their own would be considered
large defensive sites, seem to have combined incompletely, such as at Kin
Tiel Ruin, the Kluckhohn site, and perhaps the Newton site. In these instances, two room groups were attached, but in such a way that the indi-
viduality of each group was architecturally visible. That is, it appears that
social groups sometimes combined, but did not submerge their identities.

The general goal for the Late Period aggregation seemed to be to accommodate many people, but in very close quarters. And the local solution

FIGURE 6.8
A historical view of Acoma Pueblo. Unlike the prehistoric inward-facing pueblos, Acoma had rows of room blocks all facing the same direction. Shown here are the stepped rooms of the front of one block and the high back of another. Photo courtesy of the Southwest Museum, Los Angeles; photographer unknown, possibly George Warton James; photo number P7669.

varied, from everyone living in one big site to cases in which two sites were actually joined physically but remained somewhat distinct or two sites were situated immediately adjacent to each other but not joined.

Site Configurations, and Methods and Speed of Construction

The large Late Period settlements, which, having become so compact, are now often referred to as "towns," were almost ubiquitous by A.D. 1325 and had several formations. There appear to have been three different styles: The first were inward-facing towns (S. LeBlanc 1989a), also called compounds, empty-center towns, or walled towns (Stein and Fowler 1996); and plaza-oriented towns (Roney 1996). These settlements all had very large central plazas, with the room tiers highest along the outer wall, then forming stairsteps down into the plaza. They were like football stadiums with the plaza the playing field. This configuration would have provided a large, secure space for daily activities (Figures 2.1, 6.7, 6.8).

The second approach to configuring these large sites was a "honeycomb," or massed rooms, layout. In this case, there were a very large number of rooms, but plazas were relatively small or nonexistent. Daily activities would have occurred, for the most part, on the roofs or outside the walls.

Interestingly, inward-facing pueblos were found almost exclusively in what had been the Chaco Interaction Sphere area and parts of the Rio

Grande area (which probably absorbed large populations from the old interaction sphere). Exceptions include the Chavez Pass and Homolovi sites. An argument can be made that within the prior Chacoan sphere, there was an attempt to preserve the old building style, with modifications necessary for defense. The typical Chaco site—Pueblo Bonito or Aztec Ruin, for example—consisted of a high portion along the north or north-west side, which was composed of rows of rooms stairstepping down to a lower row of rooms, which then stepped down to a plaza. This plan was modified to become a high outer wall formed by multistoried rooms on all four sides, stepping down to single-storied rooms on all four sides, and then down into a central plaza.

The massed-rooms, or honeycomb sites are found outside the old Chaco area, for example, Point of Pines W:10:50, Grasshopper Pueblo, Turkey Creek, Hooper Ranch, and Besh-Ba-Gowah. These sites may have had plaza areas; but, in general, when plazas existed, they were relatively small, compared with the numbers of rooms, and the rooms did not form stairstepped tiers down into the plaza. Honeycomb sites are more like historical Taos. The significance of this difference in settlement configurations is not clear. It may have to do with prior cultural history, or with the speed of construction, or how the groups came together to build these towns. As discussed below, both types of towns could be very large, with a few hundred ground-floor rooms the norm and more than 1,000 rooms not uncommon.

The inward-facing towns sometimes were built using a very distinctive technique, most generally termed "ladder-type" construction (discussed in chapter 2). This method seemed to involve a very rapid building procedure undertaken by work gangs, rather than individual families building specific rooms. Just as the inward-facing town configuration had antecedents in the layout of the Chaco Great Houses, so did ladder-type construction. The massive outer walls and very regular room sizes and doors found in Great Houses, such as at Pueblo Bonito, Chetro Ketl, and Aztec Ruin, also suggest work gangs and an absence of independent behavior. Families were not building their own rooms in these cases. Obviously, the goal for ladder-type construction was to build rapidly and to use as little stone as possible. And, its association with earlier, stone-robbed room blocks reinforces this assertion. Ladder construction was detected for at least seven of the settlement clusters discussed below, which further suggests that the building of these large, Late Period defensive sites often took place very rapidly.

The third building style consisted of rooms or room blocks connected by freestanding walls to form unbroken exterior perimeters. Sometimes the freestanding wall was rectangular and massive, and rooms were abutted to it on the interior (for example, at Casa Grande). In other cases, much more ephemeral freestanding walls were simply built to link room blocks and to make a more irregular perimeter. This type of construction is generally limited to the southern portion of the Southwest, and additional examples are discussed when that area is considered.

A North-South Trend in Defensive Sites and Site Size

The Late Period aggregation into larger, compact settlements started first in the northern portion of the Anasazi area (southeastern Utah and southwestern Colorado), then moved south and southeast, taking about fifty years to get from the Sand Canyon Pueblo in Colorado to Grasshopper Pueblo in central Arizona—and an equivalent time to get to the Rio Grande area. The first evidence for the tight clustering of room groups is in the early to mid-1200s in the southern Colorado area, and big sites such as Sand Canyon Pueblo soon appeared. The area was abandoned between A.D. 1275 and 1288. In the El Morro Valley area, some 240 km (150 miles) south, grouping of room blocks into nearby clusters seemed to take place in the A.D. 1260–1275 interval, and the big sites followed soon after A.D. 1276 (Watson et al. 1980). In the Grasshopper Pueblo area, some 105 km (65 miles) still farther south, Chosdiastass was a small site, possibly clustered, with a date in the A.D. 1280s to 1290s. Grasshopper Pueblo dates after A.D. 1300 and its formation as a defensive site took place around A.D. 1325 (Graves et al. 1982). Similarly, the early semidefensive sites in the Chama area, such as Palisade Ruin and Riana Ruin, date to the 1310s, with the larger sites later. Any comprehensive model for this aggregation must account for the fifty-year, north-south, space-time difference in defensive site construction.

Probably closely related to this north-south trend over the fifty years is a parallel trend in site size. The farther removed from Utah and Colorado, the bigger the sites get. While community sizes may have been reasonably large in the Colorado area (Varien et al. 1996), the size of any single site was not particularly large. (For the purposes of comparisons, room counts are given here as ground-floor rooms except as noted.) Colorado's Sand Canyon, with about 400 rooms, was the largest; Goodman Point, Hedley, and Landcaster each had about 350 rooms; but the remainder were even smaller. Some of these, such as Yellow Jacket, were very large sites earlier, but were relatively small by the late 1200s. Cliff Palace, the largest cliff dwelling, had only 220 rooms. Farther south in Arizona, Bidahochi had 250 rooms; Crumbled House had 300; and Flora Vista, the largest site of this time in the area known as the Totah (where the Animas, La Plata, and San Juan river drainages converge), had 400 rooms. Long House had 350 rooms, which was by far the largest number for the Kayenta area. Even farther south was Kin Tiel with 675 rooms; and again farther south at Zuni there were 761 rooms at the Kluckhohn site; and Archeotekopta II had 807 rooms. Still farther south, there were 800 rooms at Point of Pines;

and Grasshopper and Kinishba had more than 500 rooms each. Similarly, sites in the Rio Grande area (also to the south) got quite large, with at least six having more than 1,000 rooms. The pattern only holds for the higher elevations. In the lower elevations of the Middle Verde, Tonto Basin, and Gila River areas, none of which is on the Colorado Plateau, the sites were much smaller than those to the north or east.

Thus, the largest sites more than double in size going from north to south. However, there are some anomalies to this trend. No sites in the Upper Little Colorado River area were very big: Raven, by far the largest, had only 300 rooms. Similarly, in the Silver Creek area to the west, the Fourmile site had 450 rooms and was much larger than any other in that area. Only San Pasqual, at 500 rooms, was very large in the Rio Abajo area of the Rio Grande. Nevertheless, as noted, the earliest of the large defensive sites were built in the north, and they were the smallest of the big sites. So, it seems that the later in time these fortress-like sites were built, the greater the tendency to build extremely large ones. Was this part of a learning curve?

An alternative model proposed by David Wilcox (personnal communication) would have the largest sites in the center, perhaps at Zuni, with sites getting progressively smaller the farther they were from the center. Places like the Middle Verde and Tonto basin with their smallish sites were accounted for by this model. Later, a new center of largeness formed in the Rio Grande area. Regardless of the particulars of the distribution, sites got larger over time, and they were much larger in some areas than others.

Site Clusters and Site-Size Settlement Clustering

The second aspect of the late Pueblo III and early Pueblo IV period settlement patterns was the clustering of sites. Basically, after more than a millennium of living in moderately sized communities spread reasonably evenly over the landscape, in the space of about fifty years the entire population of the Colorado Plateau moved into about 100 very large pueblos that, geographically, were very unevenly spaced. The transformation was so rapid and so complete that it is unlike anything else that occurred in the history of Southwestern settlement patterns.

This pattern, variously noted in the past (Upham 1982; Upham and Reed 1989; Jewett 1989; Duff 1996), was far more pervasive than is generally realized. Essentially, the 100 pueblos on the Plateau and in the White Mountains were coalesced into about twenty-seven settlement clusters, with the Rio Grande pueblos evolving into another dozen or so clusters. (See Table 6.1 and Figures 6.1 through 6.4.) As is discussed below, evidence for this clustering is present, but less clear for areas farther south.

The settlement clusters consisted of large pueblos generally spaced about 5 km (3 miles) apart. Clusters ranged in number from two to about eighteen sites, with line-of-sight often, but not always, important. Although some clusters contained as few as two pueblos, an initial group of five to seven large sites was more typical. On the Colorado Plateau, clusters were initially spaced about 30 to 32 km (18 1/2 to 20 miles) from the edge of one cluster to the edge of the next. However, the spacing issue was more complex in the Rio Grande area and farther south.[1]

Initially, throughout the Southwest a few single pueblos lay outside a cluster, but they soon were abandoned. Similarly, small settlement clusters of only two or three large sites were also quickly abandoned. The Petrified Forest cluster (two pueblos) was the only small cluster to survive any length of time on the Plateau; and Picuris and Taos were the only such instances in the Rio Grande area, both of which still exist today.

After clusters had formed, there began an ongoing process of settlement and cluster decline. Over time, most of the clusters declined in size and then disappeared, which resulted in no-man's-lands opening up between the surviving clusters. Finally, the entire Colorado Plateau was reduced to three clusters of sites. The Acoma area, on the extreme eastern edge, declined until it was a single pueblo. At Contact, Hopi and Zuni had six or seven pueblos each, a decline from some eighteen pueblos each. Site attrition was less severe in the Rio Grande area, but both the number of clusters and the number of sites in each cluster did decline over time (Schroeder 1992). (These overall trends are seen in Figures 6.1 through 6.4. Note that the number of settlements in clusters declined as did the number of clusters.)

The evolution of settlement clusters is the key to understanding some of the previous discussions put forth by scholars. For example, Upham (1982), Jewett (1989), and Upham and Reed (1989) variously argue for a spacing of 30 to 50 km between settlement clusters. This interpretation of distances reflects too static a perspective. The 50 km spacing occurred later in the evolution of the settlement clusters after some had disappeared. Eventually the spacing between clusters increased to around 130 km (80 miles) on the Colorado Plateau. The point is that it is possible to find a wide range of spacing simply by looking at different time intervals. However, it is the initial 30 km spacing that seems critical to understanding the initial development of the settlement clusters. This spacing distance between clusters was so pervasive over such a large area that it must represent some key element in resource use or defensive needs.

Site Clusters as Sociopolitical Units

Once the pattern of site clustering is recognized, the question arises as to what these clusters represented sociopolitically. What is clear both archeologically and ethnographically is that the single pueblo was not the

1. As the number of sites increases, it is usually impossible to determine whether all the sites in a cluster were contemporary. But there is often evidence that for at least a brief time they were occupied simultaneously.

only level of political integration. Groups of the large settlements were clearly politically integrated. This point has been made for the Western Pueblo area by Upham (1982) and for larger areas by Wilcox (1981a, 1991, 1996). It is quite clear from the early Spanish accounts of the Rio Grande area that groups of pueblos were allied in some way; and, furthermore, such groups almost always had a shared linguistic affiliation (Wilcox 1981b).

The term "alliance" has been applied to the clusters of pueblos, and initially it seems appropriate. If there were groups or clusters of sites with considerable empty space between them, then to what extent were the communities within the clusters always allies and to what extent were they sometimes competitive? Calling the site clusters "alliances" answers the question before it's asked. To further complicate the situation, Upham (1982) and others also use "alliance" to describe relationships between geographically separate clusters. Such intercluster alliances are known to have existed in the historic period, and surely they must have existed prehistorically as well. (The topic of alliances, both within and between clusters, is considered further in chapter 7.)

To me, it seems best to refer to these groups of sites simply as "site clusters" and to use the term "alliance" when there is direct evidence for military cooperation. There can be an alliance between sites within a cluster, as well as between clusters, and the nature of the alliances was probably quite fluid. The rationale for being conservative about assuming the nature of the sociopolitical relationships of the pueblos in these clusters is found in the history of some of them. While there is evidence for closely spaced pueblos being allied, there is also evidence that alliances were often fragile and could be broken. And, for example, while it does appear that the other Zuni pueblos joined in the defense of Hawikuh against Coronado, similar support does not seem to have been the case in the Rio Grande area. Communities there did not aid each other when one was attacked by the Spaniards.

Another example of how weak nominal alliances could have been is seen in the Awatovi and Sikyatki conflicts among the Hopi. Both these communities, despite being located within the Hopi cluster, were apparently destroyed by other Hopi groups. In general, it cannot be assumed that sites within clusters were politically and socially integrated, even if they have been located near each other for a century or more. For example, the community of Hano, which moved to the Hopi cluster in the late 1600s, is still not fully integrated into the Hopi political milieu even after having been there for 300 years. So, there is reason to suspect that the political relationships between the pueblos in many of the clusters may have been quite fragile. Moreover, "alliances" between clusters of pueblos seem to have been both particularly weak and disorganized in the historic period, except for a brief period of cooperation during the Pueblo Revolt.

In sum, site clusters should be seen as just that—clusters—and the question of what level of sociopolitical integration and alliance formation existed should be left open.[2]

Secure Domestic Water Supplies

Another very consistent aspect to these large Late Period towns or pueblos was the concern with domestic water supplies. The number of sites with "Springs" in their names is indicative of their locations: for example, Gallinas Springs, Mud Springs, Mitchell Springs, Big Spring Ruin, Bear Springs North, Techado Spring. Not only are sites often built next to springs (or, in some cases, right on top of them) but also other measures are frequently taken to improve the water supply. Cisterns were cut into rocks (e.g., at Atsinna) or small dams were constructed to form catch basins (e.g., at Castle Rock) and walk-in wells (e.g., at Cienega and Mirabal). The possible causeway-like steps and wall constructions between the pueblo and the spring at Chavez Pass may have been another method of protecting a domestic water supply. These examples occur from the Mesa Verde area to Grasshopper Pueblo in the White Mountains. (For a general discussion of water storage facilities see Crown [1987].)

Clearly, the water in these cases was for domestic use and not farming. Why have a walk-in well in the middle of a plaza if the water was intended for crops? It should be in the middle of the fields. Similarly, reservoirs or cisterns found at such sites as Atsinna or Kechibawa in the Zuni area were not located with respect to any possible farming areas. Also, as noted previously, there was never much concern over the location of domestic water supplies in the Middle Period even when sites were large. The Late Period efforts to protect domestic water supplies were obviously undertaken for more than just convenience. Previously, sites were often located near water, perhaps within 20 to 30 m, which would have kept the water source cleaner and allowed more choices in selecting good locations for the sites. But, during the Late Period, these concerns were often ignored, with the pueblo established directly on the water source.

Was this securing of water a mechanism for withstanding a siege? Most likely this was not the case. When Coronado's troops besieged a Tiwa pueblo, the defenders ran out of water, which suggests that the people had

2. There may have been instances of small clusters within the large site clusters. For example, within the overall Zuni cluster, this could have been the case for the group of sites in the El Morro Valley or the group of sites near Ojo Pueblo. The long string of sites along the Zuni River could possibly have consisted of two clusters. Similarly, at Hopi there were early site clusters on Antelope Mesa as well as on each of the three central Hopi mesas. Just what the relationship of the internal clusters may have been to the overall cluster is not clear. Since both Hopi and Zuni, the two geographical areas with these complex clusters, represent two of the three areas on the entire Colorado Plateau that were still occupied in A.D. 1540, it is difficult to imagine that the internal clusters were competitive with each other.

never anticipated needing to prepare for a siege—it was not the norm. The logistics of a siege and the nature of warfare at this level of social complexity would make such a maneuver unlikely. However, the presence of a secure domestic water supply is suggestive of defensive concerns. It strongly implies a severe fear of raids. Eliminating the need for women (the presumed water carriers) to venture out even a few hundred yards from the pueblo says a lot about the threat of ambushes. Enclosed plazas were another element of safety for the inhabitants. Creating a large enclosed place established a secure area in which to perform daily tasks. The combination of an enclosed plaza and a secure domestic water supply would have greatly decreased the anxiety of the inhabitants, especially the women, of these communities.

Line-of-Sight Communication

Another aspect of Late Period settlement patterns involves line-of-sight communication. As discussed previously, there is evidence for the importance of intercommunity communication for historic-period warfare. Certainly, the visual linking of pueblos within a cluster would have enhanced the ability of communities to provide aid to each other. From an archaeological perspective, the observation that pueblos were visible to each other helps define the existence of a cluster and its boundaries.

Site location based on line-of-sight communication is well documented for the Kayenta area by Haas and Creamer (1993). They made the innovative observation that line-of-sight communication linked sites *within* a cluster, but there were no visual links *between* the clusters. Just how important this pueblo-to-pueblo visibility was is apparent from the actions of the people in the Klethla Valley who removed part of an intervening cliff in order to create a visual link between two sites.

There is evidence in the El Morro area for a similar pattern of site intervisibility, especially at the aptly named Hole-in-the-Rock site, where it's possible a hole was cut into a mesa remnant to provide a view of other sites (Figures 6.9a and 6.9b). This case, however, is not well documented. Sites in the Pecos area seemed to have line-of-sight links (Genevieve Head, personal communication), as did some in the Verde Valley (Peter Pilles, personal communication) and some in the New River area (Spoerl 1984). And, there is evidence for intervisibility between towers in the Gallinas area (Sleeter 1987; A. Ellis 1991).

It is necessary to note that the presence of towers on sites does not automatically mean they were used for line-of-sight communication. Many of these towers may have simply served as general observation lookouts and as defensible "keeps." Towers in the Mesa Verde area may have served as watchtowers or the equivalent, as probably did the tower on a very inaccessible point, near the Big House site, in Manualito Canyon (Fowler et al. 1987).

FIGURE 6.9a
The Hole-in-the-Rock site in the El Morro Valley, New Mexico, was situated against a mesa remnant. A hole in the sandstone allowed viewing other large sites in the valley. To what degree the hole is natural and to what degree it was modified by the pueblo's inhabitants is not clear. In any case, the site was located to take advantage of the hole.

FIGURE 6.9b
The view from the Hole-in-the-Rock site through the hole in the sandstone.

Within many of the clusters of pueblos, there appear to have been small pueblos located on high points, so as to provide a visual link between large pueblos located in low-lying areas. While most of these small pueblos have never been examined to determine whether they do provide such a link, they were present in the Chama, Pecos, Petrified Forest, Chacra Mesa, Grasshopper, and the Upper Little Colorado River settlement clusters. In some cases, large pueblos were placed in high places, even though other pueblos of the same size in the same cluster were situated in low places. This suggests the large pueblos situated on high places were there not simply for defense, but to facilitate line-of-sight linkages between pueblos within the cluster. Clusters with such large, high sites include Zuni, Newton-Rattail, Acoma, and Anderson Mesa.

Thus, while the number of documented cases of line-of-sight communication is relatively small, the number of cases suggestive of it is quite large, implying that intervisibility could have been a very common feature of the Late Period settlement landscape. This is a badly neglected area of investigation that is of considerable interest and that needs further examination. Testing for such visual links between sites is relatively easy, and would be a productive activity.

A convincing argument can be made that the purpose of these line-of-sight settlement locations was for communication rather than surveillance—an opinion primarily based on the distance between sites. The locations of sites in El Morro Valley (S. LeBlanc 1978; Watson et al. 1980) and in the Kayenta area (Haas and Creamer 1993) meant they could have seen each other. However, since they were about 3 miles apart, it would not have been possible to observe details of activities taking place at another pueblo or even to see who's coming and going. Therefore, I think these pueblos were not situated with the intent to "spy" on potential enemies, but were located to enable signaling for mutual support.

As pointed out in chapter 2, it is not clear what methods of communication would have been used between these intervisible pueblos, but fire and smoke are the likely candidates. The only known occurrences of line-of-sight links were in sites in the Late Period and the previously discussed Chaco example. Except for the Chaco case, which is difficult to interpret, all of the examples of intervisibility were found where there was evidence for warfare; and the best documented examples included particularly good evidence for warfare. It is, therefore, difficult to ascribe another purpose for this visual linking of sites.

Burned Sites

Another independent line of evidence for Late Period warfare is the frequency of burned sites. The rationale for evaluating burned sites as evidence of warfare was taken up in chapter 2. If a consistent pattern of major burning of sites is convincing evidence, how common was such burning during the Late Period?

COLORADO PLATEAU AREA

Of the twenty-seven site clusters defined for the Colorado Plateau and immediately adjacent areas, twenty-one clusters have adequate excavation data to determine whether any pueblo in the cluster burned. Of these clusters, for two of them the data are equivocal, but for the remainder about two-thirds have one or more burned sites. (These data are summarized in Tables 6.1 and 6.2.) Given that many of these sites have very small excavation samples and that many sites in the twenty-one clusters have no excavation data, this is an extraordinarily high figure.

Although some of these data have been mentioned previously, additional comments are needed. In the McElmo Cluster, burning was very common, for example, at Sand Canyon, Castle Rock, Hedley, and Charnel House. The Mesa Verde cliff dwellings, like the Kayenta cliff dwellings, do not appear to have ever been burned. At Hopi, Sikyatki surface reconnaissance found lots of burned rooms; Hopi oral traditions say it was burned. The burning at Awatovi took place in the historic period. And, while there are some burned rooms at Kawaika-a, the evidence for massive burning is not very good.

In the Totah, both of the reoccupied Chaco sites—Aztec and Salmon Ruins—had significant late-occupation burning. This same pattern is seen for the Malpais Ruin and Stepping Stone House: Both were occupied during Chaco times, then reoccupied later. The later occupations have significant burning.

Sites in the Wide Ruins and Petrified Forest groups show evidence of major room blocks and kivas burning, which appear to have occurred at the end of their occupations. The burning at Zuni was concentrated on the slightly earlier sites, such as the Scribe S site at El Morro, and others downstream near Heshotauthla (Zier 1976). In these sites, the burning was extensive and catastrophic. At the Techado cluster of three sites, the two for which there are data were also extensively burned. This cluster and some of the sites in the Tonto Basin have the greatest proportion of burnings known to date. The Newton-Rattail two-site cluster had extensive burning on the one site for which there are data.

The evidence for burning at a number of the sites on Anderson Mesa, such as Kinnikinnick Pueblo, is clear, but it is difficult to determine the extent of burning that occurred at Chavez Pass, although there obviously was some. Similarly, some sites in the Silver Creek cluster were extensively burned, such as Showlow Ruin, but the evidence for other sites in the cluster is equivocal. The Middle Little Colorado cluster—the Homolovi area—had burned kivas and some burned rooms, but apparently no massively burned sites. However, the intensity of the pot-hunting that has taken place in some of the room blocks suggests that the inhabitants were forced to flee at the time of the burning, resulting in in situ deposits.

WHITE MOUNTAINS

In the White Mountains, there is the previously discussed burning of slightly earlier sites in the Grasshopper area and the extensive burning of the Q Ranch site of that cluster. Kinishba, however, presents a problem. There was some burning there, as noted by both Cummings (1940) and G. Baldwin (1938, 1939), but whether it was extensive is unclear. No other site of the Grasshopper cluster has any data. The famous Point of Pines example has been mentioned.

RIO GRANDE AREA

The common occurrences of burned sites in the Chama area has already been discussed. In other Rio Grande clusters, Arroyo Hondo had burned sections, Kuaua (in the southern Tiwa) burned, as did Arrowhead in the Pecos cluster. Some burning was recorded for the Rio Abajo sites. There was considerable site destruction in the Galisteo area, with one site having been destroyed just before the Spaniards arrived, but how much of the destruction was post-Contact is not clear. In sum, the majority of the Rio Grande clusters have at least some evidence for burning. Although, aside from the Chama examples, it does not seem to be quite as common as for the Colorado Plateau.

OTHER AREAS

There were also a great many instances of burning in the Tonto Basin. The burning at Gila Pueblo has been discussed, as has that at the Cline Terrace group of sites.[3] Farther to the south, in southeastern Arizona and south-

---

3. The Cline Terrace cluster covers about 5 km. Some data on burning are available for four of the six sites in the cluster. Twenty-three of thirty-five rooms tested "definitely" or "probably" burned at Cline Terrace Mound; twenty-seven of thirty-six at Indian Point Ruin; fifteen of twenty-three at U:4:9; and two of two at U:3:128. A more detailed account provides even stronger evidence for the burnings. Five of the unburned rooms at Indian Point Ruin were outside the main large room block, while within the room block twenty-seven of thirty-one rooms were probably burned. Similarly, at U:4:9, fifteen of the nineteen rooms tested within the main large room block were burned. In other words, within the entire site cluster, the majority of sites had significant burning. Outside the cluster there is similar evidence for burning. A total of six of six rooms at U:8:530 were burned, and twenty-three of fifty-nine rooms at Schoolhouse Mound were burned. Glen Rice (personal communication) notes that the unburned rooms seem to have been rapidly abandoned with floor assemblages left in situ, suggesting that the entire community was abandoned at the time of the burning. He also notes that the consistent pattern of site burnings in the Gila phase is not seen in the preceding Roosevelt phase (A.D. 1280–1320).

western New Mexico, a significant number of sites had burned. The Joyce Well site probably burned; it contained charred corn (twenty bushels of it were reported from nine different rooms). And, all of the rooms at Clanton Draw were burned (six with significant amounts of charred corn). Similarly, while the report does not specifically discuss burning per se, of the eighteen rooms at Clanton Draw, numerous burned features are described, and at least four rooms had significant amounts of burned corn in them. At the Kuykendall site, essentially the entire pueblo of 200-plus rooms was burned (some rooms with indications of intense heat) and then abandoned (J. Mills and Mills 1969). At the Dinwiddie site (J. Mills and Mills 1972), about half of the rooms had burned—some intensely, some only slightly—and there was a very high frequency of in situ materials in essentially all rooms. The excavated portion of "House 2" at the Buena Vista site, the northeastern compound, was mostly destroyed by fire, and human skeletons were found on room floors. Farther west on the upper Santa Cruz River (south of modern-day Tucson), the Paloparedo site had also burned (DiPeso 1956).

Bloom Mound, in extreme southeastern New Mexico, is worth particular mention. It dates to around 1200–1350 and appears never to have been more than about fifteen rooms. It burned, and according to Wiseman (1970) "some 30 crania along with a great number of other skeletal parts, all charred to greater or lesser degrees" were found on the floor and fill of one room. If, as is usually estimated, there were two people per room, the thirty individuals represented the entire population of this village.[4]

Outside of the Colorado Plateau and the Rio Grande area, it has been much harder to define site clusters, but there is evidence of burning. There seemed to be definite clusters in the Middle Verde, Horseshoe Reservoir, Perry Mesa, Tonto Basin, Globe-Miami, Lower San Pedro, Salt-Gila (possibly three clusters), Santa Cruz (Tucson), Pueblo Viejo, Animas, and Cliff areas. There were other sites in this same general area, but whether they formed clusters is not clear. With the exception of Perry Mesa, there is some information on burning at all of these clusters. There is at least one site with significant burning in each of the Tonto Basin, Globe-Miami, Lower San Pedro, Pueblo Viejo, Animas, and Cliff clusters. Thus, two-thirds of these clusters have known cases of burning, a finding quite comparable with that for the Colorado Plateau clusters.

As discussed in chapter 2, there is no reason why warfare should automatically lead to burned sites. There are examples of sites that were successfully attacked and not burned. Moreover, sites could have been abandoned

---

4. Jane Holden Kelley (1984) states that there were at least fifteen unburied bodies in the site. She also notes that the Bonnell site, near Bloom, which dates to the late 1200s or early 1300s, had one burial with a hole in the individual's head, another burial had a mandible but no skull, and the remains of possibly six other individuals were represented by scattered bones. There was some burning on the site, which seems more than random, but is not enough to be fully convincing. So this is an equivocal case of possible warfare.

due to pressure from enemies without ever being successfully stormed. Thus, the number of Late Period burned sites is more than what might be expected—even with considerable warfare. The warfare at this time must have been very intense.[5]

Nonformally Buried Bodies

In spite of the improbability of recovery, nonformally buried bodies are surprisingly common in the Late Period. The existence of such bodies is not always obvious, and they are often referred to as "floor" burials. When the floor burials are found without grave goods, and the remains are found in positions not usually associated with formal burials, then they must be considered as nonformally buried, regardless of the terminology used by the excavator. Of course, explanations other than warfare could account for these uncharacteristic remains. Accidental fires could catch some people before they could escape; rooms could accidentally collapse, burying individuals; and intracommunity murder or execution could also happen. However, the simultaneous occurrence of massive burning and nonburied bodies should be extremely rare unless caused by warfare (as discussed in chapter 2). The frequency of nonformal burials is listed in Table 6.2. Given the small amount of excavation undertaken on some of these sites, the overall total is quite signifcant.

The Late Period examples of nonformally buried individuals fall into two categories: those examples in which there were a few unburied bodies in a site and those in which the numbers of unburied bodies appeared to represent the entire population of the community. The difficulty with this distinction is the nature of the sample. For example, at McGimsey's Site 616—Horse Camp Mill—only two bodies were found associated with rooms: the remains of a young girl on a roof, whose arm had been cut off and who had been struck on the head with an ax-like implement, and a young male with an arrow in his leg. There was, in addition to these two, "a relative abundance of fragments of human skeletal material scattered throughout the site" (McGimsey 1980:41). However, only about 2 percent of the rooms at Site 616 were excavated. Although extrapolating from such a small sample is not very reliable, these data give a total of about 100 unburied bodies for the site as a whole.

There are similar interpretive problems with the samples from Te'ewi and Gila Pueblo. At Te'ewi, the remains of some thirty individuals trapped in a kiva were recovered; a significant portion of the rest of the site was excavated and no other bodies were encountered. And, at Gila Pueblo,

---

5. A large number of rapidly abandoned, unburned sites with everything left in situ are found in the southern part of the Southwest, such as the Salado sites of southwestern New Mexico. Even Casas Grandes was not burned when it was sacked. This seems to represent a shift in behavior. In at least some cases, the abandonment is clearly warfare related, while the rationale for others is unclear. Perhaps it was rapid abandonment under the threat of attack.

sixty unburied individuals came from one small area, although most of the rest of the site was excavated. Based on this information, what inferences can be drawn regarding events at these sites? In both cases, the best explanation is that although a large number of people were killed, there is no evidence for a massacre of the entire community. (The particular situation of unburied bodies or body parts found in kivas is discussed in chapter 2. Numerous examples of such finds come from the Late Period, including cases from Long House, Homolovi II, and Kin Tiel.)

However, at some sites, such as Sand Canyon or Castle Rock, where the samples are both larger and more systematically excavated, extrapolations using the number of nonformally buried bodies recovered are more reliable. For example, Sand Canyon's 20 unburied bodies extrapolates to more than 220 individuals, and Castle Rock's count of 42 extrapolates to about 60 (Ricky Lightfoot, personal communication). In these cases, the figures represent more than half the population in the communities. (As discussed below, a similar computation gives a comparable result for Casas Grandes.) All these examples should be considered massacres.

The cliff dwellings at Mesa Verde have a surprising number of unburied bodies and other anomalies, considering that they were believed to have experienced little or no warfare, coupled with their early, turn-of-the-century excavations. Examples of the nonformally buried individuals include at least four bodies recovered from Long House, plus isolated bones from the fill. As Nordenskiold ([1893] 1973) noted, "the inhabitants . . . were admirably prepared for defense, still there are indications to suggest that they eventually succumbed to their enemies. Human bones—ribs, vertebrae, etc.—are strewn in numbers here and there among the ruins." Another Mesa Verde unburied body, found in the kiva in nearby Ruin 16, is discussed in the Appendix. There were also about six unburied individuals in Spruce Tree House, including three skulls found in the vents of three different kivas (Fewkes 1909). "Burned bodies" were also recovered from Cliff Palace and Step House, and a possible unburied body was found at Square Tower House, as reported by the turn-of-the-century excavators.

Not only were the two reoccupied Chaco-era sites in the Totah burned to a considerable extent but Aztec Ruin also had burned bodies that appeared to be individuals who were trapped in the fire or killed just prior to it. At Salmon Ruin, one of the more tragic events of this period apparently occurred: Thirty-three children perished in a tower kiva, sometime after A.D. 1263 and before the end of the century. The best reconstruction of this catastrophy is that the children were on the roof of a tower kiva, which then burned, along with much of the site. It is not clear whether the youngsters were alive when the inferno began or were killed just before. Was this tower kiva considered a place of refuge during an attack, an attack that succeeded, and resulted in the site's burning and the children's deaths?

Guadalupe Ruin (Pippin 1987) is a Chaco Great House that was occupied in the late 1200s, presumably by people from the Mesa Verde area. The scattered remains of an adult male were found in a room that was then burned; the trash fill of another room also had disarticulated human remains. The pueblo as a whole had apparently not been burned, nor were these bones deposited at the end of its occupation. The remains may not be warfare related; there was no skeletal analysis to clarify the situation.

A good example of the difficulty in interpreting Late Period unburied remains is the case of Arroyo Hondo. Here, the site seems to have witnessed an episode of significant burning, and eleven unburied bodies were recovered, along with what were about twenty-five skulls not associated with bodies (Palkovich 1980). Arroyo Hondo appears to have been abandoned, then reoccupied at a later time, only to be abandoned again. This evidence certainly suggests warfare, and it is interesting to note that the pueblo is situated on the edge of a site cluster area. There is some evidence that sites on the edges of clusters were more likely to be destroyed than those in the center. Arroyo Hondo was on the eastern edge of its cluster, with the Pecos cluster the next group to the east. Arrowhead Ruin, the westernmost site in the Pecos cluster (i.e., the site closest to Arroyo Hondo) was also burned. So, the two sites located on the perimeters of their respective clusters, which were next to each other, were both burned.[6]

In summary, there is evidence for unburied bodies recovered from more than twenty-five Late Period sites. Several examples represent massacres in which the majority of the community's population was killed. Other cases may also represent massacres, but the data are equivocal. The frequency of these unburied bodies is unlike anything that preceded it, and they are often associated with burning and other evidence for violence.

Other Evidence for Warfare

SCALPING

Closely related to the nonformally buried bodies are incidents of scalping. The remains of scalped individuals were found at both Grasshopper Pueblo and Chavez Pass (W. Allen et al. 1985). At Chavez Pass, there were seven such cases, involving both men and women. At least two instances were recovered from "floor burials," which, as noted, often represented unburied individuals. That these nonformally buried individuals were also scalped reinforces the suspicion that they were killed, scalped, and then thrown into rooms. Incidentally, only a small number of rooms have been excavated at Chavez Pass. Of these, the Great Kiva and some nearby rooms burned, so a high proportion of the excavated rooms did burn, and this

---

6. In spite of this intriguing set of data, Creamer (1993), one of the more vocal proponents for a realistic assessment of Southwestern warfare, never addressed the issue of warfare in her work on Arroyo Hondo.

incident of scalping may relate to at least a partially successful attack that has gone unrecognized as such. In contrast, the three examples of scalping from Grasshopper Pueblo are from formal burials, and while there was burning on the site, it represents only a small portion of the site.

Along with evidence of scalping, there is some Late Period evidence of human-bone trophies. Hohmann (1985b) reports that a site from this time period in the Tonto Basin contained a room where the long bones of ten individuals were found. This find is similar to the drilled skulls, and long-bone trophies from Casas Grandes. In the Hohokam area, the few examples of violent deaths (although they were formal burials) dating to this time range have already been discussed.

BURIAL SEX RATIOS

The sex ratios of recovered remains, as discussed in chapter 2, also can provide evidence for warfare. In spite of the extensive amount of excavation in the Southwest and the large number of burials recovered over the years, it is difficult to obtain large burial samples from a single site that relate to a fairly discrete time period. For example, the Pecos Pueblo sample spans many centuries, and it most likely had a mix of time intervals when there was less warfare or comparatively more. There are, however, a few good burial samples that represent short time periods for which the sex ratios can potentially tell us about the extent of warfare. At Grasshopper Pueblo, for example, various estimates of the large sample of adult burials show that 59 to 61.5 percent were female (Hinkes 1983; D. Berry 1983). This implies that more than 25 percent of the adult males were "missing" from the burial population, which is exactly the expectation if there was significant warfare at this time and men were being killed away from the pueblo. And, at nearby and contemporary Point of Pines, AZ W:10:50, 54 percent of the adult burials were women, which, even though less skewed than Grasshopper, still implies that about 17 percent of adult males were "missing." At the earlier Turkey Creek site, where there was no evidence for significant warfare, the ratio is reversed, with only 44 percent of the adult burials being female. Why this ratio is not closer to 50 percent is unclear.

Similarly, at Casas Grandes, the sex-ratio pattern is unclear. Adult men are significantly underrepresented in the formal burial population, with 61 percent of the adult burials that could be sexed being female, about the same ratio as for Grasshopper. However, the large number (127) of unburied bodies that appear to reflect a massacre at Casas Grandes, also show too few men (the ratio was two-thirds women and one-third men). Did the men fight and die away from the town and, hence, were not part of the unburied sample? The obvious problem with this approach is that various interpretations can account for any ratio. If there were enough good burial-population samples from enough sites, a clearer pattern might emerge.

But, the best statement at this point is that there is a hint the sex ratios of recovered remains in the Late Period may indicate warfare.

In addition to Casas Grandes, the other sites with clear evidence of massacres, such as Sand Canyon, Castle Rock, Bloom Mound, and possibly Horse Camp Mill, either were just sampled, and the total number of recovered bodies was too small to draw a meaningful sex ratio, or had a total population too small to provide a meaningful sex ratio. So, there is not a good set of comparable cases on which to base an overall sex-ratio pattern for massacred communities in the Late Period.

ROCK ART AND KIVA MURALS

Evidence for an increase in Late Period warfare as seen in rock art and kiva murals is quite intriguing. The shield-bearer motif became common in Rio Grande rock art only after 1300. Similarly, the depictions on kiva murals of men with weapons—particularly shields, and even with possibly dead individuals—has been noted. According to Crotty (1995), these martial motifs were very common in the 1400s, then declined rapidly and were replaced by water imagery and similar motifs. That is, images of warriors and weapons (and possibly victims) were most common when warfare seemed to be the most intense. And, more importantly, it appears that the social role of warriors was evolving during this time. It is not just a coincidence that images such as men with shields began to appear frequently at the same time the role of the warrior elite would become prominent. There is also other evidence to suggest that leadership positions were held by warriors, who used weapons as status symbols.

WEAPONS

The evolution of Southwestern weapons was discussed earlier. It is in the Late Period that there is evidence for the sinew-backed recurved bow, the big buffalo hide shields, and the increased use of arrow-shaft straighteners or smoothers. However, as discussed in chapter 3, it would be very difficult to quantify changes in the frequency of arrowheads, knives, or club heads during this time period.

HISTORICAL ACCOUNTS

The early historical accounts of indigenous warfare in the Southwest—discussed previously—reveal several known features. First, warfare was organized and war leaders were important. Battles were fought by divisions; pueblos sent contingents to help one another; and when leaders were killed, resistance would sometimes collapse. Warriors did not wait for their enemies to enter the pueblo; they came out in the open to fight in a very organized fashion. And, if defeated on the battlefield, they would retreat to the pueblo and continue fighting there. And, if a pueblo's defenses were breached, the fighting moved inside the pueblo, where a house-to-house defense would probably take place. These tactics were in place before Contact and were quickly modified to adjust to the new realities of the Spanish military. Warfare in the Southwest also seems to have been endemic in the 1500s, and pueblo leaders repeatedly mentioned what groups they were presently at war with and tried to use the Spaniards as allies against them (much like the situation in Mexico). None of these methods and tactics was the result of occasional, minor or "ritual" warfare. The Spaniards encountered communities that were well defended and militarily organized.

A GEOGRAPHIC VIEW OF LATE PERIOD WARFARE

The previous discussion of evidence for Late Period warfare has been general and topical, with few particulars. This section briefly summarizes what is known about each of the Late Period settlement clusters in the entire Southwest, that is, how these groups of large sites evolved in terms of settlement patterns and more direct evidence for warfare. Broadly covering the region from north to south, this geographical survey traces how the clusters of pueblos developed, how long they survived, and what happened to them. A far more detailed version of this same geographical summary is presented in the Appendix. Again, it is the much more detailed evidence that is the basis for this section and the chapter as a whole.

It is difficult to detect the settlement clusters in the northern Anasazi area of southwestern Colorado and extreme southeastern Utah, and in the Totah area of northwestern New Mexico as well. While the region is relatively well known and there has been good synthetic work (Varian, et al. 1996), it was abandoned by the 1280s, and the processes described above did not have the time to develop to the extent seen farther south.

An additional problem with the northern Anasazi area is the continued use, or reuse, of major Chacoan-like and early Pueblo III sites. Some sites, such as Yellow Jacket, had massive occupations prior to A.D. 1250, and others, such as Salmon Ruin, were reoccupied after a hiatus. This greatly complicates an understanding of both the timing of site use and its degree, so determining how extensive the post-A.D. 1250 occupations were, and what their configurations might have been is very difficult.

Moreover, the movement into really large sites and the almost complete absence of small sites farther south did not completely take place in this area. Instead, there seems to have been a significant number of very small sites up to the end of the occupation. In spite of the differences, three settlement clusters are discernible: one along the McElmo drainage, one at Mesa Verde, and another in the Totah. None of these areas had sites as closely spaced as seen farther south, no sites lasted very late in the period,

FIGURE 6.10
Square Tower House, Mesa Verde. Cliff alcoves were not occupied during most of the prehistoric sequence. The famous cliff dwellings like Square Tower House were built in the mid- to late 1200s.

nor were any particularly large. If it can be assumed, based on the dating of Sand Canyon Pueblo, that the major shift to defensive sites began around A.D. 1250 and that a major exodus was underway by A.D. 1275, then the shortness of the interval (only twenty-five years) probably explains why the movement of entire populations into very large and defensive sites was never completed (Figures 6.10, 6.11).

What is important about the sites in this northern area is the evidence for massacres and other violence, in spite of the prevailing opinion that it was not common. There were burnings and massacres in the McElmo cluster, unburied bodies in Mesa Verde, and both burnings and unburied bodies in the Totah.

The Kayenta area of northeastern Arizona has many parallels to the Mesa Verde area. In each case, the area was abandoned very early, before A.D. 1300, and the evolution toward large sites never progressed very far. Each had significant numbers of cliff dwellings, and in each case the population migrated south as the shift to defensive sites was taking place there. Again, as in the Mesa Verde area, there seemed to be several site clusters evolving, but the process was truncated before they were fully established. So there was some site clustering, some large sites, some cliff dwellings, and some small sites; most, but not all, were defensively located. Several workers (Haas and Creamer 1993; Dean 1996b) have noted the begin-

FIGURE 6.11
The Castle Group at Hovenweep National Monument. A series of towers and high-walled room groups, including one tower in the canyon, surround and protect a spring. Photo ©Baker Aerial Archaeology, transparency 19C9325 #25.

nings of no-man's-lands, and while it is easy to see a Rainbow Plateau cluster and a Klethla Valley cluster, whether there were separate clusters in the Long House Valley, the Kayenta Valley, and the Tsegi Canyon is less clear. The Long House site with 350 rooms was more than twice the size of the next largest site, and most sites were closer to 50 rooms, making them very small for this time range (Figure 6.12).

The Rio Puerco of the eastern area and the rest of the southern San Juan area seems to have been a continuation of that seen for Colorado and the Totah. Population from north of the San Juan River moved into parts of the area in the 1200s. Few sites were large and by A.D. 1275 there may have been only about seven or eight sites with a total of under 250 rooms in the entire Rio Puerco area. A number of defensive sites were located on high places, which is to be expected for these small sites. There were a few site clusters such as on Chacra Mesa; and to the west along the Chuska slope, was the famous 300-room Crumbled House, a very defensive site on a mesa spur with a defensive wall and "moat," as well as a few others. In all there was never a successful movement into really large pueblos in the Rio Puerco and San Juan areas, and no communities seemed to survive past A.D. 1300 (Figure 6.13; see also Figures 6.28, 6.29).

The Zuni area contained one of the largest clusters of sites, and one of the few to survive into the historic period. It was surrounded by several

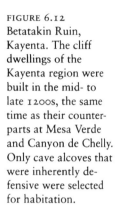

FIGURE 6.12
Betatakin Ruin,
Kayenta. The cliff
dwellings of the
Kayenta region were
built in the mid- to
late 1200s, the same
time as their counter-
parts at Mesa Verde
and Canyon de Chelly.
Only cave alcoves that
were inherently de-
fensive were selected
for habitation.

clusters extending from Cebollita Mesa to Quemado, which consisted of from two to five sites, none of which lasted past 1325. Sites in the Zuni cluster tended to be quite large, ranging from 120 to 800 ground-floor rooms, with virtually all of them having portions with two stories so that the largest sites had over 1,400 rooms. Here, the evidence for the transition to very large sites is particularly clear.

Little excavation has been done on sites in the adjacent clusters except for the one around Techado Mountain. Horse Camp Mill (McGimsey's Site 616 [1980]) and Techado Springs were both burned and had unburied bodies. For all of the Zuni-area clusters, the usual patterns are in evidence. The smaller sites were destined to be the most defensive and short-lived, as were the more isolated ones (see Figure 6.27).

Regardless of the number of sites and clusters that might have been contemporaneous at A.D. 1300, there was clearly a subsequent decline in their numbers. Soon, the three clusters nearest Zuni were gone, as were the few sites not in clusters, and within the Zuni cluster the number of sites decreased by half. By A.D. 1350 the upper reaches of the drainage were abandoned and the population moved down the Zuni River and relocated in the area of the historical seven "cities." From this period until the arrival of Coronado, there were apparently eight significant sites (Kintigh 1985; Anyon 1992). This is the only case on the Colorado Plateau where the sites in a cluster shifted *en masse* to a new location.

The transition to defensive sites was studied in the El Morro Valley by Watson et al. (1980). Prior to the mid-1200s, the valley population was small. An influx of people then formed seven communities about 3 miles apart, each consisting of groups of tightly spaced room blocks with at least

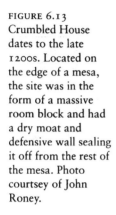

FIGURE 6.13
Crumbled House
dates to the late
1200s. Located on
the edge of a mesa,
the site was in the
form of a massive
room block and had
a dry moat and
defensive wall sealing
it off from the rest of
the mesa. Photo
courtsey of John
Roney.

one dwelling unit located as a high "lookout" where line-of-sight communication or observation would have been possible. The best studied site, Scribe S, was occupied into the late 1270s, when it was burned; most of the stone was subsequently carried away (Figures 6.14, 6.27). Although the fire was catastrophic, leaving massive amounts of burned corn and complete in situ assemblages, no unburied bodies were recovered. That the population was not killed is borne out by the rapid construction, using the ladder technique, of the massive 500-room, inward-facing Pueblo de los Muertos on low ground immediately adjacent to secure domestic water (Figure 6.15). The same process was repeated essentially simultaneously in at least five other localities in the El Morro Valley (Figure 6.16; see also Figure 7.1). Many of the earlier sites in these other communities were stone-robbed, and the resultant large inward-facing pueblos were intervisible; most also had walk-in wells or other secure water supplies. There was some relocation when two of the earlier communities were abandoned; interestingly, in two cases the later sites contained pairs of massive sites. When the transition was over, there were seven major, fort-like sites, in five locations—all intervisible. The most likely interpretation is that the Scribe S site was attacked and burned, but the bulk of the population survived and rapidly built a fortress. Most of the rest of the valley did likewise, which increased the number of people in each location and improved the line-of-sight between them. There is no evidence that any of these big sites were successfully attacked.

At Hopi, there were initially three miniclusters within the overall cluster: one with four sites and two with seven. The first group had over 1,000 rooms; the other two miniclusters had over 2,000 rooms each. There were

FIGURE 6.14
A room in the Scribe
S site in the El Morro
Valley that was
burned and stone-
robbed.

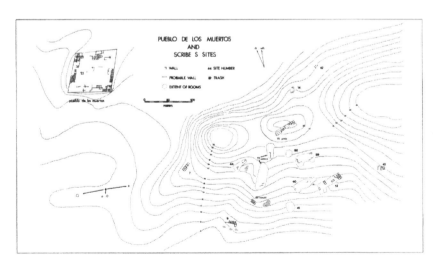

FIGURE 6.15
A map of the Scribe
S site showing its
relationship to Pueblo
de los Muertos. The
site, consisting of
spaced room blocks,
was located on a low
ridge. After it burned,
the building stone was
removed to build the
large, defensive Pueblo
de los Muertos located
next to the stream.

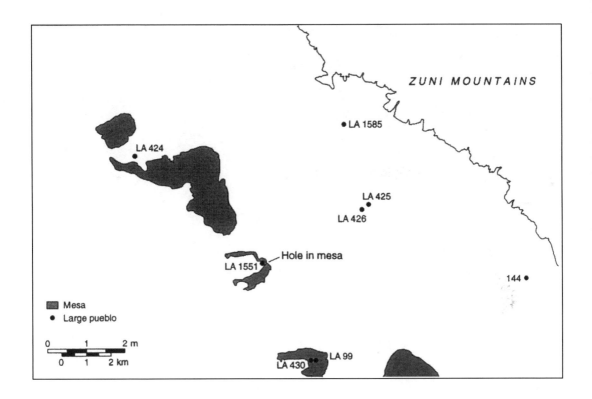

• LA 1585

LA 424

LA 425
•
LA 426

Hole in mesa
LA 1551

144 •

■ Mesa
• Large pueblo

0   1   2 m
0   1   2 km

LA 99
LA 430

FIGURE 6.16
Map of the El Morro
Valley showing the
locations of the large
late sites. All of them
had slightly earlier
dispersed room blocks
in their immediate
vicinity. All sites can
see at least one other
site, with the ex-
ception of LA424
(the Kluckholn site).
LA1585 is Pueblo de
los Muertos, LA426
is Mirabal, LA425 is
Cienega, LA99 is
Atsinna, LA430 is
North Atsinna, and
LA1551 is
Hole-in-the-Rock.

three nearby clusters (one around Kin Tiel, one around Steamboat Canyon, and one at the Hopi Buttes), and some isolated sites existed, including several in Canyon del Muerto. A number of the sites in the nearby
clusters have evidence of violence, including burning or unburied bodies
at Kin Tiel, Wide Reed, and Mummy Cave. Except for two sites at the
Hopi Buttes and those at Hopi itself, the clusters were abandoned by the
1300s.

The similarity of these patterns to Zuni is striking. The three-part central cluster was on the same scale as Zuni. The smaller clusters near Hopi
died out completely, just as those near Zuni did, and by A.D. 1350–1400,
the central cluster was reduced to twelve sites in each case.

The greater Acoma area had a large cluster around the site of Acoma,
other clusters at Cebolleta Mesa, and a small Rattail-Newton cluster. Only
one of these sites had over 300 rooms; many were small and on hilltops.
These clusters were soon abandoned, and at least the Newton site was
burned and had unburied bodies. The Acoma/middle Rio San Jose area is
unfortunately very poorly known, but there seems to have been about ten
sites. Over time they were reduced to three sites, and finally to the single
site of Acoma. A number of the sites were on high ground, and the possibility of line-of-sight links between them is very good. So, once again, the
larger central cluster outlived the smaller clusters that surrounded it.

FIGURE 6.17.
A view of the
Homolovi II site
before recent
stablization. This very
large Late Period site
sits on a knoll and is
an example of the
inward-facing pueblo.

There were three clusters along the Rio Puerco and the Little Colorado
River, and a short-lived cluster of small sites (fifty to seventy-five rooms)
on the upper Rio Puerco. The Petrified Forest cluster farther down the Rio
Puerco had several sites, including a possible small hilltop site to provide a
visual link for two large low-lying sites. The Rio Puerco site seems to have
been burned and abandoned. Farther downstream was the large, seven-
site Homolovi cluster. It was soon reduced to three sites, which lasted into
the late 1300s. This cluster had strong cultural links to Hopi, and was one
of the few to last so late in the period (Figure 6.17).

The Upper Little Colorado cluster had nine or ten relevant sites between
St. Johns and Springerville in Arizona. A number of these sites were burned
and contained some unburied bodies; the few larger or defensively located
sites lasted longer than many sites on the Colorado Plateau, surviving into
the late 1300s.

The Silver Creek area had five or six sites. Sites like Flake were small (50
rooms), and only the two largest sites (Fourmile Ruin had 450 rooms)
lasted post-A.D. 1325. Burning was associated with the abandonment of
some of the sites in this cluster. The Anderson Mesa cluster started with

three sites in the northern reaches, but soon all were abandoned, some with burning and possible unburied bodies. In the southern end, at Chavez Pass, a 100-room pueblo on a hilltop and surrounded by small room blocks was burned and a large, paired-site was then constructed. One of the pair appeared to have been rapidly built. This closely mimicked the pattern seen in El Morro Valley.

Thus, for the Colorado Plateau, there were a large number of clusters that died out early on, many with associated burning and unburied bodies. The three largest clusters, Hopi, Zuni, and Acoma, survived to the Spanish contact, although reduced in numbers, and a few other greatly reduced clusters survived to the end of the 1300s.

Outside the Colorado Plateau

South of the Mogollon Rim, but still in the "pine zone" was a series of large sites that formed several clusters. One cluster centered on Grasshopper Pueblo. It appears that there were smaller sites, some on hilltops. At least three of these (e.g., Chodistaas) burned catastrophically, at which point the sites were abandoned and the large Grasshopper Pueblo, set on a secure domestic water supply, was rapidly transformed into a large (500 rooms) defensive site. In an unusual configuration, at least nine smaller sites were built on defensive locations surrounding Grasshopper (Reid 1989). Apparently no one has looked to see if there is line-of-sight visibility between these sites.[7]

There is a poorly understood cluster centered on Kinishba (800 rooms). There were enough unburied bodies (at least twenty), in situ assemblages, and burned materials to suggest that some level of attack took place. Even farther south, Point of Pines was established in part by migrant groups from the Kayenta area. There was major burning about A.D. 1300, and a wall was constructed around the site apparently right afterwards.

In spite of dating problems, there is evidence of a linear cluster of some twenty sites along a 45-mile stretch of the Verde River. Such a long string of sites was unlike anything seen on the Colorado Plateau at this time. Also, the sites were much smaller than those on the Plateau, averaging about 100 rooms. The majority of them were either on hilltops or otherwise elevated with a good possibility of visual communication links between them, similar to that seen on much of the Plateau. The Verde sites seem to have been part of a general pattern of the level of defensiveness declining for sites not on the Plateau. Although most sites were defensively laid out and small sites were often in very defensive locations, they were

---

7. Although Tuggle (1970) found that the general locations of these sites correlated with good farmable land, their specific locations did not. They were not located with efficient access to it, but were clearly located in a good defensible position near it. So, they were able to exploit the farmable land, but be defensible, and were likely able to help defend Grasshopper Pueblo.

also smaller on average, with some smallish ones in nondefensive locations and not tightly clustered. Whether this represents a true decline in defensiveness or simply a difference in the size of the competing groups remains to be determined.

To the south of this area, the sites on Perry Mesa provide an interesting example of defense. The mesa is about 6 miles (10 km) by 9 miles (15 km). Wood (1997) maps seven site complexes, each with one big site of around 100 rooms per complex. They were spaced about 2 to 3 miles apart around the edge of the mesa. Better known sites include Squaw Creek Ruin and Pueblo Pato. The sites were the massed-room type with unbroken exteriors, but there were some plazas and freestanding enclosing walls. They were usually located on the very edge of the mesa, which would have afforded an excellent view, and the steep edges would have provided additional defense. Two of the site complexes seemed to have site pairs, where two large pueblos were very close to each other. When looked at as a whole, the sites provided a defense of the entire mesa. With this string of fort-like sites, the vulnerable mesa side of each site was somewhat protected by the existence of sites on other sides of the mesa. Any attacking force would have had to ascend the mesa in full view of one site, and men from the others could quickly have come to the defense of the exposed site.

In many ways, the Tonto Basin–Globe-Miami area was transitional between the Colorado Plateau, the White Mountains, and the Hohokam area. The period A.D. 1320–1450 witnessed a marked increase in warfare. In the Globe area, Gila Pueblo, which was part of a site cluster, was extensively burned and contained a large number of unburied bodies: at least seventy-one in a group of less than twenty rooms (McKusick 1992). Downstream in the Tonto Basin proper, there was a shift to many fewer and larger sites around A.D. 1325, together forming a couple of clusters. Unlike either the Plateau, Mogollon Rim, or Globe sites, these were not massive pueblos, but were adobe compounds that included freestanding walls and sometimes had platform mounds inside the compound. The total number of rooms in such sites was much lower than to the north. While some sites were on defensive landforms, not all were. Of six sites in the Cline Terrace cluster, major burning seems to have taken place on at least four of them, and the overall evidence for warfare is quite strong. This apparently was the beginning of a more southern pattern, where sites were smaller, and compound walls replaced massive pueblos, and secure domestic water seemed to be less important than in the north.

The Northern Rio Grande Area

The nature of settlement cluster spacing on the Colorado Plateau is strikingly clear. However, by A.D. 1540 the majority of the population was living in the Rio Grande Valley and not on the Plateau. Here, evidence for site cluster formation and evolution is far less obvious. This is due in part to the more continuous occupation of the area and the sites themselves. Wilcox (1981a, 1991) has argued that settlement clusters evolved in the Rio Grande area and no-man's-lands developed. He suggests that the Spaniards took advantage of this when they located their early settlements. Paul Reed (1990) also argues for the presence of settlement clusters. In spite of the long history of research—these sites were first plotted by Mera (1940)—the dating of a number of these sites is far from secure and makes interpretation difficult. These current data are very nicely summarized and mapped by Creamer (1996). Although the site distributions given by Creamer (1996) are not easy to reconcile with those of Schroeder (1979, 1992) for the northern Rio Grande Pueblo IV sites, a brief sketch of the potential clusters is possible.

There were clusters in the Galisteo Basin, the Pecos River area, around Albuquerque (southern Tiwa), in the Jemez area, and on the Pajarito Plateau. A group of about twenty sites (Tewa) that may have been more than one cluster existed from the Santa Fe to the Chama River area. Picuris and Taos seem to have been outliers. These sites are plotted on Figure 6.3. The inhabitants of the sites that survived into the historic period all spoke one of the Tanoan languages. There was one more cluster of sites that seem to be ancestral Keres. If this cluster is ignored, there is very clear settlement clustering. The overall spacing looks much more like a continuation of the Plateau pattern than is generally perceived. The spacing between the clusters was usually not far from the 30 km (about 20 miles) spacing seen on the Colorado Plateau.

In the middle of this rather conjectural reconstruction is a group of sites that in the historic period were occupied by Keres speakers. They essentially lie between the Jemez, Tewa, southern Tiwa, and to a lesser extent the Galisteo Basin sites. The people of Acoma speak Keres, and they and the Rio Grande Keres seem to be linguistically quite similar. Could the decline in the number of sites in the Acoma cluster be related to a late Keres movement into the Rio Grande Valley? If this is so, the Keres may have moved into a no-man's-land that formed and increased in size over time between the Tanoan-speaking clusters. (The Northern Rio Grande sites are plotted a second time in Figure 6.4, this time with the Keres sites included.) This settlement of a former no-man's-land may relate to a decline in warfare by the 1400s. If warfare declined, the no-man's-lands would have been desirable locations, and they would have been reoccupied. Alternatively, warfare may have declined and the no-man's-lands been reoccupied, which may have set off another cycle of warfare and developed a new set of no-man's-lands. It must be stressed that the dating of the presumed ancestral Keres sites is conjectural. There is simply no adequate dating to support or refute this model at present.

Going from site clusters to the number of extant sites, there are some definite trends. For the entire area, there was an overall reduction in the number of sites. Prior to A.D. 1540, the Pajarito Plateau was abandoned

(Preucel 1987), and the occupation of the Chama area was greatly reduced and almost abandoned (Beal 1987). The Galisteo Basin also had a reduction in the number of big sites. The Pecos area was down to a single site from five. Outside this immediate area, the eastern slope of the Sandia Mountains experienced a reduction in the number of sites, as did the Gran Quivira area, especially with the entire Pintada Canyon being abandoned.

The Pajarito Plateau shows evidence of the initial clustering of small sites and then further aggregation into very large pueblos (Preucel 1987). The late, big sites seemed to form two clusters. However, the spacing between the clusters appears to have been smaller than elsewhere. The details of the shift from small sites to the few large ones is obscured by the coarseness of the dating. Of particular interest is Walsh's finding (1997) that there was significant competition between the clusters of small sites prior to the formation of the really large sites. This fits nicely with the pattern found over much of the Southwest, where the slightly agglomerated communities that preceded the large sites often had a somewhat defensive aspect to them.

Using Spanish accounts and archeological data, Schroeder (1992) found that there was an 18 to 24 percent decline in the number of sites from about 1315 to the early 1400s. He attributed this to the drought of the early 1400s. He found no significant further decline until the 1600s. While his focus and interpretation differ from my formulation, the decline in sites fits well with the present model. Wilcox (1991) maintained that the overall distribution of sites implies the number of pueblos declined about 50 percent between A.D. 1400 and 1500, with another 50 percent decline between 1500 and 1600. Thus, while Schroeder and Wilcox disagree on the amount and timing of the decline in the number of large sites, both find a significant reduction.

The surviving site clusters appear to have stabilized about A.D. 1400, with any further attrition in the number of sites or groups much slower than what took place during the late 1200s and 1300s. Because the Rio Grande area was clearly gaining immigrants during a good part of this period, it reached the 1400s relatively intact, and the slow decline from the 1400s on resulted in a much lower level of cluster disappearance than it did on the Colorado Plateau. Why was the nature of warfare less intense in the Rio Grande Valley? It is possible there was less environmental stress, which both reduced the level of warfare and also lessened the impact of warfare (having crops destroyed is not as lethal for people who have stored resources as it is for those without any reserves).

In summary, these data support the idea that the shift to defensively laid out sites, the increased use of defensive locations for sites, the increase in site size, the extreme concern with domestic water supplies, the formation of settlement clusters, the increasing size of no-man's-lands, and the decline in the number of clusters all involved warfare in the Rio Grande area as it did on the Colorado Plateau.

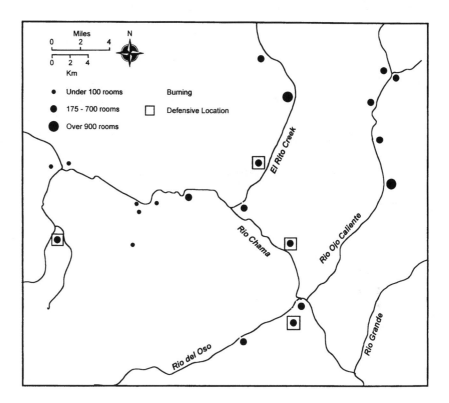

FIGURE 6.18
Map of the Chama
Valley showing Late
Period sites in the
early 1300s.

The Chama and Pecos Areas

The details of the history of several of these clusters is given in the Appendix, but two are worth a brief discussion here. The area and sites of the lower Chama River are depicted in Figure 6.18. The drainage was very lightly occupied before A.D. 1300. Between then and the mid-1500s, some twenty sites were constructed. Three of the earliest sites either were extremely defensive or had palisades and redoubt walls. The two smaller ones were both burned and short-lived. The really large sites were all over 500 rooms (some were over 1,000). These were not defensively located, although for the most part they had enclosed plazas. Middle-sized sites had plazas, and were on reasonably defensive locations. Therefore, the pattern of sites being either very big or relatively defensively located is much in evidence (see Figures 2.5, 2.6, 6.25).

Of the thirteen sites for which there are data, seven and probably eight had signs of extensive burning. The extreme upper drainage group of sites seems to have been abandoned by A.D. 1400 (including two that were burned). The middle Chama group and the Rio del Oso group were then abandoned with lots of burning; and two groups survived, each with very large sites. Does this represent in microcosm what is seen for the Southwest overall? There were initially four site clusters; one group was eliminated very early, the two groups in the middle were slowly eliminated, and the groups that survived were the largest groups, well separated from each other.

The history of the Upper Pecos River area is also revealing. It had a couple of pre-1300s nondefensive sites. After 1300, five sites were built around one or more central plazas. There may have been two small ridgetop sites that provided visual links between larger lower sites. A large site closest to the next cluster in the Rio Grande Valley was burned, the number of sites was reduced to two by A.D. 1500, and only the very defensive Pecos Pueblo existed at A.D. 1540.

Peripheral Rio Grande Areas

Site clusters in the Rio Abajo area, (the Rio Grande Valley from Socorro south) are poorly known, but "The period is characterized by the coalescence of nucleated Pueblo III village populations into large, fortified apartment complexes" (Marshall and Walt 1984:95). These include mesa-top sites with barrier walls to limit access. Over time the high locations were abandoned, and larger sites, including one of 750 rooms, were built on low ground, adjacent to the river. A major no-man's-land opened up between them and the cluster to the north around Albuquerque. Another no-man's-land appears to have developed south of the proto-Piro sites (Wilcox 1991) (Figure 6.19).

It has long been recognized that there was significant movement of population from the greater Mesa Verde area into the Rio Grande area. The evidence includes a string of sites with ceramics relating to the Mesa Verde area; they extended from the Rio Puerco in the north to Alamosa Creek in southern Socorro County and ranged in size from 40 to 500 rooms. All of them seem to have been abandoned rather early in the Pueblo IV period. While the sites may have been a stage in the movement of populations relocating into the valley proper, nevertheless, they represent an additional instance of the failure of groups to thrive outside the Rio Grande Valley.

Finally, the Largo-Gallina area is well known for its numerous burned sites, violent deaths, and defensive sites, including towers in particular. All of the sites seem to have been constructed in the 1200s, but the entire high-elevation area was abandoned by the late 1200s. Thus, the areas around the surviving Rio Grande core area were either significantly reduced in population or abandoned entirely.

The Southern Mogollon, Jornada, Casas Grandes, and Southeastern Arizona Areas

When attention shifts away from the Colorado Plateau, White Mountains, and the Rio Grande areas, the quality of archaeological information significantly diminishes. Almost all of the relevant large sites from late Pueblo III times and after on the Plateau are known. Similarly, surely almost all of

FIGURE 6.19
A Late Period site located on the hilltop far above the lower Rio Grande (Rio Abajo), New Mexico. Photo courtesy John Roney.

the Pueblo IV sites are known for the Rio Grande area. Even if a few sites have been overlooked, the patterns will not change. This is in large part because the sites were too large not to be found; many were of stone; and the pottery sequence is well worked out, establishing a reliable series of dates. This is not the case for the more southern areas—the southern Mogollon, Jornada, and Casas Grandes areas. These more southern sites were generally smaller, they were usually made of adobe (which disintegrates over time), and the ceramics did not allow for concise dating. In addition, very few sites in this region have tree-ring dates. Thus, it is difficult to find site clusters and to characterize them when they were found. What can be said is that there is considerable evidence for warfare in this southern area after A.D. 1300, and there is some evidence for the clustering of sites. But nothing in this region even begins to approach the clarity of patterns found in the north.

CASAS GRANDES

The role Casas Grandes played, along with its essential characteristics, may turn out to be key to understanding the entire southern area of the Southwest. It was certainly a very large and important site by the end of the 1200s and the early 1300s.[8] There are, basically, two models for its

8. There has been considerable debate on the dating of Casas Grandes (Wilcox and Shenk 1977; S. LeBlanc 1980; Wilcox 1986; Lekson 1984; Dean and Ravesloot 1988). I previously thought that it had declined by the early 1300s since there was a lack of late trade ceramics. However, given a better understanding of warfare and alliances, I no longer support that interpretation. I now believe Casas Grandes must have extended well into the 1300s; whether it also continued into the 1400s is debatable, but this issue is not central to the concerns here.

role in the region. One is simply that Casas Grandes was the center of a site cluster (Minnis 1989; Whalen and Minnis 1996), and had minimal impact beyond the cluster. The alternative model is that it was a regional center like Chaco and that there was a "Casas Grandes Interaction Sphere" with a continuous distribution of related sites extending out for 150 km or more (DiPeso 1974; Wilcox 1991). While this is not the place to debate the validity of these models, there is increasing evidence that the first is more accurate. In any case, there is nothing like the "*pax* Chaco" going on here during the Late Period. Rather, there is considerable evidence for warfare during the time of Casas Grandes.

Evidence for warfare at the site of Casas Grandes has been discussed by Ravesloot (1988) and Ravesloot and Sproel (1989). Their findings are repeated here for the purpose of discussion. First, and most obvious as evidence of warfare, was its destruction and abandonment. DiPeso (1974) found that of 576 individuals from the Medio Period (certainly part of my Late Period) recovered at the site, 127 were not formally buried and seemed to represent individuals killed at the very end of the occupation. While this statistic is well known, the implications have been generally ignored. Because both the buried and the unburied bodies represent only a sample of the total population of the site, it can reasonably be estimated that the entire population of the settlement—some 1,000 to 2,000 people—were killed. Casas Grandes may represent the greatest massacre—with the possible exception of Awatovi—that ever took place in the prehistoric Southwest.

I assume that the proportion of buried to unburied bodies at Casas Grandes is not biased, so the ratio of unburied to buried bodies can indicate what percentage of the extant population was killed in this event. DiPeso assumed that the annual death rate was 2.3 percent of the population. While this figure could be debated, it is a reasonable estimate to be used for determining the average extant population of the excavated portion of the site. If a Medio Period occupation of 150 years is assumed (most interpretations would have it be longer, so this assumption gives a maximal extant population), 449 burials with a 2.3 percent death rate gives a momentary population of 130 people in the excavated part of the site—almost identical to the 127 unburied bodies reported by DePeso. (An estimate based on floor area would give a larger figure using generally accepted ratios of people per square meter, but it is likely that Casas Grandes was like the big Chaco Canyon sites and had fewer people per square meter than was typical for the Southwest.) The obvious implication is that everyone in the community was killed and that the population then was not a fraction of its former peak, but was equal to the average population of the site over its existence. It is difficult to determine the proportion of the site excavated because the existence of an east plaza and eastern room blocks is in doubt. If they do not exist, then the extrapolated number of unburied bodies is around 1,000. If the size of the site is as DiPeso believed, then there were about 2,000 unburied bodies.

FIGURE 6.20
The House of the
Serpents at Casas
Grandes in Chi-
huahua, Mexico,
was probably one
of the earliest
buildings on the site
to have survived in
approximately its
initial configuration.
The structure had a
bastion corner in the
southeast, and several
sections jutted out
from the walls, which
would have provided
lines of fire along the
walls. Photo ©Baker
Aerial Archaeology,
transparency
19MX809C.

Other lines of evidence of warfare during the time frame of Casas
Grandes include skulls and other human bone used as trophies, as well as
several individuals who appear to have been injured by blows to the head
and died before the massacre. Also, several of the site's architectural features are indicative of warfare. For example, the early Mound of the Serpents, Unit 11, has a bastion corner as well as other angled exterior walls,
which would have facilitated defense (Figure 6.20).[9] Other structures at
the site have similar defensive features. The Cerro de Moctezuma site,
located about 7 km away, consisted of a tower on the top of a very high
hill, with a walled pueblo guarding the approach trail. The tower is still
standing 2.5 m high, with walls 2 m thick. While it could have served as a

9. A bastion is a corner or section of a wall that juts out beyond the rest of the wall. It
enables an archer to shoot along the axis of the wall at anyone trying to scale it—that is,
enfilading fire. The ability to shoot at someone from the side in this manner provides an
important military advantage since anyone attacking the wall will be exposed to fire from
two or even three directions. A bastion corner allows archers to shoot along either of the two
walls that form the corner. Bastions are used the world over, and are a hallmark of well-
planned defenses.

signaling tower, as DiPeso noted, this does not preclude its defensive role, as mentioned in chapter 2. The presence of a walk-in well at Casas Grandes is also of interest. Thus, at Casas Grandes, warfare was in evidence from the early occupation, during the occupation, and finally to its destruction. The question of who could have undertaken such a massacre is considered in chapter 7.

Southwestern New Mexico

In southwestern New Mexico, several site clusters have been dated into the 1300s. Some 80 miles (130 km) north of Casas Grandes was a cluster of sites in Hidalgo County and extreme southeast Arizona that may have formed one or more site clusters. That they interacted with Casas Grandes is clear; whether they were a competing polity is not clear. Some of these sites had plazas that were completely enclosed by rooms, and others had freestanding walls that probably completed the enclosure. Several of the sites had significant burning. One in particular, the Kuykendall site, with its 200-plus rooms, had both compounds and groups of rooms linked by freestanding enclosing walls and a walk-in well. The entire site was burned and then abandoned.

Another cluster, located near Cliff, New Mexico, had a mix of sites, some with massed rooms and some with plazas. One site had considerable burning, and almost all had in situ materials in nearly all of the rooms. A small number of late 1300s sites existed in the Mimbres Valley, but they were not a cluster. The largest of the Mimbres sites had a possible defensive layout, with freestanding walls joining some of the room blocks; but two smaller sites were single blocks of rooms of approximately thirty and twelve rooms, respectively. These were small sites, not tightly spaced, and not burned; they do not fit the pattern seen almost everywhere else in the Southwest. They were, however, rapidly abandoned, leaving in situ deposits (see Figure 6.26).

The difficulty is similar for interpreting the Jornada area and farther east (except for a few sites, such as the catastrophically destroyed Bloom Mound, which is discussed above). There is weak evidence for site clustering and burning in the Jornada area. Sites were generally small, were not defensively built, and they do not seem to represent patterns seen elsewhere. The pattern found here holds for much of the southern area: some evidence for warfare, but nothing to suggest it was as intense or the responses as predictable as what existed to the north.

PUEBLO VIEJO

The Gila River, near Safford, Arizona, in an area sometimes referred to as Pueblo Viejo, seems to have had a definite site cluster. There is good evidence for migrants from northern Arizona at some of these sites, an issue

FIGURE 6.21
Artistic reconstruction
of Reeve Ruin, San
Pedro River, Arizona.
Located on a high
point of land, the site
had not only a de-
fensive configuration
but also a freestanding
defensive wall at the
only point of access.
From DiPeso (1958),
courtesy of the
Amerind Foundation.

FIGURE 6.21
Artistic reconstruction
of Reeve Ruin, San
Pedro River, Arizona.
Located on a high
point of land, the site
had not only a de-
fensive configuration
but also a freestanding
defensive wall at the
only point of access.
From DiPeso (1958),
courtesy of the
Amerind Foundation.

that is considered in chapter 7. The very large Buena Vista site had multiple room blocks that seemed not to be linked together by freestanding
walls, and it is not clear whether they had enclosed plazas. Several other
sites in the Gila River area were composed of massive room blocks with
enclosed plazas. The small Goat Hill site had a circle of rooms that enclosed the summit of a knob; but, despite its very defensive nature, it had
evidence of much burning.

SAN PEDRO RIVER

To the east, there seems to have been a good cluster of sites along the
lower San Pedro River, slightly over 20 miles from the Tucson cluster.
Although it might be argued that the distances between river valleys would
dictate the spacing of clusters in the absence of warfare, the San Pedro
cluster was also about 30 miles from the Globe-Miami and the Casa Grande
clusters—for which it is harder to argue a geographically determined spacing. In the San Pedro area, there was a marked shift to defensive locations
and layouts from the preceding periods. According to Wallace and Doelle
(1997), "A number of the sites, including Flieger, Leaverton and High
Mesa are situated on the highest, most readily defended hill- or terrace-
tops in their vicinity. High Mesa is particularly dramatic in this respect.
Built atop a 67-m high terrace at the mouth of a major tributary canyon, it
is surrounded by sheer cliffs on three sides. At the narrow access point
from behind, a massive wall blocking access was constructed." The Reeve
Ruin was in a similar, but less spectacular, setting (DiPeso 1958). Situated
on the edge of a terrace spur, it had a compound wall and there was an
additional barrier wall across the spur (Figure 6.21). These San Pedro

villages were much smaller than those farther north, with fifty rooms considered a large site. Second Canyon Ruin, with a compound wall, but in a less defensible location, had only about twenty rooms; a major section of it had burned (Franklin 1980). As discussed in chapter 7, it has repeatedly been suggested that at least some of the residents of these San Pedro villages were immigrants, probably refugees from farther north. David Wilcox (personnal communication) feels that the Kayenta immigrant sites clustered within the overall group.

The difficulty with the entire preceding discussion on this portion of the southern Southwest is an incomplete knowledge of all the late sites. Certainly, other groups of sites existed that were not discussed, but it is not clear whether they were contemporary or earlier, comprised other clusters, or represented evidence for the absence of clusters in some areas. Nevertheless, in this southern area there certainly was some clustering of sites, and some sites were built with defense in mind, both in their configurations and settings. There is also considerable evidence for violence in the form of burning and unburied bodies. It is hoped that future work in this region will bring these patterns into sharper focus.

The Greater Hohokam Area

Various scholars have suggested that in the Hohokam area there is a notable increase in evidence for warfare during the Classic Period, essentially the late 1200s and 1300s (P. Fish and Fish 1989; Wilcox 1979, 1989; Rice 1998). This follows the initial evidence seen in the form of pit house burning at the end of the Sedentary period and immediately thereafter (A.D. 1100–1200), as discussed previously. There is, however, sharp disagreement over much of the possible evidence, especially site configurations. Nonetheless, there is direct evidence in the Hohokam for warfare, such as violent deaths and burned sites.

In the 1300s, the core Hohokam area apparently consisted of a major concentration of sites along the Salt River, around what is now the greater Phoenix area. To the south was a smaller group of sites centered on the Casa Buena site, and still farther southeast along the Gila River was another large concentration of sites in the neighborhood of Casa Grande. These areas were dominated by sites with adobe compounds, and the largest Hohokam sites consisted of multiple compounds. Each compound had rooms connected by freestanding walls, resulting in large rectangular structures. Inside some of the compounds were raised platform mounds (measuring anywhere from 2 to 4 m in height) with more rooms on top of them. The compound's walls generally provided an unbroken exterior wall with, in some instances, a narrow entryway on one side. The mounds themselves provided excellent views and could have functioned as keep-like strongholds. Taken as a whole, these compounds provided a level of de-

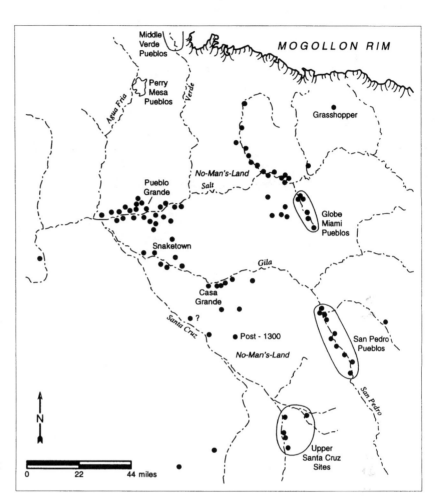

FIGURE 6.22
The distribution
of site clusters and
empty zones in central
Arizona, A.D. 1250–
1360. David Wilcox
defines this as the
Salado Macroregional
System. The number
of sites in each cluster
and the spacing
between them is quite
similar to what is seen
on the Colorado
Plateau. The largest
cluster, that on the
middle Salt, had about
the same number of
sites as the largest
Colorado Plateau
clusters, Hopi and
Zuni. Whether the
clusters had the same
number of people in
them as did their
Plateau conterparts is
not clear. After Wilcox
and Haas (1994).

fensive configuration very unlike the pit house villages that preceded them.

Outside the core Hohokam area, there is ample evidence of site clustering, defensive sites, burning, and unburied bodies. Along the northern fringe, sites became very defensive—located on hilltops or on the edges of steep mesas—in the Agua Fria and Verde Valley areas (see Spoerl 1984; Jeter 1977; Greenleaf 1975). The sites at Perry Mesa, which lies some 40 miles to the north of the major Classic Hohokam concentration on the Salt River, were good examples of defensive settlement locations. Similarly, the sites in the Tonto Basin and the Globe-Miami area provided ample evidence of the formation of clusters as well as significant amounts of burning, as previously discussed. This area was separated from the Hohokam core area by a buffer zone 25 miles across. To the south, another buffer zone about 25 miles wide opened up between the Hohokam sites centered on the Gila River and those in the Tucson area (Doelle and Wallace 1985; P. Fish and Fish 1989) (Figure 6.22).

FIGURE 6.23
The Shi-Kik *cerro de trincheras* site near Sells, Arizona. Photo courtesy of John Roney.

It is in the Late Period that, for the first time, there were numerous *trincheras* throughout the Hohokam area (Wilcox 1979; P. Fish and Fish 1989; S. Fish et al. 1984; Downum et al. 1994), and they present an interpretive problem. These terraced hillside sites extended from southern Arizona (Stacy 1974) into Sonora (Pailes 1980) and to the west of Casas Grandes in Chihuahua, Mexico (DiPeso 1974), although there they may have appeared earlier. *Trincheras* have a long history of being considered defensive (J. Hayden 1957; Fontana et al. 1959; DiPeso 1974; Spoerl 1984). Dave Wilcox (1979) persuasively argues for their having been defensive, but S. Fish et al. (1984) and Downum (1986, 1993) argue they were agricultural. Donald Dove (1970) felt a large *trinchera* on the lower Aqua Fria River was not defensive. One difficulty with the agricultural terrace argument is that many of these sites had terrace walls which were higher than needed to form farming terraces. Thus, these walls would have actually impeded farming access. This was probably the reason that Fewkes (1912a) argued that the walls at Frog Tanks Ruin, a northerly *trinchera*, were defensive features (Figure 6.23).

In Sonora, at least, some *trincheras* were habitation sites according to McGuire and Villalpando (1993), who do not seem to accept a defensive explanation for them. However, Sauer and Brand (1931) make an excellent argument for these Sonoran *trincheras* being defensive. Both Wilcox (1979) and S. Fish et al. (1984) note that villages in southern Arizona were often found on nearby flats, and Wilcox argues that *trincheras* served as a refuge in case of attack. The *trincheras* I have visited were certainly capable of providing defense, and given what is known about changes in warfare over the entire Southwest at the time they begin to appear, I believe the case for their being defensive is the stronger one (Figure 6.24).

FIGURE 6.24
The Trinchera Site in
Sonora, Mexico. The
concentric walls are
particularly clear on
this site. Photo
courtesy of John
Roney.

Thus, in the areas surrounding the Hohokam core area, there was evidence for a series of defensive sites, site clusters, broad no-man's-lands, major instances of burning, and unburied bodies. There is little doubt that people outside the core area were living in a state of significant warfare. The major issue is what was taking place within the Hohokam core area itself. There, the situation becomes much more equivocal.

There is some evidence for the formation of no-man's-lands within the core area, as mentioned in chapter 2. Most of this evidence is the existence of particular buffer zones, as discussed by Wilcox (1989), who provides the best regional perspective on this pattern. He also makes the case that it was the formation of such zones that can explain the abandonment of particular Classic Hohokam sites, such as Snaketown, Sacaton, Oldberg, Las Cremaciones, Van Liere, and the Cashion sites in the Salt and Gila river valleys (Wilcox and Haas 1994). The clearest example of a buffer zone was found between the Phoenix–Casa Grande group of sites and those centered on Tucson, where a 20-mile-wide no-man's-land opened up (Doelle and Wallace 1985; P. Fish and Fish 1989). In the Tucson area, Wilcox argues for a marked increase in defensive sites at this time (see Figure 6.22).

Because many of the Hohokam sites for this period were badly damaged or completely destroyed in the 1800s and early 1900s and because it is difficult to date sites in the low desert, the data are much less clear than they are for the Colorado Plateau. Nevertheless, it is quite clear that buffer zones did develop and were in existence over most of the area. And, certainly, a process of site abandonment and contraction of settlement clusters occurred here as well, even if it is harder to see.

Of particular interest—and especially difficult to study—is the possibility that a no-man's-land opened up between the Salt River sites and those on the Gila River. Between these major groups there were sites centered on Casa Blanca as well as small sites in the intervening areas. However, there was an 18-mile gap between the big sites in the Casa Blanca area and the large settlements on the Gila. Could this have been an evolving buffer zone and our temporal control too weak to see it developing? If not, then there may have been a massive group of allied sites stretching over 70 miles, from the Salt River to the Gila. If this is the case, it is unlike anything known for the 1300s in the entire Southwest. Such a large number of people would have dominated the entire Hohokam region, which is perhaps why the Perry Mesa cluster was so far away and the evidence for warfare so intense in the Tonto Basin. If this core group of sites held such a dominant position, there should be less evidence of warfare found within it. So long as it did not unravel politically, the group of sites would have had little to fear from outsiders.

In spite of this reasoning, there is evidence of violent deaths in the Hohokam center from La Ciudad (Wilcox 1987) and Los Colinas (Saul 1981). The evidence includes one body at Las Colinas with an embedded arrow point and two burials from La Ciudad with holes in their skulls, one with a piece of a stone ax in association. As Wilcox and Haas (1994) note, these individuals were buried in platform mounds, and only five such Hohokam mounds have ever been excavated. So, 40 percent of these mounds contained individuals that died violently.

But a more compelling issue is whether the Hohokam compounds were constructed for defense. During the interval A.D. 1150–1300, more than forty platforms were built on Hohokam sites. Beginning about A.D. 1250, the sites were surrounded by adobe compound walls, and other compounds were built that did not have mounds within them. The compound walls were high and thick, and entry was clearly restricted.[10] At Casa Grande, Pueblo Grande, La Cuidad, and possibly several other sites (Wilcox 1993b), there were very high tower-like buildings that were different from the platform mounds. In these instances, the first floor was entirely filled in with adobe, so there was no ground-level entry into the towers. Given the flat terrain, the view from all the mounds—and especially the tower-like structures—would have been very good. The towers at Pueblo Grande and Casa Grande had both burned. With a sample of only two such structures to evaluate, no firm conclusion can be drawn. However, both structures had very useful defensive features (especially good for signaling): entry was difficult (much more so than necessary from an architectural perspective), and they were enclosed by walls. That they had burned is another

---

10. At Pueblo de Los Muertos, one of the compound walls was seven feet thick. Glen Rice (personal communication) thinks that some of the compound walls in the Tonto Basin were wide enough to have served as fighting platforms and were not just barriers. It is difficult to find any other reason for such width, and the use of wide walls as fighting platforms is known from other parts of the world—in China, for example.

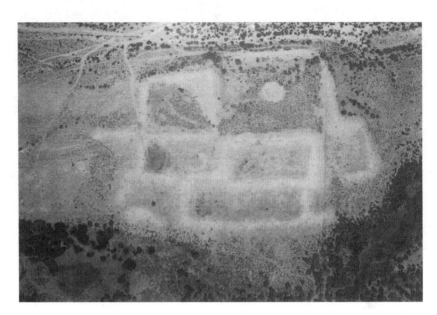

FIGURE 6.25
The Sapawe Site,
Chama Valley, a
very large site located
in a low area, near
water. Sites such as
Cerro Colorado
(Figure 2.5) and Kap
(Figure 2.6), also in
the Chama Valley,
were much smaller
and were positioned
more defensively.

indication of their defensive nature. In addition, according to Teague (1993), Piman accounts describe a great war involving these sites. She makes an excellent case that various accounts of this war are highly consistant and too accurate to be simply stories to account for the existence of the prehistoric sites in the area by later inhabitants. Moreover, the accounts make it clear that the combatants spoke the same language, and they imply that the victorious group originally lived on the Gila River and attacked and destroyed communities downstream on both the Gila and Salt Rivers, including such sites as Pueblo Grande, Pueblo de Los Muertos, and Casa Grande.[11]

It has not been a popular idea that these Hohokam compounds, tower-like structures, and mounds were built and used for defense, although early accounts of Casa Grande note its fort-like appearance. A temporal perspective adds credence to the proposition that warfare and the threat of it caused such structures to be built. Previously, at a time when there is

11. There are a number of accounts of this war, including Russell (1908) and Fewkes (1912b) who repeats some Pima historical descriptions of how these sites were destroyed: "At one time Casa Grande was beset by enemies who came from the east in several bodies." These various accounts also refer to intertribal war between the Pima of Sacaton and those of Casa Blanca. The difference between these accounts and the ones previously quoted for the Hopi and others are that the Hopi accounts discuss methods and consequences of warfare, and so their accuracy as to time and place need not be exact for them to be relevant. The Piman discussions about the warfare that destroyed Casa Grande and other sites are not so informative along these lines, which reduces their value for present purposes. There has been some debate whether the Pima in the area of the Casa Grande in the late 1800s were the direct descendants of the Hohokam, but Teague's (1993) argument about the accuracy of the accounts supports their historical derivation. It is not an issue of whether the oral tradition is describing historically known events but whether the level of detail limits their usefulness.

FIGURE 6.26
Kwellelekia Ruin,
Cliff, New Mexico,
dating to the late
1300s, consisted of
two room groups each
with a central plaza. It
was located very near
the Gila River and
may have had a walk-
in well. It was rapidly
abandoned with
artifacts left in situ.

little evidence for warfare, there was a period of everyone living in pit houses without palisades around them. Then, at a time when there is the first evidence for Hohokam warfare—as well as evidence for warfare elsewhere in the Southwest—mounds were built. Then, at a time when there is considerable evidence for warfare both in and outside the Hohokam area, adobe-walled compounds, many with platform mounds inside them, were built. And, at that point, some of the largest communities added structures that would have enhanced their defensive posture. The evolution of Hohokam compounds follows the same trajectory at the same time as the rest of the Southwest: an initial period of semidefensive construction that followed a long interval of no defensive construction; then the semidefensive construction being rapidly replaced by progressively more defensive construction. That the pattern existed in the Hohokam area seems not to be coincidental.

While it can be argued that not all the population could have lived in the compounds, that some of the platforms had earlier origins as ceremonial or special locations, and that the tower at Casa Grande had astronomical features (Wilcox and Shenk 1977), these factors do not eliminate the possibility of defensive uses. Unless it can be demonstrated that these structures were not for defensive purposes, the assumption should be that they were.[12]

David Wilcox (1989) has built an elaborate model of how Hohokam

12. An argument against the Hohokam compounds being defensive can be made by noting that these sites had many compounds. Combining into fewer, larger compounds would have provided more defense. However, it must be remembered that decisions as to the degree of risk versus the social and economic cost of defense were constantly made but were not always correct.

FIGURE 6.27
The Box S site, near
the Zuni site cluster,
was a large, five-sided,
inward-facing pueblo
located right next to a
small stream that
would have provided
a domestic water
supply.

warfare may have evolved related to changes in the social system. This is one of the few attempts by anyone working in the Southwest to construct a model for warfare. He hypothesizes that the collapse of the ball-court network was related to warfare and that the *trincheras* were another response, but that warfare may have been initiated before the time of significant conflict intensification, beginning in the late 1200s (as is proposed here). He sees intensification of Hohokam warfare as involving the rise of an elite and an increased social complexity, with intervillage social ties between the elite. Basically, he also sees much the same patterns as proposed here in that there was an increasing concentration of the population into fewer larger communities in fewer and fewer locations, with a concomitant decline in the efficiency and resiliency of the subsistence system (discussed in chapter 7). He proposes that such a system was fragile, would have been susceptible to climatic variability, and particularly would not have been able to survive the devastating floods that have been proposed for the A.D. 1350s in the Phoenix area. While there is nothing implausible about this model—and it may well have taken place—it is clear that warfare intensification was a pan-Southwestern phenomenon at this time and that it took place in much of the Anasazi area in the apparent absence of a significant increase in social complexity. Thus, Wilcox's model may illustrate how Late Period events played out in the Hohokam area, but the underlying causes must have been broader and more encompassing than what he proposes.

In summary, the Hohokam area presents the most enigmatic case for warfare in the Late Period. This does not mean that there is no evidence for warfare, just that patterns are not as clear as for other areas. The possibility that the core Hohokam area had a more complex social organization and larger population size than found anywhere else in the Southwest may have led to an asymmetric aspect to warfare not seen elsewhere in the entire region.

A SYNTHESIS OF LATE PERIOD WARFARE

The foregoing has been a review, on a topical basis, of the general evidence for the intensification of Late Period warfare in the prehistoric Southwest; the following is a discussion of the overall characteristics of several aspects of this warfare. Warfare was so intense during the Late Period that virtually everyone had to live in some type of fortress. And not only that, these fortresses also had to be situated in clusters for still more military advantage. The evolution of the settlement clusters helps in understanding the nature of the warfare at this time. That there was a significant advantage to maintaining large groups is seen in both the large size of individual sites and the existence of large groups of sites. Overall, there was a continual and concerted effort to keep the group sizes large. Also, there is the important question of whether there were people in the Southwest who were not part of the movement into large, defensive communities but who coexisted with those who did.

I am confident there was intense conflict during the Late Period, and, furthermore, I can broadly characterize the nature of this warfare. In particular, the acts of massive destruction and killing that have been documented for the Late Period go beyond what would occur in ordinary "raids." So-called hit-and-run raids occurred in the historic period, where two or three people were killed during quick attacks on villagers who had gone outside their pueblos. Certainly, the prehistoric instances of intensive burnings and the killing of numerous individuals at Salmon Ruin, Castle Rock, Sand Canyon Pueblo, Casas Grandes, or Te-ewi are not evidence of raids. Instead, these cases seem to represent a deliberate goal of killing off as much of the population as possible and often then burning the community as completely as possible. This behavior fits with conflict directed at eliminating competing groups, not just keeping them at bay. This level of conflict may have devolved into more limited-goal raids by the historic period, but initially it must have been much more purposeful and large-scale. (Incidentally, it is particularly difficult to reconcile this type of warfare with "nomad" raids.) It is against this backdrop of intense, annihilation-oriented warfare that we must look at the development of defensive settlements and settlement clusters.

Large Pueblos as Defensive Structures

In an earlier discussion on the defensive characteristics of Late Period settlements and settlement clusters, defensive sites in the Southwest were described as having two forms. The vast majority of all late habitation sites were "strongholds" or "forts." These settlements were intended for year-round habitation and were simply defensible villages or towns. However, there were a few sites that could be interpreted as likely "refuges," places the people could quickly move to when threatened, but which were not normally permanent settlements. Small hilltop sites, such as those in the Chevlon drainage (C. White 1976) and the Verde Valley (Pilles 1996) as well as some of the Hohokam *trincheras* (Wilcox 1979) are examples of refuges. These sites were so small and had so few associated artifacts, that they were probably only occasionally used. However, some of the larger *trincheras* in southern Arizona and Sonora seem to have been more permanent settlements, so the blanket characterization of *trincheras* as refuges is probably too simple.

Most of the people at this time resided in village sites that were permanent residences and could withstand a short siege or concerted attack. With secure domestic water supplies, stored food, and hundreds of defenders, the large walled villages or towns were excellent forms of defense. Moreover, the site clusters themselves can be thought of as strategic defenses. The sites were placed so as to be mutually supporting, and, not surprisingly, the larger and more well-integrated site clusters had the greatest survivability.

Key to understanding the evolution of both the villages and the clusters of villages was the need to keep the size of the group large. Even as the number of sites diminished in a given cluster of sites, the average size of the population did not decline. Rather, there seemed to be a continuous amalgamation of people to maintain the group size So, there were fewer sites, not smaller sites. The last site in the Silver Creek area—Fourmile Ruin—was the largest, as was Chavez Pass in the Anderson Mesa cluster. Similarly, Point of Pines was larger than Turkey Creek, which it outlived. The small Zuni Plateau sites, like Newton, or even Hole-in-the-Rock (Lookout), were abandoned before the biggest ones were. The small sites were either eliminated or amalgamated into larger sites.[13] This maintenance of large group sizes had very important implications for subsistence, nutrition, and social organization (a topic discussed in chapter 7). That the inhabitants of Fourmile Ruin or Point of Pines did not disperse is critical to understanding their adaptation. Equally critical is understanding why they did not disperse, since larger sites were more defensible.

The typical spacings of 4 to 5.5 km (2.5 to 3.5 miles) between sites in the settlement clusters were probably about as close as was practical. The

13. The only exceptions to the Late Period pattern of small sites being either eliminated or amalgamated into large sites were the late cliff dwellings in the Sierra Ancha and other areas off the Mogollon Rim. These small sites seem to have been relatively short-lived and may have been small population remnants of previously large communities. Group size may have been so small in these cases that there was no other choice but to live in very defensive cliff dwellings.

FIGURE 6.28
Pueblo Querencia, a
late 1200s site, was
located on a small
isolated mesa in the
eastern San Juan Basin
near San Isidro, New
Mexico. Photo
courtesy of the Bureau
of Land Mangement.

catchment areas for farming may have required such spacing in most cases, given the sizes of the communities. And, if the communities were participants in defensive alliances, then the spacing certainly makes sense. That is, the community spacing appears to have balanced the need to be close together for defense and the need to minimize travel distances to fields. Because there was room in the overall region for the sites to be more widely spaced, it seems likely that they would have located farther apart if they had been adversarial or if there had not been significant warfare. None of this implies that the particular locations of either the clusters or the sites within the clusters were not determined to some degree by the availability of resources. However, their locations were heavily constrained by the need for large spaces between clusters and for pueblos to be closely spaced within clusters.

Just what would have been the military benefit of having sites so close together? One benefit was line-of-sight visibility, which has been discussed. The closer the spacing, the greater the ability to help each other. If sites had been more dispersed, it would have been more difficult to communicate by signaling and it would have taken longer for supporting forces to reach a beleaguered pueblo. Thus, there is empirical evidence as well as theoretical reasons why the sites became so large and so closely spaced together. These patterns were being driven by military considerations, not subsistence needs. The military solution played havoc with the subsistence

FIGURE 6.29
Mesa Pueblo, a
late 1200s site, was
located on the top of
the mesa in the San
Juan Basin south of
Chaco Canyon. Photo
courtesy of John
Roney.

systems and probably caused major changes in the social organization. This
point cannot be stressed too strongly: The existence of these very large sites
that were clustered together was not "rational" from a subsistence point
of view. Their existence can only be understood as a defensive response.

The Evolution of Settlement Clusters

While it is easy to see *how* these clusters of settlements evolved, it is not
easy to see *why* the evolution worked the way it did. In summary, beginning after A.D. 1250, settlement clusters quickly formed over the entire
Southwest. Over time, the number of clusters declined and the number of
sites in each surviving cluster also declined. And there were some trends in
this process: Small clusters located between big clusters died out earlier
than big clusters. Clusters with few sites often quickly declined to just one
site, which may have lasted for some time before disappearing. And only
Acoma and Pecos had survived as single-site clusters by the 1540s. It appears that the size of the sites and their number in an initial cluster of sites,
as well as the location of the group with respect to other groups, were all
relevant to a cluster's survival.

Every Pueblo IV cluster on the Colorado Plateau, as well as most of the
other clusters, apparently experienced this evolution, although not at
the same time. The clusters died out at different times. The change was

greatest from A.D. 1250 to 1325, when most of the aggregation into big sites took place. Then, almost immediately, sites and settlement clusters began to die out and continued to do so until A.D. 1400. Small clusters—such as at the Hopi Buttes, Silver Creek, Petrified Forest, Techado, the Lower Rio Puerco of the east, Cebollita Mesa, the Chuska slope, and the Upper Rio Puerco—either died out early or contracted to just one site. It appears that most of the clusters were gone after the mid-1350s in the northern Southwest, with the remaining clusters down to one large site—such as Chavez Pass, Fourmile, Kinishba, Point of Pines, and Acoma. The two largest clusters, however, those at Hopi and Zuni, survived.

In the Rio Grande Valley, the pattern was the same, except that the initial clusters were generally larger than those on the Colorado Plateau. That is, there were more large clusters in the Rio Grande Valley and more of them survived there than elsewhere. Over the Colorado Plateau and Rio Grande Valley, Acoma and Pecos seemed to be the only communities that survived as single entities; all others appeared to be involved in alliances at some level. In the southern Southwest, the process was much the same, except the pattern seemed to start somewhat later and took longer to play out. Southern clusters—such as Pueblo Viejo, Cliff, and the Tonto Basin—declined, often became just one site, and then died out. But, they did last close to, or into, the 1400s before disappearing.

The important point is that in a great many instances, the formation of a site cluster and its evolution were not successful. Most of the initial twenty-seven clusters on the Colorado Plateau and the immediately surrounding areas—and an almost equal number elsewhere in the Southwest—did not survive. Why did so few survive? That is a critical question. The answer is best looked for on the Colorado Plateau because of its better data. With the exception of a minor settlement location shift at Zuni, and a possible more major one at Acoma, the three surviving settlement clusters on the Colorado Plateau were located in the same places at 1540 as they were at 1300. Yet, the intervening cultural landscape had changed dramatically. The number of clusters had continuously declined, and the size of no-man's-lands had grown over time. The initial 20 miles (30 km) between clusters had increased on the Colorado Plateau to 80 miles (130 km). The change in the Rio Grande Valley was less dramatic, but the trend was the same.

What possible environmental reason could there have been for such large no-man's-lands? The situation along the Little Colorado River is a case in point. From present-day Springerville downstream to the Winslow area, the Little Colorado was available for habitation. Surely, somewhere along this gradient of 185 miles (300 km) in length and 2,000 feet (625 m) in elevation there must have been a reasonably good farming zone, regardless of the climate. There was nothing about the Zuni River area, just to the east, that would have been more favorable for farming than some stretch along the Little Colorado River. Yet, the Little Colorado was abandoned and the Zuni River continued to be occupied. A host of similar arguments could be made for the other extinct clusters. The explanation lies not in ecological factors, but in political factors. It must have been the relationships between clusters that led to some surviving and others declining.

It is relatively easy to understand why large site clusters would want to—and did—form large buffer zones around themselves. But, why, for example, would the Zuni feel threatened by a few small sites some 55 km (35 miles) away along the Little Colorado? Could these relatively small communities really have been competing for resources to the point where it necessitated getting rid of them? Wouldn't it have been better to trade with them? If they were allied with the Zuni—which would have been sensible by A.D. 1400—why did these Little Colorado sites die out?

This brings up the related question: Why would hostilities continue when there was so much space between alliance groups? What could Hopi and Zuni have been competing for? While it is reasonable to see interpueblo fighting in the late 1200s and the very early 1300s as caused by resource competition, by A.D. 1350—and certainly by A.D. 1540—it makes no sense from the resource competition perspective. Of course, it isn't that it did *not* make sense, just that the reasons are not obvious. It is clear that warfare played a critical role in the relationships between the pueblos, but the development and evolution of these relationships is extremely complex and not simply a response to warfare and the threat of attack. Remember that the Quechans traveled twice the distance between Hopi and Zuni to attack the Maricopa. They thought they had a good reason to do this, even if it is not obvious to us.

The Military Advantage of Settlement Clusters

From a purely military perspective, the formation of settlement clusters was an important aspect of providing defense and conducting warfare. It is generally considered necessary to have a two-to-one or three-to-one numerical advantage in attacking a well-defended position. In addition, the attacking force must leave at home a backup defensive force to guard against a concurrent counterattack or an attack from a third quarter. Thus, it would have been definitely advantageous for a site to have the largest population of any cluster and the greatest cohesion of that population. A great military advantage could be achieved by combining combatants from multiple sites into one attack force and by ensuring mutual support between the "stay behind" defenders. A cluster of ten sites could leave a comfortably large defending force behind and still have an attack force that would adequately outnumber the defenders of clusters of only two to four sites. This seems to be exactly what happened. The largest initial clusters—Hopi, Zuni, and Acoma—survived; all others on the Colorado

Plateau eventually disappeared. Where clusters of roughly equivalent sizes existed—such as in the Rio Grande Valley—none of them seemed to dominate, and most of them continued to survive.

So, the defensive nature and spacing of the pueblos must have been part of the military equation. For example, each El Morro Valley site may have averaged about 700 people, and 160 of these would have been combatants.[14] The locations of these sites would have meant that men from nearby pueblos would have time to assist in case of an attack on any site in the cluster. If such a pueblo could be defended by 60 combatants—plus the remaining adults—until help arrived, that would leave 100 men who could travel to attack elsewhere or help defend another pueblo that was being attacked. Any single pueblo that was attacked could then expect the other four to five pueblos in its cluster to provide a total of 400 to 500 men to help with its defense. Any attacking force would need to contend with at least 60 men on the inside of the pueblo and 400-plus men on the outside—or a similar combination. The number of men necessary to attack a large cluster of large sites successfully would have been enormous. The military advantage in being a large cluster is very great and is a well-documented facet of nonstate warfare—for example, in New Guinea where the largest groups were more often the victors (Meggitt 1977). In the Southwest, this advantage probably related to the known historical cases of the willingness of the Hopi to accept outside groups that moved into the Hopi area in spite of the limited subsistence resources available to them.

Another method of warfare in which large clusters would have provided a military advantage involved harassing tactics, such as laying waste to enemy fields. If crops could be successfully destroyed, even a few times in close succession, the enemy could be defeated by starvation without the need to storm the pueblo. An attacking force could win by attrition if it could keep the inhabitants holed up in their "fort" and then destroy their fields. However, such an attacking force, unless it was extremely large, would be vulnerable to attack by overwhelming numbers from the allied pueblos in the target's cluster. That is, an effective site cluster would make such harassing tactics very dangerous. Large clusters could certainly harass small clusters, but not the reverse.

Was Everyone Involved in Warfare?

While a lot is known about Late Period warfare, the question remains whether all groups in the Southwest during this time range were involved in warfare. There are two possible situations to be considered. The first is the potential existence of small farming communities that were located

---

14. C. Lange (1978) provides what is probably a good estimate of about 23 percent of a total population being available as combatants.

FIGURE 6.30
The Citadel Ruin in
Wupatki National
Monument, Arizona,
covers a small butte
and is very defensivly
configured.

outside the warfare sphere. Could they have coexisted with the large defended sites? The second possibility is the presence of nonsedentary foragers who lived in the areas between the large pueblos.

There does not seem to be evidence of small, nondefensible sites, inhabited by pottery-using farmers, once the big pueblos came into existence.
However, there are two apparent exceptions to this statement. First, not
all big sites came into existence at the same time; for example, there were
small, nondefensible sites in the southern Mogollon Rim area after there
were none farther north. But, once the big pueblos were built in a particular area, all other sites soon became either big or very defensive. The second exceptional situation involves areas where there were no big sites at
all. Portions of the old Mimbres area and the Jornada area seemed to have
significant locations where the biggest sites consisted of only twenty to
thirty rooms. For whatever reasons, the populations there did not move
into a few large sites. Nevertheless, throughout the Southwest, there do
not seem to be any examples of areas where large defensive sites were
established and small, nondefended sites continued to be used for any
length of time. There were, however, "field houses" for use during the
farming of agricultural plots that were some distance from the large habitation sites.

It has been suggested that there were small sites contemporary with the
large sites in the Silver Creek area (K. Lightfoot 1984b) and around the
Chavez Pass sites (Henderson 1979). These assessments were all made on
the basis of surface sherds, with no fine-grained dating of either the big or
small sites and no careful tests for minor differences in pottery type frequencies between them. Given what is known about the evolution of sites,
first, into loose clusters, and then the rapid shift to large sites in the Kayenta

TABLE 6.3.
Sites, A.D.1250–1450, outside the Colorado Plateau and White Mountains that Have Evidence for Burning and/or Unburied Bodies. (Terminology is the same as for Table 6.2.)

Cluster - Site	Burning	Unburied Bodies - Number	Reference
Greater Tonto Basin			
Gila Pueblo	extensive	70+	McKusick 1992
Togetzoge		2 unburied bodies, 3 violent deaths	Hohmann and Kelley 1988
Cline Terrace	extensive		Glen Rice, personal communication
Indian Point	extensive		Glen Rice, personal communication
U:4:9	significant		Glen Rice, personal communication
U:3:128	significant		Glen Rice, personal communication
School House Point	significant		Glen Rice, personal communication
U:8:530	significant		Glen Rice, personal communication
Ash Creek U:3:49	significant	10	Hohmann et al. 1985b
Meredith Ranch Site (VIV Ruin)	extensive	some bodies	J.Mills and Mills 1975
Verde Valley			
Montezuma's Castle	significant: Unit A		Wells and Anderson 1988
Chama Area			
Palisade	very extensive		Peckham 1959, 1981
Riana	very extensive		Hibben 1937
Kap (Leaf Water)	significant		Luebben 1953
Te'ewi	significant	24 men, 6 infants	Wendorf 1953; Reed 1953
Poshu	significant		Jeançon 1923
Tsama	significant		Beal 1987
Ku	significant		Beal 1987
Pesede	significant		Jeançon 1912
Pecos			

Cluster - Site	Burning	Unburied Bodies - Number	Reference
Arrowhead	significant		Holden 1955
Southern Tiwa			
Kuaua	significant		Dutton 1963
Other Rio Grande			
Pueblo de Las Humanas		2	Hayes 1981
Pot Creek	extensive	present, at least 1 adult and 1 child	Wetherington 1968
Arroyo Hondo	some	11 bodies, 25 skulls	Palkovich 1980
Rio Abajo			
Pueblo de Arena	significant	?	Marshall and Walt 1984
Pueblo Viejo - Safford			
Buena Vista (Curtis Site)	significant	present	J.Brown 1974; J.Mills and Mills 1978
Fort Thomas			Bandelier 1892
Goat Hill	some		Woodson 1995
Lower San Pedro			
Second Canyon	extensive		Franklin 1980
Reeve Ruin	significant		DiPeso 1958
Animas - SE Arizona			
Clanton Draw	extensive		McCluney 1962
Box Canyon	some		McCluney 1962
Kuykendall	extensive		J.Mills and Mills 1969
Joyce Well	some		McCluney 1965
Cliff			
Dinwiddie	about half		J.Mills and Mills 1972
Other sites			
Paloparedo	significant		DiPeso 1956
Bloom Mound	extensive	ca. 30	Wiseman 1970

and Zuni areas—and apparently in the Grasshopper area as well—the proposed Silver Creek and Chavez Pass examples of contemporary big and small sites are not likely to prove correct.

A small site's lack of viability, once warfare became intense, can even be seen in the historic period. The Zuni, in particular, tried repeatedly to establish outlying villages in the historic period. But they never lasted due to frequent attacks by Athapaskans (T. Ferguson and Hart 1985; Quam 1972). There is no evidence of small villages being established in the 1300s or 1400s; they were as dangerous in the historic period as they had been in the Late Period. Wilcox (1978) has suggested that field houses came into use as a response to this problem: a compromise between establishing small, vulnerable sites and "commuting" from a large pueblo every day.

This lack of viability is often lost on those who try to interpret the evolution and abandonment of small sites. A good example is a suite of sites that included the Shoofly site near Payson, Arizona. This cluster consisted of four moderately sized sites, with small "hamlets" positioned around each of the largest sites in the cluster. The major sites of the group were located from 2 to 4 miles apart, and the group as a whole was 30 to 40 miles from clusters at Perry Mesa, the Verde Valley, Chavez Pass, and the Q-Ranch site of the Grasshopper cluster. These clusters seemed to outlive the Payson cluster by quite a bit, and the latter's abandonment was probably related to the formation of no-man's-lands between the other clusters.

Excavations were carried out on the fifty- to sixty-room Shoofly site, which consisted of a cluster of isolated rooms and small room groups that were enclosed by a surrounding wall (Redman 1993). The site was situated in a flat, nondefensible area. A significant portion of the site had burned, and it had been abandoned around 1225–1250. Three other larger sites in this group lasted somewhat longer; they were on the tops of hills or ridges with very good views. They seemed to consist of more massive groups of rooms than the Shoofly site, but none numbered more than 100 rooms.

Redman discounts or ignores the possibility of warfare as an explanation for the demise of these sites, but given their locations and configurations, their development and abandonment fit well with the patterns that repeatedly show up at this time. These sites seem to be a classic example of the shift to a moderately defensive posture that occurred widely over the Southwest in the early 1200s. I propose the following descriptive model of the evolution of this group of sites in the Payson area. The distance between the four sites was the same as the spacings between sites of many clusters at around this time. Each of the largest sites that was situated with a good view was surrounded by smaller sites. Then, one of the four largest sites that did not have some defensive aspect to its location was enclosed by a wall. This least defensible site burned and was abandoned, while the more defensible ones lasted another generation or so. However, this was a time when sites of even a hundred rooms were not viable and when alliances and no-man's-lands were developing. This cluster was situated in an area that became one of the buffer zones between larger site clusters, and so was abandoned. Thus, there were four sites that formed an incipient alliance, and the members began the process of increasing settlement defensibility. One site was burned, presumably due to an attack that was not repulsed because of the small size of the cluster's total population—it had not been possible to form a really large site that was the military equivalent of adjacent clusters. Either the three remaining sites were attacked and destroyed or the people migrated into one of the alliances that were forming around them. While this model is by no means demonstrated, it does account for much of what is known about Payson area sites and it places the sites in a regional context. This model rejects the possibility that these small sites could have remained untouched by the increased warfare that was taking place around them.

Also relevant to the overall question of whether all groups were involved in Late Period warfare is the idea, put forth by Upham (1984), of the possible existence in the very late prehistoric period of numerous people who lived, not as settled farmers, but as more mobile foragers. At the end of the Late Period, at about the time of Spanish contact, could there have been significant populations of nonfarmers who lived in the large spaces between the pueblos? And could not these foraging "nomads" have been the adversaries of the Pueblo people rather than other Puebloans? The strongest piece of evidence for this theory is the early historical statement by Antonio de Espejo in 1583 (Hammond and Rey 1966):

> The mountains thereabout [the vicinity of Acoma] apparently give promise of mines and other riches, but we did not go to see them as the people from there were many and warlike. The mountain people come to aid those of the settlements, who call the mountain people Querechos.

The response to this idea of nomads requires that several points be made. First, Coronado, forty years earlier, made no statements similar to Espejo's. Chronicles of Coronado's expedition mention empty zones, *despoblados*, but there are no references to nomads until the Plains are reached. Now, 1583 was not 1540, and it was certainly not 1350. Extrapolating back more than 200 years on the basis of Espejo's statement (or others of that time range) without independent lines of evidence is unwise. There is also some question about the meaning of this passage. There are no mineralized mountains near Acoma. It is located on a sandstone plateau. The nearest mountain is Mount Taylor, more than 30 miles away; the nearest mining area on the west side of the Rio Grande Valley is south of Magdalena, over twice that distance, and the Zuni Mountains, which do have copper, are equally far away. Just what was meant by "thereabout"?

The idea that there were communities—whose inhabitants did not farm or use pottery—large enough to have threatened the pueblos is in no way demonstrated. In fact, there is no site information to support it. If there were such communities in these areas throughout the Late Period, their inhabitants would have been so few that they most likely would have been used by the pueblos as spies, scouts, and auxiliaries, as the above passage suggests. And they would not have been enough of a military threat to have produced the results for which there is so much evidence.

CONCLUSION

The Late Period, beginning in the mid-1200s, ushered in several centuries of intense warfare in the Southwest. The most dramatic evidence for this increasing conflict, and its most enduring legacy, was the movement of people into large, compact communities termed "pueblos" by the Spaniards. The primary rationale for these pueblos was defense: They were walled towns. However, movement into pueblos alone was not sufficient for safety, and the pueblos then were clustered into mutually supporting groups. Archaeologically, it is possible to determine how these groups of pueblos formed and the reasons why they did or did not survive.

The underlying cause for intense Late Period warfare was probably a marked deterioration in the climate. This climatic change was so severe that farming was discontinued over much of the Southwest, and most of the pueblos and settlement clusters did not survive for long. However, those that did survive were socially and politically transformed by this process, a topic considered in the next chapter.

CHAPTER SEVEN

SOCIAL AND POLITICAL CONSEQUENCES OF LATE PERIOD SOUTHWESTERN WARFARE

In time their journey eastward led them to plains in the midst of which were great heights with large towns built upon them. The fields were many and the possessions of these people were abundant. . . . And so the ancients, the Ashiwi [Zuni], hungry from long wandering, gave them battle.

Now these people of the highland and cliffs were . . . allied to the Akakakwe, the People of Acoma. . . . Ancient Warrior Woman led the enemy with shrill cries . . . heedless of wounds to her body, [she] ran back and forth in front of her army shrieking and shaking her rattle. . . . The Two War Gods [Zuni gods] sought the counsel of the Sun Father . . . and the knowledge came to them that her heart was carried in her rattle. . . . [T]he elder War God . . . aimed his arrow and piercing her rattle, saw [the Ancient warrior Woman] fall dead. In panic her people fled the pursuing Ashiwi. . . . [T]hey found survivors [enemies hidden in the captured town] . . . . As these survivors were wiser and more comely that the common man, they spared them, and received them into the clan of the Black Corn. . . . [A]t first these people were wild of tongue.

—*War with the Black People, The Mythic World of the Zuni, as Written by Frank Hamilton Cushing* ([1896] 1988:89–90)

Unquestionably, the pervasiveness and level of warfare in the Late Period had interesting consequences on the evolution of trade, population movements, dietary needs of the people, the formation of alliances, and the development of social complexity. Some of the consequences probably also pertain to earlier times, but the situation is so much clearer in the Late Period that it is the focus of attention in this chapter. While many of the topics have been considered previously by other scholars, reexamining them in light of an environment of intensive warfare is instructive. Haas (1990) has reviewed ideas about the role of warfare in terms of social-structure evolution, and they need not be repeated. The purpose here is to consider other relevant topics.

Given the economic level of prehistoric Southwest communities, it seems unlikely one group would have had a major technological advantage over another for any extended period of time. Similarly, all of the communities were probably capable of training boys to fight, bringing them up to roughly the same levels of military skill. However, there certainly could have been major differences in the level of leadership available at the various settlements. The groups who were able to provide strong intercommunity leadership and to integrate large numbers of people into their social structures would have had a distinct advantage. Furthermore, the settlement clusters that were able to attract and assimilate other groups would have had the advantage of greater numbers. Thus, the evolution of social mechanisms designed to provide good leaders and large populations would have been necessary, and it follows that effective social changes must have occurred among the successful groups. Also, the competitive milieu caused by intense warfare would have stimulated a rapid development of social adjustments. This is an underlying thread that should be borne in mind relative to all aspects of the Late Period.

Population Movements and Abandonments

A unique aspect of the late Pueblo III and early Pueblo IV period is the level of migration that must have taken place (see S. LeBlanc, in press). Nothing like it seems to have occurred previously. Vast areas of the Southwest were abandoned—including the Kayenta (except for Hopi), Mesa Verde, and central San Juan Basin areas—and then ultimately much of the remainder of the Colorado Plateau and all of the mountain Mogollon area. Many major long-distance migrations have been recognized, in addition to the famous example at Point of Pines (Haury 1958), which involved a movement of people from the Kayenta area into south-central Arizona. Clearly, people also moved from the Kayenta area to a variety of other locales in central and southern Arizona (Lindsay 1987; Franklin and Masse 1976; DiPeso 1958; Woodson 1995). The Kayenta migrants settled in areas along the San Pedro and Gila Rivers, and B. Mills (1995) provides another example of their settling north of the Mogollon Rim in the Silver Creek area. Stark et al. (1995) persuasively argue for migration into the Tonto Basin in the 1300s, but it is not clear whether the people came from the Kayenta area; they well may have come from higher elevations in the Mogollon area. The Grasshopper site apparently had at least two ethnic groups, including one derived from the Anasazi area, living in the pueblo— a determination based on forms of skull deformation (Reid 1989).

Farther east, there was movement from the Mesa Verde, Totah, and San Juan Basin areas to the Rio Grande area (Ford et al. 1972). Emma Lou Davis (1964) made a good case for a series of sites populated by people derived from the Mesa Verde area existing along the western margin of the Rio Grande Valley (from the Rio Puerco in the north, south to the mountains above Socorro) (see also Roney 1995; Bertram et al. 1990). After a brief time period, the people in these sites then apparently migrated into the Rio Grande Valley proper (see the Appendix). Watson Smith

(1971) tentatively suggested, based on the ceramics, that there may have been a movement of people from the eastern Anasazi area to Awatovi.

Shorter migrations are suspected to have occurred from such places as the Homolovi sites to Hopi and the Upper Little Colorado River sites to Zuni, although they have not been demonstrated archaeologically. The significant presence of Gila Polychrome pottery at Table Rock Pueblo in the Upper Little Colorado and at Hawikuh probably represents some aspect of population shifts. After A.D. 1400, the movement of people seemed to slow down, and there was much greater stability for the next century or so. This may well be because the successful adaptations and relationships had been worked out and the level of warfare had diminished.

Other examples of what might be long-distance moves are more enigmatic. Based on their architecture, some sites seem very intrusive. For example, the circular pueblo under Mound 7 at Gran Quivera (Hayes 1981) had a bonding and abutting pattern executed in the "ladder" style (see Roney 1996c; Watson et al. 1980). This construction detail is almost identical to that found at sites in the El Morro Valley, the Acoma area, and elsewhere, but it is quite foreign to the Rio Grande valley. These rare and distinctive sites must represent something more than a casual copying of architectural forms.

All these examples of migration may be only one end of a continuum that represents a much broader social process. Separating long-distance migration from shorter moves may not be the best way to view this phenomenon. Migrations of great distances can be recognized by obvious material culture differences between the newcomers and the resident populations. Short-range movements are much harder to recognize, but are potentially as important as long-range movements to various aspects of social organization. Population movement would be socially significant if it resulted in people living in immediate proximity to others they had not previously lived near and, if by moving, they gave up use rights to land and abandoned traditional shrines, cemeteries, and other links to their past. Such a move would have been significant regardless of whether the migration covered a distance of 20 miles or 200.

Viewed in this way, it is clear that most of the Anasazi population embarked on significant migrations between A.D. 1275 and 1325. And, as repeatedly mentioned, small sites were abandoned, with only large sites surviving; but as the number of sites diminished, the site size did not decline. The implication is that there was a perceived need to keep Late Period community sizes large. In many, if not most, cases this must have been accomplished by combining groups that had previously been autonomous. So, if site size, site configuration, and site locations were being heavily dictated by warfare, then warfare also played a major role in how these displaced populations ultimately articulated.

There may be evidence for some of the less dramatic, short-distance population movements, and it takes several forms. One line of evidence

FIGURE 7.1
Aerial view of the two large pueblos Atsinna and North Atsinna on top of El Morro Rock in New Mexico. This site pair had a clear view of other sites in the cluster. Photo ©Baker Aerial Archaeology, transparency 19EM939.

can be seen in the configuration of a number of sites or communities where there were two separate but adjacent large-room groups or where there may have been a partial fusion of groups into one site. This "site pairing" was clearly evident in the Cienega and Mirabal sites; the North Atsinna and Atsinna sites at El Morro; Bidahochi South and Southwest, in the Hopi Buttes cluster; the Pescado Springs group along the Zuni River; the two room groups at both the Q-Ranch and Grasshopper sites; the multiple large-room groups at Kinishba; and the pair of Chavez Pass sites. These sites were very large (the smallest had several hundred rooms), and yet they were situated a maximum of a few hundred meters apart—often even less—instead of the more typical spacing of about 3 miles between sites (Figure 7.1).

In other instances, two communities seem to have combined incompletely, as at the Kin Tiel, Kluckhohn, and (perhaps) Newton sites. In these cases, two room groups were attached, but in such a way that the identity of each group was architecturally visible. It appears that the groups combined, but did not submerge their identities. For example, at the Kluckhohn site a circular and a rectangular room block were attached, but each was clearly distinctive. In the case of Kin Tiel, Mindeleff's site plan (1891) shows a generally circular site with one small section left open and a second circular site appended onto it in such a way that the unfinished portion of the first circle provided an opening into the second circle (Figure 7.2). Certainly, from a defensive point of view the communities were combined,

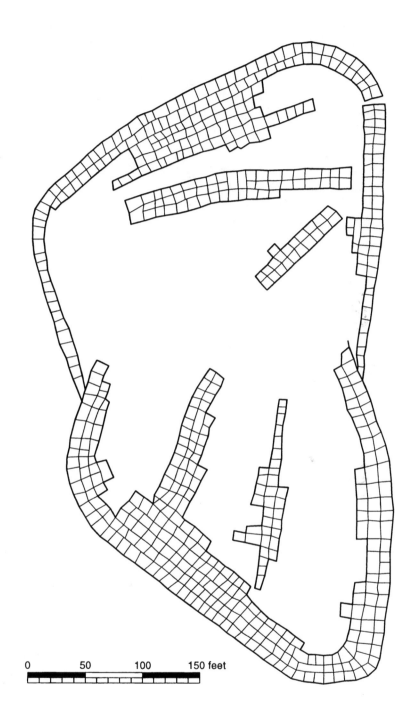

FIGURE 7.2
Map of Kin Tiel
Pueblo based on
one made by Victor
Mindeleff in the
1890s [BAE 8].
The plan seems to
indicate the partial
merging of two
basically circular sites.

0   50   100   150 feet

but from a social point of view they remained somewhat distinctive. Sites with multiple plazas, found in the Rio Grande Valley and elsewhere, may simply have reflected the same process, with the architecture not distinctive enough to show the group differences.

Sometimes it appears that a "hybridization" took place in cases where two or more groups combined into one site, but the site sections had distinctive architectural signatures, and in cases where there were close, but separate sites. Even where there were separate sites, the communities would have been so close that there must have been an overarching organization to adjudicate land tenure and so on. Interestingly, between the closely spaced Cienega and Mirabal sites, there was a large circular construction sometimes called an "unroofed Great Kiva," which was apparently a form of public architecture shared by both groups, supporting the idea that they were integrated at some level.

The same phenomenon of joining forces but not submerging identities must also have occurred in many massive sites where there was no architectural distinctiveness to the various groups of rooms. In many of these cases, the number of people in the new, larger community was much greater than the previous population in the immediate area before the construction of the site. While it cannot be demonstrated from the site plans, many people from outside an area must have migrated in to account for the large number of people residing in some sites.

In many cases, there is evidence for an initial group of people abandoning a location where a large town was later built (Watson et al. 1980; R. Lightfoot 1984b; Henderson 1979; Graves et al. 1982). Wherever there are good survey data, there never seemed to be as many people in the previous, dispersed community as were later found in the new, bigger site. In virtually every case, the big sites seemed to represent an aggregation of people who had previously lived at much greater distances from each other. When a group of people moved far enough away from its original location so that the previously used farmland was no longer convenient and then moved into an established place where others were currently farming— even if the two groups spoke the same language, had been exchanging marriage partners, etc.—it would have been necessary to reallocate farmable land and make other social adjustments. Researchers refer to these migrants as a "nonlocal population." Many of the new, large communities must have included nonlocal people, requiring some degree of social integration, even if their moves had involved only short distances.

If a significant number of the large, late Pueblo III and Pueblo IV sites on the Colorado Plateau represent nonlocal population aggregation, then this is even more the case for many of the Rio Grande sites. In some instances, such as in the Chama area, the new sites could not have been formed from the previous resident population because there were far too few people in the area prior to the formation of the large pueblos (Beal

1987). Some sites, such as Puye or Tyuonyi, had one central plaza, while other sites of about the same size, such as Sapawe, had multiple plazas. Because Sapawe, which is located in the Chama area, must have been formed from immigrant groups, it is possible that its multiple plazas resulted from people who were related in some way and who wanted to retain some form of group identity.

In virtually all the cases of these big, late pueblos, the goal seemed to be to accommodate many people living very close together. Certainly, various groups settled on a variety of solutions, from one massive site, to sites imperfectly merged, to unjoined sites adjacent to each other. Regardless of the final choice, within the fifty years between A.D. 1275 and 1325, almost all of the people living on the Colorado Plateau and in the Rio Grande Valley migrated or moved into new communities with new structures and much greater sizes. In each area, there are examples of the time it took for the resultant population integration to work out. Over the space of a generation or two, virtually the entire population of the Southwest came to live in new communities, requiring the migrants to make a significant break with the past. This is the point made by Bernardini (1996), who argues for the disruptive effects on "previous social contracts of land tenure, resource distribution, and status." He also notes settlements were generally larger and might have strained existing social mechanisms. There seems to have been no other time in the prehistoric Southwest when anything like this dramatic shift in settlement size and population relocation took place so quickly.

Given the social difficulties (discussed below) and the subsistence problems created by this aggregation, there must have been tremendous motivation for these people to move about and form such large communities. The most plausible explanation for such motivation is the outbreak of intense warfare. It would have been an extremely difficult time in which to live, what with the strains of relocation and new community structures combined with the threat—and very real consequences—of war. This fifty-year interval, which must have been very traumatic, may have set the stage for dramatic changes in the Southwest's social institutions. As Scudder (1993) has found with modern-day communities, compared to an area's long-term residents, relocated populations are more open to and inventive about new economic, as well as social, changes. In the Late Period Southwest, social and economic changes such as the rapid adoption of irrigation and use of rock mulch gardens[1] in the Rio Grande area and the overall acceptance of the Kachina cult may have been a result of this phenomenon of flexibility in crisis.

1. A rock mulch garden is the practice of carpeting the ground surface with small rocks in farming plots to reduce evaporation and collect morning dew, increasing the productivity of the plot (see D. Lightfoot and Eddy 1995).

Alliances

Clearly, as indicated by both archeological and ethnographical evidence, the Late Period site-based community was not the only level of community integration: There were integrated groups of sites. This point is convincingly made for the Western Pueblo area by Upham (1982) and for larger areas by Wilcox (1981a, 1991, 1996). It is equally clear from the Spanish accounts that in the Rio Grande area groups of sites were allied in certain ways and the alliances almost always had a linguistic aspect. Wilcox (1984) suggests the term "ethnic alliance" for each cluster. However, the term "alliance" has not always been used this way in this context. Upham and Reed (1989) review the meaning of the term and conclude that an alliance is *between* settlement clusters not *within* settlement clusters. However, I use the term to refer to relationships between the *sites* within a cluster.

Katherine Spielmann (1994) cites the importance of mechanisms to hold the clusters together in the Rio Grande area. She uses the term "confederacy" instead of "alliance" for the relationships between sites of the same clusters. (I consider her term an appropriate one.) She points out possible parallels between the Iroquois confederacy and that of the Late Period clusters in the Rio Grande Valley. The Iroquois communities were tightly clustered with empty zones between clusters, and alliances were maintained between clusters (see also Tuck 1971, 1978; Trigger 1976). There were different forms of alliance, and these alliances were closely intertwined with substantial warfare.

As discussed earlier, the Late Period clusters usually consisted of from two to eight sites, usually spaced about 3 miles apart, with distances of about 20 miles between clusters. The regularity of this spacing over quite different terrains, suggests that it has much to do with communication needs and the preferred size of a buffer zone (a buffer zone apparently had to be 20 miles wide). There must have been a dynamic trade-off between the need for sites to be dispersed for optimal food and fuel procurement and the need to be close together for defensive purposes. The trade-off would have required making decisions as to site size and the spacing between sites (see S. LeBlanc 1998).

In chapter 6, I pointed out that close spacing between sites would have increased the number of men available for both defensive and offensive operations against others. Without such spacing, it would have been harder to communicate by signaling and it would take longer for supporting forces to reach a beleaguered pueblo. However, too close a spacing or too large a community would have invited severe resource depletion and nutritional stress (a topic considered below). Thus, the population of an alliance cluster must have had to make these decisions in cooperation with each other. Site size and site spacing could not have been solely determined by each community individually.

Beyond the relationships that existed within a settlement cluster, building and maintaining relationships with other clusters would have served several purposes. To have allies in warfare and for the exchange of goods would have been the most obvious advantages to such relationships. A less obvious role would have been to ensure a distant refuge. In New Guinea, when one group was routed by another, the survivors usually found a place to live with groups to whom they were related, sometimes quite far from their original territory. Maintaining distant relationships would have been a sort of survival insurance investment. If the threat of successful attack was high enough—and given the number of successful attacks in the archaeological record, it seems to have been quite high— then the efforts to maintain long-distance relations would have been advantageous.

At a more general level, some patterns seemed to persist over time. To begin with, the formation of these alliances apparently began quite early. Site spacing, as seen in the distribution of big sites in the El Morro Valley, was practiced before these large pueblos were built. Prior to the construction of the El Morro pueblos, the communities of the Scribe S phase seemed to conform to the same spacing as the later sites, implying that the best distance between communities had been worked out by the residents of the valley before the pueblos were constructed. That is, alliance formation seemed to begin—or at least become visible—during the semidefensive stage of the process toward aggregation. Of course, the formation of alliances may have taken root even earlier; but, in any case, the movement of people into large closely spaced groups seems to have had its origins prior to the process of evolving into the formation of large pueblos.

The diachronic perspective can help clarify the importance of alliances. The Colorado Plateau area was evolving into two major population concentrations—presumably alliances—centered on Hopi and Zuni. Moreover, each of these alliances possibly had some weaker form of alliance with nearby groups: the Homolovi sites for the Hopi and the Upper Little Colorado River sites for the Zuni (discussed in the next section).

Again, while it was probably warfare that caused alliances to develop and be maintained, warfare did not necessarily govern all the relations between the allied groups. There is, of course, ample evidence for considerable interaction between these communities. The sharing of a new design style in Fourmile-Sikyatki-Matsaki polychromes, the common tendency to lighten the background color of the pottery, the common adoption of the Kachina cult, etc., all point to considerable interaction outside the context of warfare. There is no reason to expect times of total peace or all-out war—and over several hundred years there could have been significant periods of both. This is precisely what is described in ethnographic examples of tribal warfare. Of interest here is to examine what might have caused the periodic changes in aggression and cooperation.

Surviving on the Plateau—Zuni, Acoma, and Hopi

The histories of the three Colorado Plateau settlement clusters that survived to the present day are particularly interesting. The Plateau area had begun to evolve into two major population concentrations—Hopi and Zuni—with Acoma representing another larger-than-average concentration. The earliest clusters to disappear were those that lay between Hopi and Zuni or were otherwise near these two big alliance clusters. The short-lived clusters included those along the upper Rio Puerco and the Petrified Forest, Kin Tiel, and Steamboat Springs—all located between Hopi and Zuni. The area became a major no-man's-land. The clusters at Cebolleta Mesa and those situated along the San Jose River, which were not far from Acoma, also did not survive for long.

Even the clusters that survived until near the end of the 1300s, may have done so only because of their relationship with Hopi or Zuni. The Homolovi II site in the Homolovi groups (Middle Little Colorado cluster) and Hooper Ranch site in the Upper Little Colorado cluster seemed to have close ceramic ties with Hopi and Zuni, respectively, especially after 1350. That is, after the number of clusters had declined dramatically by A.D. 1350, there were probably strong relationships forming between some of the remaining clusters. The dominant alliances of Hopi and Zuni may each have had their "clients." To be fair, the ceramic ties of the Homolovi sites with Hopi were stronger than the Upper Little Colorado sites were with Zuni. Nevertheless, the same processes may have been at work, if not to the same degree.

What would be the rationale of such client/patron relations between clusters? A good example might be the Table Rock site, which, in a location at about 5,700 feet, was considerably lower in elevation than Zuni. Here, residents may have been growing cotton for the Zuni. And, while cotton presumably could have been grown at Hopi (it can be done today, but the climate was presumably colder then), surely it was easier to do so at Homolovi down on the Little Colorado (see E. Adams and Hays 1991). That is, the survivability of some clusters may have been due to their ability to forge a dependent relationship with either Hopi or Zuni.[2] (See Adams et al. [1993] on the relationship of the Homolovi sites and Hopi based on ceramics.)

In spite of their evolving dominant positions on the Colorado Plateau, there is still the question, "Why did the Zuni and Hopi clusters survive and the others did not?" They don't seem to be in particularly favorable locations with respect to other clusters. They did, however, start out as the largest clusters. Even though it may not be the case that all sites in each cluster were occupied at A.D. 1300, in the core area of each cluster

2. The history of Acoma is hard to characterize because so little is known about the other sites in the cluster and their ceramics for the time in question.

there were about seventeen to eighteen sites in the early 1300s. By around A.D. 1400 there were nine, and by A.D. 1540 there were six. The two clusters were remarkably similar in size, both were many times larger than any other clusters, and both declined in size in closely parallel ways. Were these two "megaclusters" always the focal point of groups relocating from other clusters, and so continued to maintain their dominance in size over other clusters? As discussed earlier, a large cluster size was probably a key military advantage.

The internal dynamics of the Hopi and Zuni clusters are also interestingly parallel. It is apparent, based on evidence from the historic period, that neither cluster was fully integrated. The different mesas at Hopi— and even the different Hopi towns—frequently showed animosity toward each other. Nothing so obvious existed at Zuni, but at the time of Spanish contact there did seem to be two groupings of three sites, each spaced some distance apart. If there were two Zuni groupings at Contact, they may have been better integrated and more easily combined into the one historical pueblo than was the case for Hopi. Certainly, there is no hint of significant dissension among the historical Zuni pueblos. At least some towns sent combatants to help Hawikuh against Coronado. Perhaps the survivability of the Hopi and Zuni clusters was related to their social capabilities in keeping a large group integrated, rather than to superior military ability.

I do suspect that relations between the two dominant clusters were not always cordial. In fact, the ceramic evidence points to a long history of animosity between Zuni and Hopi. For example, sherds from pottery associated with one area were not found in the other, except in the rarest of instances. Yet, they both shared, to some extent, the Fourmile-Sikyatki-Matsaki pottery design style. That is, they both seemed to participate in the same iconographic milieu. Just how to reconcile this contradiction is unclear. Upham (1982) noted a good ceramic link between Hopi and Acoma. And even potentially more interesting is the large amount of Hopi pottery found at the site of Pottery Mound. Given the location of Pottery Mound just to the west of the Rio Grande—perhaps an outpost reaching toward the Hopi cluster and the other clusters to the west—these two ceramic links suggest a strong interest by the Hopi in having Rio Grande allies.

As always, Acoma is difficult to interpret. Late in the prehistoric period, did the original Acoma cluster (with perhaps as many as ten sites) separate, with part moving to the Rio Grande area and part regrouping into the single, big Acoma pueblo? Acoma also had to relate to the large clusters along the Rio Grande, a factor different from that of Hopi and Zuni. Certainly, the Acoma mesa was far more defensive than any of the Zuni or Hopi sites, and its apparent lack of allies probably required this approach. However, do not forget that, while the Hopi and Zuni clusters had the greatest number of sites around A.D. 1300 (with about eighteen each),

Acoma, with possibly ten sites, was larger than any of the other Colorado Plateau clusters. Thus, while it declined to a single site, Acoma did survive. Again, the original size of the cluster was the best predictor of survivorship.

In summary, Hopi and Zuni appear to have dominated the Colorado Plateau from the 1300s on. They first eliminated clusters around them, and then, over time, they may have each had an allied cluster. But finally, they were the only clusters, with the exception of Acoma. With its location on the very edge of the Plateau, Acoma apparently did not compete too intensely with Zuni, and it, too, survived. Although, Acoma was the most fortified of all the pueblos in the 1500s, it obviously had to be tough going it alone.

Social Complexity and Group Size

The presence of significant Late Period warfare probably elevated the need for social complexity in the Southwest. The benefit of such complexity in maintaining cohesion between separate communities within clusters may have tipped the scale toward its development. Without the presence of warfare, development of such complexity would have been less likely. Moreover, warfare seemed to lessen after A.D. 1400, and the settlement clusters became less closely linked after the Spanish occupation and the marked decline in Pueblo population. All these factors may have undercut the impetus of the social complexity. This, of course, would have reduced its visibility in the ethnographic record, leading to conflicting interpretations of its existence and form. In the following discussion I briefly consider these issues, more for the purpose of showing the possible importance of warfare to this topic than to produce a definitive analysis.

Clearly, warfare prompted an increase in the number of people living within each community to above the previous norm. Moreover, the communities were clustered into alliances of some kind. What were the sizes of the communities and the alliances? Estimating the numbers of people in various Pueblo IV and early historic period groups has been recently undertaken (Dean et al. 1994; Kintigh 1985; Duff 1996). Analysis of population estimates (either person counts or house counts) from the early historic period has also been undertaken (Zubrow 1974; Earls 1992).

Population estimates for Hopi and Zuni at Contact range from 10,000 to 20,000 people. However, given the sizes of the sites (see Kintigh 1985; Anyon 1992), it is difficult to reconcile population estimates larger than 10,000 with the archaeology, and even that number is a stretch. Upham's estimate (1982) of 60,000 people at Zuni seems much too high, both in terms of the sites' sizes and in light of the room counts given below.

At Hopi, the sites also did not seem to be large enough to have held 20,000 people at Contact, as has sometimes been proposed. A population size similar to Zuni (10,000 people or less) seems much more appropriate.

The remaining site clusters that existed at some point during Pueblo IV in the Colorado Plateau and White Mountains areas present a different picture. The clusters had typically many fewer sites than Hopi or Zuni had, and the sites within the clusters were smaller on average.

Duff (1996) provides some room counts for the Upper Little Colorado, Silver Creek, Anderson Mesa, and Homolovi (Middle Little Colorado) areas as well as refined estimates for Hopi and Zuni. His maximum number of rooms for Hopi in Pueblo IV is under 3,500, and for Zuni it is around 5,300. The Hopi estimate seems low based on the size of Awatovi and Kawaika-a; an estimate of around 5,000 rooms is probably justified. The total for the four other less populated areas combined is around 5,300 rooms. These counts produce Pueblo IV population estimates of 8,000 to 10,000 people for Zuni, probably the same numbers for Hopi, and only 8,000 to 10,000 for the other four settlement clusters combined. On average, the other four clusters (the Upper Little Colorado, Silver Creek, Anderson Mesa, and Homolovi clusters) had populations of around 2,000 to 2,500 each.[3]

None of the settlement clusters that became extinct earlier was larger than the four small clusters, so most settlement clusters on the Colorado Plateau appear to have been under 3,000 people, with the exceptions of Hopi, Zuni, and possibly the Acoma clusters. Even for these three clusters, the maximum population for each one would have been 10,000 people. Estimates of population sizes in the Rio Grande Valley are much harder to make. However, Creamer (1996) suggests that few communities had more than 1,000 people, an estimate supported by various lines of evidence. Of these, Pecos and Taos, which may have had 2,000 people each, were two of the largest ones. If these community sizes are correct, then the population sizes of the Rio Grande settlement clusters would not have been larger than those seen for Hopi or Zuni, with the largest clusters having 10,000 people and many having less. The Spaniards estimated about 60,000 for the Rio Grande area at Contact, which seems reasonable (see Wilcox 1992) and fits well with the cluster sizes.[4]

When examined from the perspective of warfare, population sizes are

3. A rough conversion of these room counts to population estimates, using the Turner and Lofgren (1966) value of about two people per room or the refinement of Casselbury's estimates (1974) by C. LeBlanc (1981), produces a formula of 6 square meters per person. Since most rooms were under 9 square meters, this approach gives a value of 1.5 persons per room or less. Thus, two persons per room is a more generous estimate and the one and a half persons is a more conservative value.

4. Within these Southwestern clusters, the typical community probably had less than 1,000 individuals, based both on room counts and on historical accounts of community size. For example, Diego Pérez de Luxán in 1582 enumerated the number of people in various pueblos in terms of hundreds, not in the thousands (Hammond and Rey 1966). And, if there were even 8,000 Zuni combined in six pueblos at 1540, then there were just over 1,000 people in the largest Zuni settlement.

revealing. Most of the settlement clusters would have had under 700 men total (based on an estimate of 23 percent of the population as possible combatants [C. Lange 1978]). Even the clusters with populations of 5,000 people would have fielded only a little over 1,000 combatants—and only a couple of clusters could possibly have had anywhere close to 2,000 men. However, since the clusters consisted of separate, dispersed pueblos, each one had to provide for its own defense. As discussed previously, during offensive operations or when supporting the defense of another pueblo, a significant number of men must have stayed behind to defend their own pueblo against counter aggression. It is likely that most clusters could have fielded no more than 350 to 500 men at one time, with the possible upper limit of 1,000 men for a couple of clusters.

If these men were drawn from multiple pueblos, each with its own leadership, then there would have been 200 men or less under direct command of a leader. In all probablity, a small group of leaders could have provided good organization at this level. That is, there need not have been an elite level of organization in order to manage this number of men for either offense or defense. However, the coordination of groups of men from each pueblo would have been weak without strong overriding leadership. The clusters that could actually organize 1,000 men with a recognized central authority would have had a real military advantage. Sheridan (1981) discusses this type of situation for the Yaqui, and it is supported by accounts of historical intertribal warfare. Poor coordination between about 100 Quechans and an equal number of their allies apparently contributed to their defeat at the hands of the Pima in the mid-1800s (Kroeber and Fontana 1986). Accounts of Shoshone warfare discussed in chapter 2 describe groups of a few hundred men, loosely organized and with no complex tactics. These examples were not of complex societies, and their warfare reflects their overall level of organization. So, by comparison, if pueblo alliances were able to field more than 100 to 200 men, there would have been both a need and a great advantage to having a stronger and more centralized organization.

The Evolution of Social Complexity

The issue of the evolution of elite-based social organization at about the time of the Late Period has repeatedly been proposed and rejected (Upham 1982; Upham et al. 1989; Wilcox 1991; Dean 1996a). The full history of this debate need not be repeated here (see also McGuire and Saitta 1996; Cordell et al. 1987; Upham and Plog 1986; Reid and Whittlesey 1990; Whittlesey 1978). Creamer (1996) nicely reviews the arguments for social complexity in the late Prehistoric Period. She summarizes the arguments and counterarguments for complexity and concludes that the evidence for an elite-based social organization at this time is weak, but not nonexistent, and proposes some alternative models. She reviews possible causal factors for complexity, such as trade and population size, and also looks at arguments for why any posited complexity might have "devolved" by the time of good historical accounts. While Creamer discusses warfare only in passing in these models, Service (1962) and Carneiro (1970) see it as a very important factor in the formation of complex societies in general. However, with the introduction of a major increase in warfare in the Southwest during the Late Period, the possibility of social complexity appears very different.

Based on the population sizes of the settlement clusters, as discussed above, the populations of any of these clusters—or alliances—would have been at the very low end of the size of complex social organizations (Sahlins 1958; Earl 1987). This fits with Haas's argument (1990) for a typical tribal level of warfare in the Southwest. That is, based on ethnographic analogies, the likelihood that any of these clusters would have attained significant social complexity was low, except possibly for Hopi and Zuni. If the pueblo was the basic political unit, it would have been below the size expected for developing noteable social complexity. If the settlement cluster was the political unit, it would have been just barely in the size range predicted to develop some complexity. Yet, it has been repeatedly suggested that such complexity did exist.

The unique situations seen in the Late Period may have moved these societies toward more complexity than might otherwise be expected. Warfare and food stress should have encouraged the formation of some form of elite structure. The ability to organize combatants efficiently would have been a distinct advantage, both within and between communities. (Clearly, when warfare was on the rise in the historical pueblos, war leaders took control.) The tension that probably arose between war leaders and non–war-based leaders for authoritative control should have contributed toward a more complex society.

A number of scholars (see Kohler [1993] for a review) have noted that food sharing between primary economic units would have been a useful response to periodic food shortfalls. To make a long, complex argument short, suffice it to say that sharing was likely to take place when people had enough of a surplus to give some of it away without threatening their survival, but that they were less likely to share when the crisis was severe. So, just when sharing was most needed, it was most likely not to take place. Any central authority that stored surpluses, or could coerce sharing, would have been very advantageous. The greater the frequency and severity of food shortfalls, the greater the likelihood that such leadership would have evolved.

Another important role for an elite class would have been dispute adjudication within and between communities. There is considerable evidence for poorly integrated communities seen in the form of site pairs, different architectural configurations on different parts of sites, and the historical record of Hopis destroying other Hopi communities. Many of the unique site clusters may have consisted of alliances that were cultural amalgams, possibly with multiple languages being spoken.[5] Conveniently located farmland would have been in short supply because the requirements of the larger group sizes would have been greater than ever before, and so the distance to some fields would, on average, have become much greater than before. Some mechanisms would have been needed to allocate land and reallocate it based on changes in climate, field productivity, and demography in the community. This was an important role for the leadership in the historical Hopi communities, and it would have been more important prehistorically when the need for allies conflicted with the need for farmland. A strong leadership would have been an asset to the communities that had it in place.

Thus, based on all these reasons, it's to be expected that some form of elite behavior would appear. However, the above considerations ignore the time factor. Just how fast could an elite faction evolve, and how quickly would elite behavior be reflected in the archaeological record? Most likely, such an evolution would take at least a couple of generations. However, the vast majority of the sites in the Colorado Plateau and White Mountains areas, where such behavior has been posited, existed as large centers only for a couple of generations. Most communities would have become extinct before, or about the same time, elite behavior became established enough to leave evidence for it. Of the sites from the three surviving clusters—that is, where there was enough time for such behavior to evolve and develop enough archaeological manifestations to be visible—there are data only from Hawikuh, Kechipawa, Awatovi, and Kawaika-a. All of these sites were excavated a long time ago, and there has been little reanalysis of the data from them. What has been done at Hawikuh (Howell 1996) does support evidence for some form of elite, manifested in what looks like war leadership in that the signs of leadership seemed to be certain weapons.

Even at the very short-lived Grasshopper Pueblo, there was a set of grave goods for males that has been labeled "arrow society" by Whittlesey (1978) because of the use of these as social markers. Although she does not believe they were markers for an elite, they would fit with what might be expected for war leaders. However, this post-1300 evidence does not imply there were no war leaders before this time. Dated to the prior century, the "magician burial" found at Ridge Ruin was associated with artifacts that, when shown to Hopi consultants, suggested to them that "war leader"

5. As an example of an alliance being a cultural amalgam of differing languages, the Tewa speakers on First Mesa at Hopi, after about 300 years, are not linguistically integrated with the rest of the Hopi—although they apparently all can and do speak the Hopi langage. If this level of conservatism was common prehistorically, then even less linguistic unity among clusters could be expected over a much shorter period of time.

was a more accurate attribution than "magician" (McGregor 1943). And a similar argument can probably be made for the artifacts associated with the exceptionally rich male burials at Mummy Cave (see F. Lister and Lister 1986) and Aztec Ruin (E. H. Morris 1924). The question is: Did "leadership" in general become synonymous with "war leadership" beginning in the 1300s, and were these leaders becoming some type of elite?

One aspect of this debate about the level of social complexity is the long-running argument between the excavators of Chavez Pass and those of Grasshopper Pueblo, sites that are some 60 miles (100 km) apart. Both Chavez Pass and Grasshopper Pueblo are considered special cases. Some of the excavators thought there was good evidence for social stratification at both sites, and others thought there was virtually no evidence. While I have no intention of belaboring the debate, I believe evidence for warfare and its potential for increasing social complexity makes it worth looking again at these two sites.

The size of the two sites was roughly similar and the same general conditions prevailed at both.[6] As previously discussed, the Chavez Pass sites underwent a rather typical evolution in site structure in the late 1200s and early 1300s. There were originally a number of smaller sites and one fairly large site. These then seem to have been replaced by two large (paired) sites of a form seen over much of the Colorado Plateau (see chapter 6). The Chavez Pass pair of sites were apparently part of an alliance that included, at one point, three other sites, and it appears that the paired sites lasted from probably the first decade of the 1300s to around the end of that century. A ball-park estimate of their population was around 1,000 people.

My interpretation differs from the excavators' analysis of the situation at Chavez Pass. They thought that the small sites around the large site were contemporary, essentially ignoring both the existence of an alliance and the competition among alliances. Upham (1982) identified an alliance that included the Chavez Pass sites, but he did not see warfare as the probable driving mechanism in maintaining the alliance. Also, the excavators' general opinion was that the catchment around Chavez Pass was inadequate to support the pueblos' population. Well, if the carrying capacity was inadequate, why didn't the population disperse? This apparently irrational behavior suddenly makes sense if the possibility that the population had been brought together for mutual defense is considered. The population did not disperse because it was too dangerous to do so. And, under the circumstances of inadequate resources, competition within

6. The pair of sites at Chavez Pass is estimated to have contained about 900 rooms, and Grasshopper Pueblo is estimated to have had 500. However, parts of the Chavez sites are believed to have been three and even four stories high, and many more of the structures are assumed to have been two stories than those at Grasshopper (Brown 1982). I suspect that the difference in size between them is less than is generally credited, and the difference is small compared with the overall range of site sizes in the Southwest.

the community for the best land would undoubtedly have existed. These factors all point to the likelihood that leadership roles were developing.

How much inequality between the classes might be found at Chavez Pass, and how would it have been expressed? The answers probably relate to the time period under examination. It seems unlikely that a class of elites would have evolved instantly, and even more unlikely that deliberate social signaling of any such class—in terms of larger structures, more wealth, and differential burial practices—would have rapidly developed. Since the entire process—the coming together of a large population, the consequent stresses and need for elites, and the ultimate abandonment of the site or the demise of the group—would have taken no more than three generations, it is unlikely that the evolution of status symbolism would have progressed very far prior to the end of the occupation of Chavez Pass. Moreover, even if it had evolved to some considerable degree, it is most likely any such progression would have occurred in the final years.

What is the likelihood that elite individuals, at death, would have been buried in a special way, and the burials recovered? A population of 1,000 people should have resulted in about 30 burials per year, or about 2,700 burials for the maximal ninety years under consideration at Chavez Pass. If the elite represented about 5 percent of the population and if they were demonstrating their elite status via recoverable artifacts only in the final thirty years of occupation, then only 45 of the entire 2,700 burials (or about 1.3 percent of all burials) would have been elite burials. Because no more than 100 burials were recovered at Chavez Pass with adequate detail (most were from early excavations when recording was minimal), the expected number of elite burials recovered from this sample would have been one or two, and these may have gone unrecognized.

The situation at Grasshopper Pueblo is even less likely to have evolved elite behavior, and there would have been less likelihood for any elite to have been buried in a fashion demonstrating such behavior. Grasshopper Pueblo, as previously discussed, was from its beginning (around A.D. 1325–1330) a major defensive site, and probably lasted for little more than a generation. Thus, despite the possible need for an elite and the attendant elite behavior, there would hardly have been time for any of these elements to have evolved, for status symbolism to have developed, and for the status individuals to have died and been buried as an elite, all within one generation.

So, some of the large Late Period groups—but not necessarily all of them—could have benefited from a form of elite structure for enforcing and encouraging food storage and sharing, settling group disputes, and providing leadership during warfare. Such social complexity would not necessarily have been pervasive—and may have been incipient enough for it to be very hard to find and document where it did exist. This may be why there is so little consensus on the issue.

Subsistence and Survival in Large Towns

One very important aspect of the Late Period large towns that sprouted up over most of the northern Southwest was their ecological inefficiency. These large, crowded communities were a very poor solution to survival in the Southwest—particularly where irrigation was not utilized. The concentration of large numbers of people in a very small area resulted in overexploitation of local resources and underutilization of those found farther away. Not only was farmland at a premium but also the farms of a great number of people were so close together they were all susceptible to the same weather-related problems. Crop failure for one area meant the likelihood of widespread crop failure. Similarly, wild plants and animals and firewood all were collected from the same starting point. The distances people walked to gather these resources were much greater than if the population had been dispersed over the landscape. This same argument is made for the Classic Hohokam by Wilcox (1989), who thinks that such population concentration was a problem even where irrigation was dominant.

The need to keep people, especially women, protected from ambush further magnified these problems. As pointed out earlier, even short trips for water were eliminated by establishing walk-in wells. The threat of ambush would have restricted the ability of women and very small groups of men to forage far from the pueblo.[7] In sum, the nutritional disadvantages of aggregation were severe, which is presumably why it was not undertaken earlier to anything like this level. Previously, communities were smaller and more spread out over the area, with far fewer areas left underutilized as were the large buffer zones of the Late Period.

Virtually all studies show that, when compared with earlier times, there was increased nutritional stress in the Late Period (D. Berry 1983; M. Taylor 1985; P. Walker 1985; Van Gerven and Sheridan 1994). Increased evidence of disease, pathologies, and infant health problems were regularly noted. The common incidence of anemia among children at this time was particularly revealing. The findings seemed to indicate there was not enough meat nor enough of a wide variety of wild plant foods for optimum health, the exact expectation if the amount and kinds of foraging were curtailed. The subsistence problems were further exacerbated by the pattern of keeping the groups' size large, even in the face of declining

7. Kroeber and Fontana (1986) describe an incidence of a large group of Pima women going out to collect firewood. Men on horseback were posted on ridges surrounding the work group to protect them from ambush. The prohibitive hazards of foraging in multiple directions; the limited ability to do other tasks, such as collecting wild plants; and the distances people were willing to travel under these circumstances point out the significant inefficiency of living in these circumstances. Comparable fears of personal attack would undoubtedly have limited mobility in other times, but just as surely increased warfare in the Late Period intensified these problems.

population. As the population declined in many of these clusters, distances to fields shortened and hunting and foraging demands lessened. However, instead of taking advantage of the situation, the remaining populations gathered into even larger (although fewer) communities, perpetuating the problem.

If a deteriorating climate and an overall lack of resources were the ultimate causes of warfare and a decline in population, then the cultural response of aggregation was precisely the wrong one. Instead of dispersing to maximize the utilization of the remaining resources, the people aggregated to the highest degree ever seen in the Southwest. Subsistence problems were magnified, not ameliorated, by this behavior.

Individual groups probably were aware of this issue. In the historic period, as mentioned, the Zuni repeatedly tried setting up satellite villages to farm good areas located too far away to farm effectively from the main pueblo (T. Ferguson 1996; T. Ferguson and Hart 1985). However, these small communities were constantly threatened by attack, at that time by the Athapaskans (Quam 1972), and were never very heavily populated. Just because the people of a community recognized the need to disperse did not mean they were able to do so. The threat of attack seemed to override the ecological considerations, and populations stayed concentrated, with all the attendant nutritional problems as a result.[8]

This scenario leads to the subject of Southwestern population decline. There is a long history of scholarly concern about where all the inhabitants of the Colorado Plateau and the rest of the Southwest went when areas were abandoned. While a full discussion of this topic is beyond the concern here, the model of poor climate, warfare, and crowding into large towns suggests an explanation for the population dynamics of the Late Period.

Given the amount of warfare, the nutritional problems incurred by living in large towns, and the way the numbers of sites declined in the settlement clusters, it is more likely that most of the Southwest's population died and, hence, did not migrate to other areas. As noted, there is ample evidence for migrations in the late 1200s and early 1300s, but there is also evidence for death from warfare. Some clusters, such as Techado, are best understood as having been annihilated. Others may

8. The concern with traveling far from the pueblo may be relevant to understanding the famous rock mulch gardens of the Rio Grande area. They have been noted for years by a number of people (Jeançon 1912; Hibben 1937; Luebben 1953; Skinner 1965; Buge 1978, 1984; Lang 1980, 1981; Gauthier 1981; Anscheutz and Maxwell 1986; Beal 1987; D. Lightfoot and Eddy 1995). They were always seen as increasing available farmland on river terraces and on such places as the top of Abiquiu Mesa. Could they also have been a mechanism for farming near pueblos or in areas where it was not easy for enemies to destroy crops? That is, it might have been a choice between a more productive riverine field far from the pueblo or a less productive rock mulch garden near the pueblo. The latter might have been chosen, not because it was more efficient, but because the crop could be more easily safeguarded and it was simply safer to farm near the pueblo.

have dwindled in numbers until the survivors finally migrated, as at the Silver Creek cluster and the Upper Little Colorado cluster. In fact, there is little evidence for significant migrations after about A.D. 1325.

It is most likely that, of the Southwest's original population, only a small fraction ultimately survived to migrate. The population curves generated by Dean et al. (1994) strongly support this scenario. There were no surges in population in any area of the Southwest after A.D. 1325, yet there were many areas being abandoned from that time on. The abandoned areas cannot be explained by migration alone; abandonment was accompanied by a significant drop in population in the Southwest as a whole. The decline in numbers of people in this entire area was probably due to a combination of direct starvation, chronic nutritional stress, and deaths due to warfare.

Trade

As was the case with alliances, the intensification of warfare may have modified the role of trade in the Late Period. The shift to sinew-backed recurved bows seemed to result in a change in shield and bow technology. Buffalo hides apparently became necessary for well-made shields, as was buffalo sinew for the bows. Hide shields and recurved bows were clearly in use in the 1400s and possibly during the 1300s. The technological improvements in weaponry required access to such resources.

Based on a variety of evidence, I think buffalo hide was the preferred material for shields. The hump portion of a prime bull seems to have been particularly valued, but only one shield could be made from each hide. The large body shields, three feet in diameter, would not have been available to most of the Pueblo IV population except by trade. If hide shields were in use as early as the 1300s, as seems possible, then all the groups on the Colorado Plateau would have wanted access to buffalo hides. It is also possible that buffalo sinew, used for making sinew-backed bows, would have been scarce, but deer sinew could have been easily substituted for it.[9]

Not directly related to warfare, but perhaps closely intertwined with trade, is the possibility that the Little Ice Age could have increased the need for buffalo robes for warmth (as well as buffalo hide for warm footwear; bison-hide moccasins replaced sandals sometime after A.D. 1300) and for cotton mantas. The early Spanish explorers seemed to be highly driven to obtain quantities of robes and blankets because of the cold, and the Pueblos seemed to have considerable quantities on hand. Since cotton was grown only in limited areas in the Southwest and buffalo hides were in demand over most of the area, much of the trade in general at this time

9. I restrict the discussion of buffalo-hide body shields to the pueblo area, since there is no evidence for this kind of shield use by the Hohokam or other southern Southwestern people at this time.

was for "necessities" rather than "exotic" items. (See Creel [1991] for further discussion of buffalo-hide use in the Southwest, although he does not discuss its use in shields.)

Spielmann (1983), Wilcox (1984, 1991), and others believe that food was traded between the "dog nomads" of the plains areas and the Pueblos during this Late Period. However, dried meat does not contain any more calories per pound than corn. So, if meat was traded for corn, then it was for dietary variety and protein, not calories. Even if meat was traded for nonfood items, the amount traded would have been only a small percentage of the annual needs of the Pueblos. The number of Puebloans trading for necessities was probably much greater than the number of plains people supplying the items. Even as a dietary supplement, a family needed at least 50 kgm of dried meat annually. It is difficult to imagine that plains nomads, using dogs as pack animals, could have delivered much more than this on one trip. The total number of nomads seems to have been many times smaller than the total number of Pueblo people, so they could not have been supplying the entire Pueblo community with anything close to 50 kgm of meat per family, even if they made several trips a year. In these circumstances, meat would have been available to only a small portion of the Pueblo community.

However, the situation with hide shields was quite different. Two or three families of plains nomads (supplying, say, five shields each) could have brought enough hide shields to meet a typical Pueblo village's annual needs—if, in any given year, only a few adult males needed a replacement shield and if, out of 600 people, only about six to ten boys reached adulthood, thereby needing a shield. Thus, the nomads would have been bringing a very valuable commodity (per pound) and the trade would have been considered very important to the Pueblos. Of course, a secondary exchange of these hides to Pueblos without direct plains access would have been an extremely important aspect of interpueblo trade, and towns like Pecos would have wanted to corner as much of the initial trade as possible. Nevertheless, the value per pound of a shield must have been far greater than the equivalent amount of consumable meat.

Thus, technological changes in weapons and the intensification of warfare may have affected the nature of trade commodities and trade relationships. During prior periods, shell, turquoise, parrots, and other exotics may have been important for such things as social signaling. But Pueblo IV trade may have taken on a new dimension if buffalo hides and sinew were necessary both for warfare and, to a lesser extent, for warmth. In other words, prior to the Late Period the mix of trade may have been tilted more toward "exotic" items rather than "necessities," and during the Pueblo IV period there may have been a shift toward more critical resources. The need for access to buffalo resources would have created a new east-west dynamic in trade where north-south–oriented systems had been dominant; many of the previously valuable exotic items, such as shell and parrots, would have come to the pueblo area from farther south. Although there were probably instances of an earlier east-west trade as well as a later north-south trade, the intensity of trade and the most important trade associations may have caused a shift in directions.

War vs. Trade

Although interpuebloan warfare seemed to be based on settlement clusters, the clusters were not always hostile to each other. They could be expected to form alliances with other settlement clusters, but the alliances would probably have been ephemeral—unlike the relationships among the communities within a cluster. However, if the benefits were important, these alliances could have some duration. So, for example, there could have been a particularly strong relationship between Hopi and Pottery Mound for a century or more. Alternatively, the Tano might have been allied with Pecos for twenty-five years and then with the Southern Tiwa for another twenty-five years. While there might be evidence of long-term alliances reflected in the presence of such items as trade pottery, there are currently no means of recognizing short-term shifting alliances.

Furthermore, there may have been periods of relative peace between groups that were historically hostile. As discussed, Hopi and Zuni, for example, seem to have been generally antagonistic toward each other for much of the time. Yet, that doesn't mean there were no benefits to trade between them, and short-lived truces could have been common or even the norm. Ethnographic accounts show that the same groups could be both hostile and peacefully interactive, even on a yearly basis. Shared design elements in the Hopi Sikyatki and Zuni Matsatki pottery would support a suggestion of some interaction. However, it appears any such peace was considered fragile and therefore too risky to allow communities to be established in the no-man's-land between the clusters; there was never a dispersal of sites from either Hopi or Zuni.

If each site-cluster alliance group was at least nominally mutually supportive, was there support between groups? The most likely pattern of intercluster alliances is that of antagonism toward neighboring groups and positive relationships with groups farther away. This was probably the result of two factors: The old strategy that "the enemy of my enemy is my friend" and that trade had to be maintained. If the Hopi and Zuni were antagonistic, then it benefited the Hopi to have a positive relationship with Acoma or one of the Rio Grande clusters for access to buffalo hides and other items. Where would the Zuni get cotton if they did not have trading partners? Upham (1982) found that Hopi seemed to have more interaction with Pottery Mound than with Zuni, yet you have to detour around the Zuni area to get from Hopi to Pottery Mound. This finding is inexplicable if there were continuously good relations between Hopi and Zuni. As mentioned, the Zuni claimed to Coronado in 1540 to be at war with the Hopi; and when Espejo went from Zuni to Acoma in 1582, some eighty Zuni warriors accompanied him to fight the Hopi.

While it is not possible at this point to resolve the details of these relationships, the long-term trends should be made apparent. Based on ceramics, the Homolovi sites in the Middle Little Colorado cluster were found to have a long-term link to Hopi, and Table Rock and other sites along the Upper Little Colorado were linked with the Zuni. In the Rio Grande area, some decorated pottery types consistently crossed cluster boundaries and others did not (Creamer 1996). Such patterns may reflect the duration and strength of alliances between cluster groups.

Another issue is the degree to which trade was symmetric. A model of each cluster trading what it had for what it wanted may be too simplistic a view of Pueblo IV trade if some clusters were dominant over others. For example, the Hopi might have been militarily dominant over the Homolovi sites. Surely the Zuni could have been dominant over the remnants of the Upper Little Colorado cluster. These clusters may have survived as long as they did because they were useful to the Hopi and the Zuni. That is, where there was an unequal relationship beween groups, there may well have been more trade going on in some directions than others. How this would appear archaeologically is not obvious.[10]

In summary, I do not believe Pueblo IV trade can be understood without placing it within a context of significant warfare and the need for groups to maintain access to important products in such a milieu. Moreover, shifting alliances between settlement clusters would have caused trade to be an important element in helping cement such alliances. The focus of trade would have shifted as the alliances shifted, so trade should reflect such changes among alliances—that is, if the temporal control is fine enough to see it.

The Evolution of Community Integration

At some time near A.D. 1300, there were more than twenty-seven settlement clusters on the Colorado Plateau and in the White Mountains. The clusters most likely evolved their social structures somewhat independently of each other. While surely they operated within a general and shared cultural milieu, there must have been the opportunity to experiment and change. Over time, the most successful solutions developed by some groups were most likely adopted by other settlement clusters. However, over the short run, this would not have been the case. Many different approaches were probably devised and tried, some rejected and some adopted by others.

From about A.D. 1275 until A.D. 1400, the initial twenty-seven different settlement clusters declined in number to only three. During the time of

---

10. Bishop et al. (1988) found equal numbers of bowls from the Hopi area sites of Awatovi and Kawaika-a at Pottery Mound, suggesting a broad-based linkage between the two areas.

their existence, the clusters may have developed different solutions to the common problem of integrating separate groups and maintaining group cohesion. The vast majority of them died out as separate entities, and failure to develop appropriate social integrating mechanisms was possibly a significant contributing factor in their demise. They might be characterized as twenty-seven separate, or semiseparate, experiments in social evolution, with most of them failing.

When looked at in this way, arguments over whether Late Period social structure was basically egalitarian or complex become much less interesting. The answer is, very likely, both. Some settlement clusters probably did develop some form of elite behavior, while others did not. The assumption should not be that a solution developed by one group was adopted by all groups.

For example, Grasshopper Pueblo and its settlement cluster must be considered a major failure. The cluster may have consisted of Grasshopper proper, the surrounding small hilltop sites, and maybe the Q Ranch site as well. Evidence suggests that the pueblo became a large, defensively laid-out site around A.D. 1323–1325 (Reid and Riggs 1995). It was apparently abandoned about A.D. 1350. There is no evidence that the small surrounding sites lasted any later. One large room group at Q Ranch was burned and the other abandoned somewhere in this same time interval. Put in another way, the settlement cluster seems to have lasted as a major cluster for no more than twenty-five years and suffered at least one successful attack. Evidence of scalping and the underrepresentation of about 25 percent of the adult males in the burial population all suggest a considerably devastating conflict. If it is correct that the social system of Grasshopper Pueblo was essentially egalitarian (Reid 1989), then it can be said that, in this case, an egalitarian social structure was not very effective.

In contrast, the Anderson Mesa settlement cluster formed sometime around A.D. 1300 and survived late into the 1300s, even though it may have dwindled in size and scope (Upham and Bockley 1989). As a cluster, it survived at least three times as long as the Grasshopper cluster. Was this because it had a different, and perhaps more complex, social structure?

In summary, as warfare becomes more intense, it also becomes a more important factor in settlement configurations, in settlement locations, and in the formation of settlement clusters than has previously been proposed. Warfare may also be more relevant to the issue of social complexity—and to the evolution of social organizations in general and to integrating mechanisms in particular—than has been previously considered.

Social Responses to Warfare

Clearly, the 1300s were a calamitous time in the Southwest. If the Little Ice Age model is correct, the climate changed rapidly for the worse. Vast areas were abandoned and, even where regions were not abandoned, almost everyone relocated in some way. Finally, intense warfare took place, with most macrocommunities (settlement clusters) witnessing a successful attack on one or more of its member communities. In the space of 100 years, twenty-four out of twenty-seven clusters on the Colorado Plateau were abandoned. If this was not a calamity, it is difficult to image what a real crisis would look like.

As discussed, the need for large defensive sites resulted in much larger groups of people living in extreme proximity, necessitating organizational changes to accommodate the problems inherent in such social arrangements. The Kachina cult derives from this time period (E. Adams 1991), as does Crown's more broadly defined "Southwestern cult" (1994), and both are probably related to changing social issues. While warfare may not have caused the Kachina cult, it is probable that warfare set off a series of cascading causes and effects that resulted in its adoption. Warfare caused the aggregation of large groups, which was actually a poor response to the climatic conditions. The warfare and aggregation phenomena, when combined, resulted in population loss and poor health. The cults may have been crisis cults that served to mitigate and cope with the calamitous times. The cults may also have served to mitigate and dampen the warfare itself. In sum, if it is warfare that kept the groups large and aggregated, then its presence cannot be ignored, even when other aspects of the cultural systems are being considered.[11]

Alternative Interpretations

Although much of the preceding formulation is at odds with more traditional interpretations of Southwestern prehistory, I chose not to address all the alternative models and approaches. However, a few issues do require consideration. It has been suggested (P. Fish and Fish 1989) that as areas throughout the Southwest were abandoned during the Late Period, there was a concentration of settlements in more adequately watered areas, and therefore farming potential was a more important determinant of site location than defense. On a very broad basis this is clearly so: The highland areas of the Four Corners area were abandoned for the Rio Grande Valley, for example.

However, within regions, such shifts did not seem to be significant. For the entire Colorado Plateau area, after about A.D. 1275, no new site clusters formed, with the one exception of the downstream shift of the Zuni River cluster. The Plateau clusters were remarkably stable, both those that survived and those that failed. The same statement is accurate for much of the rest of the Southwest. Areas were abandoned continuously; but areas

---

11. There is a big difference between determining the origins of the form and iconographic representations of the Kachina and Southwestern cults and determining why they were adopted. The answer to the question of why people accepted these cults probably includes warfare as a factor.

which were empty at A.D. 1325 were never occupied later, and areas which were abandoned after that time were also not reoccupied. That is, after A.D. 1325 there was no shifting of locations of site clusters, only very minor establishments of sites within existing clusters.

The explanation of settlement location based on the need for access to farmland or other resources is consistently misapplied when dealing with the particulars of site locations. Several examples show how the two issues can become confused. In the early Mogollon, sites were situated on hilltops. However, the hilltops selected were near farmland. The general area was selected based on resources, but the particular land feature chosen for habitation was selected with defense in mind. The importance of the former does not negate the importance of the latter. Similarly, Tuggle (1970) showed that the small sites around Grasshopper Pueblo were deliberately located near relatively rare arable land. However, there were a great number of possible locations in a wide variety of defensible and nondefensible settings that could have been chosen for habitations to be near these fields. The particular locations that were chosen for the sites were all defensible. Moreover, none of the locations was optimally located to minimize overall travel distance to the patches of arable land. In every case, there were other locations situated closer to the middle of the arable land than the one selected. If efficiency in minimizing distance to fields was the primary overall goal in site location, then none was optimally located because all the sites could have been better placed so as to reduce the overall travel time to fields. Not only would travel time have been reduced, but so would the considerable effort required to live on a hilltop. Once again, the general location was chosen for availability of farmland, the particular location was chosen for defense.

However, for the Southwest as a whole, this was not the case. No-man's-lands did exist. It could be argued that all clusters were located on the best lands and that the no-man's-lands were merely areas that were less valuable and productive. However, the spacing is so regular that it's impossible to believe the empty buffer zones just happened to coincide with the worst land. Moreover, the very areas that were heavily populated in 1250—or even 1350—were empty in 1400. If these places were so good, why didn't the Zuni, Hopi, and others move into them? The locations of sites cannot be explained solely by their relationship to arable land. Both the overall portions of the Southwest available for habitation during the Late Period and the particulars of the precise site locations were dictated by the social—not the environmental—milieu.

Upham (1982) made a pioneering attempt at characterizing intergroup relations for the Western Pueblo area. While the formulation presented in this and the preceding chapters bears some similarities to his model, there are important differences. I believe these differences exist, in part, because his approach does not take into account the calamitous events of the fourteenth century. He took a rather static view of an extremely dynamic process, and it is the dynamics of the process that are the most interesting. This lack of a dynamic view is also discussed by E. Adams et al. (1993) concerning Upham's ceramic data.

In particular, Upham did not consider some sites as belonging to clusters, as outlined in chapter 6. For example, he did not realize that the Bidahochi site was apparently part of a separate cluster that was fast dying out and was not part of the Hopi cluster. Also, it appears that the site clusters along the upper Rio Puerco and in the Petrified Forest area were separate from both the Upper Little Colorado and Homolovi groups and were, for the most part, so short-lived that they were not part of what he was studying. Sites and site clusters including Kin Tiel, Wide Reed Ruin, the Techado cluster, Cebolleta Mesa, and several others were not considered. Also, the relationship between Hopi and Zuni was probably far different when the Bidahochi cluster, the upper Rio Puerco cluster, and the Kin Tiel cluster, and others existed than it was afterwards. Similarly, the nature of their relationships to other clusters would have changed as intervening groups died out. By the late 1300s, groups to the east and south of Zuni were essentially gone (except for Acoma), so the relationship with Silver Creek (Fourmile Ruin) and the Little Colorado (Table Rock Pueblo) groups would probably have changed significantly at that time.

By viewing Upham as examining the picture only at around A.D. 1350, and not for the entire century and beyond, his analysis becomes very important and revealing. The patterns he detected are now seen even clearer with better data that are currently available. For example, his Hopi and Upper Little Colorado clusters fit the model he proposes much better without inclusion of the sites that should not have been included in them. His most important determination is that Hopi and Zuni were antagonistic over a long period. He also shows that Hopi had a relationship with Acoma which was probably quite strategic. Both of these conclusions have been incorporated into the model proposed here. Some clusters, such as Chavez Pass and Silver Creek, seem to have been very different in their external relations (i.e., client/patron associations) from others, such as the Middle Little Colorado cluster. His analysis clearly shows that not all clusters were equal: There were not seven equivalent groups all interacting in the same ways at A.D. 1350.

If Upham's analysis is accepted as a good representation of the mid–thirteenth-century situation, then the only real problem is that many of the alliances he describes were probably much smaller than he recognizes. For all practical purposes, the Anderson Mesa–Chavez Pass group was one site, the Homolovi cluster was, by that time, probably only two large sites, and the Upper Little Colorado group was much more restricted in space and the number of sites than he indicates. This is important, because it is these differences that are significant in understanding the differences in interaction levels between the groups. So, while his work is an important initial effort, his formulation should not be used in future analyses.

CONCLUSIONS

A strong case can be made for intense warfare breaking out during the late 1200s, continuing well into the Pueblo IV period, and still taking place in 1540, although possibly at a reduced level. The implications of this warfare were profound. The most immediate effect was to concentrate people into new and very large communities, which resulted in a massive population relocation on both a regional and a subregional scale. The internal social structure of these communities would have evolved to adjust for the increased size and heterogeneity of the residents. There would have been a great adaptive advantage toward social structures that were effective in integrating these refugee communities. Also, the need for commodities to make new weapons and the necessity of secure relations with distant allies could have possibly restructured trade during this time.

The evolution of Southwestern community size and configuration provides a rare opportunity to study adaptive responses at a social level. A number of groups were variously competing and cooperating. Some chose solutions that worked, most did not. Was there a minimum site-size that worked or a minimum number of sites in a group? Perhaps it was a far more subtle and dynamic process. The implementation of integrating mechanisms to keep communities and alliances together may have been the most important determinant of survival. Or was it ecological? Did those people who chose, or held onto, locations that were situated at too high an elevation and were too restricted in resources (cotton could not be grown, for example) become relatively disadvantaged?

It appears that the Rio Grande groups were relatively more successful than those on the Colorado Plateau or in the areas south of the Plateau. Whereas the size of groups declined in the Rio Grande Valley, few died out completely. However, on the Colorado Plateau, twenty-four of twenty-seven groups failed. Was this because the Rio Grande area was more hospitable during the Little Ice Age and the competition among groups on the Plateau more severe? If this was the case, more of the groups in the lower elevations of southern Arizona and New Mexico should have survived. So, perhaps there were more failed sets of social mechanisms on the Plateau and the southern Southwest and more successful sets in the Rio Grande Valley, resulting in an overall better survival ratio for the valley sites. In all, it must have been a traumatic and unstable time for the people of the Southwest. Major changes in religion, as seen in the adoption of the Kachina and Southwestern cults, may be related to the devastating and conflict-filled fourteenth century. While it is far too simplistic to "explain" these changes with warfare, it is equally impossible to understand much of the events of the Late Period without recognizing the major role warfare played in the overall system.

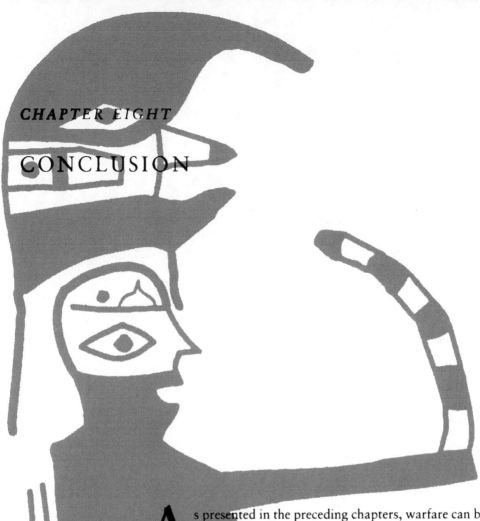

CHAPTER EIGHT

CONCLUSION

As presented in the preceding chapters, warfare can be recognized, and studied in the archaeological record; it is neither insignificant nor tangential to other aspects of society. The conclusion drawn from the data is that, instead of being almost nonexistent, warfare in the prehistoric Southwest was a driving force behind much cultural behavior. Such a conclusion requires a reassessment of the views of Southwestern society. War or its threat would have been a part of daily life, although the level of this threat seemed to change dramatically over time. It is the integration of warfare-related behavior into an overall understanding of the Southwest that is today's challenge.

A Different View of the Southwest

Security must have been an overriding concern for the early inhabitants of the Southwest. Every individual, family group, and fundamental social unit would have constantly assessed their safety and security. Their lives, their family, their stored food and other valuables, and their land were potentially always at risk. Relationships with others—alliances—and the ability to defend themselves were the only means of security. There could be no appeal to a central authority, and a "tradition" of nonhostility could not be counted on in a time of food crisis or other catastrophes. Even in peaceful times, there were boundary areas between different polities and ethnic groups. The likelihood that a peaceful tradition would have perpetually existed across those boundaries is slim. A shift in alliances was always possible, and new people could have tried to move into a given territory at any time.

Therefore, a prehistoric site should be given a security analysis, just as it gets a subsistence analysis. For example, appropriate questions would be: "Could people make a living within the site catchment and, if so, how?" "How could they ensure living safely in this community?" These are legitimate questions that force an archaeologist to come to grips with how a community might have functioned in addressing its most basic needs. And, of course, the answers would vary with different situations. Some answers might be: "They built a fort." "The larger polity was providing security, so no additional precaution was required." The purpose of this process is not to look solely for evidence of warfare; it is a way of looking to see how security needs could have been met. In other words, the issue is not whether there was warfare or, conversely, peace. Rather, it is a means of assessing a community's need for security and the measures that could have been, or were, taken to accomplish it.

This "security conscious" approach to interpretation is similar to that needed for assessing various other aspects of information about a site. Why were the rooms burned? Why were bodies not buried? Why was a palisade built or a tunnel dug from a pit structure to a tower? Archaeologists cannot simply find some categories of information and ignore their potential consequences. A burned room does not automatically signify warfare, but it cannot be ignored as a possible consequence of war. Burning, and every other similar type of evidence, needs to be assessed from the perspective that security would have been a nearly constant concern for prehistoric people and that warfare and conflict could have been contributing factors.

Review of the Models of Warfare

I began this book by demonstrating that warfare was much more common in the prehistoric past than has generally been accepted. I then argued that, if it were common, warfare would have been an important part of the cultural landscape and could have dictated where people lived, the sizes of their settlements, and might even have had major impacts on their subsistence activities. More than this, warfare would have impinged on social dynamics, from how leadership roles developed and functioned to the reasons for groups' interacting with each other and how this was accomplished.

All of these issues can be addressed simply by recognizing the existence of warfare and how it functioned. It is not even necessary to ask why it existed. However, there is much interest in why warfare would be so common. There have been a variety of models proposed to accommodate its existence. My goal for this book was not to test these models, as much as it was to characterize Southwestern warfare. But in so doing I needed to say something about the possible underlying causes of warfare.

Models that take warfare into account are essentially "materialist" or "nonmaterialist." The materialist model claims that population growth results in carrying-capacity stress or other resource limitations and that competition over these scarce resources results in warfare. The nonmaterialist models claim that warfare, instead of being rational, stems from revenge and culturally rewarded behavior and the need to gain glory and status. A middle-ground approach would be the position that warfare has materialist roots, but can, over time, become institutionalized. In such cases, even when materialistic needs dissipate (i.e., if the population declines markedly), warfare will not stop immediately; old animosities, built-in rewards for success in war, and other socially defined factors will cause the warfare to continue after it would previously have been considered irrational.

None of these models can be invalidated on their basic tenets alone. The materialists can claim that just because no one can identify which resource was scarce, doesn't mean there wasn't one. And the nonmaterialist can claim that, yes, there were resources in short supply, but other means of solving the problem were available and not used because of the need for revenge, status, and so forth. And, finally, the middle-ground approach can explain some instances of warfare by showing there were scarce resources and can argue in other instances that these were cases of residual warfare, the antecedents of which are not known. In spite of the possible explanatory problems with these models, it is still worthwhile to look at Southwestern warfare from their perspective.

A Summary of the Evidence

The suggested underlying cause of Southwestern warfare put forth here is, essentially, a climate-impelled materialist one. During the Early Period, the climate was probably generally "average" in that it neither allowed very rapid growth nor caused a resource crisis. The population did not grow unchecked, and whatever resource stress existed probably did not cause dramatic negative changes. I would expect warfare to be endemic under these circumstances. Beginning around A.D. 900, the climate improved, the carrying capacity increased and, in the Middle Period, I would expect warfare to have declined, at least initially. And, then, beginning in the 1100s, the climate seemed to revert to a more long-term average and warfare increased. Finally, in the 1200s, the Late Period, the climate deteriorated significantly and warfare became virulent.

There is a large body of evidence for prehistoric warfare in the Southwest, and it generally confirms the above scenario. I argued that evidence for warfare can be seen in site plans, site locations, and site clustering. It can also be seen in burned sites, unburied bodies, and other evidence for violence. Other indicators, such as weaponry and art, are also relevant. The ethnohistorical record can provide examples that show how warfare might have been conducted and how my model for prehistoric warfare meshes with what is known for the historic period.

And, most importantly, these independent lines of evidence reveal the same patterns. Massive burning was most intense at the same time as the greatest numbers of bodies were left unburied, which also date to when sites shifted to more defensive locations and constructions. The simultaneous occurrence of many lines of evidence for warfare in the Late Period is strong evidence for its existence. Defensively configured sites are found in defensive locations. When site clusters are found, they have been burned and there are unburied bodies. For those scholars who would interpret any of these data by other means, the burden is on them to explain the correlation among the various indicators of warfare.

Although the archaeological record underrepresents evidence for warfare, it was quite common. The massacre of some 100 people at southeastern Utah's Cave 7 (Hurst and Turner 1993) demonstrates that warfare was present by approximately A.D. 0. A long chain of data, including very defensive hilltop sites, palisades, burned sites, distinctive and well-made weapons, and scalping rounds out the evidence for warfare in the first centuries A.D. And, while the warfare was apparently chronic, it did not generally lead to everyone living in large population aggregates or clusters of sites or to areal abandonments. Warfare was a component of the Early Period social milieu, but not a dominant one.

In contrast, the last few centuries before Contact experienced not only extensive warfare but also an intense level of it, which had a major impact on other aspects of Late Period life. The most dramatic evidence for this is the change in settlement patterns. In a sharp break with the past, sites became very large, very densely occupied, and were often very well fortified. Defensive considerations dominated the formation of almost all sites at this time, and almost everyone lived in defensible communities. Not only did the sites rapidly evolve into very defensive communities but they also gathered together in clusters over the landscape. The clusters consisted of two to thirty sites, spaced about 3 miles apart, with each cluster about 20 miles from neighboring clusters. This pattern is fuzzy in some areas (in the Rio Grande Valley, for example), never fully developed before abandonment in others (as in the Four Corners area), and the clusters were more linear in a few places (such as in the Verde Valley, north of modern-day Phoenix). Nevertheless, it is clear that site clusters formed over the entire Southwest.

And then there are the unburied bodies. Although not all acts of warfare would leave unburied bodies, and not all unburied bodies would preserve (and sample excavations would not necessarily find those that did preserve), it is still possible to estimate that the number of these bodies is in the thousands. At several sites there is good evidence of the entire community being massacred, while at many others the loss was significant portions of the community. Massive burning was also widespread. From the Late Period, more than forty instances of extensive burning, spread throughout the Southwest, can be identified; no region was spared.

From the perspective of warfare, the abandonment of large areas of the Southwest begins to make sense. While some areas were probably abandoned because they were no longer inhabitable by corn farmers, others were not really abandoned at all. Instead, site clusters were eliminated. The fewer and fewer surviving groups became spaced out farther and farther apart. The severe consequences of warfare, climate deterioration, and the effects of living in massive communities all led to population decline. The result was vast areas becoming much less populated and the survivors' territories becoming much larger. The Southwest's people were adjusting to a new reality, and warfare was one of the major mechanisms driving that adjustment.

There are, in a few instances, rather detailed descriptions of what took place. In the El Morro Valley, for example, there were communities forming that followed the 3-mile spacing pattern. They consisted of small, separate room blocks lying close together. In at least one case, virtually all the room blocks were burned, and the surviving population rapidly built a massive, very defensive pueblo with over 500 rooms. Almost immediately, everyone else followed suit, and the valley ended up with seven of these large, walled towns, each carefully located to be visually linked to the others.

The El Morro Valley is one of the few areas where there is a diachronic picture of the process. In the Kayenta area, for example, people also began to congregate into communities that were defensible and mutually visible, although the timing of the process is less well understood. Direct evidence for attack is rare in the Kayenta area, but some of the sites were so defensibly located that an attack would have been practically impossible. Here, evidence exists for different, probably antagonistic, clusters of sites forming. Sites were smaller in the Kayenta area than in the El Morro Valley; the Kayenta area was abandoned and Zuni–El Morro was not. The broad pattern is the same, but the details differ. Similar pictures can probably be discovered for other parts of the Southwest, but they simply have not been adequately searched out.

Whether my proposed Southwestern model for why there was—or was not—warfare is accepted, evidence for its existence should not be judged in terms of this model. Regardless of the reasons warfare occurred, it seems inescapable that these periods of conflict were a significant cultural factor in the Southwest. In the Late Period, the combination of warfare and deteriorating climate must have resulted in a cultural crisis of major proportions. No one was immune and the population was severely affected. The survivors were forever changed, having been forced to migrate and recombine into new societies for survival. Many other aspects of life, from religion to trade, would have been directly affected. In fact, the Kachina cult, the interaction between groups, and the very political Pueblo landscape described by the Spanish at Contact were shaped by the warfare of the preceding two and a half centuries.

Explaining Warfare in the Past

The line of reasoning proposed in this book is nothing more than a standard scientific approach in which the number and degree of independent lines of argument provide strong confirmation of the hypothesis. There is not a large body of literature on how to interpret the different classes of evidence. I want this effort to spark critiques and refinements of the approaches outlined here. What I offer is an initial discussion on the subject of warfare in the Southwest, not the final word. The best response to my thoughts presented here would be to change the process of how warfare is considered.

When standard, scientific reasoning is applied to the Southwest, ample evidence exists of very significant warfare at many times. Every class of evidence that has been proposed as signaling warfare in general can be found, to at least some degree, in Southwestern material. Many classes of information—such as evidence for line-of-sight communication—have scarcely been tapped and, consequently, provide little additional information at this point. But their potential for the future is great.

Most importantly, evidence for Southwestern warfare varies through time. This change provides a comparative framework that helps in recognizing warfare and its absence, while simultaneously raising questions as to why there was this variation over time. There was not a constant level of warfare; at certain times, it was almost nonexistent and, at others, it had a tremendous impact on social systems. Going beyond simply demonstrating there was significant warfare is the actual point of this book. It is the change over time that cries out for explanation.

Of equal importance is that warfare, and the responses to it, were apparently pan-Southwestern. To the extent that this is the case, warfare and peoples' response behaviors cannot be explained by unique local factors. It is conceivable that unique events, such as a catastrophic flood, might cause famine and fighting over the remaining resources, or that a particular individual or group of elite, by some (even accidental) behavior, could cause an outbreak of warfare. But, how could such local factors have panregional consequences? When the intensification of warfare is seen to occur in a temporally patterned way over the entire Southwest, there must be much broader explanations. Indeed, there is some evidence that this Late Period of intense warfare was not just a pan-Southwestern phenomenon but a pan-North American phenomenon as well. If so, then there must be a pancontinental explanation. An accidental or idiosyncratic explanation for the occurrence of warfare of such magnitude over such an enormous area can surely be rejected.

This is the place where traditional anthropological models of warfare and the current interpretations are at their greatest divergence. Most traditional interpretations would consider humans being peaceful as the natural, normal state and would recognize the need to explain periods of warfare. However, based on the overall model proposed by Lawrence Keeley (1966) and supported by the information presented here, it is warfare that is the norm and it is long periods of peace that need explaining. In this light, a 1,000-year interval in which warfare was a factor throughout much of the Southwest, followed by ten generations of a virtual absence of war, is worthy of serious study.

Reality, as always, is more complicated than interpretive models of it. How can a period be characterized as "peaceful" when it has an overwhelming amount of evidence for very violent behavior, including possible cannibalism? While there were no forts, burned sites, or other direct evidence for intergroup conflict, the Middle Period does not seem to have been a "Garden of Eden" for many of its inhabitants. In the eastern Anasazi area, both the overall peace and the localized violence seemed intertwined with some form of evolving elite social structure. However, there is also evidence of peace elsewhere in the Southwest at this time, where evidence of an emerging social elite is equivocal or nonexistent. Missing is a major body of literature on how the formation of large political groups might have eliminated warfare within their boundaries and at the same time have used force to control the population within those boundaries. Did this ever take place within the structure of egalitarian societies? In the absence of warfare, did it take place on the boundaries of the system? Were such systems "fragile," or could they last for centuries? It is the paucity of models along these lines that makes the Middle Period's 250-year peace so difficult to understand. There is little with which to make a comparison. Until warfare is addressed realistically, explanations of particular situations will not be possible.

Warfare, Carrying Capacity, and Population Growth

The ecological model of warfare immediately requires coming to grips with ideas about carrying capacity. How do human populations grow? Are they truly limited by a region's carrying capacity, or is community growth regulated by the biological requirements of number and spacing of births and by social behavior? Can new land always be brought into production and new subsistence strategies developed or implemented to accommodate any growth that takes place? Could an area like the Southwest actually ever have filled up with people? Or, in other words, over the 2,000 years under discussion here could there have been enough growth to drastically affect the available resources, and would there have been strong reasons to fight over scarce resources?

This is probably the most fundamental question facing anthropologists today. If human populations can—and did—grow rapidly in the past, then there would be incessant carrying-capacity pressure, and human history should be read as one of incessant competition among groups for vital resouces. If not, and growth is slow and controlled, then methods of social regulation of growth would be a uniquely human attribute. How and why this social regulation of growth came to be, and how it gets lost (as seems to be the case today in many parts of the world) are equally fascinating issues.

At this point, the evidence points to Southwestern populations having been sensitive to changes in carrying capacity, with population both rising and falling with change and with warfare intimately linked to the entire process. As with evidence for warfare in general, low growth and low sensitivity to carrying-capacity limitations should not be assumed, any more than should high growth rates and constant carrying-capacity pressure. Such assumptions cannot be permitted to eliminate the question.

What does not seem to fit is the continued warfare on the Colorado Plateau after the population declined dramatically. With Hopi and Zuni separated by 80 miles, it is difficult to see what they could have been competing over. Is this a case of warfare having a materialist basis in A.D. 1300 and then warfare behavior being institutionalized within the societies? If so, even after the environmental causes were no longer applicable, the institutions and the motive of revenge would have continued the warfare for several hundred years, although at perhaps a decreasing level. It may not be possible to understand the rationale behind the level of conflict at A.D. 1500 without understanding the prior history of these people.

Social Consequences of Warfare

Studying warfare merely to demonstrate its existence is of little value. The important issue is how warfare affected the rest of the cultural system. Although much of this book has focused on the evidence of warfare, I have also been concerned with the impact of warfare on the larger social and subsistence milieu. As discussed, even in the Early Period, there was some site clustering, defenses were constructed, numerous people were killed, and perhaps no-man's-lands developed. Once warfare reached a stage where large numbers of people were being killed or forced to disband as a group, then there should have been both significant social responses to warfare and competition between groups. This would have led to the possibility of group selection. Some groups would "get it right" and survive, while others would not and hence decline in population and disband or otherwise become marginal. Such a possibility of group selection is most obvious for the Late Period and is an important aspect of the social implications of warfare at that time: There were those who survived and those who did not, and most did not.

Clearly, at some time around A.D. 1300, there were about twenty-seven clusters of sites on the Colorado Plateau, another ten or so clusters in the Rio Grande Valley, and at least that many more clusters in the southern portion of the Southwest and on the western fringe. By A.D. 1350, probably half of them no longer existed. And by A.D. 1400 or 1450, there were only three remaining on the Plateau and few anywhere else except in the Rio Grande Valley. This decline in the number of independent polities was surely accompanied by an overall population decline for the entire Southwest. The decline resulted from direct deaths due to warfare and to disease and probably famine, which were indirectly tied to warfare. So, over more than two centuries, social groups became extinct and large numbers of people died. Is it possible to determine how some groups survived and others did not? To what extent was survival due to the ecological fortunes of where people were living, and to what extent was it due to developing the social "glue" that allowed people to hang on during this catastrophic time?

In spite of the great and various idiosyncratic behaviors, unique individuals, and accidents of nature that must have occurred in the Late Period, what is surprising is the regularity of the evolutionary process. Most striking are the great similarities in the histories of Hopi and Zuni. Each started with a number of site clusters encompassing more than thirty sites; in each case the sites were spread over quite a wide area; then each group was reduced to between five and seven sites. Sometime in each area, the inward-facing pueblo plan was abandoned in favor of rows of room blocks, perhaps as the threat of attack diminished. The biggest difference is that the Hopi remained in separate pueblos, while the Zuni amalgamated into one (although it did so in the context of Spanish impact).

The Hopi and Zuni eventually dominated the entire Western Pueblo region—which was not preordained. Earlier, there were many other polities in the region. There were groups that could have merged and become as large as either Hopi or Zuni, yet they did not. Was there something special about these two areas from the beginning? Were there more sites in these two clusters than was typical for the Colorado Plateau? But, was there also a better adapted social organization or other parts of the cultural system that allowed the greater number of Hopi and Zuni sites and ensured their ability to stay together? If so, just what was it?

The Classic Hohokam of the Salt River was initially, in many ways, similar to the Hopi and Zuni. At the beginning of the 1300s, the Classic Hohokam people were by far the largest polity in their area. Soon, nearby groups disappeared. It is unclear whether they also declined in numbers during the mid-1300s. Whether there was a catastrophic flood in the 1360s that devastated their system, or some other factor that caused their demise, the Classic Hohokam community did not survive with the same level of cultural continuity as did Hopi and Zuni. This may have been due to a decline in social complexity that resulted from a decline in numbers. Or, it may have been an ability to disperse when they ran out of enemies. For whatever reasons, the survivability of the Hohokam—in broad structural terms—was very different from that of the Hopi and Zuni.

Warfare in Daily Life

Archaeology, with its wonderful time-depth perspective, tends to focus on long-term changes. This sometimes makes it difficut to discern how systems might have functioned on a daily basis. While it is easy to say that warfare was endemic or intense, what did this mean in the lives of the people? Most importantly, an outbreak of war or the presence of a conflict did not prevent other aspects of daily life from continuing. The ethnographic accounts make it clear that marriage, trade, and public events—such as fairs and ceremonies—took place between groups that were otherwise adversaries. The ramifications of the intertwining of conflict and cooperation are hard to grasp, but it seems to have been a common aspect of most warfare in the past.

Nevertheless, it is likely that the "calculus" of warfare was always present in people's minds and was included in all their decision-making processes. In an analogy with New Guinea, a visitor to a prehistoric Southwest pueblo may have automatically assessed its defensive characteristics, and the numbers of fighting-age men present, or even noted when the group was planning to undertake ceremonies and, hence, be more vulnerable to attack. Such assessments might have led to these considerations: Would these people make good allies? Were they vulnerable to attack? Every community would have known that they were under assessment by others and that such opinions were being formed about them. "Keeping up appearances" would have been very important. A reputation of strength and strong leadership would have been a valuable asset. Whom you selected as allies and whom you allowed to join your community were strategic decisions with consequences affecting lives. This kind of constant military "assessment" occurred among villages in New Guinea and other tribal-level societies, and is probably a universal phenomenon.

In the Southwest, the decision to relocate a village or to strengthen its defenses would be noted and assessed by other people. Leaders who proposed offensive operations that failed would have their status adjusted accordingly. Decisions to attack villages would be carefully weighed, determining the loss of trading partners or future allies, versus the gains that might be accrued with other allies or by access to additional resources. The degree of risk in allowing people to leave the pueblo for foraging or trading would be constantly assessed. As noted, any group must have feared they could lose a major engagement and be forced to flee. Where to go? The maintenance of long-distance relations with people with whom to seek refuge must have been a serious concern.

Peoples' concern for warfare should be reflected in its probability. The idea that settlements were expected to have a long use-life and would have been designed in fear of warfare, even if it was not immediate, has been discussed. Even trade may reflect such long-term planning. Warfare may increase trade, not decrease it, as might be initially expected. If trade was being used to build up relationships between allies, it would be expected to increase when the value of those allies increased. Also, trade may become more broad-based under conditions of warfare. There may be great value to a distant group as an ally or as intermediary. Without such added value, trade with certain groups may have been unimportant. But, with the threat of warfare, the importance of the relationship, and the role of trade in maintaining it, could rapidly increase.

Certain individuals within the community could be considered more valuable when warfare was present. Elder members of a community were usually thought to have important knowledge of how to use the landscape for subsistence. Where could good pinyon nuts be found this year? What were the consequences of farming a particular drainage in terms of the likelihood of floods or other dangers? But, even more important and crucial would have been knowing how alliances had worked out in the past, as well as knowing the individual abilities of other groups' leaders and their experience and success at both military and diplomatic strategies.

As is apparent from previous discussions, poor advice and a lack of knowledge can lead to defeat and massacres. The diplomatic leaders in New Guinea were considered so valuable that they were not allowed to fight and risk being killed. Prehistorically (as today), the ability to form truces was a critical need. A trading partner was probably much more than someone to trade with; trade provided potentially important communication channels to other groups. How to arrange a truce? How to propose a realignment of alliances, when former enemies became new allies? Having a "connection" would have been a very valuable asset. Trade may have been more a means to keep the channels open than to get the stuff itself. Humans have always lived in an "information age." In a milieu of warfare, alliances, truces and attacks, communication, and knowledge of the enemy and allies would have been critical to survival. While leadership in the Pueblos today is couched in terms of esoteric religious knowledge, in the past there must have been a great premium placed on a leader's ability to manage relationships and acquire relevant knowledge of other groups, their leadership, and past achivements and failures.

Changing Adaptations with Changing Circumstances

The warfare-related social structures, practices, and tactics had been evolving over the centuries in the Southwest, but everything changed drastically and suddenly when the Spaniards came on the scene. The Spaniards were colonizers. They brandished superior military technology (primarily in the form of metal weaponry and horses), and their troops were professional soldiers. Even though the Spanish were defeated in the Pueblo Revolt, they came back and had gained military control over the entire area by the early 1700s.

With the establishment of a well-equipped force of experienced colonizers, not only does the military situation dramatically change but so do the threats facing the Puebloans. A military response to the threat was not a viable option in the face of this new invading force. And the biggest threat was the loss of land to these colonists. So, the people of the Southwest changed tactics. After the military resistance in the 1600s and as a new coping mechanism, they responded to the onslaught by not giving the Spanish any justification—no matter how flimsy—to forcefully move them off their land. They didn't fight; they initiated nothing to cause relocation.

One way the Pueblo people accomplished this was to decrease the importance of the military in their social structures. Apparently, military leaders and previously valuable leadership qualities were now downplayed and no longer rewarded, and warrior societies lost their influence. That kind of thinking and behavior was no longer encouraged. In this new environment, the social structures that were associated with warfare were now inappropriate and dangerous.

Another way the Puebloans sought to maintain a hold on their territory was to develop an incredible sense of place. After the Spaniards gained firm control, there was only very minor relocation of pueblo communities—much more stability than was ever evidenced prehistorically. These communities and their settings became the center of the pueblo world. Everything was viewed in relation to the pueblo. This concept of the "middle place" may have evolved from the age-old notion that possession is nine-tenths of the law. If you move the pueblo, you somehow weaken your justification to occupy your own land. By even making minor shifts within your own territory, you could be opening the door to the idea that the whole community could be relocated by the Spaniards. This successful tactic became—and still is—deeply ingrained in the world view of the Pueblo people.

In a sense, staying alive depended on defending enough land to survive, not so much militarily as psychologically: "Anyone who comes to our village will immediately recognize this has been ours for centuries. It is inconceivable that you would make us move, and we do nothing to give you justification." Of course, the Puebloans were not completely successful; land loss and encroachment did occur. But their key core holdings were usually retained. As a survival tactic, an incredibly strong sense of place and an unwillingness to give the dominant power an excuse to confiscate, soon replaced fighting neighbors in order to discourage being encroached upon. The ability to recognize the real threat and respond appropriately was what led, in part, to the survival of these communities over the subsequent 300 years.

Scale and explanation

It is particularly important to realize that Southwestern warfare cut across cultural divisions and ecological zones. The differences in the three long-enduring cultural traditions of Hohokam, Mogollon, and Anasazi were substantial and significant, but, especially in the Late Period, these differences had little impact on the nature of warfare. Cluster spacing, in particular, was very regular—around 20 miles between clusters—regardless of the portion of the Southwest under review. Warfare was equally deadly everywhere. The two largest known massacres occurred at Sand Canyon, located at the very northern edge of the Southwest, and at Casas Grandes, near the southern boundary.

There were differences in response to warfare over the Southwest that may well have reflected the historical differences in cultural traditions. There were differences in community size: The Anasazi area produced, by far, the largest communities. There were differences in the way the communities were configured: Only the eastern Anasazi built inward-facing pueblos, and only people in the old Hohokam area regularly built compounds with lots of freestanding walls.

If warfare was driven by revenge or custom, or was not ultimately environmentally determined, why would all three cultural groups radically intensify conflict at the same time? In the Late Period, warfare swept across all cultural and ecological boundaries. Sites grew large and clustered, with open spaces created rather similarly over the entire Southwest. There were some exceptions, however. For example, sites were larger on the Colorado Plateau than most other places, with the largest in the Rio Grande Valley. But all areas witnessed abandonments; all areas witnessed population decline.

Is it possible to reconcile culturally driven warfare with these patterns? Yes and no. Did the lack of warfare in the Hohokam area reflect a cultural milieu that did not allow for, or need, warfare? Or, was the ecological situation such that it was not until the 1100s that carrying capacity was reached? Each of these propositions could be defended by what is known today. Nonetheless, it is an extremely weak argument that the rapid and severe intensification of warfare that swept over the Southwest in the late 1200s was simply driven by revenge and cultural rewards. The warfare took on very similar trappings from the pine-covered mountains to the low desert; no area was immune or spared. Warfare was initiated by people who had very different religions, settlement types, subsistence systems, and who must have spoken many different languages. Suddenly they were all doing the same thing: living in forts, clustering their communities, and fighting enough to eliminate many communities and even many clusters of communities. This warfare was not a fad. The level of conflict was not the result of a sudden need to prove one's manhood or to seek an eye for an eye. Something much more vitally important must have driven this pervasive change.

Outstanding Questions

The subject of early Southwestern warfare has barely been broached at the present time. The current model and evidence for warfare probably raises more questions than it answers, and some very fundamental questions are far from being answered in detail. Why was there relative peace during the 900s–1100s period and, at the same time, such overwhelming evidence for violence? Was there incipient warfare during those years in a form not presently recognizable? What was special about the Hopi and the Zuni that allowed them to survive when twenty-five other groups did not? Why did they continue to fight each other into the 1700s, even when their numbers were drastically reduced and there were great empty zones between them? Why didn't the large communities of the late Pueblo I period build defensive structures? Why, after 150 years of warfare and population decline, didn't the process reverse, and the Southwest's population begin to grow and repopulate abandoned areas? What role did nonsedentary people play in all of this? It is easy to suggest that many of the behaviors and institutions seen in the Southwest were the result of almost two millennia of adaptions to farming in a marginal environment. How many of these behaviors and traditions were also the result of warfare over this same period of time?

Final Thoughts

Warfare is, justifiably, an emotionally charged issue. It would be nice to think that peace is the natural, common human condition. But this does not seem to be the case. If warfare can be as common, and have as many consequences as proposed here, it must be addressed objectively. It cannot be ignored or relegated to a footnote, if the past is to be understood. We cannot wish away the unpleasant aspects of the human condition if we are ever to understand that condition. There will surely be individuals who react negatively to the ideas presented here, simply from reading the title of the book. Further attempts at dialogue with these individuals may be fruitless. For the rest of us, we must remember that paradigm shifts are not easy. I have a very difficult time looking at Pueblo Bonito and realizing the society that built it was apparently quite violent. However, wishing that particular society not to have been so ruthless does not further my understanding of it or other societies. We must remember that the truth, once understood, is always more interesting than fantasy. We can and will someday understand the Southwestern past and the role that warfare played in it.

APPENDIX

Details of Late Period Site Clusters

The following information provides greater detail for many of the site clusters discussed and mapped in chapter 6. Many of the summary statements and inferences are drawn from this material. The highlights of this information are in that chapter, and there has been no attempt to eliminate redundancy between this appendix and chapter 6.

COLORADO PLATEAU SITE CLUSTERS

McElmo Cluster

A McElmo cluster to the west of Mesa Verde had begun forming, but the process was probably truncated by the abandonment of the entire area in the late 1200s. A good case can be made for an initial settlement shift toward defensive sites (R. Lightfoot and Kuckelman 1995) around A.D. 1250. An excellent example is Sand Canyon Pueblo (Bradley 1992) with its enclosing wall, but Goodman Point also has an enclosing wall (Kenzle 1993). The Hedley site—the third really large site in this cluster—also seemed to have a defensive layout, but it is less clear. Many smaller sites also had enclosing walls (Kenzle 1993). The presence of towers on many of these sites and the construction of small cliff dwellings are further evidence of defensive responses at this time. Similarly, there was a settlement location shift to canyon rims and to areas immediately adjacent to springs. This often included the construction of reservoirs (R. Lightfoot and Kuckelman 1995; Fewkes 1918). These occurred at large sites such as Mud Springs and at smaller ones such as Castle Rock. Many small reservoirs have probably gone unrecognized; over time they have eroded and only remnants remain. Some small sites, such as Castle Rock, were on particularly defensive locations. Some changes in settlement patterns, such as constructing walls and towers and locating on canyon rims, began before the building of the really large defensive sites took place. This is an example of an initial shift toward slightly defensive sites and then the construction of really defensive ones, as seen elsewhere. The Hedley site is a candidate for this type of evolution. Apparently, the site initially consisted of a large, closely clustered group of room blocks on a high, but not really defensible, location that dates to the early 1200s. There is evidence for massive burning, and the site was reconfigured slightly to the east, right on a water source and with a defensive exterior.

There was a cluster of sites running between the westernmost Hovenweep group and Goodman Point farther east. Late in the 1200s this cluster had about eighteen sites, with about nine large ones of over 200 rooms each. It was a relatively linear cluster, much like the later cluster along the Zuni River (see below). With a span of some 36 km, it was similar in size to the Zuni River cluster's 40 km span, the 40 km span of the Upper Little Colorado cluster, and the 34 km span of the Silver Creek cluster, although the McElmo sites were much smaller. This cluster was about 16 1/2 miles (27 km) from the cluster at Mesa Verde. The spacing between these two was a bit closer than seen elsewhere, but the difficult topography of the mesa may have made it the equivalent of the somewhat greater spacing found elsewhere.

There are some problems with this formulation. There were a few sites between these clusters, such as Yucca House, Mud Springs, and Bowman Pueblo. However, it is thought that Mud Springs was abandoned by A.D. 1250, and the others may not be very late sites either. There were also a few sites that were not part of a cluster, and whether these sites lasted as long as those in the cluster cannot easily be determined because the area was abandoned so quickly and the time span of these clustered sites was only about twenty years.

In general, patterns seen elsewhere in the Southwest seemed to take place in this area, such as locating sites directly on domestic water and locating small sites in more defensive settings than large ones were, although the patterns are less clear due to the incomplete nature of the conversion to defense. There is an illustrative distinction between the really large sites of Sand Canyon and Goodman Point, with defensive walls, and the much smaller Castle Rock Pueblo, with both a defensive layout and a hilltop location. Massive burning and evidence for traumatic deaths and uninterred bodies at a number of sites (R. Lightfoot and Kuckelman 1995), including Sand Canyon, Castle Rock, Charnel House, and possibly Snider's Well, were discussed in chapter 6.

Mesa Verde Cluster

This site cluster consisted of the famous cliff dwellings of Mesa Verde. It was about 16 1/2 miles (27 km) from the eastern edge of the McElmo cluster (as noted above) and about 22 miles (35 km) from the northern boundary of the Totah cluster. During the 1200s, there was definitely a constriction in the area being utilized in the Mesa Verde region. Prior to the 1200s, especially, but even from A.D. 1200 to 1250, occupation sites had extended over much of the mesa top. As in other areas, there were towers and other somewhat defensive aspects to the slightly earlier sites. For example, the 499 Site was repeatedly remodeled until its rooms formed a defensive perimeter (R. Lister 1964).

The final occupation of the area was in the cliff dwellings (Rohn 1977). Essentially everyone was living in them, and all or almost all the mesa-top sites were abandoned. These cliff dwellings were actually quite small compared with other late sites. The four largest had only 220, 200, 150, and 114 rooms, respectively. While there were a number of very small sites that may well have been no more than secure food-storage places, there were only about thirteen reasonably sized habitation sites.

Haas and Creamer (1993) have shown that the cliff dwellings of the Kayenta area make sense only as defensive sites, and the same logic presumably applies to Mesa Verde although it has not been empirically tested. The demonstration that remodeling in the famous Balcony House cliff dwelling at Mesa Verde in the A.D. 1270s is best interpreted as defensively related is a case in point (Fairchild-Parks and Dean 1993). The thirty-inch-thick wall with loopholes at Alcove House (Rohn 1977) also seems to have been a defensive construction.

There is other evidence for defense and for violence. Long House has what were described as apertures in breastworks (Cattanach 1980). Kiva M burned while in use and several isolated skulls and an unburied body were found in the kivas there. Walker (1995) interpreted these remains to represent at least four individuals. Three kivas in Spruce Tree House all had skulls in their ventilator shafts, and structure 9 contained three bodies, which seemed suspiciously like unburied bodies (Fewkes 1909:24 n. B). There was also fragmentary skeletal material in Square Tower House (Fewkes 1922:57). Step House apparently had a burned body that may represent violence (Nordenskiold [1893] 1973:49). Given how early and sketchily reported some of the work is, and how small the cliff dwellings were and how few of them, this is actually quite a lot of evidence for defensive relocation and construction as well as violence. The burning of the Long House kiva is exceptional; the cliff dwellings of Mesa Verde, like those in the Kayenta area and Canyon de Chelly, rarely showed signs of burning. If burning was part of abandonment rituals, why were cliff dwellings not also burned?

One early site, Big Juniper House (Swannack 1969), a mesa-top site dating mid- to late 1100s, is enigmatic. This is the period right after the Chaco peace when there is the first evidence for increased defensiveness. It did not have a defensive configuration; there were a few burned structures, but nothing suggesting systematic massive burning. However, there was an apparently unburied body in Kiva A, which also had other disarticulated remains. There were also at least three bodies with missing body parts, such as hands and feet, found in an area of very shallow trash, without grave goods or prepared grave pits. Whether this was a continuation of the Chacoan pattern of badly treated individuals or the very beginnings of conflict in this area is unclear.

The Totah Cluster

The site cluster in the area around Farmington, New Mexico, often refered to as the Totah, is one of the most poorly known clusters. This is because almost all of the sites represent either reoccupation (or possibly continuous occupation) of Chaco Great Houses, or they have never been studied, or the relevant sites have been destroyed by modern activity (Stein and McKenna 1988). The best to be said at this point is that there was a site cluster in this area. It does not seem to have been very large, or very long-lived, and there is ample evidence for site burning and violence. The cluster included parts of Morris 41 and Morris 39 on the La Plata

River and Flora Vista, Salmon, and Aztec Ruins as well as three or four smaller sites. A site in what is now Farmington that was once referred to as the "Fort" site seems to have been another member of this cluster, although it may have been a reoccupied Great House (E. H. Morris 1939; Stein and McKenna 1988). Flora Vista seems to be the only site that was initially built in the late period that much is known about, and it had a defensive configuration (Stein and McKenna 1988).

The Salmon Ruin seems to have been catastrophically burned (at least the tower kiva and the western portion of the site), with about thirty-five unburied bodies, sometime after 1263 (R. Adams 1980; Shipman 1983:51.)—one of the most traumatic of all the catastrophes discussed in chapter 6. Both the Great Kiva and upper stories in the main room block at Aztec (west ruin) had burned at the end of the occupation, and considerable burned corn was found in the east ruin. Also, the skeleton of a female was found with a shattered pelvis and forearm; four children and an adult male were burned in a kiva fire; and an elderly female was impaled by a sharpened stake (F. Lister and Lister 1987). The Morris 41 site had at least one section of the late room area burned, and it contained charred bodies (E. H. Morris 1939). Thus, out of the four sites from which there is reasonably accurate excavation information, three have evidence of burning and violence. This cluster was abandoned before 1300, just as the other northern clusters—McElmo, Mesa Verde, and Kayenta—were.

Kayenta Area Clusters

The Kayenta area has many parallels with the McElmo–Mesa Verde area in the mid- to late 1200s. In each case, the area was abandoned very early, before A.D. 1300. The evolution toward very large sites never progressed very far. Each area also had a significant number of cliff dwellings, and in each case the population migrated south. These migrations seemed to occur before the shift to defensive sites was well-developed in the more southern areas that the migrants were moving into. Again, as in the McElmo–Mesa Verde area, there were apparently several site clusters evolving, but the process was truncated before they were well-defined spatially. So, the settlement pattern seems to have included some clustering of sites, some large sites, some cliff dwellings, and some small sites that may or may not have been defensively located. That is, not all sites were strongly clustered, not all sites were large, and most— but not all—sites were defensive.

Several workers (Haas and Creamer 1993; Dean 1996b) have noted the beginnings of no-man's-lands between settlement groupings in part of the area. It is fairly easy to see a Rainbow Plateau group and a Klethla Valley group. What is difficult to determine is whether the sites in Long House Valley, the Kayenta Valley, and in Tsegi Canyon represent one large site cluster or several smaller site clusters.

The Rainbow Plateau group had three to five reasonably large sites and at least five smaller ones. However, the largest site had only 100 rooms, and the smaller ones frequently had only 20 rooms. How many were actually contemporaneous is far from clear. Dean states they were intervisible, but provides no further information about this interesting point.

The Tsegi Canyon area had two large cliff dwellings—Kiet Siel (150 rooms) and Betatakin (120 rooms)—as well as several with 50 rooms, and a number of smaller cliff dwellings. These sites were not as tightly clustered as those on Mesa Verde, and

Haas and Creamer think that many were meant to be hidden. This does not suggest a well-integrated set of communities providing mutual defensive support, but more an "every community for itself" kind of pattern. Lindsay (1969) and Dean (1969) believe that some of the people from Kiet Siel may have been migrants from southwestern Colorado, further supporting the theory that these were not well-integrated communities.

Unlike Tsegi Canyon, the Klethla Valley had four to five major sites (Haas and Creamer 1993)—but very small compared with the later sites on the Colorado Plateau, the largest having only seventy rooms—that were located to provide mutual visibility. Haas and Creamer also think there was mutual visibility among the Long House and Kayenta Valley sites. It is possible that the Rainbow Plateau, the Klethla Valley, and the Long House–Kayenta Valley were all forming site clusters and that Tsegi Canyon was a sort of hinterland where the process of clustering had not taken place before the area was abandoned.

Interestingly, the Long House site with some 350 rooms was many times larger than any other site in these clusters. In fact, the number of rooms in Long House was more than all the rooms combined for the Klethla Valley cluster. To put this in even clearer perspective, the combined total number of rooms in sites in Tsegi Canyon, in the Kayenta Valley, and on the Rainbow Plateau was under 500. The Long House site was very close to the size of Sand Canyon and Goodman Point in the McElmo area, two significant large sites in that area. Kiet Siel and Betatakin, the two largest cliff dwellings in the Kayenta area, were also of the same magnitude as Cliff Palace and Long House, the two largest Mesa Verde cliff dwellings. It is difficult to believe that, with such striking parallels, the reasons for total abandonment of the two areas were not also parallel.

THE CIBOLA AREA CLUSTERS

What came to be known as the Cibola area contained one or more clusters in the Zuni area proper and the Jaralosa Draw and Techado clusters to the south. To the east were the Cebolleta and Rattail-Newton clusters, somewhat arbitrarily considered in the greater Acoma discussion below. Owing to the early surveys of Spier (1917) and later ones by Watson et al. (1980), Kintigh (1985), and Fowler et al. (1987), the number and spacing of sites dating to the late 1200s and early 1300s are better known than the other large clusters of Hopi and Acoma.

Kintigh notes that he was able to add only one site to Spier's initial list of large, late sites for the Zuni area, and Anyon (1992) adds only one more. That only two sites were found over the seventy-five years subsequent to Spier's work, suggests that the list of known sites must be relatively complete. Although survey is less complete farther to the south and east, there is no reason to believe that enough sites have been missed to change the observed patterns. Thirty-five large sites are known, a much larger total than for other areas. They ranged in size from about 120 to 800 ground-floor rooms. Most of them were probably at least two stories in part, so these were very big sites. For example, Kintigh estimates that Archeotekopta II had 1,412 rooms in all its stories. All of the sites were inward-facing towns with large central plazas. Less well known about this area are the sites that immediately preceded the really large towns.

The Zuni Cluster

The evolution of settlement patterns is best known from the El Morro Valley. A period where communities consisted of a cluster of small sites or room blocks with at least one site located on a high "lookout" was defined for the El Morro Valley and called the Scribe S phase (Watson et al. 1980). The phase was named for the Scribe S site, a clear example of this type of settlement pattern, near Pueblo de Los Muertos. Survey suggested a similar pattern around the Mirabal, Cienega, and Hole-in-the-Rock sites. There seemed to be a similar set of sites around Atsinna, but the data are less clear. There was an exceedingly obvious group around the Kluckhohn Ruin, with the Pettit site being the lookout (Saitta 1991). Zier (1976) excavated a probable component of such a group of sites near Heshotauthla farther downstream. There seems to have been a similar pattern of clustered room blocks near the Miller Ranch sites. Farther south, Sandstone Hill (Barnett 1974) may have been the same kind of site relating to three later sites in the Techado area (McGimsey 1980). Given the small amount of work that has been done on the issue, the number of examples of these semidefensive, loosely aggregated sites being closely associated with larger, more defensive, later sites is striking. A number of these earlier sites were significantly burned, such as the Scribe S site and the ones near Heshotauthla, and many of the earlier room blocks were stone-robbed, as were the Scribe S site and those near the Kluckhohn Ruin.

Subsequent population movement into the larger sites is overwhelmingly clear. However, the details of the occupation time spans of the sites are not. The process of movement into the large sites seemed to begin around A.D. 1285, and all of the sites were abandoned by the mid-1300s, with a new set, including the historical Zuni sites, established after that. These later sites were at a lower elevation than most of the very late, big sites of the 1200s and 1300s, which may be the only example on the Colorado Plateau of a cluster of sites shifting location over such a distance. Because this cluster was one of the few to survive, its successful strategy should be kept in mind.

The occupation span of the sites in the very late 1200s and 1300s is in question. Kintigh (1985) feels that only a portion of the sites were ever contemporaneous. I believe that most were occupied right after the transition to the big sites but that many were abandoned relatively soon thereafter. So Kintigh and I see very different settlement patterns at approximately A.D. 1300, but relatively similar ones from about A.D. 1325 onward. According to my interpretation of the sites being initially contemporaneous, the settlement distribution shows several aspects.

Several sites appear to have been isolated or on the periphery of this cluster, including the Big House site in Manualito Canyon (Fowler et al. 1987; Weaver 1978), Spier's site 61 that is north of Zuni, and the Box S site near Nutria (Spier 1917; Kintigh 1985). Each was at least 7 1/2 miles from another possibly contemporaneous site. All three sites were very close to domestic water with a possible walk-in well at Box S. Spier's 61 was small (122 rooms) and probably very short-lived. Big House, as the name implies, was quite large; but, as is usually the case for isolated sites, it did not have a long life. There was a tower on a very defensible point of land upstream from the Big House site and adjacent to a side canyon that allowed an easy entry into the canyon. It should be noted that Fowler et al. (1987) recorded a Chaco Great House at the mouth of the canyon and a later site upstream, but neither site was occupied in the late 1200s.

Closer to the Zuni drainage on the southeastern edge of the Zuni Reservation and some 18 miles away from the Jaralosa Draw cluster discussed below was a group of four sites, spaced about 3 to 4 miles apart: Jack's Lake, Archeotekopta II, Fort Site, and Ojo Pueblo. Jack's Lake, Archeotekopta II, and Ojo Pueblo were all very close to water or had a source inside the pueblo. Fort Site was relatively small (144 rooms) and the only one that was defensively located. This is an example of large sites next to water and small sites on high places. There is evidence for Scribe S phase material at Miller Ranch and perhaps at a lookout site as well (Shoemaker Ranch, a seventeen-room site on a defensive hilltop). The larger sites do not all have the same ceramic frequencies; and most likely some survived longer than others, but not by much.

Along the Zuni River were several clusters—or just a swarm of sites. The Pescado group—Lower Pescado Village, Pescado West, Lower Pescado Ruin, and Upper Pescado Ruin—represents one of the tightest clusters known. It also had one of the best water supplies (Pescado Springs). The sites were not very large. There is ceramic evidence for some of the sites lasting relatively late for the area, but they never took that expected next step: an amagamation into one big site. This may be a case similar to that of a site pair, discussed in chapter 6, although in this case there were more than two sites very close together.

Upriver, the site disturbance around the town of Ramah confuses things somewhat, but there seems to have been a site cluster made up of the Lower Deracho site, Day Ranch, and the probably much smaller (100 rooms) Ramah School House site. Finally, the El Morro group consisted of Pueblo de Los Muertos, Cienega, Mirabal, Hole-in-the-Wall (Lookout), Atsinna, and North Atsinna. These sites were spaced about 2.5 miles apart. In between, 5.5 miles from the El Morro group and 4.3 miles from the Deracho group, was the very large Kluckhohn Ruin.

Rather than seeing the sites as composing several separate site clusters, it is more accurate to see a string or swarm of sites that extended from Yellow House on the western, downstream side to El Morro, upstream to the east. This string of at least fourteen sites had no gap of more than 4.5 miles (7 km) between sites. Two slightly outlying sites—Kay Chee and Pescado Canyon—were also no more than 4.5 miles from other sites.

The usual evidence for the evolution of settlement patterns is present. The smallest sites were probably the shortest lived, as were the isolated ones. The somewhat isolated Pescado Canyon site was an exception. It was relatively large, with 413 rooms, and was on a mesa top. It lasted relatively late. This case seems to fit the rule that isolated sites must be both big and defensive to survive. Atsinna was similarly located on a mesa top, was even larger than the Pescado Canyon site, and was also long-lived. While it was not an isolated site initially, it seems to have been the last surviving site in the El Morro Valley.

The Techado and Jaralosa Draw Clusters

South of the large and complex Zuni cluster were several much smaller clusters. On the east, the Cebolleta Mesa cluster was separated by about 25 miles from the Rattail-Newton cluster (see the Acoma discussion below). About 20 miles to the west of the Rattail-Newton cluster was the Techado cluster, with spacing of 3 to 5 miles between Horse Camp Mill, Veteado Pueblo, and Techado Springs. About 29 miles north of them was the Jaralosa Draw cluster, which included Ojo Bonito (a site mentioned by Cushing, but apparently not recently recorded), and Fort Atarque. This seems to have been a linear cluster, with spaces of 5 to 6 miles between sites. There is considerable evidence for burning and unburied bodies in the Techado group's sites, with Horse Camp Mill and Techado Springs both heavily burned and containing unburied bodies. There is no excavation information on Veteado Pueblo nor on any of the Jaralosa Draw sites. Both the Horse Camp Mill and Techado Springs sites had walk-in wells or were right next to domestic water supplies. The Fort Atarque site may be associated with a Zuni oral tradition about a major battle with a site south of Zuni allied with Acoma (discussed in chapter 2).

Site Cluster Decline in the Cibola Area

Regardless of the number of sites and clusters that might have been contemporaneous at A.D. 1300 in the Cibola area, there was very soon a decline in the number of sites. The Techado, Jaralosa Draw, and Rattail-Newton clusters were completely gone, as were the isolated sites: Spier's 61, Big House, and Box S. Not much later, the Calabash cluster and the Jack's Lake–Ojo Pueblo string of sites were gone. That is, in short order, only the sites in the Zuni area proper were left. The number of sites along the Zuni River was also greatly reduced, with perhaps the only remaining ones being Heshotauthla and Lower Pescado Ruin, some 3.75 miles (6 km) apart, and Pueblo de Los Muertos, Cienega, and Atsinna—2.5 to 4.5 miles (4 to 7 km) apart—at the very upper end of the drainage some 14 miles (22 km) away. This sequence probably played itself out before A.D. 1350, at which point the upper reaches of the drainage were abandoned and the population seems to have relocated downstream to the area of the historical seven cities.

From this period until near the time of Coronado's arrival, there were apparently eight significant Zuni sites with a ninth, Hambassawa, having only thirty-nine rooms. Barbara Mills (1995) makes a case for a southern group of Chalowa, Hawikuh, and Kechipauan, spaced some 2.5 miles (4 km) apart; and a northern group of Pinnawa, Halona North, Matsaki, Ah:kya:ya (see Anyon 1992), and Kyakkima, also 2.5 miles (4 km) or less apart. The distance between these two groups was about 11 miles (18 km). In the middle was Kwakina as a possible communication link. By A.D. 1540, the eight towns had been reduced to six. In spite of the possible clustering of the remaining sites into two groups, they were all allied in A.D. 1540.

These data fit the overall late Pueblo III and Pueblo IV pattern extremely well. There was an initial period of semidefensive sites consisting of separate but clustered room blocks that seemed to have some dwelling units located for line-of-sight communication. They were rapidly replaced by extremely large and rapidly built walled towns. These occurred in clusters, typically spaced 20-plus miles apart. The number of clusters declined rapidly, and the number of sites in the surviving clusters also declined.

What followed in the Zuni area was not typical for the Colorado Plateau, however. The population of the remaining clusters moved down the Zuni River. The decline rate in the number of sites slowed down, with some nine sites in existence around A.D. 1400 and six still surviving at A.D. 1540. There is a hint of two clusters forming. Is it possible that the movement downstream in the direction of earlier westerly site clusters was possible because these other clusters had died out or had become greatly reduced? Interestingly, the Zuni could presumably have moved even farther downstream to an area where they presumably could have grown cotton, but perhaps this would have put them too close to Hopi.

Athough it may not be the case that all sites were occupied at A.D. 1300, the count of the A.D. 1300 sites compared with the later ones is very different. There were initially over thirty, by around A.D. 1400 there were nine, and by A.D. 1540 there were six. Counting only those sites along the Zuni drainage and those not very far away, there were about seventeen sites at A.D. 1300 and six at A.D. 1540. So, whether the count excludes the outlying clusters or not, the general pattern of site decline remains the same.

THE HOPI AREA CLUSTERS

The Hopi area presents many parallels to the Cibola region. Recent summaries by Gilpin (1995), E. Adams (1996), and Stein and Fowler (1996) make a case for there being three central Hopi site clusters around A.D. 1300. They included the western cluster of four sites (Orabi, Hoyapi, Kwaituki, and Huckovi); a middle cluster of at least seven sites (Chumalisko, Kwaituki, Sikyaki, Kuchaptevela, Lamehva and Old Mishongnovi and Old Shunopavi); and an Antelope Mesa group of seven sites (Lululongturqui, Kokopnyama, Nesuftanga, Pink Arrow, Chakpahu, Kawaika-a, Awatovi, and possibly Eighteen Mile Ruin). The western cluster had over 1,000 rooms; the latter two groups had over 2,000 each. These clusters were not spaced as widely apart as other clusters, and were more like the Zuni clusters in that they seemed to represent three concentrations of sites within an overall Hopi cluster. Again, it is known from the historic period that sites located in these three areas were allied with each other, although somewhat loosely. The positions of the sites are taken primarily from E. Adams (1996), but Kirt Dongoske (personal communication) believes that some are incorrently located. It is not clear whether enough locations are sufficiently in error to change the broad pattern, but I think it is unlikely.

Slightly removed from these clusters was the relatively isolated site of Many Farms. Also in the area was the Salina Springs site that Reagan (1928a, 1928b), who made some of the early descriptions of sites in very eastern Arizona, felt was built as a fort. There seems to have been a site cluster consisting of Wide Reed, Klagetoh, and Kin Tiel. However, these sites were more widely spaced than the sites in most clusters. Kin Tiel was one of the largest sites on the Colorado Plateau and seemed to consist of two circular room blocks merged together, but may have been a highly merged site pair (discussed in chapter 7). Both Wide Reed and Kin Tiel showed evidence of burning and unburied bodies. Perhaps the wide space between them resulted in a weak alliance. There was also a Steamboat Canyon cluster consisting of the Eagle Crag, Hogay, and Bear Spring North sites. And, finally, there was the Hopi Buttes cluster, which included Bidahochi, Bidahochi Southeast, and Bidahochi Southwest. Except for Bidahochi and Bidahochi Southeast, none of these sites lasted very far into the 1300s. The Bidahochi Southeast and Southwest sites were very close together, and may have been a site pair.

Sites in the Canyon de Chelly–Canyon del Muerto area may have represented another cluster, but their numbers seem small. It might be better to think of them as isolated, like the Many Farms site, that was never part of a real cluster and did not last long. The most famous of these sites, Mummy Cave (E. H. Morris 1939), did have skeletons with broken bones and bashed-in skulls in the tower. This is another example of a cliff dwelling that has evidence of violence, but not of burning.

The similarity of the settlement patterns in the Hopi area to those of Cibola is striking. First, the three central Hopi site clusters had about the same number of sites as those at Zuni. Second, there were smaller site clusters south and east of Hopi, just as there were smaller clusters somewhat removed from Zuni. The smaller clusters near Hopi died out completely, but the three central clusters survived, which was just what happened at Zuni. By A.D. 1350–1400, the best estimate is that there were twelve sites in the Hopi area: Old Oraibi, Old Shunopavi, Lamehva, Old Mishongnovi, Kuchaptuvela, Sikyaki, Awatovi, Kawaika'a, Chakpahu, Chukovi, Nesuftanga, and Kokopnyama. This number is down from at least eighteen sites fifty years earlier; by A.D. 1540, there were only seven sites (by A.D. 1580, there were only five). This decline is almost identical to that in the number of sites along the Zuni drainage. The outlying clusters together with the three central Hopi site clusters would have added up to some twenty-seven sites. This compares with the Cibola total of around thirty sites. Thus, the parallels are quite strong. Each area had around thirty sites initially; each had small clusters and isolated sites that did not survive. Each area had central clusters that did survive; each had started with about the same number of sites and had declined to about the same number. Furthermore, as discussed in chapter 7, both Hopi and Zuni seem to have had an allied remote group: the Homolovi group for Hopi and the Upper Little Colorado group for Zuni. Each of the satellite groups lasted later than most clusters, but neither lasted into the 1400s.

THE GREATER ACOMA AREA

The area east of Cibola and west of the Rio Grande Valley includes the eastern Rio Puerco and the Acoma area as well as the Cebolleta Mesa area just to the west of it. The area is of particular interest because it includes the boundary between the old Chacoan system and the Rio Grande area. It also contains one of the few communities outside the Rio Grande Valley to survive into the 1500s. It is surprising how poorly known this area is, given its proximity to much better understood areas. Recent syntheses by Roney (1995, 1996c) go a long way toward making sense out of this region, but the lack of excavations on the relevant sites makes fine-grained analysis difficult.

The Cebolleta Mesa and Rattail-Newton Clusters

In many ways, the western Cebolleta Mesa area is very similar to the Cibola area. Both areas had Chaco Great Houses and similar ceramic sequences; and they shared some architectural styles. In fact, Roney makes the case that the Cebolleta and Acoma areas really represent the extreme eastern edge of what he labels the Tularosa Black on White area.

A process of aggregation, with site size increasing rapidly, seemed to be taking place during late Pueblo III times. The population appears to have quickly moved into just a few sites. There was a northern Cebolleta Mesa group with the mesa-top Calabash Ruin (350-plus rooms) and the nearby Kowina and Ranger Station sites with 86 and 150 rooms, respectively. Apparently, the large and defensively located Calabash Ruin survived longer than the other sites. About 12 miles to the south were the Penole site (100 rooms) and several smaller sites. The Newton-Rattail cluster was another 12 miles still farther south.

A case can be made that the southern group of Cebolleta sites disappeared first (those around the Penole site), leaving the Calabash Ruin in the north and the Newton-Rattail cluster in the south. The Calabash site consisted of a large inward-facing pueblo on a small mesa, the one point of fairly easy access blocked by a wall-like block of rooms. The size and setting of this site is very similar to that of Acoma Pueblo. Even the Calabash Ruin did not last very long into the 1300s. Was this same pattern, being played out here among large site clusters, taking place on a very local scale, with the groups in the middle being eliminated and larger buffer zones developing around the surviving, more separated clusters? Perhaps the Cebolleta Mesa sites were never a true alliance, and there may have been sufficient competition among the various groups to leave the Calabash Ruin as the only survivor.

To the south, some 25 miles away from the Calabash portion of the Cebolleta Mesa cluster, the Rattail (200 rooms) and Newton (165 rooms) sites seemed to form another small cluster, as noted. As was often the case, the smaller Newton site was on a hilltop and the larger Rattail site was in a lower setting. The Newton site apparently was significantly burned, and one unburied child's skull was found in one of the twenty-eight rooms excavated. In addition, pot-hunting had exposed some skeletal material, but whether they were unburied bodies remains unclear. Because the excavated rooms were on the periphery of the site, it is possible that the pot-hunted skeletal material may have represented unburied bodies from the center of the site, an unlikely place for burials. Survey showed the presence of ten small sites spread out from the main ruin. They were judged to be roughly contemporary. This sounds very much like a slightly earlier Scribe S phase settlement, then replaced by the larger Newton site (Frisbie 1973).

The spacing between the Newton-Rattail cluster and the Techado cluster to the west was about the same as to the Calabash cluster to the north. It is noteworthy that this eastern portion of the Colorado Plateau—from the Arizona border to Acoma—initially had a large number of clusters with very regular spacing of 20 to 25 miles between them. The patterning of site clusters is perhaps clearer for this area than for any other in the Southwest.

The Acoma–Middle Rio San Jose Cluster

The Acoma–Middle Rio San Jose area is unfortunately very poorly known. No room estimates or good site plans are available for the sites of Shumatzutstya, Flour Mesa (also known as Flour Butte), Bug Mesa, Rabbit Butte, or Acoma Pueblo for this time period. The Cubero site with 175 rooms and La Mesita Redonda with 230 rooms are better known. According to Roney (1995, 1996c), Flour Mesa, Bug Mesa, and Rabbit Butte apparently did not survive after A.D. 1300. La Mesita Redonda may have lasted to A.D. 1325. Rabbit Butte, Flour Mesa, Bug Mesa, Acoma, and Shumatzutstya were all defensively located. Rabbit Butte and Flour Mesa seemed to be sites following the Mesa Verde tradition (discussed in chapter 6). Upham (1982) lists Casa Blanca, Tsiama, Locomotive Rock, and Keashkawa as Pueblo IV sites near Acoma. Of these four sites, it is possible that some are the same ones noted by Roney—although Keashkawa definitely is not the same as any of the above sites and none of the others seem to plot at the same places Roney gave for his Acoma area sites. Thus, there seems to have been an initial cluster that consisted of at least eight and probably eleven sites. Some sites were over 200 rooms, and at least half were in defensive locations. After Hopi and Zuni, this was the largest site cluster on the Colorado Plateau.

Based on Roney's analysis, it appears that by A.D. 1350 only Acoma, Shumatzutstya, and Cubero continued to be occupied. These sites were spaced 11 to 20 miles apart, which does not look like a unified site cluster. However, the sites are so poorly known that this inference may be premature. In any case, this cluster was reduced to only Acoma Pueblo by the mid-1500s. Although Acoma was considered extremely defensive by the Spaniards, and was tenaciously resistive to attack, it was not particularly large; Coronado reported only some 200 fighting-age men (Winship 1896). This estimate is probably low, however, considering later population figures for Acoma. The relatively small population size of Acoma may have been why the community continued to be located in such a defensive setting.

The Eastern Rio Puerco and the Southern San Juan Basin

The area that includes the eastern Rio Puerco and the southern or southeastern San Juan Basin displayed a site pattern very different from that seen farther south, and it was more like that seen for the more northern Anasazi areas, including McElmo, Mesa Verde, Kayenta, and Totah. Good data are provided by Stein and Fowler (1996) and Roney (1996c). Site clusters were few and of very short duration. What ephemeral site clusters did exist were not very big. Few sites were large. This paucity of large sites and site clusters may have been in part a consequence of the Chaco system collapse, which was apparently most severe in this area in terms of population decline. Also, there seems to be no question that population from north of the San Juan River moved into parts of the area in the 1200s. These groups may have been small, which would have resulted in small, short-lived sites. No communities seemed to survive past A.D. 1300. By A.D. 1275, there may have been only seven or eight sites, with a total of under 250 rooms in this entire area. In other words, all sites combined had fewer rooms than most single sites had farther south. There is significant evidence for defensive sites—expected for such small sites—and there were some site clusters.

A group of sites on Chacra Mesa date to the mid-1200s, but they were not the latest sites in the area. These may have been like the Scribe S sites at El Morro in that they consisted of several slightly defensive sites located very close together, with one being more defensive and probably acting as a focal point for the group as a whole. The Reservoir site may be an example. Also in the Chacra Mesa area were a number of late sites (not necessarily fully contemporary) that were either very defensively located, such as the Paul Longsden, Kin Nazhin, Castillejo, and Mesa Tierra sites, or that were located on a water source and were centrally focused pueblos, such as Raton Well. These sites ranged from 5 to 20 miles apart and may not represent a single cluster.

On the Rio Puerco, there was the Canada de Las Milpas site with forty-eight rooms. Roney's Salado and Coot Ridge communities had locations that seemed to be semidefensive. There were also two larger sites of sixty and ninety-five rooms that were defensively located; they were within 3 miles of each other and may have been the last sites in the area. Thus, there is some minimal evidence for sites that had some defensive attributes early on, followed by more defensive sites, with the sites reduced in number over time. What may be more interesting is that there was never a successful movement into large pueblos, and the area was abandoned earlier than those to the south and east.

Well to the west were some late 1200s sites along the Chuska slope. Crumbled House—a very defensive site on a mesa spur with a defensive wall and moat (Marshall et al. 1979)—was the largest of these, with 300 rooms. I have been unable to find useful information on the few other sites in the area.

In many ways, this region seems to have been the extreme southerly corner of an area encompassing parts of Utah, Colorado, and northeastern New Mexico that displayed a pattern of only moderate aggregation, with few really large sites. Site clusters were not very tight nor very large, and the area was abandoned rather early. Whatever went wrong in this part of the Southwest really went wrong in contrast to conditions farther south, where things changed radically, but not as catastrophically.

The Western Rio Puerco and Lower Little Colorado Area Clusters

The western Rio Puerco and the Lower Little Colorado River had several site clusters that were either short- or long-lived. The best synthesis for the area at this time range is by Gilpin (1995), although Stein and Fowler (1996) and Kintigh (1996) cover portions of it as well. There was a small and short-lived cluster of sites that included Isham, Sanders Pueblo, Emigrant Springs, and Taylor Springs, on the upper Rio Puerco. These sites were relatively small, in the range of fifty to seventy-five rooms. They had defensive layouts, but were not in defensive locations; all were abandoned prior to A.D. 1300 and perhaps by as early as A.D. 1275. Some 25 miles (40 km) down the Rio Puerco was the Petrified Forest cluster. It included Puerco Ruin (125 rooms) and Stone Axe (200 to 250 rooms), and perhaps one or two sites at Canyon Butte of under 60 rooms each, which were apparently short-lived. Puerco Ruin and Stone Axe lie some 4.3 miles (7 km) apart. Puerco Ruin was a rectangular site built around a large central plaza on a terrace above the floodplain. The site plan for Stone Axe is not clear, but it was located directly next to a spring. Between these large sites was a twelve-room site on a high butte. It appears to have provided a visibility link between the two large sites, but this has not been ground tested. The large sites seem to have lasted possibly to A.D. 1350. Puerco Ruin had significant burning, with a considerable amount of charred corn; Burton (1990, 1993) suggests it was abandoned at the time of the fire. The larger Stone Axe site lasted somewhat later.

Some 31 miles (50 km) still farther down the Rio Puerco–Little Colorado drainage was the Homolovi cluster (E. Adams 1989a, 1989b, 1996). It had seven sites: Homolovi I, II, III, and IV; Cottonwood; Jackrabbit; and Chevelon. Two of them were quite small: Homolovi III (40 rooms) and Cottonwood (50 rooms). There was clearly some mutual visibility between sites, and the small Homolovi III site was defensively located. Homolovi III and IV were very short-lived. Jackrabbit lasted until possibly A.D. 1350. Soon there were only three surviving sites of any

consequence: Homolovi I and II and Chevelon. These may have lasted until around
A.D. 1400. Homolovi I and II were quite large, with 500 and 1,000 rooms, respectively. There were burned kivas with unburied bodies and other burned rooms at
Homolovi II, but the site as a whole was not burned. There were also unburied
bodies at Homolovi I, but, again, no strong evidence for an actual attack. The
Chevelon site, however, had very signficant burning (Andrews 1982). It seems to
be a case where the smaller sites died out, but really large sites were able to exist
for a long time. This area has such strong ceramic and architectural similarities to
Hopi that it may have been a satellite cluster, a topic considered in chapter 6.

The Upper Little Colorado Cluster

Sites in the Upper Little Colorado area were initially recorded by Spier (1918) and
recently synthesized by Kintigh (1996) and Duff (1995). There were nine or ten
relevant sites between St. Johns and Springerville. At the upper end of the valley
were Casa Malpais, Hooper Ranch (which apparently included an immediately
adjacent small site on a hilltop, Danson's 146), Oscar's (which was not on the
river), and an early component at the Raven site. The Knight site may date to this
early component; it was also off the river, not far from Oscar. These upper valley
sites seem to date in the A.D. 1275 to 1325 range, and were some 2.5 to 4.0 miles
(4 to 6 km) apart. The upper valley Casa Malpais and Hooper Ranch sites were
abandoned well before the Raven site was, although the defensive hilltop component to Hopper Ranch (Danson's site 146) seems to have lasted sometime into the
1300s. DeGarmo (1975) reported on a small Pueblo III site on Coyote Creek,
several miles east of the river, that was clearly equivalent to the Scribe S site at El
Morro; it was also stone-robbed. Just how it relates to the later sites is unclear.

Near St. Johns, some 17 miles downstream, were Spier's sites 175, 176 (sixty
rooms), and nearby Table Rock (eighty rooms), with an empty zone between the
two groups. Apparently, Spier's site 175 was abandoned and survived by or replaced by Spier's 176 and Table Rock. They seem to have lasted until the late
1300s.

The data imply two separate clusters, each evolving into more defensive settings
over time. However, sometime presumably around A.D. 1325, two sites were built
between the Raven site in the upper valley and Hooper Ranch in the lower valley:
the Baca site (ninety rooms) and Rattlesnake Point (eighty-five rooms). In terms of
spacing they were about 3 miles apart, with the uppermost of the two being 3
miles downstream from the Raven site. So, they would seem to have been part of
that group. Rattlesnake Point lasted into the late 1300s, and then was heavily
burned. Apparently, the same thing happened to Baca. Sites built in what appear
to have been no-man's-lands represent a unique situation on the Colorado Plateau;
the only other instance was the downstream relocation of the Zuni River sites. In
the case of the Upper Little Colorado, the no-man's-land reoccupation sites seem
to have been destroyed.

The evidence for defensive construction is not as strong as it is for other areas.
Table Rock was in a somewhat defensive setting, and although several sites had
one edge next to a sharp drop, they were not particularly defensive. Casa Malpais
is described as defensive (Danson and Malde 1957); it had a defensive layout, but
it was not in a defensive setting. In the upper valley, the Raven Ruin (Schuster site)

seems to have been rebuilt as a large central-plaza site with about 300 rooms. This was the only bona fide large site in the entire area, and it seems to have lasted to the late 1300s. There was significant burning at the site, but when this happened is unclear.

Overall, the Upper Little Colorado cluster was very atypical. All of the sites were relatively small, with the exception of the Raven site. That sites this small were being founded at A.D. 1325 was most unusual and that they were not defensively located was even more unusual. Furthermore, the Table Rock site was one of the latest sites outside Zuni and Hopi in the entire area. Despite the uniqueness of the cluster, some of the typical patterns were in evidence. The surviving sites were either large (Raven) or defensive (Table Rock). Sites that were not large or defensive were burned (Rattlesnake Point and Baca) or they were abandoned relatively early (Hooper Ranch and Spier's 175). However, there were more anomalies than are usually encountered, and the detailed history of the area should prove interesting.

The Anderson Mesa and Silver Creek Clusters

ANDERSON MESA

The Anderson Mesa area (Pilles 1996; Wilson 1969; Upham 1982) lies on the boundary between the Colorado Plateau (Anasazi) and the Verde Valley (Sinagua) areas. The cluster was smaller than most, and some of the sites were quite small. Overall, however, it followed the Plateau settlement pattern. The cluster consisted of a set of sites at Chavez Pass and a more northerly group of sites. The Chavez Pass sites can be interpreted as consisting initially of the north pueblo, which was built on a hilltop and had only about 100 rooms. There seemed to be a number of smaller sites in the immediate area that probably date to this same time. This may represent a modified version of the Scribe S settlement pattern, where there were numerous clustered room blocks, with one site on a high point. In this case, however, the high site was much larger than any of the others. Just as in the case of other sites of this type, it had been burned and abandoned. It was replaced by two massive sites to the south on a knoll, at least one of which seems to have been rapidly built. They lasted well into the 1300s.

Some 9 to 10 miles (15 km) north was the cluster of the Kinnikinnick, Pollock, and Grapevine sites. These sites were small, with 150, 40, and 45 rooms, respectively. They were spaced 1.5 to 2.5 miles apart (2.5 to 4 km). Apparently, there was some construction at Kinnikinnick at A.D. 1308, but it is unclear how late these three sites lasted. It would appear that they did not last as long as the big sites at Chavez Pass. Grapevine Ruin had a defensive wall, but the others were not particularly defensively located. At Kinnikinnick, both of the two rooms that were excavated had burned.

Clearly, the Chavez Pass sites held almost all the population of the cluster. The Late Period site complex—the South Pueblo—could be considered either two adjacent but separate sites or two massive room blocks. They may be best thought of as being so close together that they were a site pair; combined, they contained over 1,500 rooms. The later South Pueblo was rapidly built (although it does not appear to have ladder construction), while the earlier North Pueblo had a more haphazard construction as was typical for sites that represent the transition from being semidefensive to more fully defensive. In the western room block, the Great Kiva, an adjacent room, and the upper floor of a room in the highest part of the site were all burned. As discussed in chapter 6, there were also a number of skulls showing evidence of scalping from this site. Whether this evidence points to a major successful attack is unclear.

The stairway and spring complex at South Pueblo may well have been a protected path to the domestic water supply. If so, then this was a unique solution to the problem of securing the water supply. Atsinna at El Morro seems to have tried to solve the problem with cisterns on the mesa top, but most sites were either on high points or had secure water supplies. South Pueblo may have had both.

In many ways the Anderson Mesa situation is quite parallel to the evolutionary process seen elsewhere. There was progressively more defensive construction and larger sites. Small sites were apparently abandoned earlier than the large ones. Some small sites were burned. There are differences, however. The spacing of about 10 miles between the northern and southern groups of sites was either quite large if they represent the same cluster or quite small if they do not. Also, in the case of Chavez Pass the large amount of trade pottery at the sites, especially the number of types represented, was not typical. This is really intriguing. While many of the problems of defense and aggregation were solved similarly over the Colorado Plateau, there were also many different approaches to survival. The experiment was run repeatedly. Obviously, Chavez Pass took a path with much greater trade and interaction than others. It was not a successful solution, however, and the last site apparently died out before A.D. 1400.

SILVER CREEK

The Silver Creek area had a number of relevant sites: Flake, Fourmile, Shumway, Showlow, Pinedale, and Bailey (Kintigh 1996; B. Mills 1995). Tundastusa was also part of this group from a spacing point of view since it was only 8 miles from the Showlow site, but it was not in the Silver Creek drainage. The Flake site was small (50 rooms) and was apparently abandoned rather early, while the Bailey and Shumway sites were larger with 100-plus rooms each. Still larger were Pinedale (150 rooms), Showlow (200 rooms), and Fourmile (450 rooms). Flake, Fourmile, and Shumway formed a particularly close cluster, with the sites within 3.5 miles (5.5 km) of each other. It was reduced to just Fourmile and Shumway by around A.D. 1300. With the exception of the Shumway-Fourmile pair, the remaining sites were relatively spread out, with spacing in the 9-to-11-mile (14 to 18 km) range. Interestingly, the Bailey site was relatively small and was the closest of these sites to the Grasshopper cluster (about 23 miles away); it also seems to have been the next site to be abandoned. The remaining four sites seemed to last at least post-A.D. 1325, and Fourmile, the largest, seemed to last the longest. Interestingly, these four, longer-lasting sites had been spaced generally about the same distance from each other as the Kinnikinnick-Grapevine-Pollock site group from Chavez Pass.

General patterns seen elsewhere were found here. The small sites, especially ones that were not defensively located, were not long-lived. However, the larger sites were not very large, except for Fourmile, when compared with other clusters. These middle-sized sites were defensively configured, but were not defensively located. They seemed to be too far apart to be an alliance cluster with the level of integration found with other clusters. The sites shared some of the characteristics of those found in the Upper Little Colorado cluster, but differed from those on the upper Gila River plateau and Zuni drainage.

CLUSTERS TO THE WEST AND SOUTH OF THE COLORADO PLATEAU

Away from the Colorado Plateau, both the nature of the information and the nature of the site clusters themselves begin to change. The dating of the areas is less clear and the survey is less complete, making interpretation more difficult. In addition, clusters become somewhat less distinct, and site sizes become smaller. However, the defensive aspect of the sites is still detectable, and there is still ample evidence of warfare.

The Middle Verde Valley Cluster

The Middle Verde Valley represents an interpretive problem because the sites cannot be as well dated from surface material as on the Colorado Plateau. Pillis (1996, and personal communication) provides a summary of the relevant information. In spite of the dating problems, a case can be made that around twenty sites were spread from the Tuzigoot area in the north to the junction of the East Verde River with the Verde, some 45 miles downstream. This does seem to have been a cluster of sites, although a rather linear one. It is interesting that the edge of this Middle Verde Valley site cluster was about 26 miles from both Anderson Mesa and Chavez Pass, not far different from the 20 miles between clusters seen so frequently on the Colorado Plateau to the east.

However, such a long string of sites is unlike anything seen on the Colorado Plateau at this time. Also, the Verde Valley sites were much smaller than those on the Plateau. The average site size was about 100 rooms, and only two were larger than 200 rooms (Bridgeport with 237 rooms and Mindeleff's Cavate Lodge Group with 287). The total number of rooms was over 2,200, so the population size of the cluster was not unlike some of those on the Plateau. It is the lack of agglomeration that is so different. The cluster seems to have been rather continuous, with sites every 4 miles or so, although Pilles notes that the significantly larger sites were about 20 miles apart. However, there is no evidence that they formed separate clusters.

The majority of these sites were either on hilltops or otherwise elevated, such as Tuzigoot, Hatalacva, Bridgeport, Cornville, and Brown Springs. Others, such as Montezuma Castle and Oak Creek, were fortlike, and Mindeleff's Cavate Lodge Group had a very defensive unit in it, although other parts were not very defensive. Moreover, Peter Pilles (personal communication) makes a very intriguing observation, although he does not necessarily agree with the current interpretation. He thinks it likely that the numerous hilltop sites could have provided visual communication links between them. Unit A burned at Montezuma Castle, while the castle itself was a classic defensive site (Wells and Anderson 1988). Nevertheless, in spite of this evidence for defensive aspects of these sites, there were also sites of less than 100 rooms that were not defensively located.

Although not all of these sites may have been contemporaneous and the smaller nondefensive sites may have been earlier in the sequence, the overall pattern was still not as defensive as that found on much of the Colorado Plateau. The Middle Verde seems to have been part of a new pattern. The farther away from the Colorado Plateau, the more the sites' levels of defensiveness declined. There were still large, defensively laid-out sites and there were still small sites in very defensive locations; but, overall, the degree of this defensive pattern may have been less than on the Plateau. Sites were also smaller on average, with few attaining even the average site size found on the Plateau, and were sometimes in nondefensive locations and not so tightly clustered. It is possible that the smaller, nondefensive sites were earlier. Just because the sites were smaller, does not mean there was less warfare. If, for whatever reason, all groups could have only maintained small sites, then having small sites would not have been a relative disadvantage. So, on further analysis, the Middle Verde may have had warfare as intense as the Plateau did, but with a different set of social parameters.

The Grasshopper Cluster

South of the Mogollon Rim, but still in the mountains—the "pine zone"—was a series of large sites that formed several clusters. One cluster centered around Grasshopper Pueblo and nearby sites (Longacre et al. 1982; Graves et al. 1982; Reid 1989). These sites were 20-plus miles away from the most southwesterly site in the Silver Creek site group. While the following is not the accepted interpretation of these sites, it does not seem to be in conflict with current knowledge.

Initially, there was a series of rather small sites near Grasshopper Pueblo, the Chodistaas site being a typical example with eighteen rooms (Crown 1981). The sites also included Grasshopper Spring and Glennbikii, and there seems to have been an earlier small site at the location of Grasshopper Pueblo itself. The Chodistaas site was on the highest point of a bluff, not unlike the Scribe S site at El Morro. The other sites were not defensively located. All of the sites burned, except perhaps the one at Grasshopper itself. Chodistaas and Grasshopper Spring seem to have been burned and abandoned very close to the same time during the 1290s (Crown 1981; Montgomery 1993). For both these sites burning was catastrophic, with many in situ remains. The small sites appear to have been built and added onto from around A.D. 1275 to almost A.D. 1300. At that time the small sites were abandoned and replaced by the very large Grasshopper Pueblo (500 rooms), which was set on a secure domestic water supply. Grasshopper Pueblo seems to have formed around some of these earlier small room blocks and, by A.D. 1323–1325, was rapidly transformed into a large defensive site.

In addition, a series of at least nine small sites, all on defensive locations, were built. The largest gap between the ten sites—the nine small ones and Grasshopper—was 3.75 miles (6 km), and the typical gap was about 2.5 miles (4 km). They ranged in room counts from Oak Creek, with 35 rooms, to Brush Mountain, with 140 rooms. The nine sites seemed to form a defensive ring around Grasshopper Pueblo. Apparently no one has looked to see if there was line-of-sight visibility between these sites, but it is highly likely given the landforms they were on. Tuggle (1970) found that the general locations of the sites correlated with good farmable land, but it is clear that their specific locations did not. Although they were not located with efficient access to farmable land, they were on good defensive locations in the neighborhood of it.

I suspect, but cannot show, that these hilltop sites and Grasshopper Pueblo were all initially constructed in the first decade of the 1300s. But the hilltop sites were not occupied for very long; by the 1330s, they were abandoned and the population all resided in Grasshopper, which in turn lasted until about mid-century. Thus, again there was the classic settlement pattern as found on the Colorado Plateau: Initially, there were small sites, with some on high points, which were replaced either by large sites located on domestic water supplies or by small sites on high defensive locations with regular spacing of 2.5 to 3 miles between them. Over time, the small sites were abandoned and only the large ones continued to be occupied.

A few miles south of Grasshopper and the hilltop sites were the Canyon Creek ruins, which were built against cliffs and totaled some 125 rooms (Haury 1934). They seemed to be contemporary with the terminal occupation of Grasshopper (Bannister and Robinson 1971), and were probably part of the same cluster. The nearby Q Ranch and Cibecue sites present something of a problem. They were relatively large sites and were each about 10 miles from Grasshopper Pueblo, but less than 7 miles from the nearest hilltop site in the Grasshopper group. This spacing would seem to be too close if they represented different clusters and too far away if they were part of the same site cluster. The spacing may be due to incomplete information, and perhaps there were sites—but unrecognized—in the intervening areas; or it may represent a spacing pattern unlike that seen above the Mogollon Rim. Incidentally, one of the two room blocks at Q Ranch burned catastrophically. With only 200 rooms divided into two room blocks and located on low ground, the site was neither particularly large nor particularly defensively located or constructed. It was much smaller and less defensible than its nearest potential adversary to the north, the Chavez site pair. It was, as noted, either on the very edge of a site cluster or an isolated site; in either case, it was more susceptible to being successfully attacked than many other sites were. Not surprisingly, it was apparently successfully attacked.

The Kinishba and Point of Pines Clusters

Some 20-plus miles from the edge of the Grasshopper group (if it included Cibecue Pueblo) was the very large site of Kinishba (800 rooms). It seems to have had multiple room blocks like Grasshopper, but may also have had smaller sites around it. Spier (1919) describes several sites—numbers 228, 245, 250, and 251—that appear to have been large, late sites forming a cluster that included Kinishba. To the south and east, Site 228 had 140-plus rooms arranged around a central plaza and was 4 miles from Site 245, which was a hilltop site very similar to those around Grasshopper. Site 245 was 3.5 miles from Kinishba. On the west, Site 250 consisted of a circular and a square pueblo very close together. Both had 100-plus rooms. Nearby on a point of a mesa was a rectangular site (Spier's 229) of fifteen to thirty rooms with a small central plaza and excellent views. Also nearby was Site 251 with at least sixty rooms and two plazas. These sites were about 6 miles from Kinishba. Incidentally, Kinishba was about 20 miles south of Tundastusa (at the southern end of the Silver Creek group), completing the general 20-mile spacing between site groups. Overall, this group of sites appears to have been a cluster that included large sites, site pairs, and hilltop lookout and signaling sites. Unfortunately, information about the dating of these sites is too skimpy and areal survey too spotty to do more than consider this description a good possibility.

While the report and notes on Kinishba are far from clear (Cummings 1940; Daniela Triadan, personal communication), there are enough references to unburied bodies (at least twenty), in situ assemblages, and burned materials to suggest that some kind of attack took place at the site. There is no excavation information from any of the other possible sites in this cluster.

Even farther south, but still in the mountains, the site of Turkey Creek (Lowell 1991), with what seems to have been a moderately defensive layout, was founded earlier than many of the other large sites in the mountains and was built in a more accretionary manner. Turkey Creek is a good example of a site with some burned rooms that does not show a pattern of warfare-related burning or other evidence of attack. The large, nearby Point of Pines site was formed in part by migrant groups from the Kayenta area (Haury 1958; Lindsay 1987). There was major burning at the site about A.D. 1300, and a wall was constructed around it apparently right afterwards. Close by, a string of sites along a ridge that seemed to predate the Point of Pines site was jokingly referred to as "fraternity row" (Haury 1989). The location and dating of this group of room blocks seems very similar to the Scribe S phase sites at El Morro. Overall, the same pattern of small sites being burned and replaced with more defensive sites seems to have held in this area as well. It is unclear whether these two sites should be considered a cluster and whether there were additional sites that might have been part of it.

In summary, south of the Mogollon Rim, there seems to have been a number of very large pueblos on secure domestic water, with most of the other sites being much smaller and on defensive hilltops—the same pattern observed on the Colorado Plateau. However, the number of small sites in comparison to the large ones was much greater, and there may have been a tendency for sites to be spaced farther apart.

The Tonto Basin Cluster

In many ways the Tonto Basin–Globe-Miami area is transitional between the Colorado Plateau and mountains on the one hand and the Hohokam and low desert area on the other. There seems to be strong evidence that the Gila phase (A.D. 1320–1450) witnessed a marked increase in warfare and responses to it. There appears to have been two site clusters: one in the Tonto Basin proper and the other centered in the Globe area. The Globe area site cluster included Gila Pueblo, Besh-Ba-Gowah, Pinal Pueblo, and possibly Togetzoge. Gila Pueblo and Besh-Ba-Gowah (Hohmann and Adams 1992) were relatively large and compact sites (the latter having 250 ground-floor rooms). They were like the other big sites south of the Mogollon Rim in that they had a honeycomb layout, had only small plazas, and did not have stepped-down room blocks onto the plazas. These two large sites were less than 2 miles apart and were part of a tight cluster of sites with the same close spacing often seen on the Plateau (Crary and Germick 1992). The cluster included smaller sites, like Pinal Pueblo (about fifty rooms), that were linked via line-of-sight to the larger sites (Brandes 1957).

The cluster seemed well spaced from any contemporary ones, including those in the Tonto Basin proper. Gila Pueblo had extensive burning and a large number of unburied bodies—at least seventy-one in a section of less than twenty rooms (McKusick 1992). The site of Togetzoge was about 10 miles from this cluster.

Whether this was an isolated site or whether sites that would have linked Togetzoge to the Globe cluster are now gone, making an artificial gap, is unclear. The site was on a mild rise and had very clear views in all directions; there were two unburied bodies in one room and three instances of violent deaths among seventy burials (Hohmann and Kelley 1988).

The pattern found in the Tonto Basin proper was quite different. Recent work downstream in the basin has produced a reasonably clear picture of the events in this time frame. There was a shift to many fewer and larger sites at around A.D. 1325 (the beginning of the Gila phase). Sites seemed to be in clumps, such as the group centered on Cline Terrace Mound. This cluster spanned about 3 miles (5 km). Tagg (1985) succinctly summarizes the overall settlement pattern: "Twelve to 15 major and minor, apparently contemporaneous population centers were located at regular intervals of about 3 miles (5 km) along the two major drainages in the Tonto Basin". However, the sites were quite different from those in the mountains and on the Colorado Plateau. They were much smaller, in terms of room counts, than those in the higher elevations. They were not formed by rooms alone, but employed freestanding enclosing walls. The walls had narrow entrances, and the sites contained elevated, towerlike constructions that could have been defensively oriented structures.

Although the entire Tonto Basin may represent a single cluster, within it there seemed to be clumps of sites or large sites spaced 6 or 7 miles apart. That is, the arrangement seems to have been more linear, like that of the Verde Valley, where there was a continuous distribution of sites, with the larger ones spaced some distance apart. The group of sites in the Cline Terrace area is perhaps best known. Of the six sites in the group, major burning seems to have taken place in at least four of them. Upstream from Cline Terrace, the contemporary VIV Ruin (J. Mills and Mills 1975) also had extensive burning. In addition, three projectile points were found in bodies and there were unburied bodies on room floors. There is little doubt that this village was attacked and destroyed. Glen Rice (personal communication) notes that this consistent pattern of Gila-phase site burning was not seen in the preceding Roosevelt phase (A.D. 1280–1320). Also, a room in one of the small sites in this area contained only the long bones of ten individuals, a pattern of trophy taking found at other Salado sites (Hohmann 1985a, 1985b).

A date of around A.D. 1320 for the shift to more defensive sites and direct evidence for warfare is right in line with the north-south gradient in time for the onset of major warfare in the Southwest. While there was a shift in site location and configuration toward a more defensive posture, it was not as marked as that on the Colorado Plateau insofar as the site layouts were not massive, compact groups of rooms. Moreover, the spacing between the sites and clusters was not like that farther north. Perhaps this was because rivers in the south were more critical for farming and so settlement clusters were more linearly arranged along drainages. This does not mean warfare did not exist in the south, however. Far from it.

The Upper Gila River Cluster

Clearly there was a site cluster along the Gila River near Safford, Arizona. The Safford area, sometimes referred to as Pueblo Viejo, had several sites of interest: Buena Vista, Marijilda, Earven Flat, Yuma Wash, and Goat Hill (Woodson 1995).

The Fort Thomas site was also probably part of this cluster (Bandelier 1892). The cluster of sites was about 50 miles from the cluster at Cliff, about 50 miles from the cluster at Globe, and about the same distance from the San Pedro cluster (see below). These distances are about twice those found elsewhere between clusters. Cluster spacing may have been different in this part of the Southwest, perhaps because of the distances between river systems. However, there may have been another cluster in the San Carlos Lake area that was either undetected or was inundated; other clusters may also have gone unrecognized.

The Safford area sites are broadly classified as Salado, but J. Brown (1974) argues that these "Salado" sites bear important similarities to those in the Point of Pines area and elsewhere. Lindsay (1987) makes a good case that some of these sites, as well as those from other areas, were likely occupied by migrants from the Kayenta area. Woodson (1995) also provides support for such migrants in the Safford area. This issue was considered in chapter 7.

The largest and latest site is the Buena Vista site. It had multiple rooms blocks that did not seem to be linked together by freestanding walls, and it is not clear whether they had enclosed plazas. The site seems to date in the 1300's, based on unpublished excavations from the 1930s. The excavated portion of "House 2"—the northeastern compound—had been mostly destroyed by fire, and human skeletons were found on room floors. (J. Mills and Mills 1978).

The Marijilda, Earven Flat, and Yuma Wash sites were each composed of a massive room block with an enclosed plaza. Marijilda had 50-plus rooms, Earven Flat had about 170 rooms, and Yuma Wash was between these in size. The Yuma Wash site was on a bluff across the river from the Earven Flat site. A case can be made that these three sites were occupied in the late 1200s or very early 1300s. The Earven Flat and Yuma Wash sites appear to have been a site pair similar to those found in the Colorado Plateau region.

The Goat Hill site (Woodson 1995) was on the top of a very high "knob," and the pueblo essentially enclosed the summit. It was very defensive in layout. It had about thirty-six rooms, with a central kiva. It strongly suggests a Kayenta immigrant community. At least three rooms and the central kiva burned, some with in situ deposits. Two of the burned rooms were contiguous. Since only about 25 percent of the rooms were excavated (other rooms, about which pothunters' holes revealed additional information, did not seem to show burning), the site clearly was not massively burned. Based on the assumption that about half the rooms could be characterized as having been burned or not, then about 16 percent, plus the kiva, were burned. This seems more than an accidental event, but not one of complete destruction, either. Although the data are very sketchy, it is possible to see a site cluster here that formed late in the 1200s. The initial sites were relatively small, and over time the population coalesced into the Buena Vista site, which was then successfully attacked and destroyed.

Southwestern and Southeastern New Mexico

There was a series of sites in southwestern New Mexico and the very southeastern portion of Arizona, that may have formed several clusters. While a tendency for the sites to clump together is apparent, so much of this area is unsurveyed that it is difficult to draw strong conclusions. Because the sites in this area were usually made of adobe, they do not remain as prominent as their temporal counterparts on the Colorado Plateau. In addition, the sites were in general not as large as the Plateau sites. So there is much less likelihood that all the larger sites in the southern deserts have been recorded. As a consequence, this section is rather sketchy, and more systematic work is required to clarify the situation.

Some 80 miles (130 km) north of the site of Casas Grandes was a group of sites in Hidalgo County, New Mexico, that may have formed one or more clusters. That they interacted with Casas Grandes is clear; whether they were a competing polity is not clear. Some sites had plazas enclosed by rooms, others had freestanding walls to complete the enclosures. Several burned.

The Joyce Well site (McCluney 1965) had an almost completely enclosed plaza (there may have been freestanding walls completing the enclosure that were not looked for). Three C14 dates roughly place this site in the mid-1300s to very early 1400s (as corrected and interpreted by R. E. Taylor, personal communication) although much later dates have been quoted at various times. It is difficult to determine the extent of burning from the very sketchy report, but rooms with burned corn were found from various parts of the site (at least twenty bushels of corn, from at least nine different rooms). The site was about 4.5 miles from the large Culbertson ruin. It is not known whether there is any evidence of burning at Culbertson. These two sites may have been part of a cluster.

There is the possibility of another site cluster 15 miles to the west. There, the Clanton Draw and Box Canyon sites (McCluney 1962) lie 2.5 miles (4 km) apart along Animas Creek. They had enclosed plazas and seemed to date in the 1300s. All the rooms burned at Clanton Draw, although there were few in situ deposits. Six rooms had significant amounts of charred corn in them. Box Canyon apparently had about 350 rooms, but only 18 were excavated. The report does not discuss the extent of burning, although numerous burned features are described. At least four rooms had significant quantities of burned corn in them, so the percentage of burned rooms must have been high. Again, there were few in situ deposits. However, ceramically, Clanton Draw would seem to date close to 1300 and Box Canyon well after it.

Just 8 miles south of this cluster was the Pendleton Ruin, which must have had over 100 rooms arranged around two plazas and which did not burn. This site was not clearly part of either possible cluster described above, and would seem to have been in between the two groups in time.

The Kuykendall Site (J. Mills and Mills 1969), in extreme southeastern Arizona, some 50 miles to the west of the above-mentioned sites, had 200-plus rooms and must have dated in the 1300s. It had both compounds and groups of rooms linked by freestanding enclosing walls. It had a walk-in well. Essentially, the entire site had burned (some rooms with intense heat) and then was abandoned. The excavators felt that the site had been partially abandoned at the time of the burning since only a portion of the rooms had good in situ deposits. The skeleton of one child was found unburied on a floor. The Ringo site (Johnson and Thompson 1963) was near the Kuykendall Site, and they may have been part of a cluster. The Ringo site consisted of several separate groups of rooms, each enclosing small plazas. There seemed to be little if any burning.

It is much easier to define clusters in the area near Cliff, New Mexico, some 75 miles (120 km) north of the Hidalgo County sites. Here, a clear cluster of sites dates to the mid- to late 1300s. The Dinwiddie site (J. Mills and Mills 1972) had massed rooms, but no plaza. About one-half of the rooms had burned, some intensely, others only slightly. A very high frequency of in situ materials was found in essentially all rooms. The nearby large Kwillelekia ruin was formed around two plazas; it did not burn in any significant way, but may have had one unburied body. Again, there was a very high incidence of in situ deposits, suggesting rapid abandonment. The Ormand site (Hammack et al. 1966) was also part of the cluster. Its eighty or so rooms were in four separate room blocks, and it is possible—but unlikely—that they were connected by compound walls. Data on the ceramics and the mode of abandonment indicate it may have been abandoned slightly earlier than the other pueblos and its population had moved into one of them. This would fit with its being less defensively constructed than sites like Kwillelekia.

There were a small number of late 1300s sites in the Mimbres Valley, some 35 miles from the Cliff area, but they did not cluster close to each other. The largest, the Disert site, had a possible defensive layout, with freestanding walls joining some room blocks, but the Janss and Stailey sites were single blocks of about thirty and twelve rooms, respectively. These were small sites, not tightly spaced, and had not burned; they were, however, rapidly abandoned, leaving in situ deposits.

The Jornada area and the remaining area of southeastern New Mexico farther east is difficult to address at this point. Survey is spotty, and dating difficult. In general, sites seem to have been much smaller than those to the west. Bloom Mound in very southeastern New Mexico is worth mentioning. It dates to around 1200 to 1350, and seems never to have had more than about fifteen rooms. There were "some 30 crania along with a great number of other skeletal parts; all charred to greater or lesser degrees" (Wiseman 1970) on the floor and in the fill of one room. Given the expected population of around two people per room, these thirty individuals would represent the entire population of the village. There is other minor evidence for burned sites in the Jornada area, but sites in general were small, not defensively built, and did not seem to follow any of the patterns seen elsewhere.

It should be clear that it is difficult to determine whether some of these sites were even roughly contemporaneous and whether they appear to cluster only because the intervening areas were essentially unknown. On the one hand, burning was reasonably common, and sites often had defensive layouts. On the other hand, there were some nondefensive or poorly defended sites for which there is ample evidence for rapid abandonment, leaving in situ deposits, but without being burned. This is the pattern found over much of the southern area: some evidence for warfare, but nothing to suggest it was as intense or the responses as patterned as what is found to the north.

The Greater Hohokam Area

The greater Hohokam area, including the cluster of sites along the Salt River and another two clusters along the Gila River that may have been an extension of the Salt River cluster, was discussed in chapter 6. There was a significant empty zone between this group of sites and another cluster along the Santa Cruz River near present-day Tucson. These clusters contained very large compounds, much larger than those in the Tonto Basin or San Pedro clusters. These clusters also had *trincheras*. The lower San Pedro cluster, also described in detail in chapter 6, was about 20 miles from the Tucson cluster. It included a number of sites on very defensive hills, with enclosing compound walls and additional freestanding walls. If the eleven large sites are included, then the cluster extended about 33 miles (55 km) along the river. (If the small sites are included, then the cluster was about twice that long.) Sites were spaced no more than 6 miles (10 km) apart, with most of them about half that distance apart. It is not clear whether all the sites, especially the smaller ones, were occupied the entire time. At least some of the residents of these villages were immigrants—probably refugees from farther north.

The final cluster, on Perry Mesa, essentially completed the spacing pattern between the Hohokam area, the Mogollon Rim, and the Verde Valley. This little mesa was about 6 miles wide and 9 miles long and had its perimeter fortified by seven site complexes of 100 to 300 rooms each, spaced about 2 to 3 miles apart around the edge of the mesa. The sites were discussed in chapter 6. Most interestingly, they continued the pattern of "beehivelike" layouts seen for most of the non-Plateau cluster sites that did not use the compound layout. There were a few free-standing walls, but not on the scale seen to the south. The sites totaled over 1,000 rooms, making this a relatively large cluster in terms of the number of people for clusters south of the Mogollon Rim.

SETTLEMENT CLUSTERS IN THE NORTHERN RIO GRANDE

The nature of settlement-cluster spacing in the Rio Grande Valley was discussed in chapter 6. The purpose here is to review the details about a select number of these clusters where the information is reasonably clear.

To summarize: the Galisteo cluster included eight sites. It was about 18 to 20 miles from the Pecos cluster (discussed below), and the Galisteo cluster was about the same distance from the cluster of eight sites that ultimately became recognizable as southern Tiwa. Similarly, the Jemez cluster (discussed below) was about the same distance from the southern Tiwa group and from the Biscuit Ware or Tewa cluster (between Los Alamos and Santa Fe), or about 20 miles. It is possible that the Biscuit Ware or Tewa cluster was actually two clusters, or had evolved into two clusters over time. There was a northern Biscuit Ware cluster centered on the Chama River. This cluster contained ten or so sites depending on the particular time period (discussed below). It was separated from the more southerly Los Alamos–Santa Fe group with about another ten sites, but the gap between them was only 10 miles. To the west of the Chama was the Largo-Gallina group of sites, which may or may not have been a true cluster (discussed below). Picuris was about 20 miles northeast of the Chama group, and Taos was about the same again from Picuris. South of the southern Tiwa cluster (near present-day Albuquerque) was the Rio Abajo cluster (discussed below), and to the southeast was the Tompiro cluster. I discuss about half these clusters in detail below.

Northern Tewa—The Chama and Nambe Clusters

The lower Chama River drainage presents one of the clearer pictures of the evolution of one of these clusters. The cluster area included El Rito Creek, Rio Ojo Caliente, and Rio del Oso, and had a relatively well known number of large sites, quite a few with some excavation data (e.g., Wendorf 1953; Peckham 1959, 1981; Jeançon 1911, 1912, 1923; Hibben 1937; Snow 1963). There is a good, recent summary by Beal (1987), who emphasizes the overall impact of warfare on the settlement locations, configurations, and resultant site burning—as do most of the other researchers in the area.

The drainage was very lightly occupied before A.D. 1300. Between then and the mid-1500s, some twenty sites containing twenty or more ground-floor rooms were constructed. For seventeen of these sites there are some reasonable data available. Four of the seventeen sites were relatively small and perhaps late, and are dealt with later; so thirteen sites are analyzed here.

Three of the earliest sites, Tsping, Riana, and the Palisade Ruin, were either extremely defensive, as was Tsping, or had palisades and redoubt walls, as did the Palisade site. All could be described as particularly defensive. Riana and Palisade were small, with twenty-three to forty-eight rooms; both were burned and short-lived. Tsping was quite large, with 400 rooms, and extremely defensive, being on a mesa top and having a wall across the one reasonable point of access. Its location was very poor for access to farmland and apparently to domestic water as well. Interestingly, it did not seem to last as late as other sites. Thus, the common pattern of early defensive sites being not as defensive and not as successful as later ones existed in the Chama region.

The really large sites, such as Sapawe, Howiri, Pose, Nute, Te'ewi, Ponsipaaker, Poshu, and Tsama, were all over 500 rooms, with some over 1,000. They were not defensively located, although for the most part they had enclosed plazas, usually multiple ones. Middle-sized sites, such as Kap (Leaf Water) with 175 rooms, Cerro Colorado with 350 rooms, and Ku with 300 rooms, were both plaza-oriented and in reasonably defensive locations—particularly Ku, which Beal considers to have been highly defensive. Therefore, the pattern of sites being either very big or relatively defensively located was quite prevalent.

What is of perhaps more interest, is that of the thirteen sites, seven and probably eight had signs of extensive burning (no data are available for several of the others), including the smaller sites of Riana and Palisade. The entire group of Te'ewi, Ku, and Pesede ruins on the Rio del Oso had evidence for burning, and so did all the middle Chama group of sites—Kap, Tsama, and Poshu. This means that there is evidence for significant burning from well over 50 percent of the relevant sites, including three sites that had more than 500 rooms.

There is also an interesting aspect to the settlement pattern over time. The twenty sites were spread throughout the drainage. The upper drainage group of sites seems to have been abandoned by A.D. 1400 (including two that were burned). The middle Chama group of three sites all showed signs of burning, as did the Rio del Oso group of three. (Incidentally, each group had one small site that was a hilltop site.) On El Rito Creek there was the big site of Sapawe and the undescribed site of El Rito. A third site, Cerro Colorado, was on a hill. This group survived until quite late, as did a group on the Rio Ojo Caliente. The latter group had five sites, all over 400 rooms in size. They were spaced 3 miles or less apart, none had evidence of burning, and all were well away from the other later sites in the drainage: 10 km (6 miles) over mountains, or 13 km (8 miles) via drainages to the next group.

This settlement pattern evolution may represent in microcosm what is seen for the Southwest overall. There were initially four site groups; one group was eliminated very early, the two groups in the middle were slowly eliminated, and the groups that survived were the larger ones, well separated from each other.

A final set of four small (thirty to eighty rooms) sites are of note: Buena Vista, Buena Vista II, Abiquiu, and Abiquiu Canyon. They seem to have been late and not particularly defensive. Beal suggests that warfare declines after A.D. 1450—the pattern seen for the entire Southwest. These sites may be a reoccupation of a buffer area after the threat of warfare declined enough to make it viable. Why these sites, and the remaining clusters, were largely abandoned before the 1600s is not clear.

The area around the modern single pueblo of Nambe in the Tewa cluster to the east is of interest, although the data are somewhat sketchy. Florence Ellis (1964) reports that there were some five ancestral villages in close proximity to the present Nambe Pueblo, which was probably also inhabited at least intermittently in the A.D. 1300 to 1500 time frame. The five sites were all located with respect to defense. They all seem to have been abandoned prior to Coronado's arrival, and only the Nambe Pueblo continued to be occupied. This would suggest that Rio Grande groups were declining in numbers and that by the 1500s the process of attrition due to warfare was diminishing. Otherwise, the defensive sites would not have been abandoned in favor of a nondefensive one.

The Jemez Cluster

The Jemez area has been considered by Schroeder (1979), Mera (1940), and Crown et al. (1996). Most usefully, the larger sites in this region have been summarily described by Elliott (1982). He notes that Coronado reported seven settlements in the immediate Jemez area and three in the Aguas Calientes area slightly to the east. Elliott has seven good candidates for the Jemez area sites. Yet, known to have been in the same area were around thirty Pueblo IV sites, including about twenty sites with 300 or more rooms. Even assuming that not all sites were initially in existence during the 1300s, it is difficult not to think that there must have been a reduction in the number of sites (and presumably room counts) from the 1300s' peak to A.D. 1540.

Again, the same pattern holds that is seen elsewhere. Small sites were more defensively located than big sites. Interestingly, there were some large Pueblo V sites established to resist the Spaniards, and at least a few of these were very defensively located. Thus, bigness alone may have been an adequate defense against other Indian groups, but it was not against the Spaniards. It seems that as the Spaniards successfully attacked and subdued pueblos regardless of their size, the Pueblo people soon realized that something else was needed to defend their homes against the Spaniards. They began to build large sites that were in very defensible locations. Although the Spaniards did ultimately conquer sites like Acoma, the settlements at Jemez and Hopi were located inaccessibly in the historic period, and some settlements were never defeated.

The Rio Abajo Cluster

Marshall and Walt (1984) provide a good summary of the later period sites of the Rio Abajo—the Rio Grande Valley from Socorro south—building on earlier work by Mera (1940). Wilcox (1991) interprets these data for the protohistoric period overall, and once more emphasizes the evolution of no-man's-lands between site clusters.

The beginning of the clustering process in the Rio Abajo followed the patterns observed elsewhere. There was the usual pattern of defensive sites in the late Pueblo III period. "The period is characterized by the coalescence of nucleated Pueblo III village populations into large, fortified apartment complexes" (Marshall and Walt 1984:95). The sites are not as datable as those on the Colorado Plateau, so it is not possible at this time to work out the subtleties of the settlement shifts. In general, the late Pueblo III sites showed a strong tendency to be on mesa tops: for example, the Bowling Green, El Nido de Las Piedras, and Piedras Negras sites. These sites often included major barrier walls to limit access to the mesa tops (e.g., Bowling Green and Piedras Negras). Almost all known sites of this interval were fortified. One site at the end of this period, Pueblo de Arena, appears to have been built in an orderly manner (bonding and abutting wall patterns are not discernible from the map), as expected in "ladder construction". Interestingly, it was not a big site—only thirty-six rooms—nor was it defensively laid out or in a defensive location. It did show evidence of burning. Perhaps this site represents a failed strategy.

These late Pueblo III sites were not very large, with room estimates of 20, 30, 40, 50, 55, 65, and 150, in terms of those sites for which relatively good estimates can be given. The following Pueblo IV Glaze A–D period (ancestral Piro) sites tended to be much larger: four sites were in the 50-to-100-room range; eight had 100 to 200 rooms; and four had over 200 rooms, including one with 750 rooms. The largest sites were located in low settings, adjacent to the river. There were also some smaller sites that retained a defensive setting, such as Cerro Indio Pueblo, San Pasqualito, and La Jara Peak Pueblo, that seemed to be contemporary with the large river sites.

In some cases, there may have been site groups that included a large river's edge site and a small hilltop site, perhaps for signaling or lookout purposes (e.g., the low-lying San Pasqual with 750 rooms and the nearby hilltop site of San Pasqualito with 37 rooms). It should be noted that the river sites were usually built around a plaza, but they did not appear to be completely enclosed as were sites found farther north and on the Colorado Plateau. The lack of excavation precludes determining whether freestanding enclosing walls may have been present. Nevertheless, the overall site layouts did not seem to show the same concern with a very safe domestic space. It would appear that, although the population increased, presumably due to immigration during the Glaze Ware period, there was not the same level of resource stress found in higher elevations, and there was much less intense warfare.

Nevertheless, the same general pattern seen elsewhere is found here: initial small sites, very defensively located, with a transition to larger sites, still generally defensively laid out very near water. Also, as Wilcox (1991) clearly notes, there was a significant no-man's-land between the Rio Abajo sites (Piro) and the southern Tiwa sites upstream. This gap was on the order of 20 miles, the distance seen so commonly elsewhere. Wilcox also sees a no-man's-land with another group of sites to the south.

The sites in the Gran Quivira area (Tompiro) are not analyzed except for a couple of points. The early pueblo at Gran Quivira was circular in form, very similar in size and shape to the big circular sites in the Zuni area, and was built with the same 'ladder' construction seen on those sites, extending the time and spatial distribution of this construction pattern. Late in the time period, Gran Quivira had two bodies on the floor of burned Kiva N (Hayes 1981:53).

The Upper Pecos Cluster

Spielmann (1996) provides a brief summary of the upper Pecos River area, which had about seven sites that spanned the late Pueblo III and Pueblo IV time range. The Forked Lightning site and Dick's Ruin seem to have been pre-1300s nondefensive sites; how long into the 1300s they were occupied is unclear. After A.D. 1300, the sites of Pecos, Rowe, Arrowhead, Loma Lothrop, and Hobson-Dressler were built. Most or all were built around one or more central plazas. On the ridge above Glorieta Pass, the small Hobson-Dressler site was apparently a lookout or signaling site. Interestingly, it provided a view toward the Rio Grande area to the west and not to the plains to the east. The small Loma Lothrop site also was a hilltop site, likely used as a lookout or for signaling. The Arrowhead ruin, a relatively small site, and the one closest to the next site cluster in the Rio Grande area was burned. Apparently, only Rowe and Pecos survived until A.D. 1500, and only Pecos existed at A.D. 1540. Whether the Tecolote site farther out toward the plains was part of this cluster is unclear, but it did not last into the historic period.

The general pattern of nondefensive sites giving way to defensive ones and only a few, larger sites surviving holds for the Pecos. Also, the sites at the edge of the cluster were abandoned first, and the cluster contracted toward its center, with the surviving sites being the largest.

Largo-Gallina Area

The Largo-Gallina area is well known for its burned sites, violent deaths, and defensive sites—in particular, towers. Mackey and Holbrook (1978) provide a good summary. They found that 62 of 183 habitation sites surveyed were burned. At least 127 of the 183 sites were in defensive locations. Out of a sample of 116 bodies, 49 were found unburied on floors of burned habitation structures. The presence in these sites of numerous bodies with arrowpoints in them and skulls crushed from blows by a club is well known. There is also good evidence for at least some degree of line-of-sight communication links between some of these sites (A. Ellis 1991; Sleeter 1987).

Sites were tiny—often only a few rooms and an associated tower. Sleeter sorts most of these sites into five spatial groups. Each group had perhaps sixty sites, with a probable total of under 200 rooms, so these groups were not large. Virtually all the dated sites from this phase seem to have been constructed in the 1200s. Of sixteen sites, where reasonably good abandonment dates can be determined (generally associated with massive burning), with only one exception dated to A.D. 1213, they were abandoned between A.D. 1253 and A.D. 1280. There is little doubt that major warfare took place in the 1200s in this area, but it is not clear whether the five spatial clusters were competitors or allies. Given the very high incidence of successful attacks, it is likely that people from one of the larger site clusters, such as the Chama or Jemez groups, methodically eliminated these mountain people.

Mesa Verde Migrant Sites

Following the movement of significant population from the greater Mesa Verde area into the Rio Grande area (which seems quite strongly supported, as noted in chapter 6), a string of relevant sites could have been found just to the west of the

Rio Grande Valley area (E. L. Davis 1964; Lekson 1985). The sites ranged along the Rio Puerco in the north (Roney 1995, 1996c) to at least two sites in the Acoma area—all previously discussed—to the Gallinas Springs site complex farther south (Bertram et al. 1990), and finally to a small cluster at Ojo Caliente on Alamosa Creek in southern Socorro County (Laumbach 1992). The Gallinas Springs site has been estimated to have had some 500 rooms. At Ojo Caliente, the very defensive Pinnacle Ruin had around 50 rooms, LA1131 had some 60 to 80 rooms, and LA1134 had between 40 and 70 rooms. The latter two sites were on high ground, but consisted of well-spaced room blocks. They looked much more like the Scribe S phase sites on the Colorado Plateau than the later highly defensive sites. It appears that the relatively undefensive LA1131 and LA1134 were abandoned, and then the very defensive Pinnacle Ruin was constructed.

All these sites apparently had ceramics that somehow related to the Mesa Verde area, and they all seem to have been abandoned early in the Pueblo IV period if not before. Was this a failure of these sites to survive or simply a stage in the population movement, with the people relocating into the valley proper slightly later? In either case, it was an additional instance of failure of groups to thrive outside the Rio Grande Valley.

BIBLIOGRAPHY

Accola, Richard M.

1981 Mogollon Settlement Patterns in the Middle San Francisco River Drainage, West-Central New Mexico. *The Kiva* 46(3):155–68.

Adams, E. Charles

1973 Dead Horse Site. Master's thesis, Department of Anthropology, University of Colorado, Boulder.

1989a Homol'ovi III: A Pueblo Hamlet in the Middle Little Colorado River Valley, Arizona. *The Kiva* 54(3):217–30.

1989b The Homol'ovi Research Program. *The Kiva* 54(3):175–94.

1991 *The Origin and Development of the Pueblo Katsina Cult.* Tucson: University of Arizona Press.

1996 The Pueblo III–Pueblo IV Transition in the Hopi Area, Arizona. In *Pueblo Cultures in Transition*, edited by Michael A. Adler. Tucson: Arizona University Press.

Adams, E. Charles, and Kelley Ann Hays

1991 *Homol'ovi II: Archaeology of an Ancestral Hopi Village, Arizona.* Anthropological Research Papers, no. 55. Tucson: University of Arizona Press.

Adams, E. Charles, Miriam Stark, and Deborah Dosh

1993 Ceramic Distribution and Exchange: Jeddito Yellowware and Implications for Social Complexity. *The Journal of Field Archaeology* 20:3–21.

Adams, Rex K.

1980 Salmon Ruin: Site Chronology and Formation Processes. In *Investigations at the Salmon Site: The Structure of Chacoan Society in the Northern Southwest*, edited by Cynthia Irwin-Williams and Phillip H. Shelley, 1:186–272. Final report to funding agencies. Portales: Eastern New Mexico University.

Adler, Michael A.

1996 *The Prehistoric Pueblo World, A.D. 1150–1350.* Tucson: University of Arizona Press.

Aikens, C. Melvin

1966 *Virgin-Kayenta Cultural Relationships.* University of Utah Anthropological Papers 79. Salt Lake City: University of Utah Press.

Akins, Nancy J.

1986 *A Biocultural Approach to Human Burials from Chaco Canyon, New Mexico.* Reports of the Chaco Center, no. 9. Branch of Cultural Research, U.S. Department of the Interior, National Park Service. Santa Fe, New Mexico.

1987 Human Remains from Pueblo Alto. In *Investigations at the Pueblo Alto Complex, Chaco Canyon, New Mexico 1975–1979*, vol. 3, pt. 2, edited by Frances Joan Mathien and Thomas C. Windes, 789–92. Publications in Archaeology 18F. Chaco Canyon Studies. Santa Fe, New Mexico: National Park Service, U.S. Department of Interior.

Aldred, Cyril

1984 *The Egyptians.* 2d ed. London and New York: Thames & Hudson.

Allen, Christina G., and Ben A. Nelson, eds.

1982 *Anasazi and Navajo Land Use in the McKinley Mine Area near Gallup, New Mexico*, vol. 1, *Archeology.* Albuquerque: Office of Contact Archeology, University of New Mexico.

Allen, Wilma H., Charles F. Merbs, and Walter H. Birkby

1985 Evidence for Prehistoric Scalping at Nuvakwewtaga (Chavez Pass) and Grasshopper Ruin, Arizona. In *Health and Dis-*

ease in the Prehistoric Southwest, edited by C. F. Merbs and R. J. Miller, 23–42. Arizona State University Anthropological Research Papers 34. Tempe.

Anderson, Bruce A.
1990   *The Wupatki Archeological Inventory Survey Project: Final Report*. Professional Paper no. 35. Santa Fe, New Mexico: Southwest Regional Office, Division of Anthropology, Southwest Cultural Resources Center.

Anderson, D. G.
1990   Political Change in Chiefdom Societies: Cycling in the Late Prehistoric Southeastern United States. Ph.D. diss., University of Michigan.

Andrews, Michael J.
1982   An Archaeological Assessment of Homolovi III and Chevelon Ruin, Northern Arizona. Ms on file, Department of Anthropology, Northern Arizona University, Flagstaff.

Anscheutz, Kurt, and Timothy Maxwell
1986   The Multidisciplinary Investigations of Prehistoric Puebloan Gardens in the Lower Chama Valley, New Mexico. Paper presented at the 9th annual ethnobiology conference of the Society of Ethnobiology, University of New Mexico, Albuquerque, March 21–23, 1986.

Anyon, Roger
1983   Divergent Mogollon Evolution and the Development of Ceremonial Structures. Master's thesis, Department of Anthropology, University of New Mexico.
1992   The Late Prehistoric and Early Historic Periods in the Zuni-Cibola Area, A.D. 1400–1680. In *Current Research on the Late Prehistory and Early History of New Mexico*, edited by Bradley J. Vierra, 75–84. Albuquerque: New Mexico Archaeological Council.

Anyon, Roger, Susan M. Collins, and Kathryn H. Bennett
1983   *Archaeological Investigations between Manuelito Canyon and Whitewater Arroyo, Northwest New Mexico*. Zuni Archaeology Program Report, Number 185. Zuni, New Mexico.

Anyon, Roger, and Steven A. LeBlanc
1980   The Architectural Evolution of Mogollon-Mimbres Communal Structures. *The Kiva* 45:253–77. (eds.)
1984   *The Galaz Ruin: A Prehistoric Mimbres village in Southwestern New Mexico*. Contributions by Paul Minnis, James Lancaster, and Margaret C. Nelson. Albuquerque: University of New Mexico Press.

Atkins, Victoria M., ed.
1993   *Anasazi Basketmaker: Papers from the 1990 Wetherill–Grand Gulch Symposium*. Cultural Resources Series no. 24. Salt Lake City: Bureau of Land Management.

Baker, S. A.
1990   Rattlesnake Ruin (42Sa18434): A Case of Violent Death and Perimortem Mutilation in the Anasazi Culture of San Juan County, Utah. Master's thesis, Department of Anthropology, Brigham Young University, Provo, Utah.

Baldwin, Gordon C.
1938   Excavations at Kinishba Pueblo, Arizona. *American Antiquity* 4(1):11–21.
1939   The Material Culture of Kinishba. *American Antiquity* 4(4):314–27.

Baldwin, Stuart J.
1997   *Apacheans Bearing Gifts: Prehistoric Influence on the Pueblo Indians*. The Arizona Archaeologist no. 29. Phoenix: Arizona Archaeological Society.

Balée, William
1984   The Ecology of Ancient Tupi Warfare. In *Warfare, Culture, and Environment*, edited by Brian R. Ferguson, 241–66. Orlando, Florida: Academic Press.

Bamforth, Douglas B.
1994   Indigenous People, Indigenous Violence: Precontact Warfare on the North American Great Plains. *Man* 29:95–115.

Bandelier, Adolph F. A.
1892   *Final Report of Investigations among the Indians of the Southwestern United States, Carried out mainly in the Years from 1880 to 1885*. Papers of the Archaeological Institute of America, pts. 1 and 2. Cambridge.

Bannister, Bryant, and William J. Robinson
1971   *Tree-Ring Dates from Arizona U-W:*

Gila-Salt River Area. Tucson: Laboratory of Tree-Ring Research.

Barnett, Franklin
1974   *Sandstone Hill Pueblo Ruin: Cibola Culture in Catron County, New Mexico*. Albuquerque: Albuquerque Archaeological Society.

Basso, K. H., ed.
1971   *Western Apache Raiding and Warfare*. Tucson: University of Arizona Press.

Beaglehole, Ernest
1935   Notes on Hopi Warfare. In *Hopi of the Second Mesa*. Memoirs of the American Anthropological Society 44:17–24. Washington, D.C.

Beal, John D.
1987   *Foundations of the Rio Grande Classic: The Lower Chama River* A.D. *1300–1500*. Southwestern Project no. 137. Southwest Archaeological Consultants. Santa Fe, New Mexico.

Beals, Ralph L.
1932   *The Comparative Ethnology of Northern Mexico before 1750*. Ibero-Americana no. 2. Berkeley: University of California Press.

1933   *The Acaxee: A Mountain Tribe of Durango and Sinaloa*. Ibero-Americana no. 2. Berkeley: University of California Press.

Benedict, Ruth
1934   *Patterns of Culture*. Boston and New York: Houghton Mifflin. 4th printing. New York: Mentor Books.

Bergman, Christopher A., and Edward McEwen
n.d.   Sinew-Reinforced and Composite Bows: Technology, Function and Social Implications. Ms in the possession of the author.

Bergman, Christopher A., Edward McEwen, and R. Miller
1988   Experimental Archery: Projectile Velocities and Comparison of Bow Performances. *Antiquity* 62(237):658–70.

Berman, Mary Jane
1978   *The Mesa Top Site: An Early Mogollon Village in Southeastern Arizona*. Cultural Resources Management Division Report 280. Las Cruces: Department of Sociology and Anthropology, New Mexico State University.

Bernardini, Wesley
1996   Transitions in Social Organization: A Predictive Model from Southwestern Archaeology. *Journal of Anthropological Archaeology* 15(4):372–402.

Berndt, Ronald M.
1964   Warfare in the New Guinea Highlands. *American Anthropologist* 66(4):183–203.

Berry, D. R.
1983   Disease and Climatic Relationship among Pueblo III and Pueblo IV Anasazi of the Colorado Plateau. Ph.D. diss. University of California, Los Angeles.

Berry, Michael S.
1982   *Time, Space, and Transition in Anasazi Prehistory*. Salt Lake City: University of Utah Press.

Bertram, Jack B., Andrew R. Gomolak, Steven R. Hoagland, Terry L. Knight, Emily Garber, and Kenneth J. Lord
1990   Excavations in the South Block of Gallinas Springs Ruin (LA1178), a Large Town of the Gallinas Mountains Phase (Late Pueblo III–Early PIV) on the Mogosazi Frontier. Ms on file, Cibola National Forest, Albuquerque, New Mexico.

Billman, Brian R.
1997   Cannibalism in Cowboy Wash, pt. 3: The Colorado Plateau in the Twelfth Century A.D. Paper presented at the 62d annual meeting of the Society for American Archaeology, April 2–6, Nashville, Tennessee.

Bishop. Ronald L., Veletta Canouts, Suzanne De Atley, Alfred Qoyawayma, and C. W. Aikins
1988   The Formation of Ceramic Analytical Groups: Hopi Pottery Production and Exchange, A.D. 1300–1600. *The Journal of Field Archaeology* 15:317–37.

Blackburn, Fred M., and Ray A. Williamson
1997   *Cowboys and Cave Dwellers: Basketmaker Archaeology in Utah's Grand Gulch*. Santa Fe, New Mexico: School of American Research Press.

Blake, Michael, Steven A. LeBlanc, and Paul E. Minnis
1986   Changing Settlement and Population in the Mimbres Valley, S. W. New Mexico. *The Journal of Field Archaeology* 13(4):439–64.

Blick, J. P.

1988   Genocidal Warfare in Tribal Societies as a
        Result of European-Induced Culture Con-
        flict. *Man*, n.s., 23:654–70.

Blitz, John H.

1988   Adoption of the Bow in Prehistoric North
        America. *North American Archaeologist*
        9(2):123–45.

Bluhm, Elaine A.

1960   Mogollon Settlement Patterns in the Pine
        Lawn Valley, New Mexico. *American An-
        tiquity* 25(4):538–46.

Boehm, Christopher

1996   Emergency Decisions, Cultural-Selection
        Mechanics and Group Selection. *Current
        Anthropology* 17(5):763–93.

Bolton, Herbert E.

1964   *Coronado, Knight of Pueblos and Plains.*
        Albuquerque: University of New Mexico
        Press.

Boulding, Kenneth E.

1963   *Conflict and Defense: A General Theory.*
        New York: Harper Torchbooks.

Bourke, John G.

1884   *The Snake-Dance of the Moquis of Ari-
        zona.* London: Sampson Low, Marston,
        Searle, and Rivington.

Bradbury, Andrew P.

1997   The Bow and Arrow in the Eastern Wood-
        lands: Evidence for an Archaic Origin.
        North American Archaeologist 18(3):207–
        34.

Bradfield, Wesley

1931   *Cameron Creek Village: A Site in the
        Mimbres Area in Grant County, New
        Mexico.* Monographs of the School of
        American Research no. 1. Santa Fe, New
        Mexico.

Bradley, Bruce A.

1992   Excavations at Sand Canyon Pueblo. In
        *The Sand Canyon Archaeological Project:
        A Progress Report*, edited by William
        Lipe, 79–97. Occasional Papers no. 2.
        Cortez, Colorado: Crow Canyon Ar-
        chaeological Center.

Brandes, Raymond

1957   An Archaeological Survey within Gila
        County, Arizona. Ms on file, Western Ar-

cheological and Conservation Center, Tucson, Arizona.

Breternitz, Cory D., David E. Doyel, and Michael P.
Marshall, eds.

1982   *Bis sa'ani: A Late Bonito Phase Commu-
        nity on Escavada Wash, Northwest New
        Mexico.* Navajo Nation Papers in Anthro-
        pology, no. 14. Window Rock, Arizona.

Brew, John O.

1946   *Archaeology of Alkali Ridge, Southeastern
        Utah, with a Review of the Prehistory of
        the Mesa Verde Division of the San Juan
        and Some Observations on Archaeologi-
        cal Systematics.* Papers of the Peabody
        Museum of American Archaeology and
        Ethnology vol. 21. Cambridge.

Brody, J. J.

1977   *Mimbres Painted Pottery.* Albuquerque:
        University of New Mexico Press.

Brody, J. J., Catherine J. Scott, and Steven A. LeBlanc

1983   *Mimbres Pottery: Ancient Art of the
        American Southwest.* New York: Hudson
        Hills Press.

Broecher, Wallace S.

1992   Global Warming on Trial. *Natural History*
        4:6–14.

Brown, Gary M.

1982   Preliminary Report on Archaeological Re-
        search During 1981 at Nuvakwewtaqa
        (Chavez Pass). Interim report prepared for
        the National Science Foundation, Wash-
        ington, D.C. and the USDA Forest Service,
        Southwestern Regional Office, Albuquer-
        que, New Mexico. Department of Anthro-
        pology, Arizona State University.

Brown, Jeffrey L.

1974   Pueblo Viejo Salado Sites and Their Rela-
        tionship to Western Pueblo Culture. *The
        Artifact* 12:1–49.

Buge, David E.

1978   Preliminary Report: 1978 Excavations at
        NM-01-1407, Ojo Caliente, New Mexico.
        Ms submitted through Department of So-
        ciology/Anthropology, Occidental Col-
        lege, Los Angeles. Ms on file, Laboratory
        of Anthropology, Museum of New
        Mexico, Santa Fe.

1979   Preliminary Report: 1979 Excavations at

Ponsipa-akeri, Ojo Caliente, New Mexico. Ms submitted through Department of Sociology/Anthropology, Occidental College, Los Angeles. Ms on file, Laboratory of Anthropology, Museum of New Mexico, Santa Fe.

1984 Prehistoric Subsistence Strategies in the Ojo Caliente Valley, New Mexico. In *Prehistoric Agricultural Strategies in the Southwest*, edited by S. K Fish and Paul R. Fish, 27–34. Anthropological Research Paper no. 33. Tempe: Arizona State University.

Bullard, William Rotch, Jr.
1962 *The Cerro Colorado Site and Pithouse Architecture in the Southwestern United States Prior to A.D. 900*. Papers of the Peabody Museum of Archaeology and Ethnology, vol. 44, no. 2. Cambridge.

Bullock, Peter Y.
1991 A Reappraisal of Anasazi Cannibalism. *The Kiva* 57:5–16.
1992 A Return to the Question of Cannibalism. *The Kiva* 58:203–5.

Bunker, C. J., and D. D. Dykeman
1991 *A Cultural Resources Inventory of the Phillips San Juan 32-7 Unit Gathering System Located on Burnt Mesa, San Juan County, New Mexico*. Daggett and Chenault Report no. 91-DCI-043. Farmington, New Mexico.

Burton, Jeffrey F.
1990 *Archeological Investigations at Puerco Ruin, Petrified Forest National Park, Arizona*. Publications in Anthropology no. 54. Tucson: Western Archeological and Conservation Center, National Park Service.
1991 *The Archaeology of Sivu'uvi*. Publications in Anthropology no. 55. Tucson: Western Archeological and Conservation Center, National Park Service.
1993 *Days in the Painted Desert and the Petrified Forests of Northern Arizona*. Publications in Anthropology no. 62. Tucson: Western Archeological and Conservation Center, National Park Service.

Cameron, Catherine M., and Steve A. Tomka, eds.
1993 *Abandonment of Settlements and Regions: Ethnoarchaeological and Archaeo-logical Approaches*. New York: Cambridge University Press.

Canouts, Veletta
1975 *An Archaeological Survey of the Orme Reservoir*. Archaeological Series 92. Tucson: Arizona State Museum.

Carlson, Roy L.
1963 *Basketmaker III Sites near Durango, Colorado*. University of Colorado Studies, Series in Anthropology 8. Denver.

Carneiro, R.
1970 A theory of the Origin of the State. *Science* 169:733–38.

Casselberry, Samuel E.
1974 Further Refinement of Formulas for Determining Population from Floor Area. *World Archaeology* 6(1):117–22.

Castleton, Kenneth B.
1987 *Petroglyphs and Pictographs of Utah*, vol. 2, *The South, Central, West and Northwest*. 2d enlarged ed. Salt Lake City: Utah Museum of Natural History, Salt Lake City.

Cater, J. D., and William L. Shields
1992 *A Cultural Resources Inventory of the Phillips San Juan 29-6 Unit Gathering System Located in the Greater Gobernador Area, Rio Arriba County, New Mexico*. Daggett and Chenault Report no. 91-DCI-044. Farmington, New Mexico.

Cattanach, George S., Jr.
1980 *Long House, Mesa Verde National Park, Colorado*. With contributions by R. P. Wheeler, C. M. Osborne, C. R. McKusick, and P. S. Martin. Publications in Archeology 7H. Wetherill Mesa Studies. Washington, D.C.: National Park Service, U.S. Department of the Interior.

Chagnon, Napoleon A.
1968 Yanomamö Social Organization and Warfare. In *War: The Anthropology of Armed Conflict and Aggression*, edited by Morton Fried, Marvin Harris, and Robert Murphy, 85–91. Garden City, New York: Natural History Press.

Chartkoff, Joseph L., and Kerry Kona Chartkoff
1984 *The Archaeology of California*. Stanford: Stanford University Press.

Cole, Sally

1990   *Legacy on Stone: Rock Art of the Colorado Plateau and Four Corners Region.* Boulder, Colorado: Johnson.

1993   Basketmaker Rock Art at the Green Mask Site, Southeastern Utah. In *Anasazi Basketmaker: Papers from the 1990 Wetherill-Grand Gulch Symposium*, edited by Victoria M. Atkins, 193–222. Cultural Resource Series 24. Salt Lake City: Bureau of Land Management.

Colton, Harold S.

1932   *A Survey of Perhistoric Sites in the Region of Flagstaff, Arizona.* Bureau of American Ethnology Bulletin no. 104. Washington, D.C.

1946   *The Sinagua: A Summary of the Archaeology of the Region of Flagstaff, Arizona.* Museum of Northern Arizona Bulletin 22. Flagstaff.

1960   *Black Sand: Prehistory in Northern Arizona.* Albuquerque: University of New Mexico Press.

Conner, Sidney

1943   Excavations at Kinnikinnick, Arizona. *American Antiquity* 8(4):376–79.

Cordell, Linda S.

1984   *Prehistory of the Southwest.* Orlando, Florida: Academic Press.

1989   Warfare: Some Issues from the Prehistoric Southwest. In *Cultures in Conflict: Current Anthropological Perspectives*, edited by D. C. Tkaczuk and B. C. Vivian, 173–74. Calgary, Alberta, Canada: Archaeological Association of the University of Calgary.

1994   *Ancient Pueblo Peoples.* Washington, D.C.: Remy Press and Smithsonian Institution.

1997   *Archaeology of the Southwest.* 2d ed. Orlando, Florida: Academic Press.

Cordell, Linda S., Steadman Upham, and Sharon L. Brock

1987   Obscuring Cultural Patterns in the Archaeological Record: A Discussion from Southwestern Archaeology. *American Antiquity* 52(3):565–77.

Cosgrove, H. S., and C. B. Cosgrove

1932   *The Swarts Ruin: A Typical Mimbres Site in Southwestern New Mexico.* Papers of the Peabody Museum of American Archaeology and Ethnology, vol. 15, no. l. Cambridge.

Cosner, A. J.

1951   Arrowshaft-Straightening with a Grooved Stone. *American Antiquity* 17:147–48.

Crary, Joseph S., and Stephen Germick

1992   Late Classic Period Cultural and Subsistence Patterns of the Upper Pinal Creek Drainage. Ms on file, U.S. Forest Service, Tonto National Forest, Phoenix, Arizona.

Creamer, Winifred

1993   *The Architecture of Arroyo Hondo Pueblo, New Mexico.* Arroyo Hondo Archaeological Series, vol. 7. Santa Fe, New Mexico: School of American Research Press.

1996   Developing Complexity in the American Southwest: Constructing a Model for the Rio Grande Valley. In *Emergent Complexity: The Evolution of Intermediate Societies*, edited by Jeanne Arnold, 91–106. International Monographs in Prehistory, Archaeological Series no. 9. Ann Arbor: University of Michigan.

Creel, Darrell

1989   A Primary Cremation at the NAN Ranch Ruin, with Comparative Data on Other Cremations in the Mimbres Area, New Mexico. *The Journal of Field Archaeology* 16:309–29.

1991   Bison Hides in Late Prehistoric Exchange in the Southern Plains. *American Antiquity* 56(1):40–49.

Crotty, Helen Koefoed

1995   Anasazi Mural Art of the Pueblo IV Period, A.D. 1300–1600: Influences, Selective Adaptation, and Cultural Diversity in the Prehistoric Southwest. Ph.D. diss., Department of Art History, University of California, Los Angeles.

Crown, Patricia L.

1981   Variability in Ceramic Manufacture at the Chodistaas Site, East-Central Arizona. Ph.D. diss., Department of Anthropology, University of Arizona, Tucson.

1987   Water Storage in the Prehistoric Southwest. *The Kiva* 52:209–28.

1994 *Ceramics and Ideology: Salado Polychrome Pottery*. Albuquerque: University of New Mexico Press.

Crown, Patricia L., and W. James Judge, eds.

1991 *Chaco & Hohokam: Prehistoric Regional Systems in the American Southwest*. Santa Fe, New Mexico: School of American Research Press.

Crown, Patricia L., Janet D. Orcutt, and Timothy A. Kohler

1996 Pueblo Cultures in Transition: The Northern Rio Grande. In *Pueblo Cultures in Transition*, edited by Michael A. Adler. Tucson: Arizona University Press.

Culbert, T. Patrick

1988 The Collapse of Classic Maya Civilization. In *The Collapse of Ancient States and Civilizations*, edited by Norman Yoffee and George L. Cowgill, 69–101. Tucson: University of Arizona Press.

Cummings, Byron

1940 *Kinishba, A Prehistoric Pueblo of the Great Pueblo Period*. Tucson, Arizona: Hohokam Museums Association.

Cunliffe, B., ed.

1994 *The Oxford Illustrated Prehistory of Europe*. Oxford: Oxford University Press.

Cushing, Frank Hamilton

[1882] *My Adventures in Zuni*. Reprint, Palo
1970 Alto, California: American West Publishing Company. Reprint 1941, Santa Fe, New Mexico: The Peripatetic Press.

[1896] *The Mythic World of the Zuni, as Written*
1988 *by Frank Hamilton Cushing*. Reprint, edited and illustrated by Barton Wright, Albuquerque: University of New Mexico Press.

d'Anglure, Bernard Saladin

1984 Inuit of Quebec. In *Handbook of North American Indians*, vol. 5, *Arctic*, edited by David Damas, 476–507. Washington, D.C.: Smithsonian Institution Press.

Danson, Edward B.

1957 *An Archaeological Survey of West Central New Mexico and East Central Arizona*. Papers of the Peabody Museum of Archaeology and Ethnology, vol. 44, no. 1. Cambridge.

Danson, Edward B., and Harold E. Malde

1957 Casa Malpais: A Fortified Site at Springerville, Arizona. *Plateau* 22(4):61–67.

Darling, J. Andrew

1995 Mass Inhumation and the Execution of Witches in the American Southwest. Paper presented at the 60th annual meeting of the Society for American Archaeology, Minneapolis, Minnesota.

Davis, Carolyn O'Bagy

1995 *Treasured Earth: Hattie Cosgrove's Mimbres Archaeology in the American Southwest*. Tucson, Arizona: Sanpete Publications and Old Pueblo Archaeology Center.

Davis, Emma Lou

1964 Anasazi Mobility and Mesa Verde Migrations. Ph.D. diss., Department of Anthropology, University of California, Los Angeles.

Dean, Jeffrey S.

1969 *Chronological Analysis of Tsegi Phase Sites in Northeastern Arizona*. Papers of the Laboratory of Tree-Ring Research no. 3. Tucson: University of Arizona Press.

1988 Dendrochronology and Paleoenvironmental Reconstruction on the Colorado Plateau. In *The Anasazi in a Changing Environment*, edited by George J. Gumerman, 119–67. Cambridge: Cambridge University Press.

1994 The Medieval Warm Period on the Southern Colorado Plateau. *Climatic Change* 26:225–41.

1996a Demography, Environment, and Subsistence Stress. In *Evolving Complexity and Environmental Risk in Prehistoric Southwest*, edited by J. Tainter and B. B. Tainter, 25–56. Santa Fe Institute Studies in Scientific Complexity 24. Reading, Massachusetts: Addison-Wesley.

1996b Kayenta Anasazi Settlement Transformations in Northeastern Arizona: A.D. 1150–1350. In *The Prehistoric Pueblo World, A.D. 1150–1350*, edited by Michael A. Adler, 29–47. Tucson: University of Arizona Press.

Dean Jeffrey S., William H. Doelle, and Janet D. Orcutt

1994 Adaptive Stress, Environment, and Demography. In *Themes in Southwest Prehistory*, edited by George J. Gumerman,

33–86. Santa Fe, New Mexico: School of American Research Press.

Dean, Jeffrey S. and Gary S. Funkhouser
  1995 Dendroclimatic Reconstructions for the Southern Colorado Plateau. In *Climatic Change in the Four Corners and Adjacent Regions: Implications for Environmental Restoration and Land-Use Planning*, edited by W. J. Waugh, 85–104. Grand Junction, Colorado: Campbell College Center, Mesa State College.

Dean, Jeffrey S., and John C. Ravesloot
  1988 The Chronology of Cultural Interaction in the Gran Chichimeca. Paper prepared for the American Advanced Seminar: Culture and Contact, Charles C. DiPeso's Gran Chichimeca. Dragoon, Arizona.

Debowski, Sharon, A. George, Richard Goddard, and D. Mullon
  1976 *An Archaeological Survey of the Buttes Reservoir*. Archaeological Series no. 93. Tucson: Arizona State Museum.

DeGarmo, Glen D.
  1975 Coyote Creek, Site 01: A Methodological Study of a Prehistoric Pueblo Population. Ph.D. diss., Department of Anthropology, University of California, Los Angeles.

Demarest, Arthur A.
  1992 Ideology in Ancient Maya Cultural Evolution: The Dynamics of Galactic Polities. In *Ideology and Pre-Columbian Civilizations*, edited by Arthur A. Demarest and Geoffrey W. Conrad, 135–57. Santa Fe, New Mexico: School of American Research Press.

Dice, Michael H.
  1993a A Disarticulated Human Bone Assemblage from Leroux Wash, Arizona. Master's thesis, Department of Anthropology, Arizona State University, Tempe.
  1993b Disarticulated Human Remains from the Hansen Pueblo, 5MT3976, Cortez, Colorado. Ms on file, Woods Canyon Archaeological Consultants, Yellow Jacket, Colorado.
  1993c *Disarticulated Human Remains from Reach III of the Towaoc Canal, Ute Mountain Ute Reservation, Montezuma County, Colorado*. Four Corners Archaeological Project Report no. 22. Yellow Jacket, Colorado: Complete Archaeological Consultants.

Diehl, Michael W.
  1994 Subsistence Strategies and Emergent Social Differences: A Case Study from the Prehistoric North American Southwest. Ph.D. diss., Department of Anthropology, State University of New York at Buffalo.

Diehl, Michael, and Steven A. LeBlanc
  n.d.   *Early Pithouse Villages of the Mimbres Mogollon and their Regional Context*. Albuquerque: University of New Mexico, Maxwell Museum. In press.

DiPeso, Charles C.
  1951 *The Babocomari Village Site on the Babocomari River, Southeastern Arizona*. The Amerind Foundation Paper no. 5. Dragoon, Arizona.
  1956 *The Upper Pima of San Cayatano del Tumacacori: An Archaeo-Historical Reconstruction of the Ootam of Pimera Alta*. The Amerind Foundation Paper no. 7. Dragoon, Arizona.
  1958 *The Reeve Ruin of Southwestern Arizona: A Study of a Prehistoric Western Pueblo Migration into the Middle San Pedro Valley*. Amerind Foundation Paper no. 8. Dragoon, Arizona.
  1974 *Casas Grandes: A Fallen Trading Center of the Gran Chichimeca*. Amerind Foundation Publications no. 9. Flagstaff, Arizona: Northland Press.

Dittert, Alfred E., Jr., F. W. Eddy, and B. L. Dickey
  1966 LA 4195, Sambrito Village. In *Prehistory in the Navajo Reservoir District, Northwestern New Mexico*, edited by F. W. Eddy, 230–54. Papers in Anthropology no. 15, pt. 1. Santa Fe, New Mexico: Museum of New Mexico.

Doelle, William H., and Henry Wallace
  1985 Rincon Phase Community Re-Organization in the Tucson Basin. Paper presented at the annual meeting of the American Association for the Advancement of Science, Southwest and Rocky Mountain Division, Tucson, Arizona.

1991   The Changing Role in the Tucson Basin in the Hohokam Regional System. In *Exploring the Hohokam: Prehistoric Desert Peoples of the Southwest*, edited by G. J. Gumerman, 279–346. Albuquerque: University of New Mexico Press.

Dohm, Karen M.

1994   The Search for Anasazi Village Origins: Basketmaker II Dwelling Aggregation on Cedar Mesa. *The Kiva* 60(2):257–76.

Dongoske, Kurt

1997   Comments as symposium discussant on "Debating Anasazi Cannibalism: Recent Evidence from the Northern San Juan Basin." 62d annual meeting of the Society for American Archaeology, Nashville, Tennessee.

Dove, Donald E.

1970   A Site Survey along the Lower Aqua Fria River, Arizona. *Arizona Archaeologist* 5:1–36. Phoenix: Phoenix Archaeological Society.

Downs, James F.

1972   *The Navajo*. New York: Holt, Rinehart and Winston.

Downum, Christian E.

1986   The Occupational Use of Hill Space in the Tucson Basin: Evidence from Linda Vista Hill. *The Kiva* 51(4):219–33.

1993   *Between Desert and River*. Anthropological Papers of the University of Arizona no. 57. Tucson: University of Arizona Press.

Downum, Christian E., Paul R. Fish, and Suzanne K. Fish

1994   Refining the Role of *Cerros de Trincheras* in Southern Arizona Settlement. *The Kiva* 59(3):271–96.

Doyel, David E., ed.

1992   *Anasazi Regional Organization and the Chaco System*. Papers of the Maxwell Museum no. 5. Albuquerque, New Mexico.

Dozier, Edward P.

1954   *The Hopi-Tewa of Arizona*. University of California Publications in American Archaeology and Ethnology 44(3):259–376. Berkeley.

Duff, Andrew I.

1995   Excavations at Rattlesnake Point Pueblo on the Upper Little Colorado River. Paper presented at the 60th annual meeting of the Society for American Archaeology, Minneapolis, Minnesota.

1996   When Is a Region? Issues for Late Pueblo Prehistory. Paper presented at the Southwest Symposium, February 1996, Tempe, Arizona.

Durham, W.

1976   Resources, Competition and Human Aggression, pt. 1: A Review of Primitive War. *The Quarterly Review of Biology* 51:385–415.

Dutton, Bertha P.

1963   *Sun Father's Way: The Kiva Murals of Kuaua, a Pueblo Ruin, Coronado State Monument, New Mexico*. Albuquerque: University of New Mexico Press.

Earl, Timothy

1987   Chiefdoms in Archaeological and Ethnohistorical Perspective. *Annual Reviews of Anthropology* 16:279–308.

Earls, Amy C.

1992   Raiding, Trading, and Population among the Piro Pueblos, A.D. 1540–1680. In *Current Research on the Late Prehistory and Early History of New Mexico*, edited by Bradley J. Vierra, 75–84. Albuquerque: New Mexico Archaeological Council.

Eddy, F. W.

1966   *Prehistory in the Navajo Reservoir District Northern New Mexico*. Papers in Anthropology no. 15. Tucson: Museum of New Mexico.

1972   Culture Ecology and the Prehistory of the Navajo Reservoir District. *Southwestern Lore* 38:1–75.

1974   Population Dislocation in the Navajo Reservoir District, New Mexico and Colorado. *American Antiquity* 39(1):75–84.

1977   *Archaeological Investigations at Chimney Rock Mesa: 1970–1972*. Memoirs of the Colorado Archaeological Society no. 1. Boulder, Colorado.

Elliott, Michael L.

1982   *Large Pueblo Sites near Jemez Springs, New Mexico*. Cultural Resources Report no. 3. Santa Fe, New Mexico: Santa Fe National Forest.

Ellis, Andrea

1991 Towers of the Gallina Area and Greater Southwest. In *Puebloan Past and Present: Papers in Honor of Stewart Peckham*, edited by Meliha S. Duran and David T. Kirkpatrick, 57–70. Publications of the Archaeological Society of New Mexico no. 17. Albuquerque.

Ellis, Florence Hawley

1951 Patterns of Aggression and the War Cult in Southwestern Pueblos. *Southwestern Journal of Anthropology* 7(2):177–201.

1964 Archaeological History of Nambe Pueblo, 14th Century to the Present. *American Antiquity* 30(1):34–42.

1967 Use and Significance of the Tchamahia. *El Palacio* 74(1):35–43.

Ember, Carol R., and Melvin Ember

1992 Resource Unpredictability, Mistrust, and War: A Cross-Cultural Study. *Journal of Conflict Resolution* 36(2):242–62.

Errikson, Mary

1994 *Prehistoric Archaeological Investigations on Prehistoric Sites, Reach III of the Towaoc Canal, Ute Mountain Ute Reservation, Montezuma County, Colorado*. Four Corners Archaeological Project Report no. 21. Cortez, Colorado: Complete Archaeological Services Associates.

Ezell, Paul H., and Alan P. Olson

1955 An Artifact of Human Bone from Eastern Arizona. *Plateau* 27(3):8–11.

Fairchild-Parks, James, and Jeffrey S. Dean

1993 Analysis of Tree-Ring Dates from Balcony House—Mesa Verde National Park, Colorado. Ms on file, Laboratory of Tree-Ring Research, Tucson, Arizona.

Fairley, Helen C.

1989 Culture History. In *Man, Models and Management: An Overview of the Archaeology of the Arizona Strip and the Management of Its Cultural Resources*, edited by J. H. Altschul and H. C. Fairly, 85–152. Tucson: Statistical Research.

Farmer, Malcolm F.

1955 Awatovi Bows. *Plateau* 29(1):8–10.

Fathauer, George H.

1954 The Structure and causation of Mohave

warfare. *Southwestern Journal of Anthropology* 10:97–118.

Fay, P. M., and Klein, P. Y.

1988 A Reexamination of the Leroux Wash Skeletal Material for Evidence of Human Modification. Ms on file, Museum of Northern Arizona, Flagstaff, Arizona.

Fenenga, Franklin, and Fred Wendorf

1956 Excavations at the Ignacio, Colorado, Field Camp: Site LA2605. In *Pipeline Archaeology*, edited by Fred Wendorf, Nancy Fox, and Orian L. Lewis, 207–14. Santa Fe, New Mexico, and Flagstaff, Arizona: Laboratory of Anthropology and Museum of New Mexico.

Ferguson, R. Brian

1992 A Savage Encounter: Western Contact and the Yanomami War Complex. In *War in the Tribal Zone: Expanding States and Indigenous Warfare*, edited by Ferguson, R. Brian and Neil L. Whitehead, 199–227. Santa Fe, New Mexico: School of American Research Press. (Ed.)

1984 *Warfare, Culture, and Environment*. Orlando, Florida: Academic Press.

Ferguson, R. Brian, and Neil L. Whitehead, eds.

1992 *War in the Tribal Zone: Expanding States and Indigenous Warfare*. Santa Fe, New Mexico: School of American Research Press.

Ferguson, T. J.

1996 *Historic Zuni Architecture and Society: An Archaeological Application of Space Syntax*. Anthropological Papers of the University of Arizona no. 60. Tucson: University of Arizona Press.

Ferguson, T. J., and E. Richard Hart

1985 *A Zuni Atlas*. Norman: University of Oklahoma Press.

Fetterman, Jerry, and Linda Honeycutt

1987 *The Mockingbird Mesa Survey*. Colorado State Office, Bureau of Land Management Cultural Resource Series 22. Denver.

Fewkes, Jesse Walter

1893 A-Wa-To-Bi: An Archaeological Verification of a Tusayan Legend. *American Anthropologist* 6:363–75.

1898a Archeological Expedition to Arizona in 1895. In *Seventeenth Annual Report of the Bureau of American Ethnology, 1895–*

96, pt. 2:519–742. Washington, D.C.: Smithsonian Institution.

1898b Preliminary Account of an Expedition to the Pueblo Ruins near Winslow, Arizona, in 1896. In *Annual Report of the Smithsonian Institution for 1896*, 517–39. Washington, D.C.: Smithsonian Institution.

1904 Two Summers' Work in Pueblo Ruins. In *Bureau of American Ethnology, 22nd Annual Report, 1900–1901*, 1–197. Washington, D.C.: Smithsonian Institution.

1909 *Antiquities of the Mesa Verde National Park: Spruce Tree House*. Bureau of American Ethnology Bulletin no. 41. Washington, D.C.: Smithsonian Institution.

1911 *Antiquities of the Mesa Verde National Park, Cliff Palace*. Bureau of American Ethnology Bulletin no. 51. Washington, D.C.: Smithsonian Institution.

1912a Antiquities of the Upper Verde River and Walnut Creek Valleys, Arizona. In *Bureau of American Ethnology 28th Annual Report*, 181–220. Washington, D.C.: Smithsonian Institution.

1912b Casa Grande, Arizona. In *Bureau of American Ethnology 28th Annual Report for 1906–1907*, 1–180. Washington, D.C.: Smithsonian Institution.

1918 *Prehistoric Ruins of Southwestern Colorado and Southeastern Utah*. Smithsonian Miscellaneous Collections 68(12):108–33. Washington, D.C.

1922 *Field Work on the Mesa Verde National Monument Park, Colorado*. Smithsonian Miscellaneous Collections 72(1):47–64. Washington, D.C.: Smithsonian Institution.

Fish, Paul R., and Susanne K. Fish
1989 Hohokam Warfare from a Regional Perspective. In *Cultures in Conflict: Current Anthropological Perspectives*, edited by D. C. Tkaczuk and B. C. Vivian, 112–29. Calgary, Ontario, Canada: Archaeological Association of the University of Calgary.

Fish, Paul R., and Godfrey Whiffen
1967 Arizona N:4:6 (ASU): The Excavation of an Early PIII Site near Perkinsville, Ari-

zona. Ms on file, Department of Anthropology, Arizona State University, Tempe.

Fish, Suzanne K., Paul R. Fish, and Christian Downum
1984 Hohokam Terraces and Agricultural Production in the Tucson Basin. In *Prehistoric Agricultural Strategies in the Southwest*, edited by S. K. Fish and P. R. Fish, 55–72. Anthropological Research Papers no. 33. Tempe: Arizona State University.

Fletcher, Thomas F., preparator
1994 *Archaeological Data Recovery Excavations at the Sanders Great House and Six Other Sites along US Highway 191, South of Sanders, Apache County, Arizona*. Zuni Archaeological Program Report no. 471, Research Series no. 9. Pueblo of Zuni.

Flinn, L., C. G. Turner, II, and A. Brew
1976 Additional Evidence for Cannibalism in the Southwest: The case of LA 4528. *American Antiquity* 41(3):308–18.

Fontana, B. L., J. C. Greenleaf, and D. D. Cassidy
1959 A Fortified Arizona Mountain. *The Kiva* 25(2):41–53.

Ford, Richard I., Albert H. Schroeder, and Stewart L. Peckham
1972 Three Perspectives on Puebloan Prehistory. In *New Perspectives on the Pueblos*, edited by Alfonso Ortiz, 19–40. Albuquerque: University of New Mexico Press.

Fowler, Andrew P., and John R. Stein
1992 The Anasazi Great House in Space, Time and Paradigm. In *Anasazi Regional Organization and the Chaco System*, edited by David E. Doyel, 101–22. Anthropological Papers no. 5. Albuquerque: Maxwell Museum of Anthropology.

Fowler, Andrew P., John R. Stein, and Roger Anyon
1987 An Archaeological Reconnaissance of West-Central New Mexico: The Anasazi Monuments Project. Ms on file, New Mexico Historic Preservation Division, Santa Fe.

Franklin, Hayward H.
1980 *Excavations at Second Canyon Ruin, San Pedro Valley, Arizona*. Contributions to Highway Salvage Archaeology in Arizona no. 60. Tucson: Arizona State Museum, University of Arizona.

Franklin, Hayward H., and W. B. Masse
  1976   The San Pedro Salado: A Case of Prehistoric Migration. *The Kiva* 42(1):47–56.
Fried, Morton, Marvin Harris, and Robert Murphy
  1968   *War: The Anthropology of Armed Conflict and Aggression.* Garden City, New York: Natural History Press.
Frisbie, Theodore R.
  1967   The Excavation and Interpretation of the Artificial Leg Basketmaker III–Pueblo I Sites near Corrales, New Mexico. Master's thesis, University of New Mexico, Albuquerque.
  1973   Field Report: The Newton Site, Catron County, New Mexico. *Awanyu* 1(4):31–36.
  1978   High Status Burials in the Greater Southwest: An Interpretive Synthesis. In *Across the Chichimec Sea. Papers in honor of J. Charles Kelley*, edited by C. L. Riley and C. B. Hedrick, 202–27. Carbondale: Southwestern Illinois University Press.
Fuller, Steven L.
  1988   *Cultural Resource Inventories for the Animas–La Plata: The Wheeler and Koshak Borrow Sources.* Four Corners Archaeological Project Report no. 12. Cortez, Colorado: Complete Archaeological Service Associates.
Fuller, Steven L., and James N. Morris
  1991   Excavations at Knobby Knee Stockade (Site 5MT2525), A Basketmaker III–Pueblo III Habitation. In *Archaeological Excavations on the Hovenweep Laterals*, by James N. Morris, 59–325. Four Corners Archaeological Project Report no. 16. Cortez, Colorado: Complete Archaeological Service Associates.
Gauthier, Rory P.
  1981   National Register of Historic Places Inventory, Nomination Form: Abiquiu Mesa Grid Gardens (LA 4934). Ms on file, New Mexico Historic Preservation Bureau.
Geib, Phil R.
  1990   A Basketmaker II Wooden Tool Cache from Lower Glen Canyon. *The Kiva* 55(3):265–77.
Geib, Phil R., and Peter W. Bungart
  1989   Implications of Early Bow Use in Glen Canyon. In *Utah Archaeology, 1989*, 32–47. Salt Lake City.
Gilpin, Dennis
  1988   The 1987 Navajo Nation Investigations at Bidahochi Pueblo, a Fourteenth Century Site in the Hopi Buttes, Navajo County, Arizona. Paper presented at the 1988 Pecos Conference, August 18–21, Cortez, Colorado.
  1989   Great Houses and Pueblos in Northeastern Arizona. Paper presented at the 1989 Pecos Conference, August 17–20, Bandelier National Monument, Los Alamos, New Mexico.
  1995   Anasazi Community Architecture on the Lower Puerco River. Paper presented at the 60th annual meeting of the Society for American Archaeology, Minneapolis, Minnesota.
Gilman, Patricia A.
  1987   Architecture as Artifact: Pit Structures and Pueblos in the American Southwest. *American Antiquity* 52(3):538–64.
Gladwin. Harold S.
  1943   *A Review and Analysis of the Flagstaff Culture.* Medallion Papers no. 31. Globe, Arizona: Gila Pueblo.
  1945   *The Chaco Branch, Excavations at White Mound in the Red Mesa Valley.* Medallion Papers no. 33. Globe, Arizona: Gila Pueblo.
Gladwin, Harold S., Emil W. Haury, Edwin B. Sayles, and Nora Gladwin
  1937   *Excavations at Snaketown I: Material Culture.* Medallion Papers no. 25. Globe, Arizona: Gila Pueblo.
Glennie, Gilbert D.
  1983   Replication of an A.D. 800 Anasazi Pithouse in Southwestern Colorado. Master's thesis, Washington State University, Pullman.
Graves, Michael W., William A. Longacre, and Sally J. Holbrook
  1982   Aggregation and Abandonment at Grasshopper Pueblo, Arizona. *The Journal of Field Archaeology* 9:193–206.
Greenleaf, J. Cameron
  1975   The Fortified Hill Site near Gila Bend, Arizona. *The Kiva* 40: 213–82.
Grove, Jean
  1990   *The Little Ice Age.* London: Routledge.

Guernsey, Samuel James, and Alfred Vincent Kidder
1921   *Basket-Maker Caves of Northeastern Arizona: Report on the Explorations, 1916–1917.* Papers of the Peabody Museum of American Archaeology and Ethnology, vol. 8, No. 2. Cambridge.

Gumerman, George J., ed.
1994   *Themes in Southwest Prehistory.* Santa Fe, New Mexico: School of American Research Press.

Gunnerson, James H.
1969   *The Fremont Culture: A Study in Culture Dynamics on the Northern Anasazi Frontier.* Papers of the Peabody Museum of Archaeology and Ethnology, vol. 59, no. 2. Cambridge.

Haas, Jonathan
1990   Warfare and Tribalization in the Prehistoric Southwest. In *The Anthropology of War,* edited by Jonathan Haas, 171–89. New York: Cambridge University Press.
1990   *The Anthropology of War.* New York: Cambridge University Press.

Haas, Jonathan, and Winifred Creamer
1993   *Stress and Warfare among the Kayenta Anasazi of the 13th Century* A.D. Fieldiana, Anthropology New Series, no. 21. Chicago: Field Museum of Natural History.
1995   A History of Pueblo Warfare. Paper presented at the 60th annual meeting of the Society for American Archeology, Minneapolis, Minnesota.
1996   The Role of Warfare in the Pueblo III Period. In *Pueblo Cultures in Transition,* edited by Michael Adler. Tucson: University of Arizona Press.
1997   Warfare among the Pueblos: Myth, History, and Ethnology. *Ethnohistory* 44(2):235–61.

Haase, William R.
1985   Domestic Water Conservation among the Northern San Juan Anasazi. *Southwestern Lore* 51(2):15–27.

Hall, E. T., Jr.
1944   *Early Stockaded Settlement in the Governador, New Mexico.* Columbia Studies in Archeology and Ethnology, vol.

2, no. 1. New York: Columbia University.

Hall, Edwin S.
1984   Interior North Alaska Eskimo. In *Handbook of North American Indians,* vol. 5, *Arctic,* edited by David Damas, 338–46. Washington, D.C.: Smithsonian Institution.

Hallasi, Judith A.
1979   Archaeological excavation at the Escalante Site, Dolores, Colorado, 1975 and 1976. In *The Archaeology and Stabilization of the Dominguez and Escalante Ruins,* by A. D. Reed, J. A. Hallasi, A. S. White and D. A. Breternitz. Cultural Resources Series no. 7. Denver: Colorado State Office, Bureau of Land Management.

Hammack, Laurens C., Stanley D. Bussey, and Ronald Ice
1966   LA 5793—Ormand Site. *In* The Cliff Highway Salvage Project, assembled by Alfred E. Dittert, Jr. Ms on file, Laboratory of Anthropology, Museum of New Mexico, Santa Fe, New Mexico.

Hammond, George P., and Agapito Rey, eds.
1928   *Obregon's History of Sixteenth Century Explorations in Western America. Entitled: Chronicle, Commentary, or Relation of the Ancient and Modern Discoveries in New Spain, New Mexico and Mexico, 1584.* Los Angeles: Wetzel.
1940   *Narratives of the Coronado Expedition 1540–1542.* Albuquerque: University of New Mexico Press.
1953   *Don Juan de Oñate: Colonizer of New Mexico, 1959–1628.* Albuquerque: University of New Mexico Press.
1966   *The Rediscovery of New Mexico 1580–1594. The Explorations of Chamuscado, Espejo, Castaño de Sosa, Morlete, and Leyva de Bonilla and Humana.* Albuquerque: University of New Mexico Press.

Hargrave, Lyndon L.
1931   *Excavations at Kin Tiel and Kokopnyama.* Smithsonian Miscellaneous Collections, vol. 82:80–120. Washington D.C.: Smithsonian Institution.
1933   *Pueblo II Houses in the San Francisco Mountains.* Museum of Northern Arizona Bulletin, no. 4. Flagstaff.

Harrill, Bruce
 1973   The Dobell Site: Archaeological Salvage near Petrified Forest. *The Kiva* 39:35–67.
Harriman, Raymond G.
 1990   Archaeological Excavations on Reach III of the Dove Creek Canal. Ms on file, Complete Archaeological Service Associates, Cortez, Colorado.
Haury, Emil W.
 1934   *The Canyon Creek Ruin and the Cliff Dwellings of the Sierra Ancha*. Medallion Papers no. 11. Globe, Arizona: Gila Pueblo.
 1936   *The Mogollon Culture of Southwestern New Mexico*. Medallion Papers no. 20. Globe, Arizona: Gila Pueblo.
 1958   Evidence at Point of Pines for a Prehistoric Migration From Northern Arizona. In *Migrations in New World Culture History*, edited by R. H. Thompson, 1–8. University of Arizona Bulletin, vol. 29, no. 2. Tucson: University of Arizona Press.
 1976   *The Hohokam, Desert Farmers and Craftsmen: Excavations at Snaketown, 1964–1965*. Tucson: University of Arizona Press.
 1985   *Mogollon Culture in the Forestdale Valley*. Tucson: University of Arizona Press.
 1989   *Point of Pines, Arizona: A History of the University of Arizona Archaeological Field School*. Anthropological Papers of the University of Arizona no. 50. Tucson: University of Arizona Press.
Haury, Emil, and Lyndon L. Hargrave
 1931   *Recently Dated Pueblo Ruins in Arizona*. Smithsonian Miscellaneous Collections, vol. 82, no. 11. Washington, D.C.: Smithsonian Institution.
Haury, Emil W., and E. B. Sayles
 1947   *An Early Pithouse Village of the Mogollon Culture*. Social Science Bulletin no. 16. Tucson: University of Arizona.
Hayden, Irwin
 1930   *Mesa House*. Southwest Museum Papers no. 4:26–92. Los Angeles.
Hayden, Julian D.
 1957   *Excavations, 1940, at University Indian Ruin, Tucson, Arizona*. Southwestern Monuments Association Technical Series

no. 5. Globe, Arizona: Gila Pueblo.
Hayes, A. C.
 1981   *Excavation of Mound 7*. National Park Service Publications in Archaeology no. 16. Washington, D.C.
Hayes, A. C., and J. Lancaster
 1975   *Badger House Community*. Washington, D.C.: National Park Service.
Heider, Karl
 1979   *Grand Valley Dani: Peaceful Warriors*. New York: Holt, Rinehart and Winston.
Heizer, Robert F.
 1942   Ancient Grooved Clubs and Modern Rabbit-sticks. *American Antiquity* 8(1):41–56.
 1974   Studying the Windmiller Culture. In *Archaeological Researches in Retrospect*, edited by Gordon R. Willey, 179–206. Cambridge: Winthrop.
Henderson, T. Kathleen
 1979   Archeological Survey at Chavez Pass Ruin, Coconino National Forest, Arizona: The 1978 Field Season. Ms on file, Coconino National Forest, Flagstaff, Arizona.
Herrington, Lavern C.
 1979   Settlement Patterns and Water Control Systems of the Mimbres Classic Phase, Grant County, New Mexico. Ph.D. diss., Department of Anthropology, University of Texas at Austin.
Herrmann, N. P., M. D. Ogilvie, C. E. Hilton, and K. L. Brown
 1993   *Human Remains and Burial Goods*, vol. 18: *Across the Colorado Plateau*. Anthropology Studies for the Transwestern Pipeline Expansion Project. Albuquerque: Office of Contact Archeology and Maxwell Museum of Anthropology, University of New Mexico.
Hibben, Frank C.
 1937   *Excavation of the Riana Ruin and Chama Valley Survey*. The University of New Mexico Bulletin, Anthropological Series, vol. 2, no. 1. Albuquerque.
 1975   *Kiva Art of the Anasazi at Pottery Mound*. Las Vegas, Nevada: K. C. Publications.
Hickerson, Harold
 1967   *Land Tenure of the Rainy Lake Chippewa at the Beginning of the 19th Century*.

Smithsonian Contributions to Anthropology, vol. 2, no. 4. Washington, D.C.: Smithsonian Institution.

Hill, James N.

1970   *Broken K. Pueblo: Prehistoric Social Organization in the American Southwest.* Anthropological Paper no. 18. Tucson: University of Arizona Press.

Hinkes, M. J.

1983   Skeletal Evidence of Stress in Subadults: Trying to Come of Age at Grasshopper Pueblo. Ph.D. diss., Department of Anthropology, University of Arizona, Tucson.

Hinsley, Curtis M., and David R. Wilcox, eds.

1996   *The Southwest in the American Imagination: The Writings of Sylvester Baxter, 1881–1889.* Tucson: University of Arizona Press.

Hohmann, John W.

1985a   Archaeological Evidence for Raiding and Warfare in the Salado Heartland. Paper presented at the 29th annual meeting of the Arizona-Nevada Academy of Science, Las Vegas, Nevada.

1985b   *Hohokam and Salado Hamlets in the Tonto Basin, Site Descriptions.* Arizona State University Office of Contract Archaeology Report no. 64. Tempe.

Hohmann, John W., and Christopher D. Adams

1992   Salado Site Configuration and Growth: The Besh-Ba-Gowah Example. In *Proceedings of the Second Salado Conference, Globe, AZ. 1992,* edited by Richard C. Lange and Stephen Germick, 109–24. Phoenix: Arizona Archaeological Society.

Hohmann, John W., and Linda B. Kelley

1988   *Erich F. Schmidt's Investigations of Salado Sites in Central Arizona: The Mrs. W. B. Thompson Archaeological Expedition of the American Museum of Natural History.* Bulletin Series no. 56. Flagstaff: Museum of Northern Arizona Press.

Holden, Jane

1955   A Preliminary Report on the Bloom Mound. *Texas Archaeological Society Bulletin* 26:165–81.

1955   A Preliminary Report on Arrowhead Ruin. *El Palacio* 62:102–19.

Holmer, Richard N.

1986   Common Projectile Points of the Intermountain West. In *Anthropology of the Desert West: Essays in Honor of Jesse D. Jennings,* edited by Carol J. Condie and Don D. Fowler, 89–115. Salt Lake City: University of Utah Press.

Holmer, Richard N., and Dennis G. Weder

1980   Common Post-Archaic Projectile Points of the Fremont Area. In *Fremont Perspectives,* edited by David B. Madsen, 55–68. Antiquities Section Selected Papers no. 16. Salt Lake City: Utah State Historical Society.

Hough, Walter

1903   Archaeological Field Work in Northeastern Arizona, the Museum-Gates Expedition of 1901. In *Annual Report of the U.S. National Museum for 1901,* 279–358. Washington, D.C.

1907   *Antiquities of the Upper Gila and Salt River Valleys in Arizona and New Mexico.* Bureau of American Ethnology Bulletin no. 35. Washington, D.C.

1930?   Exploration of Ruins in the White Mountain Apache Indian Reservation, Arizona. In *Proceedings of the U.S. National Museum,* vol. 78, art. 13:7–8. Washington, D.C.

Howard, Julie, and Joel C. Janetski

1992   Human Scalps from Eastern Utah. *Utah Archaeology* 5(1):125–32.

Howell, Todd L.

1996   Identifying Leaders at Hawikku. *The Kiva* 62(1):61–82.

Huckell, Bruce B.

1995   *Of Marshes and Maize: Preceramic Agricultural Settlements in the Cienega Valley, Southeastern Arizona.* Anthropology Papers of the University of Arizona no. 59. Tucson: The University of Arizona Press.

Hughes, Charles C.

1984   Asiatic Eskimo: Introduction. In *Handbook of North American Indians,* vol. 5, *Arctic,* edited by David Damas, 243–46. Washington, D.C.: Smithsonian Institution.

Hurst, Winston B., and Joe Pachak
1989 *Spirit Windows: Native American Rock Art of Southwestern Utah.* Blanding, Utah: Spirit Window Project.

Hurst, Winston B., and Christy G. Turner II
1993 Rediscovering the "Great Discovery": Wetherill's First Cave 7 and its Record of Basketmaker Violence. In *Anasazi Basketmaker: Papers from the 1990 Wetherill–Grand Gulch Symposium*, edited by Victoria M. Atkins, 143–91. Cultural Resource Series no. 24. Salt Lake City: Bureau of Land Management.

Irwin-Williams, Cynthia
1973 *The Oshara Tradition: Origins of the Anasazi Culture.* Eastern New Mexico University Contributions in Anthropology no. 5. Portales.

Irwin-Williams, Cynthia, and Philip H. Sheley
1983 *Investigations at the Salmon Site: The structure of Chacoan Society in the Northern Southwest.* 4 vols. Portales: Eastern New Mexico University.

Jeançon, Jean A.
1911 Explorations in the Chama Basin, New Mexico. In *Records of the Past* 10(2):92–108.
1912 Ruins at Pesedeuingue. In *Records of the Past* 11(1):28–37.
1923 *Excavations in the Chama Valley, New Mexico.* Bureau of American Ethnology Bulletin no. 81. Washington, D.C.

Jelinek, Arthur J.
1961 Mimbres Warfare? *The Kiva* 27(2):28–30.

Jeter, Marvin D., ed.
1977 *Archaeology in Copper Basin, Yavapai County, Arizona: Model Building for the Prehistory of the Prescott region.* Anthropological Research Paper no. 11. Tempe: Arizona State University.

Jett, Stephen
1964 Pueblo Indian Migrations. *American Antiquity* 29:281–300.

Jewett, Roberta
1989 Distance, Interaction, and Complexity: A Pan-Regional Comparison of the Spatial Organization of Fourteenth-Century Settlement Clusters in the American Southwest. In *Sociopolitical Structure of Prehistoric Southwestern Socieies*, edited by Steadman Upham, Kent Lightfoot, and Roberta Jewett. Boulder, Colorado: Westview Press.

Johnson, A. E., and Raymond H. Thompson
1963 The Ringo Site: Southern Arizona. *American Antiquity* 28:465–81.

Judd, Neil M.
1931 The Excavations and Repair of Betatakin. *United States National Museum Proceedings*, vol. 77, art. 5. Washington, D.C.
1952 A Pueblo III War Club from Southwestern Utah. *The Masterkey* 26(2):60–62.
1954 *The Material Culture of Pueblo Bonito.* Smithsonian Miscellaneous Collections vol. 124. Washington, D.C.: Smithsonian Institution.
1959 *Pueblo del Arroyo, Chaco Canyon, New Mexico.* Smithsonian Miscellaneous Collections vol. 38, no. 1. Washington, D.C.: Smithsonian Institution.

Kane, Allen E.
1989 Did the Sheep Look Up? Sociopolitical Complexity in Ninth Century Dolores Society. In *The Sociopolitical Structure of Prehistoric Southwestern Societies*, edited by S. Upham, K. G. Lightfoot, and R. A. Jewett, 307–62. Boulder, Colorado: Westview Press.

Kane, A. E., and C. K. Robinson
1988 *Dolores Archaeological Program: Anasazi Communities at Dolores, McPhee Village.* Denver: U.S. Department of the Interior, Bureau of Reclamation.

Keegan, John
1993 *A History of Warfare.* New York: Alfred A. Knopf.

Keeley, Lawrence H.
1996 *War Before Civilization.* New York and Oxford, England: Oxford University Press.

Kelley, Ellen A.
1978 The Temple of the Skulls at Alta Vista, Chalchihuites. In *Across the Chichimec Sea: Papers in Honor of J. Charles Kelley*, edited by C. L. Riley and B. C. Hedrick, 102–26. Carbondale: Southern Illinois University Press.

Kelley, J. Charles
1952 Factors Involved in the Abandonment of

Certain Perhiperal Southwestern Settlements. *American Anthropologist* 54:356–87.

Kelley, Jane Holden

1984 *The Archaeology of the Sierra Blanca Region of Southeastern New Mexico.* Anthropological Papers no. 74. Ann Arbor: Museum of Anthropology, University of Michigan.

Kenzle, Susan C.

1993 Enclosing Walls: A Study of Architectural Function in the American Southwest. Master's thesis. Department of Archaeology, University of Calgary, Alberta, Canada.

Kidder, Alfred Vincent

1932 *The Artifacts of Pecos.* Papers of the Southwestern Expedition no. 6. New Haven, Connecticut: Published for the Phillips Academy by Yale University Press.

1958 *Pecos, New Mexico, Archaeological Notes.* Papers of the Robert S. Peabody Foundation for Archaeology no. 5. Andover, Massachusetts.

[1924] 1962 *An Introduction to the Study of Southwestern Archaeology with a Preliminary Account of the Excavations at Pecos.* Reprint, New Haven, Connecticut: Yale University Press.

Kidder, Alfred Vincent, and Samuel James Guernsey

1919 *Archaeological Explorations in North-Eastern Arizona.* Bureau of American Ethnology Bulletin no. 65. Washington, D.C.: U.S. Government Printing Office.

Kintigh, Keith W.

1985 *Settlement, Subsistence, and Society in Late Zuni Prehistory.* University of Arizona Anthropological Papers no. 44. Tucson: University of Arizona Press.

199 The Cibola Region in the Post-Chacoan Era. In *Pueblo Cultures in Transition*, edited by Michael A. Adler. Tucson: University of Arizona Press.

Kirch, P.

1984 *The Evolution of Polynesian Chiefdoms.* Cambridge: Cambridge University Press.

Kluckhohn, Clyde

1939 The Excavations of Bc 51 Rooms and Kivas. In *Preliminary Report on the 1937*

Excavations, Bc 50–51., *Chaco Canyon, New Mexico*, edited by Clyde Kluckhohn and Paul Reiter, 30–48. University of New Mexico, Bulletin no. 345, Anthropological Series, vol. 3, no. 2. Albuquerque.

Knauft, Bruce M.

1992 Warfare, Western intrusion and ecology in Melanesia. *Man*, n.s., 27:399–403.

Kohler, Timothy A.

1993 News from the Northern American Southwest: Prehistory on the Edge of Chaos. *Journal of Archaeological Research* 1(4):267–321.

Kroeber, Clifton B., and Bernard L. Fontana

1986 *Massacre on the Gila: An Account of the Last Major Battle between American Indians, with Reflections on the Origin of War.* Tucson: University of Arizona Press.

Kuckelman, K., and J. N. Morris

1988 *Archaeological Investigations on South Canal*, vol.1. Four Corners Archaeological Project Report no. 11. Cortez, Colorado: Complete Archaeological Service Associates.

Kuijt, Ian

1996 Negotiating Equality through Ritual: A Consideration of Late Natufian and Prepottery Neolithic A Period Mortuary Practices. *Journal of Anthropological Archaeology* 15(4):313–36.

Lamb, Hubert H.

1995 *Climate, History and the Modern World.* 2d ed. London: Routledge.

Lambert, Patricia M.

1997a Cannibalism in Cowboy Wash, pt. 2: The Osteological Evidence. Paper presented at the 62d annual meeting of the Society for American Archaeology, April 2–6, Nashville, Tennessee.

1997b Patterns of Violence in Prehistoric Hunter-Gatherer Societies of Coastal Southern California. In *Prehistoric Evidence for Interhuman Violence*, edited by D. Martin and D. Frayer. Langhorne, Pennsylvania: Gordon and Breach.

Lancaster, James A., Joan M. Pinkley, Philip F. Van Cleave, and Don Watson

1954 *Archaeological Excavations in Mesa Verde National Park, Colorado, 1950.* Archeological Research Series no. 2. Washington, D.C.: National Park Service. U.S. Department of the Interior.

Lang, Richard W.

1980   *Archaeological Investigations at a Pueblo Agriculture Site, and Archaic and Puebloan Encampments on the Rio Ojo Caliente, Rio Arriba County, New Mexico.* School of American Research Contract Archaeology Program, Report no. 007. Santa Fe, New Mexico.

1981   *A Prehistoric Pueblo Garden Plot on the Rio Ojo Caliente, Rio Arriba County, New Mexico: Ojo Caliente Site 7, Features 1–2.* School of American Research Contract Archaeology Program, Report no. 065. Santa Fe, New Mexico.

Lange, Charles H.

1978   The Spanish-Mexican Presence in the Cochiti-Bandelier Area, New Mexico. In *Across the Chichimec Sea: Papers in Honor of J. Charles Kelley,* edited by Carroll L. Riley and Basil C. Hedrick. Carbondale: Southern Illinois University Press.

Lange, Frederick, Nancy Mahaney, Joe Ben Wheat, Mark L. Chenault, and John Cater

1988   *Yellow Jacket: A Four Corners Anasazi Ceremonial Center.* Rev. ed. Boulder, Colorado: University of Colorado, Johnson Publishing Company.

Lange, Richard C.

1992   Pots, People, Politics, and Precipitation: Just Who or What are the Salado Anyway? In *Proceedings of the Second Salado Conference, Globe, Arizona,* edited by Richard C. Lange and Stephen Germick, 325–33. Arizona Archaeological Society Occasional Paper. Phoenix, Arizona.

Lantis, Margaret

1984a Aleut. In *Handbook of North American Indians,* vol. 5, *Arctic,* edited by David Damas, 161–84. Washington, D.C.: Smithsonian Institution.

1984b Nunivak Eskimo. In *Handbook of North American Indians,* vol. 5, *Arctic,* edited by David Damas, 209–23. Washington, D.C.: Smithsonian Institution.

Larralde, Signa

1992   On Beating Swords into Plowshares: A functional Analysis of the Anasazi Tchamahia. Paper presented at the Third Southwestern Symposium, "Interpreting Southwestern Diversity: Underlying Principles and Overarching Patterns," January 1992, Tucson, Arizona.

Larralde, Signa, and Sarah Schlanger

1994   Large Hafted Tools, Technical Report, Draft no. 2. La Plata Highway Project, Museum of New Mexico. Ms in possession of the author.

Larson, Lewis H., Jr.

1972   Functional Considerations of Warfare in the Southeast during the Mississippi Period. *American Antiquity* 37(3):383–92.

Laumbach, Karl

1992   *Reconnaissance Survey of the National Park Service Ojo Caliente Study Area, Socorro County, New Mexico.* Human Systems Research Project no. 9132. Tularosa, New Mexico.

LeBlanc, Catherine J.

1981   Late Prehistoric Huanca Settlement Patterns in the Yanamarca Valley, Peru. Ph.D. diss., Department of Anthropology, University of California, Los Angeles.

LeBlanc, Steven A.

1978   Settlement Patterns in the El Morro Valley, New Mexico. In *Investigations of the Southwestern Anthropological Research Group,* edited by Robert C. Euler and George J. Gumerman, 45–52. Flagstaff, Arizona: Museum of Northern Arizona.

1980   The dating of Casas Grandes. *American Antiquity* 45(4):799–806.

1986   Aspects of Southwestern Prehistory: A.D. 900–1400. In *Ripples in the Chichimec Sea,* edited by Randall H. McGuire and Frances J. Mathien, 105–34. Carbondale: Southern Illinois University Press.

1989a Cibola: Shifting Cultural Boundaries. In *Dynamics of Southwestern Prehistory,* edited by Linda S. Cordell and George J. Gumerman, 337–69. Washington, D.C.: Smithsonian Institution Press.

1989b Cultural Dynamics in the Southern

Mogollon Area. In *Dynamics of Southwestern Prehistory*, edited by Linda S. Cordell and George J. Gumerman, 179–207. Washington, D.C.: Smithsonian Institution Press.

1996   The Impact of Warfare on Southwestern Regional Systems after A.D. 1250. Paper presented at the Southwest Symposium, February 1996, Tempe, Arizona.

1997   Modeling Warfare in Southwestern Prehistory. *North American Archaeologist* 18(3):235–76.

1998   Settlement Consequences of Warfare during the Late Pueblo III and Pueblo IV Period. In *Migration and Reorganization: The Pueblo IV Period in the American Southwest*, edited by Katherine A. Spielmann. Arizona State University Anthopology Papers. Tempe, Arizona. In Press.

n.d.   The Impact of Warfare on Southwestern Regional Systems after A.D. 1250. in *The Archaeology of Regional Interaction in the American Southwest*, edited by Michelle Hegmon. Boulder: University of Colorado Press. In press.

Lekson, Stephen H.

1984   Dating Casas Grandes. *The Kiva* 50(1):55–60.

1985   *Archaeological Reconnaissance of the Rio Grande Valley, Sierra County, New Mexico*. Santa Fe: New Mexico State Historic Preservation Division.

1986   *Great Pueblo Architecture of Chaco Canyon*. Albuquerque: University of New Mexico Press.

1992   Scale and Process in the Southwest. Paper presented at the Third Southwestern Symposium, January, Tucson, Arizona.

1996   Chaco and Casas Grandes. Poster session presented at the 61st annual meeting of the Society for American Archaeology, New Orleans, Louisiana.

Lekson, Stephen H., and Catherine M. Cameron

1995   The Abandonment of Chaco Canyon, the Mesa Verde Migrations, and the Reorganization of the Pueblo World. *Journal of Anthropological Archaeology* 14(2):143–69.

Leonard, Banks L.

1997   Cannibalism in Cowboy Wash, pt. 1: The Archaeology of 5MT10010. Paper presented at the 62d annual meeting of the Society for American Archaeology, April 2–6, Nashville, Tennessee.

Leonard, Robert D., Janet E. Belser, David A. Jessup, and James Carucci

1984   Arizona D:7:3133. In *Excavations on Black Mesa, 1982: A Descriptive Report*, edited By Deborah L. Nichols and Francis E. Smiley, 371–94. Center for Archaeological Investigations, Research Paper no. 39. Carbondale: Southern Illinois University.

LeRoy Ladurie, Emmanuel

1988   *Times of Feast, Times of Famine: A History of Climate Since the Year 1000*. Translation of 1971 edition by Barbara Brey. New York: Noonday Press.

Lightfoot, Dale R., and Frank W. Eddy

1995   The Construction and Configuration of Anasazi Pebble-Mulch Gardens in the Northern Rio Grande. *American Antiquity* 60(3):459–70.

Lightfoot, Kent G.

1984a   *The Duncan Project: A Study of the Occupation Duration and Settlement Pattern of an Early Mogollon Pithouse Village*. Anthropological Field Studies no. 6. Tempe: Office of Cultural Resource Management, Department of Anthropology. Arizona State University.

1984b   *Prehistoric Political Dynamics: A Case Study from the American Southwest*. Dekalb: Northern Illinois University Press.

Lightfoot, Ricky R., and Mary C. Etzkorn

1993   *The Duckfoot Site*, vol. 1, *Descriptive Archaeology*. Occasional Paper no. 3. Cortez, Colorado: Crow Canyon Archaeological Center.

Lightfoot, Ricky R., and Kristin A. Kuckelman

1995   Ancestral Pueblo Violence in the Northern Southwest. Paper presented at the 60th annual meeting of the Society for American Archaeology, Minneapolis, Minnesota.

Lincoln-Babb, Lorrie

1994   Revered Ancestors or Slain Enemies at La Quemada: A Review of the Evidence.

Copy at http://www.eas.asu.edu/~voegele/
bioarchy/lorrie.html.

Lindsay, Alexander, Jr.

1969   The Tsegi Phase of the Kayenta Cultural
Tradition in Northeastern Arizona. Ph.D.
diss., Department of Anthropology, University of Arizona, Tucson.

1987   Anasazi Population Movements to Southeastern Arizona. *American Archaeology*
6(3):190–98.

Linton, Ralph

1944   Nomad Raids and Fortified Pueblos.
American Antiquity 10(1):28–32.

Lipe, William D.

1978   The Southwest. In *Ancient Native Ameri-
cans*, edited by Jesse D. Jennings, 327–
401. San Francisco: W. H. Freeman and
Company.

Lipe, William D., and R. G. Matson

1971   Human Settlement and Resources in the
Cedar Mesa Area, SE Utah. In *The Distribution of Prehistoric Population Aggregates*. Prescott College Anthropological
Reports no. 1. Prescott, Arizona.

Lipe, William D., James N. Morris, and Timothy A.
Kohler

1988   *Dolores Archaeological Program: Anasazi
Communities at Dolores, Grass Mesa
Village*. Denver: U.S. Department of the
Interior, Bureau of Reclamation.

Lister, Robert H.

1964   *Contributions to Mesa Verde Archaeol-
ogy: I, Site 449, Mesa Verde National
Park, Colorado*. University of Colorado
Studies, Series in Anthropology no. 9.
Boulder: University of Colorado Press.

1965   *Contributions to Mesa Verde Archaeol-
ogy: II, Site 875, Mesa Verde National
Park, Colorado*. University of Colorado
Studies, Series in Anthropology no. 11.
Boulder: University of Colorado Press.

1966   *Contributions to Mesa Verde Archaeology: III, Site 866, and the Cultural Sequence at Four Villages in the Far View
Group, Mesa Verde National Park, Colorado*. University of Colorado Studies, Series in Anthropology no. 12. Boulder:
University of Colorado Press.

Lister, Robert H., J. Richard Ambler, Florence C.
Lister, Lyndon L. Hargrave, and Christy G. Turner, II

1959–   *The Coombs Site, pts. 1, 2, and 3*. Univer-
1961   sity of Utah Anthropology Papers 41, Glen
Canyon Series 8. Salt Lake City: University of Utah Press.

Lister, Florence C., and Robert H. Lister

1986   *Earl Morris and Southwestern Archaeology*. Albuquerque: University of New
Mexico Press.

1987   *Aztec Ruins on the Animas: Excavated,
Preserved and Interpreted*. Albuquerque:
University of New Mexico Press.

Lockett, H. Claiborne, and Lyndon L. Hargrave

1953   *Woodchuck Cave, a Basketmaker II Site in
Tsegi Canyon, Arizona*. Museum of Northern Arizona Bulletin no. 26, Flagstaff.

Loendorf, Lawrence L., and Stuart W. Conner

1993   The Pectol Shields and the Shield-Bearing
Warrior Rock Art Motif. *Journal of California and Great Basin Anthropology*
15(2):216–24.

Lomatuway'ma, Michael, Lorena Lomatuway'ma,
and Sidney Namingha, Jr.

1993   *Hopi Ruin Legends*. Collected, translated
and edited by Ekkehart Malotki. Lincoln:
University of Nebraska Press.

Longacre, William

1962   Archaeological Reconnaissance in Eastern
Arizona. *In* Chapters in the Prehistory of
Arizona, I. *Fieldiana: Anthropology* 53.

1964   A Synthesis of Upper Little Colorado Prehistory, Eastern Arizona. *In* Chapters in
the Prehistory of Arizona, II, by Paul S.
Martin, John B. Rinaldo, et al. *Fieldiana:
Anthropology* 55:201–15.

1970   *Archaeology as Anthropology: A Case
Study*. Anthropological Papers of the University of Arizona no. 17. Tucson.

Longacre, William, Sally J. Holbrook, and Michael
W. Graves

1982   *Multidisciplinary Research at Grasshopper Pueblo, Arizona*. Anthropology Papers of the University of Arizona no. 40.
Tucson: University Arizona Press.

Lounsbury, Floyd G.

1978   Iroquoian Languages. In *Handbook of
North American Indians*, vol. 15, *North-*

east, edited by B. G. Trigger, 334–43. Washington, D.C.: Smithsonian Institution Press.

Lowell, Julie C.

1991   *Prehistoric Households at Turkey Creek Pueblo, Arizona.* Anthropology Papers of the University of Arizona no. 54. Tucson: University of Arizona Press.

Luebben, Ralph A.

1953   Leaf Water Site. In *Salvage Archaeology in the Chama Valley, New Mexico,* complied by Fred Wendorf, 9–33. Monograph of the School of American Research no. 17. Santa Fe.

1983   The Grinnell Site: A Small Ceremonial Center near Yucca House, Colorado. *Journal of Intermountain Archeology* 2(2):1–26.

Luebben, Ralph A., and Paul R. Nickens

1982   A Mass Interment in an Early Pueblo III Kiva in Southwestern Colorado. *Journal of Intermountain Archeology* 1:66–79.

Lutonsky, Anthony F.

1992   Anasazi Wooden "Paddles" Sometimes Called "Digging Sticks." Paper presented at the Third Southwestern Symposium, "Interpreting Southwestern Diversity: Underlying Principles and Overarching Patterns," January 1992, Tucson, Arizona.

Lyneis, Margaret M.

1992   *The Main Ridge Community at Lost City: Virgin Anasazi Architecture, Ceramics, and Burials.* University of Utah Anthropological Papers no. 117. Salt Lake City: University of Utah Press.

McCluney, Eugene B.

1962   *Clanton Draw and Box Canyon: An Interim Report on Two Prehistoric Sites in Hidalgo County, New Mexico.* School of American Research Monograph no. 26. Santa Fe, New Mexico.

1965   The Excavation of the Joyce Well site, Hidalgo County, New Mexico. Ms on file, School of American Research, Santa Fe, New Mexico.

McCoy, Ronald

1984   Circles of Power. *Plateau* 55(4).

McDonald, James A.

1976   *An Archeological Assessment of Canyon De Chelly National Monument.* Western Archeological Center Publications in Anthropology no. 5. Tucson, Arizona.

McEwen, Edward, Robert L. Miller, and Christopher A. Bergman

1991   Early Bow Design and Construction. *Scientific American* 264(6):76–82.

McGimsey, Charles R., III

1980   *Mariana Mesa: Seven Prehistoric Sites in West Central New Mexico.* Papers of the Peabody Museum of Archaeology and Ethnology vol. 72. Cambridge.

McGregor, John C.

1943   Burial of an Early American Magician. *Proceedings of the American Philosophical Society* 86(2):270–98.

McGuire, Randall H., and Dean J. Saitta

1996   Although They Have Petty Captains, They Obey Them Badly: The Dialectics of Prehispanic Western Pueblo Social Organization. *American Antiquity* 61(2):197–216.

McGuire, Randall H., and Maria Elisa Villalpando C.

1993   *An Archaeological Survey of the Altar Valley, Sonora, Mexico.* Arizona State Museum Archaeological Series no. 184. Tucson: Arizona State Museum, University of Arizona.

McKenna, Peter J.

1984   *The Architecture and Material Culture of 29SJ1360.* Reports of the Chaco Center no. 7. Albuquerque: Division of Cultural Research, National Park Service.

McKenna, Peter J., and John R. Stein

1989   Wide Reed Ruin: Hubble Trading Post National Historical Site, Apache County, Arizona. Ms map in possession of the authors.

Mackey, James C., and Sally J. Holbrook

1978   Environmental Reconstruction and the Abandonment of the Largo-Gallina Area, New Mexico. *The Journal of Field Archaeology* 5:29–49.

McKusick, Charmion

1992   Evidences of Hereditary High Status at Gila Pueblo. In *Proceedings of the Second Salado Conference, Globe, Arizona, 1992,* edited by Richard C. Lange and Stephen Germick, 86–91. Phoenix: Arizona Archaeological Society.

McNamee, William D.

1992   Excavations at Cloud Blower Stockade (5DL121b), a Late Basketmaker III Habitation. In *Archaeological Excavations on Reach III of the Dove Creek Canal*, edited by William D. McNamee and Nancy S. Hammack, 3.1–3.33. Four Corners Archaeological Project Report no. 18. Cortez, Colorado: Complete Archaeological Services Associates.

McNamee, William D., and Nancy S. Hammack

1992   *Archaeological Excavations on Reach III of the Dove Creek Canal*. Four Corners Archaeological Project Report no. 18. Cortez, Colorado: Complete Archaeological Services Associates.

McNamee, William D., Raymond G. Harriman, and Richard W. Yarnell

1992   Excavations at Palote Azul Stockade (5DL112), a Late Basketmaker III Habitation. In *Archaeological Excavations on Reach III of the Dove Creek Canal*, edited by William D. McNamee and Nancy S. Hammack, 2.1–2.48. Four Corners Archaeological Project Report no. 18. Cortez, Colorado: Complete Archaeological Services Associates.

Madsen, David B.

1994   Mesa Verde and Sleeping Ute Mountain: The Geographical and Chronological Dimensions of the Numic Expansion. In *Across the West: Human Population Movement and the Expansion of the Numa*, edited by David B. Madsen and David Rhode, 24–31. Salt Lake City: University of Utah Press.

Malotki, Ekkehart

1993   The Destruction of Awat'ovi. In *Hopi Ruin Legends*, by Michael Lomotuway'ma, Lorena Lomatuway'ma, and Sidney Namingha, Jr., 275–97. Collected, translated and edited by Ekkehart Malotki. Lincoln: University of Nebraska Press.

Malville, N. J.

1989   Two Fragmented Human Bone Assemblages from Yellow Jacket, Southwestern Colorado. *The Kiva* 55(1):3–22.

Marshall, Michael P., John Stein, Richard W. Loose, and Judith E. Novotny

1979   *Anasazi Communities of the San Juan Basin*. Albuquerque and Santa Fe: Public Service Company of New Mexico and New Mexico Historic Preservation Division.

Marshall, Michael P., and Henry J. Walt

1984   *Rio Abajo: Prehistory and History of a Rio Grande Province*. Santa Fe: New Mexico Historical Preservation Program.

Martin, Deborah L., Nancy J. Akins, Alan H. Goodman, and Alan C. Swedlund

n.d.   *Harmony and Discord: Bioarchaeology of the La Plata Valley*. Santa Fe: Museum of New Mexico Press. In press.

Martin, Paul S.

1959   *Digging into History*. Chicago: Field Museum of Natural History.

1967   Hay Hollow Site. *Field Museum of Natural History Bulletin* 38(5):6–10.

Martin, Paul S., Carl Lloyd, and Alexander Spoehr

1938   *Archeological Work in the Ackmen-Lowry Area, Southwestern Colorado, 1937*. Field Museum of Natural History Publication no. 419, Anthropological Series 23(2):219–304. Chicago.

Martin, Paul S., William A. Longacre, and James N. Hill

1967   Chapters in the Prehistory of Eastern Arizona, III. *Fieldiana: Anthropology* 57.

Martin, Paul S., and Fred Plog

1973   *The Archaelogy of Arizona*. Garden City, New York: Doubleday/Natural History Press.

Martin Paul S., and John B. Rinaldo

1939   Modified Basket Maker Sites, Ackmen-Lowry Area, Southwestern Colorado, 1938. *Fieldiana: Anthropology* 23(3).

1947   *The SU Site: Excavations at a Mogollon Village, Western New Mexico, Third Season, 1946*. Anthropological Series, Field Museum of Natural History, vol. 32, no. 3. Chicago.

1950   Turkey Foot Ridge: A Mogollon Village, Pine Lawn Valley, Western New Mexico. *Fieldiana: Anthropology* 38(2).

Martin, Paul S., John B. Rinaldo, and Ernst Antevs

1949   Cochise and Mogollon Sites, Pine Lawn

Valley, Western New Mexico. *Fieldiana: Anthropology* 38(1).

Martin, Paul S., John B. Rinaldo, William A. Longacre, Constance Cronin, Leslie G. Freeman, Jr., James Schoenwetter

1962   Chapters in the Prehistory of Eastern Arizona, I. *Fieldiana: Anthropology* 53.

Martin, Paul S., John B. Rinaldo, William A. Longacre, Leslie G. Freeman, Jr., James A. Brown, Richard H. Hevly, and M. E. Cooley

1964   Chapters in the Prehistory of Eastern Arizona, II. *Fieldiana: Anthropology* 55.

Maschner, H. D. G.

1991   The Emergence of Cultural Complexity on the Northern Northwest Coast. *Antiquity* 65:924–34.

Matson, R. G.

1991   *The Origins of Southwestern Agriculture.* Tucson: University of Arizona Press.

1994   Anomalous Basketmaker II Sites on Cedar Mesa: Not so Anomalous after All. *The Kiva* 60(2):219–37.

Matson, R. G., William D. Lipe, and William R. Haase IV

1988   Adaptational Continuities and Occupation Discontinuities: The Cedar Mesa Anasazi. *The Journal of Field Archaeology* 15:245–64.

Meggitt, M.

1977   *Blood Is Their Argument.* Palo Alto, California: Mayfield.

Mellaart, James

1967   *Çatal Hüyük: A Neolithic Town in Anatolia.* London: Thames and Hudson.

Mensforth, Robert P.

1996   Observations on the Antiquity and Geographic Distribution of Trophy-Taking and Warfare Related Behaviors among Archaic Hunter-Gatherers of the Eastern United States. Paper presented at the 65th annual meeting of the American Association of Physical Anthropologists, April 1996, Durham, North Carolina.

Mera, H. P.

1935   *Ceramic Clues to the Prehistory of North Central New Mexico.* Laboratory of Anthropology Technical Series Bulletin no. 8. Santa Fe.

1940   *Population Changes in the Rio Grande Glaze Paint Area.* Laboratory of Anthropology Technical Series no. 9. Santa Fe.

Mills, Barbara J.

1995   Reconsidering Migration, Integration, and Aggregation in the Silver Creek Area of East-Central Arizona. Paper presented at the Fall meeting of the Arizona Archaeological Council, October 1995, Flagstaff.

Mills, Jack P., and Vera M. Mills

1969   *The Kuykendall Site.* El Paso Archeological Society, Special Report no. 6. El Paso, Texas.

1972   The Dinwiddie Site: A Prehistoric Salado Ruin on Duck Creek, Western New Mexico. *The Artifact* 10(2):i–iv, 1–50.

1975   The Meredith Ranch Site (VIV Ruin): A Prehistoric Salado Pueblo in the Tonto Basin, Central Arizona. Ms on file, Arizona State Museum Library, University of Arizona, Tucson.

1978   *The Curtis Site: A Prehistoric Village in the Safford Valley.* Privately printed.

Milner, G., E. Anderson, and V. G. Smith

1991   Warfare in Late Prehistoric West-Central Illinois. *American Antiquity* 56:581–603.

Mindeleff, Victor

1891   A Study of Pueblo Architecture in Tusayan and Cibola. In *Eighth Annual Report of the Bureau of American Ethnology for the Years 1886–1887,* 3–228. Washington, D.C.

Minnis, Paul E.

1985   *Social Adaptation to Food Stress: A Prehistoric Southwestern Example.* Chicago: The University of Chicago Press.

1989   The Casas Grandes Polity in the International Four Corners. In *The Sociopolitical Structure of Prehistoric Southwestern Societies,* edited by S. Upham, K. G. Lightfoot, and R. A. Jewett, 269–305. Boulder, Colorado: Westview Press.

1992   Earliest Plant Cultivation in the Desert Borderlands of North America. In *The Origins of Agriculture,* edited by C. Wesley Cowan and Patty Jo Watson. Washington, D.C.: Smithsonian Institution Press.

Montgomery, Barbara Klie

1993   Ceramic Analysis as a Tool for Discovering

Processes of Pueblo Abandonment. In *Abandonment of Settlements and Regions: Ethnoarchaeological and Archaeological Approaches*, edited by Catherine M. Cameron and Steve A. Tomka, 157–64. New York: Cambridge University Press.

Moratto, Michael J.
1984   *California Archaeology.* Orlando, Florida: Academic Press.

Morren, George E. B., Jr.
1984   Warfare on the Highland Fringe of New Guinea: The Case of the Mountain Ok. In *Warfare, Culture, and Environment*, edited by R. Brian Ferguson. Orlando, Florida: Academic Press.

Morris, Ann Axtell
1933   *Digging in the Southwest.* Chicago: Cadmus Books, E. M. Hale and Co.

Morris, Earl H.
1919   *The Aztec Ruin.* American Museum of Natural History Anthropological Papers, vol. 26, pt. 1. New York.
1924   *Burials in the Aztec Ruin and Aztec Ruin Annex.* American Museum of Natural History Anthropological Papers, vol. 26, pts. 3 and 4. New York.
1929   *Field Notes, Canyon del Muerto, 1929.* Tucson: Western Archeological Center, National Park Service.
1938   Mummy Cave. *Natural History* 42(2:127–38.
1939   *Archaeological Studies in the La Plata District, Southwestern Colorado and Northwestern New Mexico.* Carnegie Institution of Washington Publication no. 519. Washington, D.C.

Morris, Earl H., and Robert F. Burgh
1931   *The Temple of the Warriors.* Carnegie Institution of Washington Publication no. 406. Washington, D.C.
1941   *Anasazi Basketry, Basket Maker II through Pueblo III.* Carnegie Institution Publication no. 533. Washington, D.C.
1954   *Basket Maker II Sites near Durango, Colorado.* Carnegie Institution of Washington Publication no. 604. Washington, D.C.

Morris, Elizabeth Ann
1980   *Basketmaker Caves in the Prayer Rock District, Northeastern Arizona.* Anthropological Papers of the University of Arizona no. 35. Tucson: University of Arizona Press.

Morris, J. N.
1991   *Archaeological Investigations of the Hovenweep Laterals.* Four Corners Archaeological Project Report no. 16. Cortez, Colorado: Complete Archaeological Service Associates.

Morss, Noel
1931   *The Ancient Culture of the Fremont River in Utah.* Papers of the Peabody Museum of American Archaeology and Ethnology, vol. 12, no. 3. Cambridge.

Moss, Madonna L., and Jon M. Erlandson
1992   Forts, Refuge Rocks, and Defensive Sites: the Antiquity of Warfare along the North Pacific Coast of North America. *Arctic Anthropology* 29(2):73–90.

Mount, James E., Stanley J. Olsen, John W. Olsen, George Teague, and B. Dean Treadwell
1993   *Wide Reed Ruin: Hubbell Trading Post National Historic Site.* Southwest Cultural Resources Center Professional Papers no. 51. National Park Service, Southwestern Region. Washington, D.C.: Government Printing Service.

Nelson, Ben A., J. Andrew Darling, and David A. Kice
1992   Mortuary Practices and the Social Order at La Quemada, Zacatecas, Mexico. *Latin American Antiquity* 3(4):298–315.

Nelson, Ben A., and Steven A. LeBlanc
1986   *Short-Term Sedentism in the American Southwest: The Mimbres Valley Salado.* Albuquerque: University of New Mexico Press.

Nesbitt, Paul H.
1931   *The Ancient Mimbrenos: Based on Investigations at the Mattocks Ruin, Mimbres Valley, New Mexico.* The Logan Museum Bulletin no. 4. Beloit, Wisconsin: Beloit College.

Nickens, P. R.
1975   Prehistoric Cannibalism in the Mancos Canyon, Southwestern Colorado. *The Kiva* 40(4):283–93.

Nordenskiold, Gustaf E. A.
[1893] *The Cliff Dwellers of the Mesa Verde*

1973   *Southwestern Colorado, Their Pottery and Implements.* Translated by D. Lloyd Morgan, with a new Introduction by Watson Smith. Antiquities of the New World, vol. 12. Reprint, New York: AMS Press.

Oakeshott, Ewart

[1960] *The Archaeology of Weapons: Arms and*
1994   *Armor from Prehistory to the Age of Chivalry.* Reprint, New York: Barnes and Noble.

Olsen, Sandra L.

1979   A Study of Bone Artifacts from Grasshopper Pueblo, AZ P:14:1. *The Kiva* 44(4):34–73.

Olson, Alan P., and William W. Wasley

1956   An Archaeological Traverse Survey in West-Central New Mexico. In *Pipeline Archaeology*, edited by Fred Wendorf, Nancy Fox, and Orian L. Lewis, 256–390. Santa Fe, New Mexico, and Flagstaff, Arizona: Laboratory of Anthropology and The Museum of Northern Arizona.

Olszewski, D.

1984   Arizona D:11:2023. In *Excavations on Black Mesa, 1982: A Descriptive Report*, edited by D. L. Nickols and F. E. Smiley, 209–22. Center For Archaeological Investigations Research Paper no. 39. Carbondale: Southern Illinois University.

Orcutt, Janet D., Eric Blinman, and Timothy A. Kohler

1990   Explanations of Population Aggregation in the Mesa Verde Region prior to A.D. 900. In *Perspectives on the Prehistoric Southwest*, edited by P. E. Minnis and C. Redman, 196–212. Boulder, Colorado: Westview Press.

Owsley, Douglas W., H. Berryman, and W. Bass.

1977   Demographic and Osteological Evidence for Warfare at the Lawson Site, South Dakota. *Plains Anthropologist Memoir* 13:119–31.

Owsley, Douglas W., and R. L. Jantz

1994   *Skeletal Biology in the Great Plains: Migration, Warfare, Health, and Subsistence.* Washington, D.C.: Smithsonian Institution Press.

Owsley, Douglas W., Robert W. Mann, and Timothy G. Baugh

1994   Culturally Modified Human Bones from the Edwards I Site. In *Skeletal Biology in the Great Plains: Migration, Warfare, Health, and Subsistence*, edited by Douglas W. Owsley and R. L. Jantz, 363–75. Washington, D.C.: Smithsonian Institution Press.

Page, Robert C., Jr.

1970   Primitive Warfare in the Prescott Area. *Arizona Archaeologist* 5:47–56. Phoenix: Arizona Archaeological Society.

Pailes, Richard A.

1980   The Upper Sonora Valley in Prehistoric Trade. *Transactions of the Illinois Academy of Science* 72(4):20–39.

Palkovich, Ann M.

1980   *The Arroyo Hondo Skeletal and Mortuary Remains.* Arroyo Hondo Archaeological Series, vol. 3. Santa Fe, New Mexico: School of American Research Press.

Peckham, Stewart

1959   *The Palisade Ruin LA 3505 Archaeological Salvage Excavations near the Abiquiu Dam, Rio Arriba County, New Mexico.* Santa Fe: School of American Research and the Museum of New Mexico in cooperation with the National park Service, Region 3 (Southwestern Region), United States Department of the Interior.

1963   *A Basket Maker III Site near Tohatchi, New Mexico.* Highway Salvage Archaeology, vol. 4:73–82. Assembled by Stewart Peckham. Santa Fe, New Mexico: Museum of New Mexico.

1981   Palisade Ruin (LA 3505): A Coalition Period Pueblo near Abiquiu Dam, New Mexico. In *Collected Papers in Honor of Erik Kellerman Reed*, edited by A. H. Schroeder, 113–47. Papers of the Archaeological Society of New Mexico no. 6. Albuquerque.

Peckham, Stewart, Fred Wendorf, and Edwin N. Ferdon, Jr.

1956   Excavations near Apache Creek, New Mexico. In *Highway Salvage Archaeology*, vol. 2, edited by Fred Wendorf, 17–86. Santa Fe, New Mexico: Museum of New Mexico.

Pepper, George H.

1909   The Exploration of a Burial Room in

Pueblo Bonito, New Mexico. In *Putnam Anniversary Volume: Anthropological Essays*, edited by Franz Boas, 196–252. New York: G. E. Stechert.

1920   *Pueblo Bonito.* Anthropology Papers of the American Museum of Natural History, vol. 27. New York.

Peterson, K. L.

1988   *Climate and the Dolores River Anasazi.* University of Utah Anthropology Papers 113. Salt Lake City: University of Utah Press.

1994   A Warm and Wet Little Climatic Optimum and a Cold and Dry Little Ice Age in the Southern Rocky Mountains. *Climatic Change* 26:243–69.

Pickering, Robert B.

1974   A Preliminary Report on the Osteological Remains from Alta Vista, Zacatecas. In *Archaeology of West Mexico*, edited by Betty Bell, 240–52. Ajijic, Jalisco, Mexico: West Mexican Society for Advanced Study.

Pilles, Peter J., Jr.

1996   Pueblo III along the Mogollon Rim: The Honanki, Elden, and Turkey Hill Phases of the Sinagua. In *Pueblo Cultures in Transition*, edited by Michael Adler. Tucson: University of Arizona Press.

Pippin, Lonnie C.

1987   *Prehistory and Paleoecology of Guadalupe Ruin, New Mexico.* University of Utah Anthropological Papers 107. Salt Lake City: University of Utah Press.

Plog, Stephen

1997   *Ancient Peoples of the American Southwest.* London: Thames and Hudson.

Pope, Saxton T.

1923   *A Study in Bows and Arrows.* University of California Publications in American Archaeology and Ethnology, vol. 13, no. 9. Berkeley.

Preucel, Robert Washington

1987   Settlement Succession on the Pajarito Plateau, New Mexico. *The Kiva* 53:3–33.

Quam, Alvina, translator

1972   *The Zunis, Self-Portrayals by the Zuni People.* Albuquerque: University of New Mexico Press.

Ragir, S. R.

1972   *The Early Horizon in central California.* Contributions of the University of California Archaeological Research Facility, vol. 15. Berkeley.

Ravesloot, John

1988   *Mortuary Practices and Social Differentiation at Casas Grandes, Chihuahua, Mexico.* Anthropological Papers of the University of Arizona no. 49. Tucson: The University of Arizona Press.

Ravesloot, John, and Patricia M. Spoerl

1989   The Role of Warfare in the Development of Status Hierarchies at Casas Grandes, Chihuahua, Mexico. In *Cultures in Conflict: Current Archaeological Perspectives*, edited by D. C. Tkaczuk and B. C. Vivian, 130–37. Proceedings of the 20th Chacmool Conference. Calgary, Ontario, Canada: Archaeological Association of the University of Calgary.

Raymond, A.

1986   Experiments in the Function and Performance of the Weighted Atlatl. *World Archaeology* 18(2):153–77.

Reagan, Albert B.

1928a Further Notes on the Archaeology of the Navajo Country. *El Palacio* 25(1):2–26, 35, 36.

1928b Some Notes on the Archaeology of the Navajo Country. *El Palacio* 24(18):334–46, 354, 359.

Redman, Charles L.

1993   *People of the Tonto Rim: Archaeological Discovery in Prehistoric Arizona.* Washington, D.C.: Smithsonian Institution Press.

Reed, Alan D., and Jonathan C. Horn

1990   Early Navajo Occupation of the American Southwest: Reexamination of the Dinetah Phase. *The Kiva* 55(4):283–300.

Reed, Erik K.

1953   Human Skeletal Remains from Te'ewi. In *Salvage Archaeology in the Chama Valley, New Mexico*, edited by Fred Wendorf, 104–18. Santa Fe, New Mexico: School of American Research.

Reed, Paul F.

1990   A Spatial Analysis of the Northern Rio

Grande Region, New Mexico: Implications for Sociopolitical and Economic Development from A.D. 1325–1540. In *Economy and Polity in Late Rio Grande Prehistory*, edited by Steadman Upham and Barbara D. Staley, 1–89. The University Museum Occasional Papers no. 16. Las Cruces: New Mexico State University.

Reid, J. Jefferson
1989   A Grasshopper Perspective on the Mogollon of the Arizona Mountains. In *Dynamics of Southwestern Prehistory*, edited by Linda S. Cordell and George J. Gumerman. Washington, D.C.: Smithsonian Institution Press.

Reid, J. Jefferson, and Charles R. Riggs, Jr.
1995   Dynamics of Pueblo Architecture. Paper presented at the 60th annual meeting of the Society for American Archaeology, April 9, 1995, Minneapolis, Minnesota.

Reid, J. Jefferson, and Stephanie M. Whittlesey
1990   The Complicated and the Complex: Observations on the Archaeological Record of Large Pueblos. In *Perspectives on Southwestern Prehistory*, edited by P. Minnis and C. Redman, 184–95. Boulder, Colorado: Westview Press.

Reid, J. Jefferson, John R. Welch, Barbara K. Montgomery and Maria Nieves Zedeno
1996   A Demographic Overview of the Late Pueblo III Period in the Mountains of East-central Arizona. In *Pueblo Cultures in Transition*, edited by Michael A. Adler. Tucson: University of Arizona Press.

Reiter, Paul
1938   *The Jemez Pueblo of Unshagi, New Mexico*. Monographs of the School of American Research nos. 5 and 6. Albuquerque: University of New Mexico Press.

Reyman, Jonathan E.
1978   Pochteca Burials at Anasazi Sites? In *Across the Chichimec Sea: Papers in Honor of J. Charles Kelley*, edited by Carroll L. Riley and Basil C. Hedrick, 242–59. Carbondale: Southern Illinois University Press.

Rice, Glen
1974   Were the Early Mogollon Sedentary Agriculturalists? Paper presented at the 73d annual meeting of the American Anthropological Association, November 1974, Mexico City.
1975   A Systematic Explanation of Mogollon Settlement Pattern Changes. Ph.D. diss., Department of Anthropology, University of Washington. University Microfilms, Ann Arbor.
1998   War and Water: An Ecological Perspective on Hohokam Irrigation. *The Kiva*. In press.

Riley, Carroll
1987   *The Frontier People: The Greater Southwest in the Protohistoric Period*. Rev. and expanded ed. Albuquerque: University of New Mexico Press.

Roberts, Frank H. H., Jr.
1929   *Shabik'eschee Village, A Late Basketmaker Site in the Canyon, New Mexico*. Bureau of American Ethnology Bulletin no. 92. Washington, D.C.: Smithsonian Institution.
1930   *Early Pueblo Ruins in the Piedra District, Southwestern Colorado*. Bureau of American Ethnology Bulletin no. 96. Washington, D.C.: Smithsonian Institution.
1931   *The Ruins at Kiathulanna Eastern Arizona*. Bureau of American Ethnology Bulletin no. 100. Washington, D.C.: Smithsonian Institution.
1932   *The Village of the Great Kivas on the Zuni Reservation, New Mexico*. Bureau of American Ethnology Bulletin no. 111. Washington, D.C.: Smithsonian Institution.
1939   *Archaeological Remains in the Whitewater District, Eastern Arizona: Part I*. Bureau of American Ethnology Bulletin no. 121. Washington, D.C.: Smithsonian Institution.
1940   *Archaeological Remains in the Whitewater District, Eastern Arizona: Part II, Artifacts and Burials*. Bureau of American Ethnology Bulletin no. 126. Washington, D.C.: Smithsonian Institution.

Rohn, Arthur H.
1971   *Mug House, Mesa Verde National Park, Colorado (Wetherill Mesa Excavations)*. Archeological Research Series 7-D. Washington, D.C.: National Park Service.

1974   Payne Site Investigations. *Southwestern Lore* 40:50–52.

1975   A Stockaded Basketmaker III Village at Yellow Jacket, Colorado. *The Kiva* 40(3):113–20.

1977   *Cultural Change and Continuity on Chapin Mesa.* Lawrence: Regents Press of Kansas.

1989   Warfare and Violence among the Southwestern Pueblos. In *Cultures in Conflict: Current Anthropological Perspectives*, edited by D. C. Tkaczuk and B. C. Vivian, 147–52. Proceedings of the 20th Chacmool Conference. Calgary, Ontario, Canada: Archaeological Association of the University of Calgary.

Roney, John R.

1995   Mesa Verdean Manifestations South of the San Juan River. *Journal of Anthropological Archaeology* 14:170–83.

1966a   Cerro Juanaquena: A Late Archaic Cerros de Trincheras in Northwestern Chihuahua. Paper presented at the Archaic Prehistory of the North American Southwest, October 25, Albuquerque, New Mexico.

1996b   Late Archaic Cerros de Trincheras in Northwestern Chihuahua. Paper presented at the 61st annual meeting of the Society for American Archeology, New Orleans, Louisiana.

1996c   The Pueblo III Period in the Eastern San Juan Basin. In *Pueblo Cultures in Transition*, edited by Michael A. Adler. Tucson: University of Arizona Press.

Russell, Frank

1908   The Pima Indians. In *Twenty-Sixth Annual Report of the Bureau of American Ethnology*, 3–289. Washington, D.C.: Smithsonian Institution.

Sahlins, Marshall D.

1958   *Social Stratification in Polynesia.* Seattle: University of Washington Press.

Saitta, Dean J.

1991   Room Use and Community Organization at the Pettit Site, West Central New Mexico. *The Kiva* 56(4):385–409.

Sandor, John A.

1990   Prehistoric Agricultural Terraces and Soils in the Mimbres Area, New Mexico. *World Archaeology* 22:70–86.

Sauer, Carl O.

1932   The Road to Cibola. *Ibero-Americana* 3.

Sauer, Carl O., and Donald D. Brand

1931   *Prehistoric Settlements of Sonora, with Special Reference to Cerros de Trincheras.* University of California Publications in Geography, vol. 5, no. 3. Berkeley.

Saul, Marilyn B.

1981   Appendix B: Disposal of the Dead at Las Colinas Ruins. In *The 1968 Excavations at Mound 8, Las Colinas Ruins Group, Phoenix, Arizona*, edited by Laurence B. Hammack and Alan P. Sullivan, 257–68. Arizona State Museum Archaeological Series no. 154. Tucson: University of Arizona.

Sayles, E. B.

1945   *The San Simon Branch Excavations at Cave Creek and in the San Simon Valley.* Medallion Papers no. 34. Globe, Arizona: Gila Pueblo.

Schaafsma, Polly

1972   *Rock Art of New Mexico.* Santa Fe, New Mexico: State Planning Office.

1980   *Indian Rock Art of the Southwest.* Albuquerque: School of American Research and University of New Mexico Press.

1994   *Rock Art of Utah.* Rev. ed. Salt Lake City: University of Utah Press.

Schellback, Louis, III

1926   *An Unusual Burial in Mesa House Ruin, Overton, Clark County Nevada.* Southwest Museum Papers no. 4:93–105. Los Angeles.

Schroeder, Albert H.

1947   Did the Sinagua of the Verde Valley Settle in the Salt River Valley? *Southwestern Journal of Anthropology* 8(3):230–46.

1955   *Archaeology of Zion National Park.* University of Utah Anthropology Papers 22. Salt Lake City: University of Utah Press.

1972   Rio Grande Ethnohistory. In *New Perspectives on the Pueblos*, edited by Alfonso Ortiz, 41–70. Albuquerque: University of New Mexico Press.

1979   Pueblos Abandoned in Historic Times. In *Handbook of North American Indians*, vol. 9, *Southwest*, edited by Alfonso Ortiz, 236–54. Washington, D.C.: Smithsonian Institution Press.

1992   Protohistoric Pueblo Demographic Changes. In *Current Research on the Late Prehistory and Early History of New Mexico*, edited by Bradley J. Vierra, 29–36. Albuquerque: New Mexico Archaeological Council.

Schroeder, Albert H., and Dan S. Matson

1965   *A Colony on the Move: Gaspar Castano de Sosa's Journal 1590–1591*. Santa Fe, New Mexico: School of American Research.

Schulman A.

1950   Pre-Columbian Towers in the Southwest. *American Antiquity* 15:288–97.

Schwartz, D. W.

1956   Demographic Changes in the Early Periods of Cohonina Prehistory. In *Prehistoric Settlement Patterns in the New World*, edited by Gordon R. Willey, 26–34. Publications in Anthropology no. 23. New York: Viking Fund.

Scudder, T.

1993   Development-Induced Relocation and Refugee Studies: 37 Years of Change and Continuity among Zambia's Gwembe Tonga. *Journal of Refugee Studies* 6(2):123–52.

Scutt, Jeanne A., Richard C. Chapman, and June-el Piper

1991   *The Cuchillo Negro Archaeological Project: On the Periphery of the Mimbres-Mogollon*. Albuquerque: Office of Contract Archeology, University of New Mexico.

Secoy, Frank Raymond

1953   *Changing Military Patterns on the Great Plains: 17th Century through Early 19th Century*. Monographs of the American Ethnological Society no. 21. Locust Valley, New York: J. J. Augustin.

Service, Elman R.

1962   *Primitive Social Organization: An Evolutionary Perspective*. New York: Random House.

1975   *Origins of the State and Civilization: The Process of Cultural Evolution*. New York: Norton.

Shafer, Harry J.

1991   Archaeology at the NAN Ranch (LA15049) 1985 Interim Report. *The Artifact* 29(1):1–29.

Shankman, Paul

1991   Culture Contact, Cultural Ecology, and Dani Warfare. *Man*, n.s., 26:229–321.

Sheridan, Thomas E.

1981   Prelude to Conquest: Yaqui Population, Subsistence, and Warfare during the Protohistoric Period. In *The Protohistoric Periods in the North American Southwest*, edited by D. R. Wilcox and W. B. Masse, 71–93. Research Paper no. 24. Tempe: Arizona State University.

Shimkin, Demitri B.

1986   Ethnology: Eastern Shoshone. In *Handbook of North American Indians*, vol. 11, *Great Basin*, edited by Warren L. D'Azevedo, 308–35. Washington D.C.: Smithsonian Institution Press.

Shipman, Jeff H.

1983   Human Skeletal Remains from the Salmon Ruin (LA8846), New Mexico. In *Investigations at the Salmon Site: The Structure of Chacoan Society in the Northern Southwest*, edited by Cynthia Irwin-Williams and Philip H. Sheley, 47–58. Portales: Eastern New Mexico University.

Shutler, Richard, Jr.

1961   *Lost City, Pueblo Grande de Nevada*. Nevada State Museum Anthropological Papers no. 5. Carson City.

Sillitoe, Paul

1977   Land Shortage and War in New Guinea. *Ethnology* 16:71–81.

Sink, Clifton W., Douglas M. Davy, A. Trinkle Jones, Laura Michalik, and Diane Pitz

1982   Arizona D:7:262. In *Excavations on Black Mesa, 1980: A Descriptive Report*, edited by Peter P. Andrews, Robert W. Layhe, Deborah L. Nichols, and Shirley Powell, 87–108. Research Paper no. 24. Carbondale: Center for Archaeological Investigations, Southern Illinois University.

Sink, Clifton W., J. Manson, B. J. Baker, and J. K. Feathers

1984   Arizona D:11:2062. In *Excavations on*

Black Mesa, 1982: A Descriptive Report, edited by D. L. Nichols and F. E. Smiley, 255–80. Research Paper no. 39. Carbondale: Southern Illinois University.

Skinner, Alan S.

1965   A Survey of Field Houses at Sapawe, North Central New Mexico. *Southwestern Lore* 31:18–24.

Sleeter, Richard S.

1987   Cultural Interaction of the Prehistoric Gallina: A Study of Settlement Patterns in North-Central New Mexico. Master's thesis, New Mexico State University, Las Cruces.

Smith, Watson

1952a   *Excavations in Big Hawk Valley, Wupatki National Monument, Arizona.* Museum of Northern Arizona Bulletin no. 24. Flagstaff.

1952b   *Kiva Mural Decorations at Awatovi and Kawaika-a, with a Survey of other Wall Paintings in the Pueblo Southwest.* Papers of the Peabody Museum of Archaeology and Ethnology, vol. 37. Cambridge.

1971   *Painted Ceramics of the Western Mound at Awatovi.* Papers of the Peabody Museum of Archaeology and Ethnology, vol. 38. Cambridge.

Snow, David H.

1963   A Preliminary Report on Excavations at Sapawe, New Mexico. Ms on File, Laboratory of Anthropology, Museum of New Mexico, Santa Fe.

Spicer, Edward H.

1962   *Cycles of Conquest.* Tucson: University of Arizona Press.

Spielmann, Katherine A.

1983   Late Prehistoric Exchange between the Southwest and Southern Plains. *Plains Anthropologist* 28:246–72.

1991   Coercion or Cooperation? Plains-Pueblo Interaction in the Protohistoric Period. In *Farmers, Hunters and Colonists, Interaction between the Southwest and the Southern Plains*, edited by K. A. Spielmann, 36–50. Tucson: University of Arizona Press.

1994   Clustered Confederacies: Sociopolitical Organization in the Protohistoric Rio Grande. In *The Ancient Southwestern Community: Models and Methods for the Study of Prehistoric Social Organization*, edited by W. H. Wills and Robert D. Leonard, 45–54. Albuquerque: University of New Mexico Press.

1996   Impressions of Pueblo III Settlement Trends among the Rio Abajo and Eastern Border Pueblos. In *Pueblo Cultures in Transition*, edited by Michael A. Adler. Tucson: University of Arizona Press.

Spier, Leslie

1917   *An Outline for a Chronology of Zuni Ruins.* Anthropological Papers of the American Museum of Natural History no. 18:205–331. New York.

1918   *Notes on Some Little Colorado Ruins.* Anthropological Papers of the American Museum of Natural History no. 18:333–62. New York.

1919   *Ruins in the White Mountains, Arizona.* Anthropological Papers of the American Museum of Natural History no. 18:363–87. New York.

Spoerl, Patricia M.

1984   Prehistoric Fortifications in Central Arizona. In *Prehistoric Cultural Developments in Central Arizona: Archaeology of the Upper New River Region*, edited by Patricia M. Spoerl and George J. Gumerman, 261–76. Center for Archaeological Investigations Occasional Papers no. 5. Carbondale: Southern Illinois University Press.

Stacy, V. K. Pheriba

1974   "Cerros de Trincheras" in the Arizona Papegueria. Ph.D. diss., Department of Anthropology, University of Arizona, Tucson.

Stark, Miriam T., Jeffrey J. Clark, and Mark D. Elson

1995   Causes and Consequences of Migration in the 13th Century Tonto Basin. *Journal of Anthropological Archaeology* 14(2):212–46.

Stein, John, and Andrew P. Fowler

1996   Pueblo III in the San Juan Basin and its Peripheries. In *Pueblo Cultures in Transition*, edited by Michael A. Adler. Tucson: University of Arizona Press.

Stein, John, and Peter J. McKenna

1988   *An Archaeological Reconnaissance of a*

Late Bonito Phase Occupation near Aztec Ruins National Monument, New Mexico. Santa Fe, New Mexico: Division of Anthropology, Southwest Cultural Resources Center, National Park Service.

Steward, Julian H.
1941   *Archeological Reconnaissance of Southern Utah*. Anthropological Paper 18, Bureau of American Ethnology Bulletin 128. Washington, D.C.: Smithsonian Institution.

Stewart, Yvonne G.
1980   *An Archeological Overview of Petrified Forest National Park*. Western Archeological and Conservation Center Publications in Anthropology no. 10. Tucson: National Park Service.

Swannack, Jervis D., Jr.
1969   *Big Juniper House, Mesa Verde National Park, Colorado (Wetherill Mesa Excavations)*. Archeological Research Series no. 7-C. Washington, D.C.: National Park Service.

Tagg, Martyn D.
1985   *Tonto National Monument: An Archeological Survey*. Western Archeological and Conservation Center Publications in Anthropology no. 31. Santa Fe, New Mexico: National Park Service.

Tanner, Clara Lee
1976   *Prehistoric Southwestern Craft Arts*. Tucson: University of Arizona Press.

Taylor, Mark
1985   The Paleopathology of a Southern Sinagua Population from Oak Creek Pueblo, Arizona. In *Health and Disease in the Prehistoric Southwest*, edited by Charles F. Merbs and Robert J. Miller, 115–18. Arizona State University Anthropological Research Papers no. 34. Tempe.

Taylor, W. W.
1958   *Two Archaeological Studies in Northern Arizona*. Museum of Northern Arizona Bulletin no. 30. Flagstaff.

Teague, Lynn S.
1993   Prehistory and the Traditions of the O'Odham and Hopi. *The Kiva* 58(4):435–54.

Thomas, David H.
1978   Arrowheads and Atlatl Darts: How the Stones Got the Shaft. *American Antiquity* 43:461–72.

Thompson, David
1916   *David Thompson's Narrative of His Explorations in Western North America, 1784–1812*. Edited by Joseph B. Tyrrell. Publications of the Champlain Society no. 12. Toronto, Ontario, Canada: The Champlain Society.

Thompson, Laurence C., and M. Dale Kinkade
1990   Languages. In *Handbook of North American Indians*, vol. 7, *Northwest Coast*, edited by Wayne Suttles, 30–51. Washington, D.C.: Smithsonian Institution Press.

Thompson, Marc
1994   The Evolution and Dissemination of Mimbres Iconography. In *Kachinas in the Pueblo World*, edited by Polly Schaafsma, 93–105. Albuquerque: University of New Mexico Press.

Titiev, Mischa
1944   *Old Orabi: A Study of the Hopi Indians of Third Mesa*. Papers of the Peabody Museum of American Archaeology and Ethnology, vol. 22, pt. 1. Cambridge.

Tkaczuk, D. C., and B. C. Vivian, eds.
1989   *Cultures in Conflict*. Proceedings of the 20th Annual Chacmool Conference. Calgary, Ontario, Canada: Archaeological Association of the University of Calgary.

Toulouse, Joseph H., Jr.
1939   Arrow-Shaft Tools (with Notes on Their General Distribution). In *Preliminary Report on the 1937 Excavations, Bc 50–51, Chaco Canyon, New Mexico, with Some Distributional Analyses*, edited by Clyde Kluckhohn and Paul Reiter, 80–89. The University of New Mexico Bulletin no. 345, Anthropological Series, vol. 3, pt. 2. Albuquerque.

Trigger, Bruce G.
1976   *The Children of Aataentsic, I*. Montreal, Quebec, Canada: McGill-Queen's University Press.

Tuck, James A.
1971   The Iroquois Confederacy. *Scientific American*. 224(2):32–49.
1978   Northern Iroquoian Prehistory. In *Handbook of North American Indians*, vol. 15,

Northeast, edited by B. G. Trigger, 322–33. Washington, D.C.: Smithsonian Institution Press.

Tuggle, H. David
1970   Prehistoric Community Relationships in East-Central Arizona. Ph.D. diss., Department of Anthropology, University of Arizona, Tucson.

Turner, Christy G., II
1983   Taphonomic Reconstructions of Human Violence and Cannibalism Based on Mass Burials in the American Southwest. In *Carnivores, Human Scavengers and Predators: A Question of Bone Technology*, edited by G. M. LeMoine, and A. S. MacEachern, 219–40. Calgary, Alberta, Canada: Archaeological Association of the University of Calgary.
1988   Appendix 2H. Another Prehistoric Southwest Mass Human Burial Suggesting Violence and Cannibalism: Marshview Hamlet, Colorado. In *Dolores Archaeological Program: Aceramic and Late Occupations at Dolores*, edited by G. T. Gross, and A. E. Kane, 81–83. Denver: Bureau of Reclamation.
1989   Teec Nos Pos: More Possible Cannibalism in Northeastern Arizona. *The Kiva* 54(2):147–52.
1993   Cannibalism in Chaco Canyon: The Charnel Pit Excavated in 1926 at Small House Ruin by Frank H. H. Roberts, Jr. *American Journal of Physical Anthropology* 91(4):421–39.

Turner, Christy G., II, and Laural Lofgren
1966   Household Size of Prehistoric Western Pueblo Indians. *Southwest Journal of Anthropology* 22(2):117–32.

Turner, Christy G., II, and Jacqueline A. Turner
1990   Perimortem Damage to Skeletal Remains from Wupatki National Monument, Northern Arizona. *The Kiva* 55(3):187–212.
1992   The First Claim for Cannibalism in the Southwest: Walter Hough's 1901 Discovery at Canyon Butte Ruin 3, Northeastern Arizona. *American Antiquity* 57(5):661–82.
1995   Cannibalism in the Prehistoric American Southwest: Occurrence, Taphonomy, Ex-

planation, and Suggestions for Standardized World Definition. *Anthropological Science* 103:1–22.
1999   *Man Corn: Cannibalism and Violence in the Prehistoric American Southwest*. Salt Lake City: University of Utah Press.

Turner, Christy G., II, Jacqueline A. Turner, and Roger C. Green
1993   Taphonomic Analysis of Anasazi Skeletal Remains from Largo-Gallina Sites in Northwestern New Mexico. *Journal of Anthropological Research* 49(2):83–110.

Turney-High, H.
[1949] *Primitive War: Its Practice and Concepts.*
1971   Reissue with new preface and afterword, Columbia: University of South Carolina Press.

Tuthill, Carr
1947   *The Tres Alamos Site on the San Pedro River, Southeastern Arizona*. Amerind Foundation Publications no. 4. Dragoon, Arizona.

Underhill, Ruth
1979   *Papago Woman*. New York: Holt, Rinehart, and Winston.

Upham, Steadman
1982   *Polities and Power: An Economic and Political History of the Western Pueblo*. New York: Academic Press.
1984   Adaptive diversity and Southwestern Abandonment. *Journal of Anthropological Research* 40(2):235–56.

Upham, Steadman, and Gail M. Bockley
1989   The Chronologies of Nuvakwewtaqa: Implications for Social Processes. In *Sociopolitical Structure of Prehistoric Southwestern Societies*, edited by Steadman Upham, Kent Lightfoot, and Roberta Jewett. Boulder, Colorado: Westview Press.

Upham, Steadman, Kent G. Lightfoot, and Roberta A. Jewett
1989   *Sociopolitical Structure of Prehistoric Southwestern Societies*. Boulder, Colorado: Westview Press.

Upham, Steadman, and Fred Plog
1986   The Interpretation of Prehistoric Political Complexity in the Central and Northern

Southwest: Toward a Mending of Models. *Journal of Field Archaeology* 13:223–31.

Upham, Steadman, and Paul F. Reed
1989 Inferring the Structure of Anasazi Warfare. In *Cultures in Conflict: Current Archaeological Approaches*, edited by D. C. Tkaczuk and B. C. Vivian, 153–62. Proceedings of the 20th Annual Chacmool Conference. Calgary, Ontario, Canada: Archaeological Association of the University of Calgary.

Upham, Steadman, and Lori Stevens Reed
1989 Regional Systems in the Central and Northern Southwest: Demography, Economy, and Sociopolitics Preceding Contact. In *Colombian Consequences: Archaeological and Historical Perspectives on the Spanish Borderlands West*, edited by David Hurst Thomas, 57–76. Washington, D.C.: Smithsonian Institution Press.

Van Dyke, Ruth M.
1997 The Andrews Great House Community: A Ceramic Chronometric Perspective. *The Kiva* 63(2):137–54.

Van Gerven, Dennis P., and Susan Guise Sheridan
1994 *The Pueblo Grande Project: The Bioethnography of a Classic Period Hohokam Population*. Soil Systems Publications in Archaeology, vol. 6, no. 20. Phoenix, Arizona.

Varien, Mark
1990 *Excavations at Three Prehistoric Sites along Pia Mesa Road, Zuni Indian Reservation, McKinley County, New Mexico*. Zuni Archaeological Program Report no. 233, Research Series no. 4. Zuni Pueblo.

Varien, Mark D., William D. Lipe, Michael A. Adler, Ian M. Thompson, and Bruce A. Bradley.
1996 Southwest Colorado and Southeast Utah Settlement Patterns: A.D. 1100–1300. In *Pueblo Cultures in Transition*, edited by Michael A. Adler. Tucson: University of Arizona Press.

Vayda, Andrew P.
1968 Hypotheses about Functions of War. In *War: The Anthropology of Armed Conflict and Aggression*, edited by Morton Fried, Marvin Harris, and Robert Murphy, 85–91. Garden City, New York: Natural History Press.

Wallace, Henry D., and William H. Doelle
1997 From Ballcourts to Platform Mounds to Rancherias: A Comparison of Three Organizational Strategies on the Lower San Pedro River. Paper presented at the 62d annual meeting of the Society for American Archaeology, April 2–6, Nashville, Tennessee.

Walker, Phillip L.
1985 Anemia among Prehistoric Indians of the American Southwest. In *Health and Disease in the Prehistoric Southwest*, edited by Charles F. Merbs and Robert. J. Miller, 139–63. Arizona State University Anthropological Research Papers no. 34. Tempe.

Walker, William Howard
1995 Ritual Prehistory: A Pueblo Case Study. Ph.D. diss., Department of Anthropology, University of Arizona, Tucson.
1996 Ritual Deposits: Another Perspective. In *River of Change: Prehistory of the Middle Little Colorado River Valley, Arizona*, edited by E. Charles Adams, 75–92. Arizona State Museum Archaeological Series no. 185. Tucson: University of Arizona.

Walsh, Michael Richard
1997 Lines in the Sand: Competition and Territoriality in the Northern Rio Grande, A.D. 1150–1325. Ph.D. diss., Department of Anthropology, University of California, Los Angeles.

Watson, Patty Jo, Steven A. LeBlanc, and Charles Redman
1980 Aspects of Zuni Prehistory: Preliminary Report on Excavations and Survey in the El Morro Valley of New Mexico, with Patty Jo Watson and Charles Redman. *The Journal of Field Archaeology* 7:201–18.

Weaver, Donald E., Jr.
1978 Prehistoric Population Dynamics and Environmental Exploitation in the Manuelito Canyon District, Northwestern New Mexico. Ph.D. diss., Department of Anthropology, Arizona State University, Tempe.

Webster, David
1975 Warfare and the Evolution of the State: A Reconsideration. *American Antiquity* 40:464–70.

Weiner-Stodder, Ann Lucy

1985 *The Physical Anthropology and Mortuary Practices of the Dolores Anasazi: An Early Pueblo Population in Local and Regional Context.* Dolores Archaeological Program Technical Reports. Final report submitted to the U.S. Bureau of Reclamation, Upper Colorado Region. Salt Lake City, Utah.

1988 Appendix 2D. Human Remains from Marshview Hamlet. In *Dolores Archaeological Program: Aceramic and Late Occupations at Dolores*, edited by G. T. Gross, and A. E. Kane, 71–72. Denver: Bureau of Reclamation.

Wells, Susan J., and Keith M. Anderson

1988 *Archeological Survey and Architectural Study of Montezuma Castle National Monument.* Western Archeological and Conservation Center Publications in Anthropology no. 50. Santa Fe, New Mexico: National Park Service.

Wendorf, Fred

1953 *Archaeological Studies in the Petrified Forest National Monument.* Museum of Northern Arizona Bulletin no. 27. Flagstaff.

1953 *Salvage Archaeology in the Chama Valley, New Mexico.* Monograph of the School of American Research no. 17. Santa Fe, New Mexico.

1956 Some Distributions of Settlement Patterns in the Pueblo Southwest. In *Prehistoric Settlement Patterns in the New World*, edited by Gordon R. Willey. Viking Fund Publications in Anthropology no. 23. New York.

Wetherill, Richard

1894a Letter about Snider's Well. *Archaeologist* (Ohio Archaeological and Historical Society) 2(9):288–89.

1894b Untitled letter to Talbot Hyde, December 20. Copy on file at the Wetherill–Grand Gulch Archives, Edge of the Cedars Sate Park, Blanding, Utah.

Wetherington, Ronald K.

1968 *Excavations at Pot Creek Pueblo.* Fort Burgwin Research Center Publication no. 6. Taos, New Mexico.

Whalen, Michael E., and Paul E. Minnis

1996 Ballcourts and Regional Organization the Casas Grandes Region. *American Antiquity* 61(4):732–46.

Wheat, Joe Ben

1955 *Mogollon Culture prior to* A.D. *1000.* American Anthropological Association Memoir no. 82. Washington, D.C.

White, Christopher W.

1976 Prehistoric Warfare in the Chevlon Creek Area: An Ecological Perspective. In *Chevlon Archaeological Research Project*, edited by Fred T. Plog, James N. Hill, and Dwight W. Read, 127–45. Archaeological Survey Monograph no. 2. Los Angeles: Department of Anthropology, University of California.

White, Tim D.

1988 Appendix C. Cottonwood Wash, Southeastern Utah: Human Osteology of Feature 3, FS #27, Site 42SA12209. In *Salvage Excavations of 42SA12209*, edited by J. K. Fetterman, L. Honeycutt, and Kristin Kuckelman. Yellow Jacket, Colorado: Woods Canyon Archaeological Consultants.

1992 *Prehistoric Cannibalism at Mancos 5MTUMR-2346.* Princeton: Princeton University Press.

Whittlesey, Stephanie M.

1978 Status and Death at Grasshopper Pueblo: Experiments toward an Archaeological Theory of Correlates. Ph.D. diss., Department of Anthropology, University of Arizona, Tucson.

Wilcox, David R.

1978 The Theoretical Signficance of Field Houses. In *Limited Activity and Occupation Sites, A Collection of Conference Papers*, edited by Albert E. Ward, 25–32, Contributions to Anthropolocial Studies no. 1. Albuquerque: Center for Anthropological Studies.

1979 The Warfare Implications of Dry-Laid Masonry Walls on Tumamoc Hill. *The Kiva* 45(1&2):15–38.

1981a Changing Perspectives in the Protohistoric Pueblos, A.D. 1450–1700. In *The Protohistoric Periods in the North American Southwest*, edited by D. R. Wilcox and W. B. Masse, 378–409. Research Paper no. 24. Tempe: Arizona State University.

1981b The Entry of Athapaskan Speakers into the American Southwest: The Problem Today. In *The Protohistoric Periods in the North American Southwest*, edited by D. R. Wilcox and W. B. Masse, 213–56. Research Paper no. 24. Tempe: Arizona State University.

1984   Multi-Ethnic Division of Labor in the Protohistoric Southwest. In *Collected Papers in Honor of Harry L. Hadlock*, edited by Nancy L. Fox, 141–56. New Mexico Archaeological Society Papers no. 9. Albuquerque.

1986   A Historical Analysis of the Problem of Southwestern-Mesoamerican Conections. In *Ripples in the Chichimec Sea: New Considerations of Southwestern-Mesoamerican Interactions*, edited by Francis Joan Mathien and Randall H. McGuire, 9–44. Carbondale: Southern Illinois University Press.

1987   *Frank Midvale's Investigations of the Site of La Ciudad*. Arizona State University Anthropological Field Studies no. 19. Tempe.

1988a Avonlea and Southern Athapaskan Migrations. In *Avonlea Yesterday and Today: Archaeology and Prehistory*, edited by Leslie B. Davis, 273–80. Saskatoon, Saskatchewan, Canada: Saskatchewan Archaeological Society.

1988b The Regional Context of the Brady Wash and Picacho Area Sites. In *Hohokam Settlement along the Slopes of the Picacho Mountains, Synthesis and Conclusions, Tucson Aqueduct Project*, edited by R. Ciolek-Torrello and D. R. Wilcox, 244–67. Museum of Northern Arizona Research Papers, vol. 35, pt.6. Flagstaff

1989   Hohokam Warfare. In *Cultures in Conflict: Current Archaeological Perspectives*, edited by D. C. Tkaczuk and B. C. Vivian, 163–72. Proceedings of the 20th Annual Chacmool Conference. Calgary, Ontario, Canada: Archaeological Association of the University of Calgary.

1991   Changing Contexts of Pueblo Adaptations, A.D. 1200–1600. In *Farmers, Hunters, and Colonists: Interaction between the Southwest and the Southern Plains*, edited by

Katherine A. Spielman, 128–54. Tucson: University of Arizona Press.

1992   Discussion of Pueblo Research. In *Current Research on the Late Prehistory and Early History of New Mexico*, edited by Bradley J. Vierra, 101–7. Albuquerque: New Mexico Archaeological Council.

1993a The Evolution of the Chaco Polity. In *The Chimney Rock Archaeological Symposium*, edited by J. McKim Malville and Gary Matlock, 76–90. Rocky Mountain Forest and Range Experiment Station, Forest Service General Technical Report RM-227. Fort Collins, Colorado.

1993b Pueblo Grande in the Nineteenth Century. In *Archaeology of the Pueblo Grande Platform Mound and Surrounding Features*, edited by Christian E. Downum and Todd W. Bostwick, 43–71. Pueblo Grande Museum Anthropological Papers no. 1. Phoenix.

1994   Three Macroregional Systems in the North American Southwest and Their Relationships. Paper presented at the Advanced Seminar on "Great Towns and Regional Polities: Cultural Evolution in the U.S. Southwest and Southeast," Amerind Foundation, March 5–12. Dragoon, Arizona

1995   *The Wupatki Nexus: Chaco-Hohokam-Chumash Connectivity, A.D. 1150–1225*. Proceedings of the 25th Annual Chacmool Conference. Calgary, Alberta, Canada: Archaeological Association of the University of Calgary.

1996   Pueblo III: People and Polity in Relational Context. In *Pueblo Cultures in Transition*, edited by Michael Adler, 241–54. Tucson: University of Arizona Press.

Wilcox, David R., and Jonathan Haas

1994   The Scream of the Butterfly: Competition and Conflict in the Prehistoric Southwest. In *Themes in Southwest Prehistory*, edited by George J. Gumerman, 211–38. Santa Fe, New Mexico: School of American Research Press.

Wilcox, David R., Jerry B. Howard, and Rueben H. Nelson

1990   *One Hundred Years of Archaeology at La Ciudad de Los Hornos*. Soil Systems Publications in Archaeology no. 16. Phoenix, Arizona.

Wilcox, David R., Thomas R. McGuire, and Charles Sternberg
1981   *Snaketown Revisited.* Arizona State Museum Archaeological Series no. 155. Tucson.

Wilcox, David R., and Lynette O. Shenk
1977   *The Architecture of the Casa Grande and Its Interpretation.* Arizona State Museum Archaeological Series no. 115. Tucson.

Wilcox, David R., and Charles Sternberg
1983   *Hohokam Ballcourts and Their Interpretation.* Arizona State Museum Archaeological Series no. 160. Tucson.

Willey, P.
1990   *Prehistoric Warfare on the Great Plains: Skeletal Analysis of the Crow Creek Massacre Victims.* New York: Garland Publishing.

Wills, W. H.
1988   *Early Prehistoric Agriculture in the American Southwest.* Santa Fe: School of American Research Press.

Wills, W. H., and Thomas C. Windes
1989   Evidence for Populations Aggregation and Dispersal during the Basketmaker III Period in Chaco Canyon, New Mexico. *American Antiquity* 54(2):347–69.

Wilshusen, Richard H.
1986   The Relationship between Abandonment Mode and Ritual Use in Pueblo I Anasazi Protokivas. *The Journal of Field Archaeology* 13:245–54.
1991   Early Villages in the American Southwest: Cross-Cultural and Archaeological Perspectives. Ph.D. diss., Department of Anthropology, University of Colorado, Boulder.
1995   *The Cedar Hill Special Treatment Project: Late Pueblo I, Early Navajo, and Historic Occupations in Northwestern New Mexico.* La Plata Archaeological Consultants Research Papers no. 1. Dolores, Colorado.

Wilson, John P.
1969   The Sinagua and Their Neighbors. Ph.D. diss., Harvard University.

Winship, G. P.
1896   The Coronado Expedition, 1540–1542. In *Fourteenth Annual Report of the Bureau of American Ethnography, 1892–1893,* pt. 1:329–613. Washington, D.C.: U.S. Government Printing Office.

Wiseman, Regge N.
1970   Artifacts of Interest from the Bloom Mound, Southeastern New Mexico. *The Artifact* 8(2):1-10.
1977   *The Blackrock Project: Archeological Excavations on the Zuni Indian Reservation, McKinley County, New Mexico.* Museum of New Mexico Archeological Research Papers no. 3. Santa Fe.
1982   *The Tsaya Project: Archaeological Excavations near Lake Valley, San Juan County, New Mexico.* Laboratory of Anthropology Note no. 308. Santa Fe: Museum of New Mexico.

Wood, J. Scott
1997   Field Trip to Perry Mesa. Ms on file, Museum of Northern Arizona, Flagstaff.

Woodbury, Richard
1954   *Prehistoric Stone Implements of Northeastern Arizona.* Papers of the Peabody Museum of American Archaeology and Ethnology, vol. 34. Cambridge.
1956   *The Antecedents of Zuni Culture.* Transactions of the New York Academy of Sciences, series 2, vol. 18:557–63. New York.
1959   A Reconsideration of Pueblo Warfare in the Southwestern United States. In *Actas del XXXIII Congreso Internacional de Americanistas,* vol. 2:124–33. San Jose, Costa Rica: Editorial Lehmann.

Woodbury, Richard, and Natalie F. S. Woodbury
1956   Zuni Prehistory and El Morro National Monument. *Southwestern Lore* 21:56–60.

Woodbury, Richard B., and Ezra B. W. Zubrow
1979   Agricultural Beginnings, 2000 B.C.–A.D. 500. In *Handbook of North American Indians,* vol. 9, *Southwest,* edited by Alfonso Ortiz, 43–60. Washington, D.C.: Smithsonian Institution Press.

Woodson, Michael Kyle
1995   The Goat Hill Site: A Western Anasazi Pueblo in the Safford Valley of Southeastern Arizona. Master's thesis, University of Texas at Austin.

Woodward, Arthur.
1933   A Man's Way. *The Masterkey* 7(6):165–67.

Wormington, H. M.

1947 *Prehistoric Indians of the Southwest.* Denver: The Denver Museum of Natural History.

1955 *A Reappraisal of the Fremont Culture with a Summary of the Archaeology of the Northern Periphery.* Proceedings of the Denver Museum of Natural History, vol. 1. Denver.

Wright, Barton

1976 *Pueblo Shields from the Fred Harvey Fine Arts Collection.* Flagstaff, Arizona: Northland Press.

1979 *Hopi Material Culture: Artifacts Gathered by H. R. Voth in the Fred Harvey Collec-* *tion.* Flagstaff and Phoenix, Arizona: Northland Press and The Heard Museum.

Zier, Christian J.

1976 *Excavations near Zuni New Mexico: 1973.* Museum of Northern Arizona Research Paper no. 2. Flagstaff.

Zimmerman, L., and R. Whitten

1980 Prehistoric Bones Tell a Grim Tale of Indian v. Indian. *Smithsonian* 11:100–107.

Zubrow, Ezra B.

1974 *Population, Contact and Climate in the New Mexico Pueblos.* University of Arizona Anthropology Papers no. 24. Tucson: University of Arizona Press.

INDEX